MONGOLIA

in the 21st Century

Society, Culture and International Relations

HIMALAYAN RESEARCH AND CULTURAL FOUNDATION

The Himalayan Research and Cultural Foundation, NGO in Special Consultative Status with ECOSOC, United Nations, is a multi-disciplinary research, cultural and development facilitative organization engaged in appraising and creating awareness about various issues related to the Himalayan and trans-Himalayan regions in South and Central Asia, or parts thereof connected with its environment, biodiversity, regional development, human resources, history, culture, art and literature, social structures, economies, human rights, peace processes etc., thus contributing to sustainable development and promotion of human, educational and economic advancement of the peoples of the region, besides preserving and enriching their rich and variegated cultural heritage. The Foundation has evolved as a vibrant national centre specialized on the Hindu Kush-Himalayan and trans-Himalayan regions in South and Central Asia. By means of its publications and activities, the Foundation has been providing a specialized input and expert analyses on a wide range of issues.

OUR PUBLICATIONS

BOOKS

Afghanistan Factor in Central and South Asian Politics
Edited by K. Warikoo (New Delhi, 1994), 73pp.
Society and Culture in the Himalayas
Edited by K. Warikoo (New Delhi, 1995), 316pp.
Central Asia : Emerging New Order
Edited by K. Warikoo (New Delhi, 1995), 352pp.
Jammu, Kashmir and Ladakh : Linguistic Predicament
Edited by P. N. Pushp and K. Warikoo (New Delhi, 1996), 224pp.
Artisan of the Paradise : A Study of Art and Artisans of Kashmir
By D.N. Dhar (New Delhi, 1999), 230pp.
Gujjars of Jammu and Kashmir
Edited by K. Warikoo (Bhopal, 2001), 317pp.
Bamiyan: Challenge to World Heritage
Edited by K. Warikoo (New Delhi, 2002), xviii, 313pp. 61plates.
The Afghanistan Crisis : Issues and Perspectives
Edited by K. Warikoo (New Delhi, 2002), xxvi, 523pp.
Mongolia-India Relations
By O. Nyamdavaa (New Delhi, 2003), 228pp.
Child Labour Rehabilitation in India
Edited by B. Zutshi and M. Dutta (New Delhi, 2003), 257pp.
Mongolia-China Relations
By Sharad K. Soni (New Delhi, 2006), xix, 328pp.
Afghanistan: The Challenge
Edited by K. Warikoo (New Delhi, 2007), 377pp.
Drugs Production and Trafficking in Afghanistan
By Deepali Gaur Singh (New Delhi, 2007), 380pp.
Afghanistan: Challenges and Opportunities (set of 3 volumes)
Edited by K. Warikoo (New Delhi, 2007).
L. Berzenczey, Adventures in Central Asia: A Hungarian in the Great Game
Edited by P.J.Marczell (New Delhi, 2007).
Cultural Heritage of Jammu and Kashmir
Edited by K. Warikoo (New Delhi, 2009)
Cultural Heritage of Kashmiri Pandits
Edited by S. S. Toshkhani and K. Warikoo (New Delhi, 2009)

JOURNAL

Himalayan and Central Asian Studies
(Quarterly being published regularly since 1997)

MONGOLIA
in the 21st Century

Society, Culture and International Relations

Edited by

K. Warikoo *and* Sharad K. Soni

Issued under the auspices of

HIMALAYAN RESEARCH AND CULTURAL FOUNDATION

and

CENTRAL ASIAN STUDIES PROGRAMME
School of International Studies, Jawaharlal Nehru University, New Delhi

PENTAGON PRESS

Mongolia in the 21st Century: Society, Culture and International Relations
K. Warikoo *and* Sharad K. Soni (Eds)

ISBN 978-81-8274-485-1

First Edition 2010

Published in India by
PENTAGON PRESS
206, Peacock Lane, Shahpur Jat,
New Delhi-110049
Phones: 011-64706243, 26491568
Telefax: 011-26490600
email: rajan@pentagonpress.in
website: www.pentagonpress.in

Published in UK by
PENTAGON BOOKS UK LTD
2-8, Longcroft House,
Victoria Avenue, Liverpool Street,
London England EC2M 4NS

Printed at
New Elegant Printers, New Delhi (India)

PREFACE

Mongolia occupies a unique place in the geographical heartland of Asia. Bordered by Siberia in the north and Gobi desert in the south and surrounded by two powerful neighbours – Russia and China, Mongolia has had a peculiar geo-strategic situation of being land-locked. Its location at the crossroads of Central Asia, North East Asia, Far East, China and Russia further enhances the importance of Mongolia. Having an area as big as 1,566,500 sq. kms. with little over 2.6 million population, Mongolia is the seventh largest country in Asia in terms of its territory but populationwise it is one of the smallest. Its significance, however, lies in the territory rather than in population, which contributed much to the shaping of its distinct nomadic civilisation and its history. The Mongol expansion under Chinggis Khan left a significant impact of the nomadic peoples of Inner Asia on the sedentary world. In fact the Mongol led campaigns not only threatened the security of major settled regions of Eurasian continent but also brought a vast zone stretching from the China Sea to the banks of Dnieper under the unified Mongol rule led by Chinggis Khan himself and later on by his successors.

At the turn of the twenty first century, Mongolia has been trying to overcome its geographical disadvantage of being a landlocked state and is striving to open itself to the outside world despite being surrounded by two giant powers – Russia and China. Moreover, in the post-Cold War security environment of Mongolia, bilateral and multilateral cooperation has become the key factor of regional dynamism in the Asia-Pacific. With the collapse of the USSR and the end of the Cold War the geopolitical situation of Mongolia was altered. This encouraged China to consider its future relations with Mongolia in the framework of new geopolitical realities on the northern side of its border. There have also been concerns about Mongolia's search for a Third Neighbour, such as the United States or Japan which could act as a balancing power vis-à-vis Russia and China.

Mongolia now seeks to ensure the security of its own existence by strictly observing the policy of not allowing the use of the country's territory against other States; ensuring its Nuclear-Weapon-Free-Zone status at the international level and making it an important element of strengthening the country's security by political means. China, on the other hand, wants to build up its power base in North East Asia due to its geo-strategic and geo-economic importance.

As regards India and Mongolia, both countries have had civilisational links spanning over a period of 2,700 years despite being geographically far away. The two countries are the southern and northern ends of a Buddhist arch which provides the cultural foundation of a political and cosy strategic relationship. It is this cultural compatibility that has defined the interests of India and Mongolia. Almost 90 per cent of the Mongolians are Buddhists who consider India as the land of the Budhha's birth and hence affectionately they call India their "Spiritual neighbour." Mongolia's new freedom of strategic choice has further highlighted the commonality of interests. With the signing of the Treaty of Friendly Relations and Cooperation in 1994, a solid foundation was laid down for further development of bilateral relations and cooperation in regional and global affairs.

Both Mongolia and India are involved in several activities including expansion of their multipronged cooperation in diverse areas. Mongolia has some untapped assets which can attract participation by Indian businessmen. Mongolia's assets include abundant mineral resources, broad opportunities to utilise solar and wind energy, a large livestock economy, an agricultural area totalling 130 million hectares, a geographical bridge between Central Asia and Northeast Asia, and a strong commitment to a market economy. Besides, Mongolia's geopolitical location makes it very special for India's Asian strategy.

India's traditional security thrust in South East Asia is now being extended to East Asia and the Pacific and Mongolia figures prominently in this initiative, particularly if it goes beyond to include North East Asia. The new role of India in East Asia for regional cooperation is expected to have its impact on Mongolia as well. Mongolia has been reiterating its support for India's candidature for permanent membership of the UN Security Council. That India and Mongolia have been maintaining closer ties, notwithstanding the physical barriers is also evident from the fact that in December 2005 the two sides agreed in principle to launch a new joint project for the establishment of a satellite-based e-network for tele-education and tele-medicine in Mongolia. The present status of India-Mongolia relations can be described as the "most friendly, cordial and trouble-free."

Inner Mongolia Autonomous Region, the first national minority autonomous region in Chinese history, has also been playing a significant role. In terms of geopolitical importance, Inner Mongolia occupies 3,193 kms., i.e., 70 per cent of the borderland area of the 4,677 kms. long Sino-Mongolian border. With its 15 banners (*hoshuns*) sharing common borders with Mongolia and having five trading ports of first and second-class categories, Inner Mongolia plays a sort of bridge between China and Mongolia. Although the Mongols in Inner Mongolia and Mongolia are living in two different countries, ethnically they belong to the one group sharing same language, culture and the lifestyle. While relations between Mongolia and China have reached a high point, there are some risk factors in their relations. Mongolian notion of potential Chinese threat to reoccupy its "lost territory" is still prevailing as Mongolia had been the Chinese frontier province under the Qing dynasty from 1691 to 1911. The issue of "Pan-Mongolism" or Mongolian nationalism is still a bone of contention between the two sides. China is increasing its economic leverage in Mongolia in order to ensure the non-involvement of Mongolia in any kind of ethnic resurgence of Inner Mongols for the Pan-Mongolist cause.

So far as the Russian Federation is concerned, the indigenous groups having close ethnic affinities with Mongols are concentrated in the Republics of Buryatia, Tuva and Kalmykia. The intellectuals and Buddhist clergy from these Republics have been traditionally wielding considerable influence in Russia particularly in its dealings with Mongolia and Tibet. The post-Cold War era has signified the end of strategic conflict and heralded the end of viewing international politics purely through the geopolitical perspective. New security agenda of states is comprehensive and broad, economics and politics often playing major roles in the individual country's internal and external security interests. Mongolia's international relations have now "shifted from predominantly political and military fields to economic, scientific-technological and information sectors, in other words, from geopolitics to geo-economics." As such Mongolia recently has become a centre of attraction for not only its two neighbours but also the US, Europe, Japan and others.

It is in this background that this book deals with both the historical, cultural, economic, geopolitical perspectives on Mongolia and also its relations with direct and third neighbours. The book is based on the papers presented by eminent academics and Mongolists from India, Mongolia, Russia, USA, Kazakhstan, China, Japan and Turkey at an International Seminar organized in November 2007 by the Central Asian Area Studies Programme, Centre for South, Central, South East Asian & South West Pacific Studies, School of International Studies, Jawaharlal Nehru University, New Delhi.

First three chapters provide historical perspectives on the statehood traditions of Mongolian nomads, Mongolian influences on the economic, military, social and cultural life during Mongolian rule in Anatolia, besides shedding light on the documents in Turkish Archives related to Mongolia. Fourth chapter traces the Mongolic elements in the Hazaragi language of Afghanistan. Issues of Mongolian nationalism and importance of Mongolian language and culture in the identity formation in Mongolia are analysed in chapters five to six. Chapter seven while surveying the literature related to Chinggis Khan, his life and exploits, analyses the revival of Chinggis cult and its importance for the historical and cultural heritage and political identity in Mongolia. Whereas the evolving national security interests of Mongolia, particularly in Northeast and Central Asia are explored in eighth chapter, the following chapter delves into the vulnerability of the economic security of Mongolia. Chapter ten analyses the position of Mongolian women not only in the pre and post-1921 periods, but also during the post-socialist economic transition period. Five chapters (eleven to fifteen) deal with India-Mongolia relations in a comprehensive manner, tracing their civilisational ties from ancient to modern times, contribution of Prof. Raghuvira to the promotion of Mongolian studies, links between Indian and Mongolian literature with particular reference to the Buddhist influences, and the problems and prospects of economic cooperation between the two countries.

Whereas chapter sixteen deals with Sino-Mongolian relations in contemporary times, three chapters (seventeen to nineteen) explore the relations between Mongolia and Russia, particularly after the break-up of former USSR. Chapter twenty provides insight into the political and economic relations between the United States and Mongolia during the past two decades.

Mongol culture areas outside Mongolia in Inner Mongolian Autonomous Region of China, Buryatia, Kalmykia and Tuva Republics of Russian Federation are dealt with separately and in detail in seven chapters (twenty-one to twenty-seven). The study is rounded up by a chapter focusing on the issue of migration of ethnic Kazakh diaspora (*Oralmans*) from Mongolia to Kazakhstan.

Editors

CONTENTS

CONTRIBUTORS

1. **Prof. K. Warikoo** is Director, Central Asian Studies Programme, School of International Studies, Jawaharlal Nehru University, New Delhi.
2. **Dr. Sharad K. Soni** teaches at Central Asian Studies Programme, School of International Studies, Jawaharlal Nehru University, New Delhi.
3. **Academician B. Enkhtuvshin** is President, Academy of Sciences, Mongolia and Director of International Institute for the Study of Nomadic Civilizations, Ulaanbaatar, Mongolia.
4. **Dr. A. Melek Özyetgin** is in the Faculty of Letters, Department of Turkish Languages and Literature, Ankara University, Turkey.
5. **Dr. A. Merthan DUNDAR** is in the Faculty of Letters, Department of Japanese Language and Literature, Ankara University, Ankara, Turkey.
6. **Andrew Shimunek** is a Doctoral student in Linguistics and Mongolian Studies at Indiana University, Bloomington, USA, where he also serves as a Chinese language instructor.
7. **Olzvoi Battumur** is Director of the "Ikh Tenger" complex, Ulaanbaatar, Mongolia.
8. **Dr. B. Uranchimeg** is associated with Institute of International Studies, Academy of Sciences, Mongolia.
9. **Dr. Sindhu Rao** teaches at Bangalore University, Bangalore.
10. **Prof. A. Tuvshintugs** is Deputy Director, Institute for Strategic Studies, Ulaanbaatar, Mongolia.

11. **Dr. J. Gulgou** is formerly Ambassador of Mongolia to India.
12. **Dr. Maqsooda Shitoni** is Visiting Faculty, Centre of Central Asian Studies, University of Kashmir, Srinagar.
13. **Gauri Shankar Gupta** is Joint Secretary (Establishment), Ministry of External Affairs, Government of India and former Ambassador of India to Mongolia.
14. **Dr. Lokesh Chandra,** an eminent Indologist, is Director, International Academy of Indian Culture, New Delhi.
15. **Prof. Yü. Mönkh-Amgalan** is Chair of the Academician Sh. Luwsanwandan Department of Mongolian Linguistics, School of Mongolian Language and Culture, National University of Mongolia, Ulaanbaatar, Mongolia.
16. **Dr. G. Galbayar** teaches at the Department of Literature, School of Mongolian Language and Culture, National University of Mongolia, Ulaanbaatar, Mongolia.
17. **Dr. O. Nyamdawaa,** former Ambassador of Mongolia to India is Head of Protocol, Government of Mongolia and President, Centre of Indian Studies, Ulaanbaatar, Mongolia.
18. **Dr. Nawal K. Paswan** is Assistant Professor, Central Asian Studies Progrmame, School of International Studies, Jawaharlal Nehru University, New Delhi.
19. **Dr. Srikanth Kondapalli** is Professor of Chinese Studies at the Centre for East Asian Studies, Jawaharlal Nehru University, New Delhi.
20. **Prof. Luvsan Khaisandai** is Director, Institute of International Studies, Academy of Sciences, Mongolia.
21. **Dr. Elena Boykova** is associated with Institute of Oriental Studies, Russian Academy of Sciences, Moscow.
22. **Dr. Ilyas Kamalov**, an Expert of Russian Studies is working with Center for Eurasian Strategic Studies, Ankara, Turkey.
23. **Dr. Alicia Campi,** a former diplomat with the US Department of State is President of The Mongolia Society,

President of the U.S.-Mongolia Advisory Group, and President of the Chinggis Khan Foundation, all in USA.

24. **Ms. Baohua** is a Doctoral candidate at Beijing Normal University, Beijing, China.
25. **Prof. Marina N. Baldano** is Head, Department of History, Sociology and Ethnology, Institute for Mongolian, Buddhist and Tibetan Studies, Siberian Branch, Russian Academy of Sciences, Ulan Ude, Russia.
26. **Dr. Victor M. Mitypov** is associated with Economic Ministry, Republic of Buryatia, Ulan Ude, Russia.
27. **Dr. Yelena B. Pokaninova** is based in Elista, Kalmykia.
28. **Dr. L. K. Shotbakova** is associated with the Faculty of History and International Politics, E.A. Buketov Karaganda State University, Karaganda, Kazakhstan.

CHAPTER 1

STATEHOOD TRADITIONS OF MONGOLIAN NOMADS

B. Enkhtuvshin

First of all, it must be made clear that being civilized does not ultimately mean urbanized. Majority of researchers and scholars in the field of civilization study define a civilization as a harmonious coherence of social life, administration, law, letters and culture, education, technology, science and art. According to this definition, state, governance and statehood traditions are the elements of civilization. Therefore, there is no ground to regard nomads, who had their own state and a highly developed statehood doctrine as uncivilized, uncultured or barbarian. The statehood tradition of Mongolian nomads has a history of 2,200 years and they influenced the establishment of a distinct nomadic civilization which belongs to the treasure of civilizations created by the humanity.

Derived from their way of living, traditions, religion, mentality and values, the statehood tradition of Mongolian nomads is the intellectual foundation of their state. While we consider the statehood traditions from the point of view of civilization studies, the statehood is regarded as implementation of the governance idea expressed by the state writing, the ways of treatment by state of its subjects and people, the rules, concept, policy and ideology of perception by citizens of their state. Secondly, we cannot consider the statehood traditions of Mongolian nomads separately from the history of establishment of the Mongolian state.

The history of the classic statehood traditions of Mongolian nomads (3rd century BC – 13th century AD) can be classified into three inter-related periods, namely birth, heritage and restoration. Following this principle and from the point of view of civilization development, this paper presents an overview of the establishment and development of classic statehood traditions of Mongolian nomads through following periods:

- Ancient period (3rd century BC – 3rd century AD)
- Early states established on the Mongolian soil (3rd century AD-11th century AD)
- The Mongol State Empire (12th-13th centuries AD)

PERIOD OF THE HUN EMPIRE

The period of the Hun Empire (3rd century BC – 3rd century AD) and establishment of Great Mongol State and the Mongol Empire are of our particular interest. It was during this period that the classical statehood tradition of Mongolian nomads was established and developed and that Mongolians left their traces in the development of world civilization. The Hun State was founded in 209 BC. It is believed that the statehood traditions of Mongolian nomads originated from this time.

Firstly, these traditions based on culture originated from nomadic husbandry and customs derived from particular geographic and natural conditions. The sky was the supreme belief of the Hun Empire and became essential spiritual content of Central Asian nomadic people. Introduction of writing had an extraordinary impact on the state development of Hunnus. Hunnus had a state seal and used a special seal in their relations with other states. The Hun Empire maintained official contacts with neighboring states and concluded treaties of friendship. Preservation of territorial integrity was the foundation of statehood concept. We consider that development of this concept formed one of the key elements of statehood, which is protection and development by the state of its society, civilization and culture.

Secondly, to compare with sedentary states, Hunnus established a relatively simple system, and organized their governance to be able to conduct independent domestic and foreign affairs. They developed an army organized into a system of 10, 100, 1000 and 10000 units, divided the country into the central, eastern and western administrative parts and promoted the view of heaven above, which meant the respect for state power. This leads to a conclusion that during the time of the Hun Empire another key element of statehood was formulated, which is perception, trust and attitude of citizens towards the state.

Thirdly, Hunnus ensured security of the famous Silk Road and developed the world trade network. They reached cultural centers of Mesopotamia from western China through mountainous and steppe regions of Central Asia. The great road linking Rome, Muslim countries and Western Europe served as the road for interaction of nomads. City-states emerged along this road in Asia, Arabia and Africa. Besides, Buddhism, Muslim, Daos and Christian religions peacefully co-existed along this road. The nomads used this road to introduce the Chinese paper-making technology in Egypt and Europe and the modern military technology in Eurasia.

STATEHOOD OF ANCIENT MONGOLIAN AND OTHER STATES ON MONGOLIAN TERRITORY

Although subsequent Mongolian ancestor states, such as kingdoms of Hsianbi (1st-3rd centuries AD), Jujani (4th-6th centuries AD), Khyatan (8th-12th centuries AD) and Tureg (6th-8th centuries AD) emerged as successors of previous states and inherited statehood traditions to some extent, certainly they brought their own peculiarities of statehood due to their unique culture and writing.

Firstly, historical evidence shows that the notion of *qagan* came into being during the Hsianbi state period. The Hsianbi state just like the Hun empire divided its territory into the central, east and western administrative parts, had decimal unit system, state and laws. This state was a nomadic civilization with its own script, shamanism, nomadic customs and morals. Elevation to royal rank was introduced in Hsianbi era which was inherited by the Great Mongol State in the 13th century AD.

Secondly, the Jujani State introduced the state tradition to decide important state affairs such as proclamation of *qagan* by a *quraldai* (council) of nobles. A *qagan* of the Jujani State as a supreme leader conducted foreign affairs, sent envoys, maintained correspondence, determined the priorities of foreign relations and used state representation credentials *Gerege*. The Jujani State had its own script and an official in charge of public affairs. At early stage shamanism dominated the state affairs, and the king was considered as an emissary of the sky. Later on, Buddhism prospered and became the state religion developing the idea of dual state tradition.

Thirdly, kingdoms of Tureg, established on the territory of Mongolia (6th century AD), inherited many ideas from the statehood traditions of the Jujani State. The chief of the Tureg State possessed the title of *qagan*, the territory was divided into the eastern and western administrative parts and had military organization of society. According to historical documents, there were 28 civilian and military grades under the king. It shows that this state had sophisticated governance procedure and traditions. They advanced the nomadic culture and left rich literature and poetry heritage. The state affairs were conducted and their history was written in a sound script called *Orkhon-Enisei*. Turegs believed in shamanism and worshipped the father sky.

Fourthly, the Uighur Kingdom was established on the Mongolian territory after the Tureg Kingdom. They adopted the script from Central Asian civilized Sogdians, adapted it to their own language sound, developed and made the Uighur script as the state writing, conducted official correspondence, wrote books in this script and translated *satras* from foreign languages. Uighurs unlike other nomads built cities and villages. Archaeological findings at the site of the Uighur capital – "Khar balgas" in Orkhon valley show that the city had a royal palace and had developed artisan mode of production and trade.

Fifthly, the Khyatan state developed industries, art and technology in addition to animal husbandry, promoted intellectual education to a level higher than previous states, and combined nomadic culture with sedentary culture. In the 7th century AD they elaborated their own script, recorded state affairs and made the state writing in the 10th century AD which became known later as *Yeke bičig* (Big letter). A scientific institute was established to collect the papers of Uighur state. In addition to Uighur writings, libraries of nobles and royal palaces contained manuscripts in Chinese, Indian and Korean languages. The state power was in the hands of the *qagan* and implemented by various ministers having different civilian and military ranks. Rashid Al-Din wrote that Khyatans and Mongolians had little difference before and became similar in their language and customs.

Development of Statehood during the Period of Great Mongol State

In the early 13th century, Mongolian nomads formed "Qamag" Mongol and then the Great Mongol State was established in 1206 AD. *The Secret History of Mongols*, which is considered as a true mirror of then nomadic Mongols' life and civilization and the great monument of oriental history and poetry, noted that the great *khuraldai* of Mongolian nobles convened in 1206 AD, raised the 9 support white banner, conferred on Temujin the title of Chinggis Khan and established the United Mongol State. "The most important part of the statehood traditions of the Great Mongol state was the idea of unity as a state priority, integrity and greatness of the country. According to the scholar Ch.Dalai, the idea of unity originated in the era of Hunnus. After break up of the Hun Empire, Mongols lost their unity, disintegrated and fought with each other." Perception of this idea became even more strong in the period of united Mongolia and it was realized and became a component concept of the statehood traditions during the period of Great Mongol State established by Chinggis Khan, according to the last will of Alangua Borte Ujin. The idea of the sky, which was the basic concept of statehood since the period of the Hun empire, was connected and developed with the concept of state governance by genius intellectual approach during the Great Mongol period.

Chinggis Khan established a Council of Wise Men (*Seced-ün zöblel*) from intelligent and experienced people who gave their advice and assisted in the formulation and implementation of the state policy. This was a new concept of Mongolian statehood to run the state by the power of wisdom. Chinggis Khan made the *uighurjin* as the official script which was inherited till then. The concept of eternal heaven, which became one of the foundations of the classical statehood traditions of Mongolian nomads, was the expression of further development of the idea of trusting and respecting the state by citizens.

Since the era of Chinggis Khan the Mongolian nomads have honored their *qagan* as "destined from heaven", and that became an ideological component of statehood traditions of nomads and formed a distinctive system of governance. It can be said that regulated social relations were set up from the time of Great Mongol State which adopted the traditional system of 10 units ensuring the governance of 10s, 100s, 1000s and 10000s and the administrative division into the central, eastern and western parts. In addition to the power of "Holy master" Chinggis Khan used the special state consultative body known as *quraldai* or *khuraldai* to implement his governance. The *khuraldai* discussed and advised on the most important state affairs such as proclamation of new *khagans* (Khans), wars, battles, etc. Besides, establishment of an early social organizational unit of nomads- *khishigten* as a privileged military-administrative body at the *qagan* strengthened the nomadic statehood during the period of Great Mongol State. The institution of *khishigtens* included court, soldiers, clerks, decree-criers, litigation administrators and served as a foundation of administrative staff of Great Mongol State.

One of the innovations brought by Chinggis Khan to develop the nomadic statehood was introduction of the first Mongolian state litigation (*zarqachi*) and law enforcement administration (*qauli yosu-yig keregjigülügči*). The ability of Chinggis Khan to consolidate the foundations of the state through law was a new phenomenon of the Mongolian nomadic statehood. Adoption of the state basic law – *Yeke Jasa* legally strengthened the social relations. The *Yeke Jasa* law was a written law which had codified ancient nomadic customs and norms. The *Yeke Jasa* was the supreme law and contained specific provisions on procedures of elevation to the rank of *khagan*, rules of conducting foreign relations, state great *khuraldai*, duties of people, immunities, military service, battle, finance, taxation, criminal and civil law, family and heritage law.

The state symbol was renewed during the period of Great Mongol State developing the content of the statehood traditions of Mongols. The big white and black banners were the state banners of Chinggis Khan's Mongolia. The big white banner with 9 tails flew at each ceremony of proclamation of new *khagan* or assembly of *khuraldai*. This tradition is maintained to some extent now in the form of "banner of honor". The black banner of Chinggis Khan served as a symbol of might and ability of nomads to defend their country. The state seal was created after the establishment of the state by Chinggis Khaan, though it did not reach us today. Scholars believe that the seal put on the letter addressed by Guyuk Khan to the king of France and the Pope in 1248, was the state seal used since Ogodei Khaan and the letter contained the following text: "In the power of the eternal heaven, the order of the oceanic khaan of the people of the Great Mongol State, the conquered people must respect it and fear them." The capital city of Great Mongol State was established in the valley of Orkhon where the Hun empire had its capital. Chinggis Khan founded *Qorum-a saguhu balgasun* or the capital of Great Mongol State in 1220 AD.

CONTRIBUTION OF CHINGGIS KHAN AND HIS STATE TO WORLD CIVILIZATION

It is obvious that development of classic statehood traditions of Mongolian nomads during the period of Great Mongol State contributed not only to the progress of the Mongolian but also the world civilization.

Firstly, several writings have portrayed the said push of the Mongolian nomadic society from the point of view of waging wars and impeding national development of some nations. It is true, the Mongolian Empire conducted conquests but it performed great deeds for the development of world civilization which any previous empires did not accomplish.

Secondly, from the historical moment of establishment of Great Mongol State it became impossible to rule the Mongolian nomadic society by old means, and hence to put in order many tribes residing on such a big territory became a challenge. It was, in fact, a historical demand which required fundamental changes in the development of the nomadic society and establishment of Mongolia as a true nation state. Chinggis Khan was the first to grasp this moment, and he initiated and organized great changes of social, political, military, economic and intellectual life combining statehood traditions of Mongolian nomads and renovations.

Great Mongol State founded by Chinggis Khan and after that the Mongol Empire, which occupied the half of the world, fully qualified the main requirements of a civilized society. The basic standards of a modern civilization include:

- A "civilized" state upholds the fundamental rights such as the right to life, reputation, property, and especially the freedom of tourism, trade and religion;
- A "civilized" state must be able to defend itself and have a political machinery to efficiently conduct state affairs;
- A "civilized" state must have a judiciary and a legal system compatible with the universally recognized international law, including the rules of war, which guarantee legal fairness for foreigners under its jurisdiction and its own citizens;
- A "civilized" state maintains permanent and appropriate diplomatic relations enabling fulfillment of international obligations.

Thirdly, the main policy of Chinggis Khan was to renovate and develop the political and economic life of nomads using material and intellectual assets of advanced civilizations. Although he was a genuine product of the nomadic civilization, as a great statesman he was able to appreciate and apply achievements of foreign advanced civilizations in the state policy and activities. The fact that he used intellect of educated and skillful people of many nations in the conduct of state affairs and consulted foreign scholars and religious personalities, proves this.

Chinggis Khan linked the east and the west through cultural relations and formulated a distinct philosophy of international relations. He became a driving force of the whole human development through interaction of economies, intellectual culture, means and technologies of eastern and western people, introduction of pluralism, openness and freedom. The capital of Great Mongol State not only showed application of achievements of sedentary civilizations but also became a refined harmony of different civilizations.

Fourthly, Mongolians created a horse relay system throughout the territory of the Empire which was the most expeditious mean of transportation of that time. Western and eastern traders, tourists, the clergy, political and military people traveled using this network, and the relations between Asia and Europe flourished as never before during the period of Great Mongol State. Furthermore, new maritime routes were discovered whereby in addition to land transportation European traders reached India and China via Persian harbors, and Russian traders went to Italy, Mediterranean and Asia Minor through the sea of Azov. Besides the flow of western goods to the east and vice versa, there was an increase in the circulation of coined and paper currencies, and trading and handicrafts, and cities and ports were built. The policy of the Mongol Empire to promote free trade had an important influence on interaction of different cultures and strengthening relations between different nationalities. In this sense the transportation network and the trade route, which were situated on the territory of the Mongol Empire and linked major parts of Europe, Asia and Middle East, served as a bridge between many civilizations in the eastern part of the globe. History provides evidence that new food, inventions and ideas used to follow only this road.

CONCLUSION

The Hun Empire founded classical statehood traditions in the civilizations. The statehood traditions of Mongolian nomads were developed during the Great Mongol State. The Mongolian empire founded by Chinggis Khan and his successors played a significant role in the history of world civilization and left its deep impact. Respect for democracy, which has become an important principle in international relations, and that globalization is gaining momentum, requires Mongolia to preserve its national culture and civilization to boost its economy and strengthen its independence, to learn from its own statehood traditions and successfully build a civil society.

REFERENCES

1. *Cultures and Civilizations*, UNESCO Publishing, 1994, pp. 8, 9.
2. *Nomads and use of Pastures Today*, Ulaanbaatar, 2000, pp. 5-19.
3. G. Sukhbaatar, *Mongolchuudyn ertnii ovog*, Ulaanbaatar, 1980, pp. 204-213, 216-217.
4. *Mongol ulsyn tuukh*. First volume, Ulaanbaatar, 2003, pp. 195-244, 279-288, 313-328, 365-380.
5. A.J. Toynbee, *A Study of History*, I, NY-London, 1965, p. 667.
6. N. Ishjamts, "Mongol tor yosni ulamjlalyn asuudal", *Issues on Oriental Studies*, 1986, 42/33/, pp. 47-51.
7. O.I. Bichurin, *Istoriya o narodakh obitavshih v Srednei Azii v drevnie vremena*, Pt-1, 1851, pp. 27-28.
8. "Nomadism", *International Study*, Ulaanbaatar, 2002, pp. 8-26.
9. G. Sukhbaatar, *Syanbi*, Ulaanbaatar, 1971.
10. G.Sukhbaatar, *Mongol Nirun uls*, Ulaanbaatar, 1992.
11. H. Perlee, *Hyatan guren tednii mongolchuudtai holbogdokh ni*, Ulaanbaatar, 1959.
12. Rashid Al-Din Tahib, *Sbornik letopicei*, Vol.III, kn. 1, pp.103.
13. *Mongoliin nuuts tovchoo*, Ulaanbaatar, 1990, p. 202.
14. Ch. Dalai, *Ikh Mongol uls (1206-1260)*, Ulaanbaatar, 1994.
15. *Mongol ulsyn tuukh*, Second volume, Ulaanbaatar, 2003, pp.25-104.
16. Sh. Bira, "Early Mongolian Political Concepts, (13th-14th Centuries)", *Studies in Mongolian History, Culture and Historiography*, Ulaanbaatar, 2001, pp. 375-377.
17. Sh.Bira, "Mongolin tort yosni uusel hogjil", *Studies in Mongolian History, Culture and Historiography*, Ulaanbaatar, 2001, pp.209-216.
18. Ch. Jugder, *Mongold pheodalizm togtokh ueiin setgelgee*, Ulaanbaatar, 2002, p.155.
19. M. Sanjdorj, *Mongol toriin tuukhees*, Ulaanbaatar, 1998, pp.153-159.
20. B. Enkhtuvshin, "Nomadic Society and Some Aspects of Civilizations Studies", *Chinggis Khaan and Contemporary Era*, Ulaanbaatar, 2003, pp.65-84.
21. *Harmony between Nomadic and other Civilizations*, Ulaanbaatar, 2003, pp. 8-14.

CHAPTER 2

MONGOLIAN INFLUENCE ON THE OTTOMAN INSTITUTIONAL STRUCTURE

A. Melek Özyetgin

Mongolians, who became a great power in the world history from 13th century, did influence the Ottomans. The terms related to various institutional structures of Turco-Mongolian states have similarities to the Ottoman world. As it is known, activities of the states founded by Chinggis Khan and his sons led to dramatic changes in the social, economic and cultural life in Central Asia, where the majority were Turks. The Chinggis influence created a new period which extended to Eastern Europe from Central Asia and had some political and cultural results in terms of world history. The Great Mongolian Empire, founded by Chinggis Khan, developed under the Turco-Uighur tradition with the nomadic Mongolian customs that were taking on a shape in the Buddhist and Islamic cultures and gained a universal quality. This strong state tradition of Chinggis Khan also extended to other Chinggis nation states, which were founded on different lands with different cultures, and uninterruptedly continued and expanded with slight differences. Thus, the rules about administrative, economic and military systems of those states were mainly the same.[1]

In the 13th century, Anatolia, the main land of the Ottoman State, underwent the reign of Ilkhanid for nearly a century. Ilkhanids were the dominant component in Iran and Azerbaijan. In the 14th century, Ottomans became the settled dominating power on this land after the decline of Anatolian Seldjukids.

They actually were the heirs of Seldjukids and inherited a strong institutional structure.

The one-century long Mongolian reign in Anatolia had important influences on the economic, military, social and cultural life of the area and these influences can be seen even today. Mongolian influence on the Ottoman institutional structure is visible at various extents. Some of the Mongolian components included in the organizational structure that the Ottomans inherited were not of permanent quality, but only the results of diplomatic relations with Turco-Mongolian States. For instance, the Uighur script was used in the Ottoman Divan (the Supreme Council) correspondence. Very few documents which show that the Ottomans used the Uighur script in their official correspondence with the Chinggis nations are available today. The *yarlik* (correspondence) written in the Uighur script that (Uzun) Hasan Bey, the ruler of Aq Quyunlu's sent to declare the Ottoman victory to his lands, after Fatih the Conqueror won the Battle of Otlukbeli in 1473, is a fine example of that kind.[2] Its main text is in the Uighur script and just under the lines, the text in Arabic script is found. This practice of chancellery tradition is not directly related to structure, but is a formal interaction as a result of the diplomatic relations between the Ottomans and the Turco-Mongolian nations. One should consider the reason of alphabetical and stylistic changes in letters addressed to Mongolian states as part of the Ottoman Divan tradition. The Ottomans used the Uighur script in their correspondence with the Turco-Mongolian nations.[3]

The Mongolian influence is most felt in financial practices of the Ottomans. From the mid-13th century, Ilkhanids defeated Anatolian Seldjukids and became dominant in Central Anatolia. They had considerable influence especially on economics in Anatolia. Despite a certain prejudice against Mongolians under the influence of Islam in Anatolia, Ilkhanid components were still included in the Turkic state tradition. The Mongolian (Ilkhanid) reign laid the groundwork for economic prosperity and wellfare of Iran and Anatolia. There was a chaotic financial situation in Anatolia before the Mongolian reign, which was proved by the changing currency and taxation systems from region to region under the same government. The financial instability in the region had an adverse effect on commercial life. However, through a monetary system and a taxation system introduced by Ilkhanids, the same commercial laws and financial system prevailed everywhere.[4] Thus, the Ilkhanid influence on the Ottoman financial organization is strongly felt. During the period of its emergence, the Ottoman State was a small *beylik* that was paying taxes and it was situated on the western border of the Ilkhanid State. During the early years of the Ottoman State, Ilkhanids were in the process of their decline. Under the reign of Ilkhanids, *beyliks* in western Anatolia adopted administartive and financial organizations of that state and kept their traditions.[5]

Common things in financial practices, especially tax related terms are remarkable. The following taxes were also levied in Anatolia: *qupčur,* a typical Turco-Mongolian livestock tax dating back to the Ilkhanid period, *qalan,* the land tax, and *tamga,* related to commerce.[6]

Qupčur was a typical Mongolian sheep farming tax which was collected from farmers. The inscription on the door of Camî-i Kebir (the Grand Mosque in Nigde) to the marketplace, shows that *qupčur* system in Anatolia lived up to the reign of Mehmed II. This inscription was carved by order of the last Karaman amirs, Pir Ahmed Khan and Kasım Khan, between 1469 and 1470. This is the last known document related to Mongolian *qupčur* system.[7] The term was again used in the following statement in *Tārih-i Al-i Selčuk* written in the 15th century: "...Muslims paid x*arač, qalan and qapčur"*. We can see the traces of *qupčur* in modern Turkish as *qapčur* (~*qapcur*) "livestock tax; cattle tax" in Anatolian dialects. The word has one more variation; that is *qamčor* "livestock tax".

Tamga, one of the characteristic Turco-Mongolian taxes, was used to mean "customs tax" especially in the Golden Horde, Ilkhanids and Chaghatai. The tax levied upon those who were dealing with commerce at borders and customs was also prevalent in the Ottoman state as a civil tax. In the Ottoman resources, terms like *damgacı, damgalı kile, damgalı urgan, damga zabit eri, damga-yı agnam* were used.[8]

Yasama "salma vergisi" in the Ottoman taxation system must be of the same origin as ***yasaq***, used in Turco-Mongolian taxation system. *qapčur* (*qupčur*) and *tagar* taxes are mentioned in Aşık Pasha's *Garipname* written in the 14th century: "*Gah yasama gāh qapčur geh tagar, qoşuna qoşmuş ili her dem sagar*"(TTS VI, 4365). Moreover, *yasaq* is mentioned in Turkish historical dictionary: *yasa* (*yasaq* ~ *yasag*) "Code, act, law, ban (1. Kanun, ferman, kaide, töre, emir; 2. Memnu, memnuiyet (yasak); 3. Tertibat, tabiye; 4. Ödev olarak verilen iş" (TTS VI, 4361-62).[9]

Qalan, another typical land tax of the Turco-Mongolian period, is mentioned in the vocabulary of ancient Anatolian Turkish: *kalan* is expressed as *Şirvan vilâyetinde bir nevi Salgundur (tax)* (a kind of Salgun in Şirvan province) (TTS V, 3265).

In our studies on old Turkic taxation terms, we find parallelism between the Ottoman taxation practices and those of Ilkhanids and the Golden Horde. ***Tütün,*** a household tax in practice from the ancient Uighur period was called the same particularly in the Golden Horde and the Ottomans. However, its content was changed in the Ottoman State. For them, *tütün* (~ *dütün*) was a kind of tax paid by strangers who temporarily settled in the land of a *sipahi* (Ottoman cavalryman), but these strangers were not dealing with farming. According to the Ottoman Codes, the tax was for married foreigners who settled in a land and they did not pay the taxes levied upon the residents.[10]

Another remarkable point is that the Ottomans had a similar practice to *tarkhan* (privileged families/people) that created privileged classes in the Golden Horde. Tarkhan *yarliks* are the civil documents which gave social and economic privilege to its owner. The privilege seen in traditional societies and granted to individuals who worked for the benefit of the society was always granted in various Turkic states in Central Asia and Middle East. The grant of *tarkhan* title of privilege in the Ottoman State is a continuation of that tradition.[11] It is known that Ottoman Sultans granted certain individuals titles of privilege and deeds of assignment that entailed some tax exemptions. For instance; in

1366, Murad I. granted a man called Ahî Musa a *waqf* deed, which showed that the owner of the deed was tax-free and exempted from all civil taxes and *avārız* taxes (a series of extraordinary taxes on the rural population). The taxes and services mentioned in these documents were entirely of civil quality, in other words, they were based on tacit law. It seems that the exemptions given in this document and other deeds of assignment were related to the old Turco-Mongolian *tarkhan* institution in terms of structure and content.[12] Furthermore, a title of privilege granted to a Jewish merchant called Andriya and his son by Suleiman the Magnificent in 1524 entitled its owners free commerce rights in the Ottoman lands and certified that they were exempted from many taxes as privileged men.[13] A *Tarkhan yarlik*/ediçt in 1580 stated that Ebu Ali Oglu Mehmed, an Egyptian mercant, was granted the title of privilege upon the letter by Mesih Pahsa, the Egyptian governor.[14] All these documents are noteworthy in that they indicate the traces of *tarhanid* institution in the Ottoman State. Although the institution was not a direct one in the Ottoman State, it was included as an exemption.

Military and administrative matters also came under the Mongolian influence. Special military and administrative titles used in Turco-Mongolian states were also found in the Ottoman resources. For example, the word ***daruga***, originated in Mongolian language, which means "general governor", that is a person with important duties in the administrative organization in Turco-Mongolian states and a typical Chinggis position was also mentioned in an imperial edict by Mehmed II in 1473: *taruga* ~ *darga* "vali". The text shows that the term *daruga* was in use in East Anatolia, today's Iran and thereabouts in the 15th century.[15] We find the term ***basqaq*** ~ *basqaqlıq* (general governorship), the Turkic correspondent of the term used again in Chinggis world in the 15th century in *Tarih-i Ali-Selçuk* (TTS I, 409).

Čagdavul (rearguard, rear troop) (<Mo. čagadavul) in the Golden Horde[16] meant the same as ***čandavul***[17] in the Ottoman world, which originated from Mongolian. Another military term ***čapavul*** (raider),[18] formed with the same suffix, was used in the

Ottoman world and it originated from Mongolian. ***Yasaul*** (mounted guards escorting a very important officer);[19] ***yasavul*** (repressor, guard)[20] (the 16th century, the 18th and the 19th centuries) (TTS VI, 4367); ***kevteval*** ~ (<Mo. *kebte'ül*) (guard, warden)[21] were also mentioned in the organization.

Again in the Ottoman organization, ***noyan*** (commander, ruler);[22] originated from Mongolian (the 15th and the 16th centuries); ***nöker*** (servant, aider, company, fellow wife in a polygamous household)[23] were used. In the Golden Horde state organization, ***qaravuls*** (<Mo. *qaragul*) (TMEN I 276; Arat 1987: 615) which meant "watchman, guard; scouting patrol outside the military camp to prevent the army from a sudden raid, dispatch rider" served at strategic points as early warnings against the enemy. In the Ottoman State, it meant "watchman, guard, patrol".[24]

Other military terms like ***cebeci*** (arsenalman, military man) (TTS II, 758) (the 16th century); ***cebelü*** (an armed odd man with sipahis) (TTS II, 759) (the15th century); ***yasakčı*** (escort, guard, the minion of the law) (TTS VI, 4363). Ott. ***yasaqčıbaşı*** (head guard, chief police) (TTS VI, 4363) were used in the Ottoman military organization.

As for the influences on the administrative structure, *sultanic* (tacit) rules that shaped the state law in the Ottoman State trace back Turco-Mongolian tradition. After Ilkhanids, laws enacted by the Sultan himself were known as *Yasa* or *Yasakname* both in the Ottoman State, and Aq quyunlu State and Qara quyunlu State, which were founded in East Anatolia and Iran.[25] On this account, Turco-Mongolian originated words in the Ottoman basic concepts of law and enactment are remarkable: Ott. ***yosun*** (law, custom, practice, system) (TTS VI, 4674) (the 14th and the 15th centuries); Ott. ***yasak ~ yasa*** (law, imperial edict, regulation, custom, order) (TTS VI, 4361). Moreover, ***yargu*** (judgement, reasoning) (TTS VI: 4343-4344) which refers to the Turco-Mongolian course of law, though originated from Turkish and ***yargucu*** (a judge adjudicating court cases and hostility) (TTS VI: 4344) is a term that belonged to the Ottoman civil law.

It is observed that administrative terms that were used in the Golden Horde *tarhan* edicts like ***quščı, barsčı, kemiči, köprükči*** and ***yamčı*** were also included in the Ottoman non-activity supply services behind the front: Ott. ***Qušču*** is the name of a policeman of the members of the Sultan's bodyguards. Instead of *Bostancibasi*, the head of the security, he is responsible for the discipline and reprimand of the member of the Sultan's bodyguards to be imprisoned and disciplined due to a fault.[26] Ott. ***köprücü*** "(mil.) is a term used for those who worked to build bridges. An organization established to build bridges over rivers, repair and maintain them";[27] Ott. ***Gemici.***[28]

Mo. ***keleči*** means "remark" in Ottoman. The word which was a delegacy term in the Golden Army was used to mean "delegate" in Anatolia. It is interesting to see that ***ilči keleči ıyıš-*** was used in the edict addressed to Murad II from Uluğ Muhammed, the Khan of the Golden Horde in 1428.[29] Here, it is clear that there is a status difference between *elçi* and *keleçi* in legal and official terms.

Mongolian influence can also be seen on the Ottoman communication organization. Post or ***ulaq*** system (~ *messengers on horseback*), the most common and fastest way of communication in old times, was a system used by Turks from the Kokturk period. From the early times of Islam, *berîd* in Selcuks and Memluks, *menzil* in the Ottoman Empire, and ***Yam*** post organization in Turco-Mongolian Empire were the main institutions of communication, which was the case in all the Islamic states. The organization called *Yam* in Ilkhanids had great influence on *menzil,* the Ottoman organization of way stations. These communication practices started by Chinggis Khan influenced all Turkic areas and the sound institutional structure lived up to the Ottoman period.[30]

Some of the terms related to the Ottoman *menzil* organization were originated from Mongols. One of them was ***čapar*** (TMEN III, 1033) used in the doubleword *čapar ulaq*. *Čapar ulaq* means "the post whose rider and horse were changed at every station for quick communication, tatar" (Tsö I, 146). Fuat Köprülü stated that the word *čapar* dated back to Selcuks and added that the term *čapar-hane* was used to mean 'post station, menzil'.[31]

It is known that those who were responsible for post were

called ***tatar,*** before the establishment of post in the Ottoman State. This case could be related to the Mongolian influence on communication institution. The word *yam,* which originated from Mongolian language, was also used as "horse, horse at stations" in the Ottoman State with a semantic restriction.[32]

One can suggest that ***tutqavulluq,*** an organization for the security of roads and gates, in Turco-Mongolian states played a role in the establishment of *derbend* organization (founded for the security of roads and gates) in the Ottoman State.[33] ***Tutqavulluq***[34] is a kind of guard organization. *Tutqavul* is frequently mentioned in the *tarkhan yarliks* (edicts) of the Golden Horde as an important service.[35] The organziation started for the security of international trade caravans also existed in Selcuks. In the organization, trade caravans were provided with security with a guard troop under the command of a *rahdar* or ***tutqavul.***[36]

Turco-Mongolian practices also influenced the Ottoman practices of land organization. ***Soyurgal*** (a kind of land property, a land granted by the emperor), which originated from Mongolian language, was also used in the Ottoman Empire. It is possible to take these *soyurgals* into account for the basis of the Ottoman land organization.[37] The term ***Inčü,***[38] which was used for land property by Ilkhanids, was used by the Ottomans with a change in meaning: "captive, subject, dependent on land." *Inčü* was used by Ilkhanids as a land in return for a kind of manor within the land regime. It is known that *inčüs* were secured in various regions in Anatolia, under the Ilkhanid reign and revenues belonged to the Ilkhanid treasury.[39]

It is possible to increase the number of the terms examined here, which are related to various fields. The Ottoman case is remarkable in that it shows the common Mongolian influence and fields of application in history. It is essential to understand well and take Turco-Mongolian organization into account, particularly to determine and understand the resources of the institutional history of the universal Ottoman Empire. In conclusion, Mongols were able to extend their sound state organizations through conquests from their own land to remote regions and this structure was considered and adopted as a continuation of "steppe" tradition over the Turkic-Islamic lands.

REFERENCES

1. Fuat Köprülü, "Orta Zaman Türk Hukuku Müesseseleri", *Belleten*, Vol. II, Issue 5-6, Ankara 1938, pp. 66-67.
2. See Reşit Rahmeti Arat, "Fatih Sultan Mehmet Yarlığı", *Türkiyat Mecmuası*, Vol. VI, 1939, p. 288; A. Melek Özyetgin, "Eski Türk Yazışma Geleneğine Dair: Timürlü Hükümdarı Ebu Sa'id Küregen'e Ait Uygur Harfli 1468 tarihli Bitik", *Orta Zaman Türk Dili ve Kültürü Üzerine İncelemeler*, Ötüken Ankara, 2005, p. 61.
3. M.A. Usmanov, "XIV.-XVI. Yüzyıllarda Coçı Ulusu'nun Osmanlı Devleti'yle Kançılarya İşlerindeki Temaslarının İncelenmesi Üzerine", *X. Türk Tarih Kongresi (22-26 Eylül 1986), Bildiriler,* Vol. III, Ankara Türk Tarih-Kurumu Yayınları, Ankara, 1991, pp. 903-906
4. A. Zeki Velidi Togan, "Moğollar Devrinde Anadolu'nun İktisadî Vaziyeti", *Türk Hukuk ve İktisat Tarihi Mecmuası*, C.I., İstanbul, 1931, pp. 15, 18.
5. İ. Hakkı Uzunçarşılı, "Osmanlı Devleti Maliyesinin Kuruluşu ve Osmanlı Devleti İç Hazinesi", *Belleten*, Vol. XLII, Issue 165, Ankara, 1978, p. 67.
6. V.V. Barthold, "İlhanlılar Devrinde Malî Vaziyet", *Türk Hukuk ve İktisat Tarihi Mecmuası*, C.I., İstanbul, 1931, pp. 24-44; Abdülkadir Yuvalı, "İlhanlıların Anadolu Politikası ve Doğu Anadolu Şehirlerinin Vergi Potansiyeli", p. 585.
7. A. Zeki Velidi Togan, "Moğollar Devrinde Anadolu'nun İktisadî Vaziyeti", *Türk Hukuk ve İktisat Tarihi Mecmuası*, C.I., İstanbul, 1931, pp. 20-21; W. Hinz "Ortaçağ Yakın Şarkına Aid Vergi Kitabeleri", *Belleten*, Vol. 13, Issue 52, 1945, p. 782; A. Melek Özyetgin, *Eski Türk Vergi Terimleri*, KÖKSAV: Tengrim Türklük Bilgisi Araştırmaları Dizisi:4, Ankara, 2004, pp. 86-91.
8. Yusuf Halaçoğlu, "Damga", Türk Diyanet Vakfı, *İslâm Ansiklopedisi*, Vol.8, 1993, p. 455; A. Melek Özyetgin, *Ibid.*, pp. 103-108.
9. W. Hinz, "Ortaçağ Yakın Şarkına Aid Vergi Kitabeleri", *Belleten*, 1945, Vol. 13, Issue 52, p. 774, 11dn.; A. Melek Özyetgin, *Eski Türk Vergi Terimleri*, KÖKSAV: Tengrim Türklük Bilgisi Araştırmaları Dizisi:4, Ankara, 2004, pp. 121-125.
10. Halil İnalcık, "Osmanlılarda Raiyyet Rüsumu", *Osmanlı İmparatorluğu Toplum ve Ekonomi Üzerinde Arşiv Çalışmaları, İncelemeler,* Eren Yayıncılık, İstanbul, 1993, p. 48; A. Melek Özyetgin, *Eski Türk Vergi terimleri*, KÖKSAV: Tengrim Türklük Bilgisi Araştırmaları Dizisi:4, Ankara, 2004, pp. 112-120.
11. İlber Ortaylı "Osmanlı Toprak Düzeninin Kaynakları (15. yy'da İran toprak rejiminde Görülen Muafiyet ve İmtiyaz Sistemi Üzerine)", *Toplum ve Bilim*, 4 (Kış 1977), p. 76.
12. Halil İnalcık, *Osmanlı İmparatorluğu Toplum ve Ekonomi Üzerinde Arşiv Çalışmaları, İncelemeler,* Eren Yayıncılık, İstanbul, 1993, pp. 324-325.

13. Adnan Sadık Erzi, "Türkiye Kütüphânelerinden Notlar ve Vesikalar I", *Belleten*, C. XIV, Sayı: 53, 54, 55, 56, Türk Tarih Kurumu: Ankara, 1950, pp. 92-94.
14. Cengiz Orhonlu, *Osmanlı İmparatorluğunda Derbend Teşkilatı*, Eren Yayıncılık: İstanbul, 1990, p. 15.
15. Reşit Rahmeti Arat, "Fatih Sultan Mehmet Yarlığı", *Türkiyat Mecmuası*, İstanbul, 1939, Vol. VI, p. 307; also see (TMEN I, 165: G. Doerfer, *Türkische und mongolische Elemente im Neupersischen*, 4 c., Wiesbaden (1963-75); Claus Schönig, *Mongolische Lehnwörter im Westoghusischen*, Turcologica 47, Harrassowitz Verlag, Wiesbaden, 2000, p. 113.
16. A. Melek Özyetgin, *Altın Ordu, Kırım ve Kazan Sahasına Ait Yarlık ve Bitiklerin Dil ve Üslûp İncelemesi*, Türk Dil Kurumu Yayınları, Ankara, 1996, p. 113.
17. Schönig 78, TMEN I, 309.
18. Mehmet Zeki Pakalın, *Osmanlı Tarih Deyimleri ve Terimleri Sözlüğü*, I.C., Milli Eğitim Basımevi, İstanbul, 1983, p. 324.
19. Schönig 112, TMEN IV, 166.
20. RSl. III, 215.
21. There are different spellings of the word in the Ottoman State. It is found in the 16th, 18th and 19th century texts. See Schönig 122, TMEN I, 456.
22. Schönig 140, TMEN I, 526.
23. Schönig 141, TMEN I 521. It is found in the 15th and the 16th century resources. The word today is in Anatolian dialects.
24. It is found in the 14th and the 18th century texts. Today the word has a different meaning in our language. See Schönig 152, TMEN I, 399.
25. Halil İnalcık, "Osmanlı Hukukuna Giriş, Örfî-Sultanî Hukuk ve Fatih'in Kanûnları", *Osmanlı İmparatorluğu Toplum ve Ekonomi Üzerinde Arşiv Çalışmaları, İncelemeler,* Eren Yayıncılık, İstanbul, 1993, p. 323; also see Ahmet Akgüdüz, *Osmanlı Kanunnameleri ve Hukuki Tahlilleri*, Book I., İst. 1990, p. 79.
26. Mehmet Zeki Pakalın, *Osmanlı Tarih Deyimleri ve Terimleri Sözlüğü*, II.C., Milli Eğitim Basımevi, İstanbul, 1983, p. 329.
27. *Ibid.*, p. 302.
28. Ömer Lütfi Barkan, *XV ve XV inci Asırlarda Osmanlı İmparatorluğunda Ziraî Ekonominin Hukukî ve Malî Esasları, Birinci Cilt Kanunlar*, İstanbul Üniversitesi Yayınlarından Edebiyat Fakültesi Türkiyat Enstitüsü Neşriyatı, İstanbul, 1943, p. 448.
29. A. Melek Özyetgin, "Altın Orda Devlet Teşkilatında Elçilik Terminolojisi", *Orta Zaman Türk Dili ve Kültürü Üzerine İncelemeler*, Ötüken Yayınları: Ankara, 2005, p. 229.
30. A. Melek Özyetgin, "Eski Türklerde Haberleşme ve Posta Teşkilatı", *Orta Zaman Türk Dili ve Kültürü Üzerine İncelemeler*, Ötüken Yayınları: Ankara, 2005, p. 212.
31. Fuat Köprülü, "Eski Türk Unvanlarına Ait Notlar", *Türk Hukuk ve İktisat Tarihi Mecmuası*, Vol. II., p. 29.

32. A. Melek Özyetgin, "Eski Türklerde Haberleşme ve Posta Teşkilatı", *Orta Zaman Türk Dili ve Kültürü Üzerine İncelemeler*, Ötüken Yayınları: Ankara, 2005, p. 217.
33. Cengiz Orhonlu, *Osmanlı İmparatorluğu'nda Derbend Teşkilâtı,* Eren Yayınları, İstanbul, 1990, pp. 15-16.
34. See TMEN I, 124.
35. A. Melek Özyetgin, *Altın Ordu, Kırım ve Kazan Sahasına Ait Yarlık ve Bitiklerin Dil ve Üslûp İncelemesi*, Türk Dil Kurumu Yayınları, Ankara, 1996, pp. 106, 175.
36. Osman Turan, *Selçuklular tarihi ve Türk İslam Medeniyeti,* Ötüken yayınları, Ankara, 2003, p. 356.
37. See Halil İnalcık "Autonomous Enclaves in Islamic States: Temlîk, Soyurghal, Yurdluk-Ocaklık, Mâlikâne-Mukata'as and Awqaf", *History and Historiography of Post-Mongol Central Asia and the Middle East, Studies in Honor of John E. Woods,* Ed. Judith Pfeiffer, Sholeh A. Quinn, Harrassowitz Verlag, Wiesbaden, 2006, pp. 119-124.
38. See TMEN II 670, ED173a. Clauson stated that the origin of the word was problematic and that it was first used in Uighur documents most probably at the Mongolian period, and also compared the word with *ince* "a maid-servant given to a bride at her marriage" in Mongolian language and *ying* in Chinese (ED173a-b),
39. Ismail H. Uzunçarşılı, *Osmanlı Devleti Teşkilâtına Medhal*, Atatürk Kültür, Dil ve Tarih Yüksek Kurumu, Türk Tarih Kurumu Yayınları VIII. Dizi-Sa. 10[a2], Türk Tarih Kurumu Basımevi, Ankara, 1988, pp. 235-236.

CHAPTER 3

DOCUMENTS RELATED TO MONGOLIA IN TURKISH ARCHIVES AND JAPAN-MONGOLIA RELATIONS

A. Merthan Dundar

Mongolia is important in that it hosted Turkic people found in a large area extending from Balkans to Anatolia, from the Caucasus to Central Asia over a certain period. Inscriptions pertaining to the Kok Turks (Blue Turks) period especially in the Orkhun valley, point to the continuation of the historical and cultural ties between Turkey and Mongolia until today. Political structures known as Turco-Mongolian states in history have also caused those two nations to become closer in many aspects. Raids by Chinggis Khan and his successors reaching Europe caused to so many Turkic groups join the army in those lands, thus leading to an increase in the existing population of Turks in the Middle East and Anatolia.

There exists important correspondence in the Ottoman archives particularly about Chaghatay, Ilhanids and the Golden Horde period.[1] In the republican period Turkish archives, there are very few documents about Mongolia. However, there is some interesting information especially about Japanese policy about Mongolia during 1930s. This case is of course related to the active international policy of the Turkish government during Ataturk period.

As of 1919, the Japanese government let Idil-Uralian Turco-Tatar groups who were escaping from Russia, settle down in

Japan. Afterwards, Turco-Tatar communities in Tokyo were used to propogandize Japan among the Turkic groups (Muslims) living in Russia and China.[2] On the establishment of Manchuko State in Manchuria by Japan in 1932, Turkish Ministry of Foreign Affairs started to pay attention to the Far East closely. Turkey carefully followed the relationship of certain anti-Kemalist groups in Japan with Manchuko State and their activities in the Middle East. In 1933, the Turkish government reacted against Japan when Şehzade Abdülkerim Efendi (Prince Abdulkarim), grandson of Abdülhamid II, the Ottoman Sultan who was well-known among Muslims and considered as the founder of the movement called Pan-Islamism by Europeans, was invited to Japan.[3] The Prince's efforts to re-establish the Ottoman Dynasty in Xinjiang, which was called Eastern Turkistan by the native people, in collaboration with Japanese caused Turkey to intervene in the case.

Because of the above mentioned reasons, the Turkish Embassy in Tokyo very closely examined Japanese policies and activities of Asian states and reported their results to Ankara. Their examination and research was largely about the Japanese policy on China. However, there are some other reports prepared by Turkish diplomats on Japanese-Mongolian relations and Japanese plans on that country. These documents relating the period between 1930 and 1935, are important in that they show the interpretation of the Turkish government concerning the Japanese policy on Asia and accordingly reflect upon the attitude of the Turkish Ministry of Foreign Affairs.[4]

This paper examines the related reports and points out how the Japanese-Mongolian relations of that time are reflected in Turkish archives.

Three documents prepared by the Turkish Foreign Affairs about Japanese relations to Mongolia, in other words, Japanese plans over Mongolia are of importance. Among them, particularly the report dated December 30, 1931 on Chinese-Japanese conflict is striking in terms of the information that it provides about Japanese view about Mongolia.[5] In this document, the Japanese policy over Mongolia is directly shown through quoting extracts from declarations of the Japanese statesmen at that time. A report submitted to the imperial office by Baron Tanaka,[6] one of the Japanese Prime Ministers, is mentioned in the following way in the document sent to Ankara by the Turkish Ambassador in Tokyo:

> "... it is necessary to occupy China in order to reign over Central Asia, and to conquer Manchuria in order to get the control of China. If this happens, the whole world as far as the Near East will give into demands of Japan..."

> "... When the current situaiton and any kinds of possibility are properly considered, it will be clear that the best way is to gain hegemony and privileges over Manchuria and Mongolia as much as possible. Later, we may have all the natural resources in China, particularly through commercial relations, using Manchuria and Mongolia as operational bases. After gaining hegemony over China in this way, we may then be able to conquer India, Malaya, Anatolia, Central Asia, even Europe..."

This plan was interpreted by the Turkish Foreign Affairs as follows:

> "...The policy described by Baron Tanaka is an imperialist view, some parts of which is ridiculous, but it has become a national policy to be followed by the Japanese nationalists for the development of the country. It was the need of Japan that determined the national policy, not the style of Baron Tanaka. Even if the governmets change, it is the main Japanese policy over China, despite slight differences..."

In 1931, with the Japanese operation over Manchuria, some Mongolian states declared their independence. As far as it is understood, the topics described as the national policy by Baron Tanaka were put into practice by the Japanese army. In the report of the Turkish Embassy, it was stated that extending the Japanese military invasion to Manchuria would enliven the Mongolian question. The Mongolian question was substantially mentioned in the document as follows:

> "... One of the most sensitive and important issues of Central Asia is the Mongolian question. Tsarist Russia first felt the necessity to control Mongolia, when Russians wanted to occupy the center of Asia, and always desired these lands with greed. However, the

interventions of England and America in favour of China prevented such a desire. During World War I, Russia put a pressure on its allies and imposed the condition that Mongolia and Turkestan were dominions of the Russian Empire and got the condition affirmed. However, after the collapse of Tsarist Russia, they were territorially claimed by the Russians. After the war, the Chinese declared sovereignty rights over Mongolia and Turkestan again.

Today, Russians have again won upon a part of Mongolia, as in the case of Manchuria. Even a Soviet system has been set up in northern Mongolia, under the influence of Russia. The only Soviet government in the world apart from the USSR is here. After the 1905 Russian-Japanese War, the Japanese started to influence the eastern parts of İnner Mongolia through railways, after they gained ascendance over these parts. According to the latest news, there are states in South Mongolia that claim independence with the encouragement of Japan. As well as the Manchuria question, there is the Mongolian one, which is an important Asian question..."

According to the Turkish Ambassador, who wrote the report, Japan was making efforts to make an agreement with the anti-Russian states, since Japan estimated that they could come up against the Soviet Union because of Manchuria and Mongolia. Even a secret alliance was being prepared against Poland and Russia. The final comment in the report is that although the big states, even the League of Nations were tackling that problem, the problem was not relieved, but grew even more serious.

Another document that we consider important about the Japanese policy over Mongolia is dated January 9, 1936.[7] This report consists of secret information sent to Ankara by Zekayi Apaydın,[8] the Turkish Ambassador in Moscow between November 17, 1935 and December 22, 1935. In the introduction of the document, it is stated that autonomy was declared in Heibei and Caharar[9] (the two states are contiguous to today's İnner Mongolia) as a result of the Japanese pressure and the Japanese gained ascendance over a richest and a most crowded part of China pursuant to the recognition by the Nanking Government. According to the report, the declaration of autonomy was supposed to be demanded for the five states in Northern China included Heibei and Caharar. However, Chang

Kai-shek opposed the situation due to the opposition of England and the protests by the Chinese intellectuals and students. Also, Russia declared that in such a case, if Japan would have a military operation over those autonomous lands, Russians would not observe it passively. According to the Turkish Ambassador, this case was confirmed by Sergeant M. Istamanyakof of the Russian Foreign Affairs, whom he had met the previous day. It also highlighted that the Soviet Union made great effort so as not to lose Mongolia to Japan and that particularly Russians tried to connect the railway being constructed towards Xinjiang and Trans-Siberia line. According to the report, with the connection of these railway lines, Outer Mongolian trade would entirely pass into the hands of Russia. However, Japan gained ascendance over Caharar state, with the occupation of Jehol, a part of Mongolia, by the Japanese and the autonomy of Northern China. In the report, the Ambassador also states that Moscow adopted a protective position on Outer Mongolia against the Japanese attack. He quotes the following statements by M. Istamanyakof as evidence: "*There is nothing to hide, Mongolia is our close friend. We cannot meet the Japanese attack calmly*". Finally, Ankara was informed that there were rumours in Moscow about an attack on Outer Mongolia by the Japanese together with the Manchurian army.

Another document is the *Annual Report* by the Embassy in Tokyo,[10] which included information collected in 1934 and sent to Ankara. The 33-page report was prepared by Minister Nebil Bey.[11] In this document, the possible Chinese measures to be taken against the Japanese actions in order to establish new governments in İnner Mongolia and Xinjiang are also briefly mentioned. Accordingly, China would follow a policy to ensure the prevention of autonomy demands pacifically through the leading local people in the lands under Japanese control. Otherwise, China would change the policy for the desired autonomy and try not to have problems with the Japanese. At the same time, Japan would secretly maintain any propoganda with those whom they trusted among the local people and try to keep its relations with China at a normal level so as not to disturb Russia.

In relation to the Japanese policy over Mongolia, one can draw the following conclusions from the brief study in which we examined the documents in the Republic archives of Turkey:

1. Turkish Foreign Affairs considered the relations between Mongolia and Japan and the Japanese policy over Mongolia generally in the context of the Chinese-Japanese relations.
2. As it is clear from the report written in 1931, Turkey carefully watched the political attacks and activities of Japan concerning Mongolia at that time. Not only the Turkish embassies in Japan, but also the ones in Moscow and European capitals tried to collect relevant information.
3. In the reports written after 1933, it is quite possible that the Turks were trying to understand the Japanese plans about Xinjiang as well as their policy over Mongolia. This is also due to the anxiety that some Turks in the region created through their activities in Xinjiang in cooperation with Japan.

REFERENCES

1. The documents found in the Ottoman archive, where the name "Mongolia" was directly mentioned are as follows: Tarih: 08/Ş /1300 (Hicrî), Dosya No: 6, Gömlek No: 39, Fon Kodu: Y..PRK.TKM. "The coronation ceremony of Alexander III. held, Russia and the necessity for Russia and France to become allies against the three allied governments and Russian military power."
Tarih: 29/Z /1300 (Hicrî), Dosya No: 7, Gömlek No: 28, Fon Kodu: Y..PRK.HR.. "The natural, economic and historical aspects of China, population, military organization and geographical area *(tt)*"
Tarih: 28/Ş /1322 (Hicrî), Dosya No: 46, Gömlek No:81, Fon Kodu: Y..PRK.EŞA. "*Information about the wars between Japan and Russia.*"
Tarih: 29/Z /1310 (Hicrî), Dosya No: 29, Gömlek No: 11, Fon Kodu: Y..PRK.TKM. "*A stage of the historical course of Northern Africa and the Middle East (French) (tt)*"
Tarih: 30/Z /1320 (Hicrî), Dosya No: 9, Gömlek No: 110, Fon Kodu: Y..PRK.SGE. "*Settlement of Osmanogullari in Söğüd. a.g.y.tt.*"
Tarih: 20/Ş /1337 (Hicrî), Dosya No:51/-2, Gömlek No: 9, Fon Kodu: DH.KMS. "*the memorandum sent by the special commission in Kilis concerning the retention of Kilis in the Ottoman Empire.*"

For detailed information about the documents see *http://www.devletarsivleri.gov.tr.*

2. For the Turco-Tatar communities in the Far East, see Nadir Devlet, *Yırak Künçıgıştagı Tatar-Başkortlarda Ni Buldı*, Kazan Devlet Ünivesitesi, Kazan, 2005.
3. For detail information, see Selçuk Esenbel, "Japan's Global Claim to Asia and the World of Islam: Transnational Nationalism and World Power, 1900-1945," *The American Historical Review*, Vol. 109, No. 4, October 2004 and A. Merthan Dundar, *Pan-İslamizim'den Büyük Asyacılığa: Osmanlı İmparatorluğu, Japonya ve Orta Asya*, Ötüken Yayınları, İstanbul, 2006.
4. The documents found in the Republic archive, whose titles directly included the name "Mongolia" are as follows:
   Tarih: 1/6/1925, Sayı: Dosya: 43182, Fon Kodu: 30..10.0.0, Yer No: 247.672..17. "In the secret clause of the agreement between Japan and Russia, in return for the Japanese concessions, Mongolia is to join the Union, and Turkestan in China is to recognise the free movement of the Russian Government."
   Tarih: 15/8/1934, Sayı:, Dosya: 400-3265, Fon Kodu: 30..10.0.0, Yer No: 221.490..17. "The news in the copy dated May 17, 1934, of the Japanese Times published in Japan, about the agreement between the Chinese Government and the Soviet Union concerning the Russian schools in Inner Mongolia."
   Tarih: 9/1/1936, Sayı:, Dosya: 43431, Fon Kodu: 30..10.0.0, Yer No: 257.727..15. "Japanese activities in China and Mongolia, Chinese financial situation."
5. Tarih: 30/12/1931Sayı:, Dosya: 434A7, Fon Kodu: 30..10.0.0, Yer No: 257.728..7. "A Report on the Chinese-Japanese Conflict."
6. *Tanaka Giichi (*1864-1929), 26th Prime Minister of Japan from 1927 to 1929.
7. Tarih: 9/1/1936, Sayı:, Dosya: 43431, Fon Kodu: 30..10.0.0, Yer No: 257.727..15. "Japanese activities in China and Mongolia, Chinese financial situation".
8. Zekayi Apayadın was appointed as the Ambassador in Moscow for the second time on July 9, 1935 and voluntarily retired in September 1939.
9. It was abolished as a province in 1952; most of it was incorporated in the Inner Mongolian Autonomous Region, and the rest was divided between Shanxi and Hebei provinces.
10. Tarih:, Sayı:, Dosya: 434B, Fon Kodu: 30..10.0.0, Yer No: 257.729..30. *The Annual Report* by the Embassy in Tokyo.
11. Nebil Bey worked for the Embassy in Tokyo as the permanent Chargé d'affairs between December 17, 1931 and February 13, 1936.

CHAPTER 4

MONGOLIC ELEMENTS IN THE HAZARAGI LANGUAGE OF AFGHANISTAN AND THEIR VALUE FOR RECONSTRUCTING WESTERN MIDDLE MONGOL

Andrew Shimunek

It has long been suggested that the Hazara people of Afghanistan are descendants of the Mongols. While ethnicity is a thorny and complicated question, and in all reality, the Hazaras are almost certainly descendants of Mongols, Turks, and their Tajik neighbors, there are in fact a large number of Mongolic and some Turkic elements in the Hazaragi language, which is best classified as an Iranian language with a Mongolic substratum. In addition to their value for the history of the Hazaragi language and language contact studies, this Mongolic stratum in Hazaragi is also quite useful for increasing our understanding of the Middle Mongol lexicon, and can supplement the somewhat small corpus of Middle Mongol lexicographical sources we have available to us in Arabic, Armenian, Chinese, Georgian, and Persian transcriptions, and *Phags-pa* (Square Script) and Pre-Classical Mongolian orthography. In particular, most, if not all, of these Mongolic elements in Hazaragi are Western Middle Mongol elements.

Given my background in Mongolian Studies and Mongolic linguistics in particular, this paper sheds some insight into the Mongolic elements in Hazaragi. This study would not have been possible were it not for the native Hazara scholar Tariq

Malistani's important dictionary of Hazaragi (1993). All of the Hazaragi forms in this paper are taken from his work. This paper should be seen as supplement to Ligeti's pioneering work on Mongolic elements in Hazaragi, and Dulling's (1973) work. I have noted Moghol forms from Weiers and extant Middle Mongol forms, with emphasis placed on western Middle Mongol sources.

SEMANTICS OF MONGOLIC ELEMENTS IN HAZARAGI

Most of the Mongolic elements in Hazaragi come from the sphere of so-called "basic vocabulary" – lexical items that are largely stable over time and tend to resist borrowing. This fact in and of itself is a good reason for considering the Mongolic elements in Hazaragi not as loanwords or borrowings, but rather as substratal elements from Middle Mongol – the original language of the population, which was later obscured by an Iranian superstratum.

Some of the identifiable basic vocabulary items of Mongolic origin include kinship terms such as 'maternal grandmother', 'uncle', 'wife', etc.; color terms such as 'red', 'brown', and 'black'; body part terms such as 'hip', 'heel', 'shoulder blade', 'thumb, big toe', 'stomach', etc.; and personal pronouns such as 'your'. Note the forms presented below:

Kinship terms

[ɒˈd͡ʒʌ] ~ [ˈɒd͡ʒʌj] 'maternal grandmother' < wMM **eje* ~ **ejei* 'mother'

[ʌbˈʁʌ] ~ [ʌbʌˈʁʌ] 'uncle, father, brother' < wMM *abaqa* ~ *abaγa* 'uncle'

[boˈlʌ] 'cousin belonging to mother's sister' < wMM **höle* (cf. Khalkha **бөл** *pɵɮ* 'children of sisters')

[χɒˈto] 'wife' < wMM *qatun* 'queen'

Color terms

[ʌˈlɒn] 'red' < wMM *hula'an* ~ *hulān* 'red'

[boɾ] 'brown' < wMM *bora* 'gray'

[qʌˈɾʌ] 'black' < wMM *qara* 'black'

Body part terms

[be'jʌ] 'body, stature' < wMM *beye* 'body'

[bok'sʌ] 'hip' < wMM *bökse* 'buttocks, posterior'

[boɾ'bi] 'heel' < wMM **borbi* 'heel'

[dɒ'lu] 'shoulder blade' < wMM *dalu* 'shoulder blade'

[eɾ'kʌ] 'thumb, big toe' < wMM *erke* 'thumb, big toe' (glossed 'finger' in the Leiden manuscript)

[qo'tʌ] 'stomach (human)' < wMM **qota* id.

[ʁo'jʌ] 'thigh' < wMM *γuya* 'thigh'

[tol'ʁʌ] 'top of the head' < wMM **tol(u)γa* 'head'

[t͡ʃʌ'bi] 'body part below the ribs (soft)' < wMM **čabi* 'groin'

[t͡ʃe'd͡ʒin] 'bosom, chest, lap' < wMM *če'eji* 'chest'

[t͡ʃe'mʊk] 'joint (of bones), thighbone (femur), upper arm (humerus) bone' < wMM **čemük* 'bone marrow'

[t͡ʃo'qu] 'forehead' < wMM **čoqu* 'forehead'

Pronouns

[tʌ] 'your' < wMM *ta* 'you (plural)'

VALUE OF HAZARAGI FOR RECONSTRUCTING WESTERN MIDDLE MONGOL LEXICON

The Mongolic elements in Hazaragi are also of value for reconstructing the lexicon of western Middle Mongol. Simply put, the Middle Mongol corpus is very limited. The extant lexicographical and other materials on the western variety of Middle Mongol, or "Western Middle Mongol", are especially impoverished. However, Hazaragi gives us a chance to reconstruct some of the lexicon of Western Middle Mongol that was not documented in contemporary sources, since the Mongolic elements in Hazaragi are certainly of Western Middle Mongol stock. Among the Mongolic elements in Hazaragi which are not attested in the Western Middle Mongol corpus, we may note the following including such words as [ɖom] 'beneficial medicine', from western Middle Mongol **dom* 'folk medicine';

[be'lʌj] 'gloves for reaping thorns', from western Middle Mongol **be'elei* 'gloves'; and [bu'dʌ] 'domestic animals', from western Middle Mongol **buda* 'large livestock':

Table 1. Western Middle Mongol lexical items reconstructed from Hazaragi

Western Middle Mongol	Hazaragi
**ača*	[ɒ't͡ʃʌ] 'forked stick'
**aqta*	[ʌχ'tʌ] 'castrated animal'
**aryali*	[ʌɾʁʌ'li] 'one-year-old female deer'
**be'elei*	[be'lʌj] 'gloves for reaping thorns'
**book*	[bo'ko] 'camel hump'
**bökse*	[bok'sʌ] 'hip'
**bole*	[bo'lʌ] 'cousin belonging to mother's sister'
**borbi*	[boɾ'bi] 'heel'
**buda*	[bu'dʌ] 'domestic animals'
**čabi*	[t͡ʃʌ'bi] 'body part below ribs (soft)'
**čalči-*	[t͡ʃʌl't͡ʃʌl] 'loquacious, talkative, wordy'
**čabči-*	[t͡ʃʌp't͡ʃi kʌ'do] 'slash (kill with a sword)'
**čibil*	[t͡ʃʌ'bʌl] 'dirt, uncleanliness'
**čemük*	[t͡ʃe'mʊk] 'joint (of bones), femur, humerus'
**čimqo-*	[t͡ʃɪm'qo kʌn'do] 'pinch'
**čoqu*	[t͡ʃo'qu] 'forehead'
**dāyan*	[dɒ'ʁɒn] 'ass (of two years of age)'
**darui*	[dʌɾ'ɾʌw] 'now, just now, right now, at present'
**dom*	[ɖom] 'beneficial medicine'
**duta'a-*	[dʊ'tɒ kʌ'do] 'escape'
**engger*	[eŋ'gʌɾ] 'shirt collar'
**ebse-/*ebsi-ye-*	[ep'sʌ] 'yawning'
**yolo-*	[ʁol'd͡ʒi kʌ'do] 'refuse, reject'
**yorqi/*yoryi*	[ʁoɾ'ʁi] 'hook, ring, link'
**yunaji*	[ʁun'd͡ʒi] 'cow (young, which newly bears a calf)'
**hala / *ala*	[hɒ'lʌ] 'multicolored'
**kenje*	[kɒnd͡ʒ] 'cross-eyed'

**mergen*	[meɾˈgʌn] 'hunter (very experienced)'
**qabi* / **qabu*	[qɒˈbu] 'near'
**qabqu*	[qʌbˈqu] 'fox trap, snare (for foxes and wolves)'
**qada*	[qɒˈdʌ] 'cliff'
**qadu'ur/*qada'ur*	[qɒˈduɾ] 'sickle'
**qaljan/*qaljon*	[qʌlˈd͡ʒo] 'white spot on forehead (of cows), baldness on forehead, receding hair'
**qarγana*	[qʌɾʁʌˈnʌ] 'wild bush (creeping)'
**qima*	[qiˈmʌ] 'ground meat (cut very finely by hand)'
**qoriγ/*quriγ*	[qʊˈɾiʁ] 'prohibition'
**qota*	[qoˈtʌ] 'stomach (human)'
**qoto*	[qoˈto] 'manger, trough, feeding trough'
**qungqar*	[quŋˈqɒr] 'brown cow'
**quru'ut*	[qʊˈɾut] 'dried sour milk product'
**sabda-*	[sʌbˈdʌ kʌˈdo] 'beat with a stick'
**sača-*	[sʌˈt͡ʃi kʌˈdo] 'scatter, strew, sprinkle'
**širaja*	[ʃiɾˈd͡ʒʌ] 'impure milk'
**sona*	[soˈnʌ] 'horsefly'
**teke*	[ʈʌˈkʌ] 'young male goat'
**tala*	[tɒˈlʌ] 'meadow, pasture, strip of grass (land)'
**ungγi*	[ũˈʁi] 'hole for handle in axe or hammer'
**yara*	[jɒˈɾʌ] 'injury, wound'

CONCLUSION

So far I have identified approximately 150 Hazaragi words of Mongolic origin, occurring within a number of different semantic domains, including the kinship terms, color terms, pronouns, and body part terms mentioned above, as well as animal names (zoonyms), plant names, verbs, words for tools, clothing items, dairy products and other foods, adjectives, words related to medicine, hunting terminology, words for natural phenomena (such as the Hazaragi words for 'cliff', 'cloud', 'spring', 'meadow', 'desert', etc.), and types of dwellings, among others. Although this study is in all likelihood not comprehensive, as other Mongolic elements are sure to be found in the Hazaragi language, the lexical items identified here present a clear picture of the Mongolic substratum of the Hazaragi language, and serve as testament to the lasting ethnolinguistic impact the Mongols have had on Afghanistan.

LEXICON OF MONGOLIC ELEMENTS IN HAZARAGI

Abbreviations
eMM.ZYYY = Zhi Yuan Yi Yu (Kuribayashi 2003)
MM = Middle Mongol
Mog. = Moghol (Weiers 1972)
WM = Written Mongol
wMM = Western Middle Mongol
wMM.I = Istanbul Manuscript (Ligeti 1962)
wMM.Ibn = ibn-Muhannā (Poppe 1938-9)
wMM.L = Leiden Manuscript (Poppe 1927-8)
wMM.M = Muqaddimat al-Adab (Poppe 1938-9)
wMM.R = Rasulid Pentaglot (Golden 2000)

Note: All Hazaragi forms cited here are from Malistani (1993); all reconstructed wMM forms are my own proposals. Other wMM forms are cited according to their source. Eastern Middle Mongol (eMM) forms are for the most part cited only when no attested wMM form exists in the extant source materials. Note also that I have not attempted to provide all the attested Middle Mongol and Written Mongol forms for every Hazaragi word; rather, it should suffice that I have provided at least one attested wMM form when such an attested cognate exists. Western Middle Mongol forms were only reconstructed for Hazaragi words whose Mongolic cognates are not attested in wMM sources.

Table 2

Hazaragi form (in IPA and Arabic orthography)			Mongolic origin
ɒ'd͡ʒʌ	آجه	grandmother (maternal)	wMM **eje* 'mother'
'ɒd͡ʒʌj	آجی	grandmother (my, maternal); old woman	wMM **ejei* 'mother'

ɒlo'ʁʌ	آلوغه	hammer	wMM.Ibn *haluγa* [هلغا] 'hammer'
ɒ'ɾɒl	آرال	wet land	wMM.M *aral* [ارال] 'island'
ɒ't͡ʃʌ	آچه	forked stick	wMM **ača*
ɒ'wuɾ	آوور	cloud	wMM *a'ur* [آوور]
ʌb'ʁʌ ~ ʌbʌ'ʁʌ	ابغه	uncle; father's brother	wMM.L *abaqa* [اباقا] 'uncle', wMM.R *abaqa* [آبقا] 'paternal uncle', wMM.M *abaγa* [اباغا]
ʌd'li ~ ʌdʌ'li	ادلی	alike, resembling	wMM.M *adali* [ادالی]; WM *adali*, Mog. [ɔdɔ'li] 'alike, similar'
ʌ'lɒn	الان	red	< wMM.Ibn *hulān*, wMM.M *hula'an* 'id.' (cf. Mog. [u'lɒm] id.[1])
ʌp't͡ʃi	اپچی	influenza, grippe	wMM.L *ebčin* [ابْجين] 'Krankheit', wMM.R *ebečin* [ابجين] 'disease', wMM.M *ebečin*
ʌɾʁʌ'li	ارغلی	deer (female, one year old)	wMM **arγali* ; cf. WM *arγali* 'female wild sheep'
ʌɾ't͡ʃi	ارچی	milk product from churned sour milk (after removing water)	wMM.R *ārči* [ارجی] 'sour milk dried (cream) cheese' ; WM *aγarča*
ʌɾ't͡ʃu	ارچو	cloth (thin co-vering, used like a shawl); veil	< wMM.M *arči'ur* [آرجيور]
ʌχ'tʌ	اجته	castrated animal	wMM **aqta* 'gelding' ; cf. wMM.I *aqtači* [آقتاجي] 'hostler, wrangler', WM *aγta*
ʌχtɪl'd͡ʒi kʌ'do	اختلجی کدو	castrate	

[1] This is the form Weiers cites in his lexicon of Moghol. However, when one examines the sentential context of the word, it seems more likely that this [m] is simply due to assimilation with the bilabial consonant of the existential verb which follows it. Thus, it is more likely that the underlying form is /u'lɒn/.

bɒ'tuɾ	باتور	brave; valiant; bold; intrepid	wMM *ba'atur/*bahatur* 'hero', wMM.Ibn *bahadur* [بهادُر] 'id.'
bʌ'jo	بيو	rich; wealthy	wMM.M *bayan* [بايان], wMM.Ibn *bayan* [باين]
bʌ'sʌ	بسه	again; once more	wMM.I *basa* [بَاسَا], wMM.Ibn *basa* [باصا] 'id.'
be'jʌ	بييه	body; stature	wMM.Ibn *beye* [بَيا] 'body', wMM.M *beye* [بيه]
be'lʌj	بيلى	gloves for reaping thorns	< wMM *be'elei/*bēlei* ; cf. WM *begelei* 'gloves'
bo'ko	بوكو	camel hump	wMM **bökö* 'id.'
bok'sʌ	بوكسه	hip	wMM.M *bökse* [بوكسه]; WM *bögse* 'buttocks, posterior'
bo'lʌ	بوله	cousin belonging to mother's sister	wMM **böle*
bol'd͡ʒʌ	بولجه	appointment; promise (to visit)	cf. wMM.M *boljal* [بولجال]
bol'ʁʌ	بولغه	caution; care; circumspection	cf. wMM.M *bolγa-*
boɾ	بور	brown	wMM.M *bora* [بوره] 'gray'
boɾ'bi	بوربى	heel	wMM **borbi* 'id.'; cf. WM *borbi*
bu'dʌ	بوده	domestic animals; tame animals	wMM **buda*
bu'ʁʌ	بوغه	young cow	wMM.M *buγu* [بوغو] 'stag'
bʊ'lɒʁ, bʊ'lɒq	بلاق ~ بلاغ	spring; drain (e.g. water from under the ground)	wMM.I *bulaq* [بُولاَق] 'source', wMM.M *bulaq* [بولاق]; cf. WM *bulaγ* 'spring'

bʊ'ɾʌw	برو	cow (yearling)	wMM.M *bura'u*; WM *birayu*
bʊr'gʊt	برگد	eagle; royal falcon	wMM.M *bürküt* [بورکوت] 'чапрак'
bʊrʁʊ'so	بورغوسو	red willow	wMM.M *buryasun* [بورغاسون]
dɒ'lu	دالو	shoulder blade	wMM.I *dalu* [دَالوُ] 'id.', wMM.M *dalu* [دالو], wMM.IM *dalu* [دَالو]; cf. WM *dalu*
dɒ'ɾi	داری	wound; injury	cf. wMM.R. *dāritu* [دارتو] 'having a wound on the back (under the saddle)'; WM *dayir*
dɒ'ʁɒn	داغان	ass (of two years of age)	wMM **dāyan*
dʌ'bʌ kʌ'do	دبا کدو	pass a mountain pass	cf. wMM.R *dabān* [دبان] 'mountain pass' ; WM *daba-* 'go through a mountain pass', *dabay-a* 'mountain pass'
dʌɾ'ɾʌw	دررو	now; just now; right now; at present	WM *darui* 'immediately'
del	دیل	mane of a horse	wMM.M *del* 'id.'; cf. WM *del*
do'tʌɾ	دوتر	lining (of clothing)	wMM.M *dotar* [دوتار]
dʊ'tɒ kʌ'do	دتا کدو	escape	wMM **duta'a-* 'flee, escape'; cf. Mog. [dɔtɔ-] ~ [dutɔ-] ~ [tutɔ-] 'fliehen, weglaufen'
ɖom	ڈوم	beneficial medicine; medicine which is effective, useful	wMM **dom*; cf. WM *dom*
d͡ʒɒ'ʁʌ	جاغہ	edge; side; collar	wMM.M *jaqa* [جقا]; WM *jaq-a* ; cf. Mog. [dʒʌʀʌ] 'Seite, Ufer'

d͡ʒʌɾ'jʌ	جریہ	porcupine	wMM.I *jaryasun* [جَرْیاسُون] 'hedgehog', wMM.M *jarya* [جاریا]; cf. WM *jaraγ-a*
d͡ʒuɾ	جور	wing	wMM.I *jibür* [جبوُرْ] 'wing'; cf. WM *jigür*
eŋ'gʌɾ	اینگر	shirt collar	wMM **engger*
ep'sʌ	ایپسہ	yawning	wMM **ebse-/*ebsi-ye-*
eɾ'kʌ	ایرکہ	thumb; big toe	wMM.L *erke* [ارگهْ] 'finger [sic!]' ; WM *erekei* 'thumb, big toe'
et'kʌ	ایتکہ	trust; reliance; confidence	cf. wMM.M *itegel* ; wMM.L *itegiltü* [اتكلتو] s'zuverlässig'
hɒ'lʌ	ہالہ	multicolored	wMM **hala* (?); cf. wMM.M *ala* [الا], eMM.ZYYY *alaq*, WM *alaγ* (cf. also OT *ala*, Khalaj *hāla* 'id.')
il'jʌ	ایل یہ	hawk (which hunts small chicks)	wMM.R *helie* [هيليه] 'hawk, kite, vulture'
il't͡ʃi	ایلچی	messenger; courier; carrier	wMM.I *elči* [اَلچى] 'prophet', wMM.R *elči* 'messenger, angel', wMM.M *elči*
jɒ'ɾʌ	یارہ	injury; wound	wMM.Ibn *yara* [يارا]; cf. wMM.R *yaratu* [يرتو] 'wounded'
kɒɾ	کار	horse (brown)	wMM **keher* ; cf. WM *keger* 'dark chestnut, brown (of a horse)'
kɒnd͡ʒ	کانج	crosseyed	wMM **kenje* ; WM *kenje*

kɪl'gʌj	کلگی	stammerer	wMM.M *kelegei* [کیلاکای]; cf. wMM.M *kilen* [کیلن], wMM.I *kelen* [گیْلن], WM *kelegei* 'having a speech impediment'
meɾ'gʌn	میرگن	hunter (very experienced, a champion)	wMM **mergen*
nʌχ'͡tʃi (nʌʁʌ'͡tʃi)	نخچی (نغہ چی)	sister of mother; brother of mother	wMM.R *naqaču* [نقاجو] 'maternal uncle', wMM.M *naγaču* [نغاجو]
nɪl'ʁʌ	نلغہ	1. nursing child; baby 2. new grown plant; sprout	wMM.M *nilqa* [نیلقه]
ol'͡dʒʌ	اواجہ	booty; spoil	wMM.M *olja*
qɒ'bu	قابو	near	wMM **qabi/*qabu* ; cf. WM *qabi* 'vicinity'
qɒ'dʌ	قاده	cliff	wMM **qada* ; WM *qada* 'cliff; rock'
qɒ'duɾ	قادور	sickle	wMM.R *qadūr*, wMM.M *qadūr* 'scythe, sickle' ; cf. WM *qadaγur*
qɒ'lo	قالو	beaver	wMM.R *qaliun* [قليون] 'beaver', wMM.M *qali'un* [قالیوون]; wMM.I *qaliun* [قلیُونْ] 'red roan'; cf. WM *qaliγu*
qɒw'ɾi ~ qo'ɾʌ	قاوری ~ قوره	file (for metal)	wMM.Ibn *qa'ūra(i)* [قُورا]
qʌb'qu	قبقو	fox trap; snare (for foxes and wolves)	wMM **qabqu*
qʌl'͡dʒo	قلجو	white spot on forehead of cows; baldness on forehead; receding hair	wMM **qaljan/*qaljon* (?); cf. WM *qaljan*

qʌnd͡ʒi	قنجی	soaked	wMM.M *qana-*
qʌnd͡ʒu'ʁʌ	قنجوغہ	saddle strap	wMM.R *qanjuqa* [قنجوقا] 'saddle thongs'; cf. WM *γanjuγ-a*
qʌ'ɾʌ	قره	black	wMM.M *qara* [قرا] 'id.'; cf. WM *qara* 'id.'; cf. Mog. [qʌ'rɔ] ~ [qɒ'rɒ] 'schwarz; dunkel'
qʌɾʁʌ'nʌ	قرغنہ	wild bush (creeping)	wMM **qarγana*; cf. WM *qarγana*
qi'mʌ	قیمہ	ground meat (cut very finely hand)	wMM **qima* ; cf. MoKh x^j*aam* 'sausage', WM *kim-a*, eMM *kima* 'ground meat'
qo'ʃo	قوشو	beak	wMM.R *qošūn* [قوشون] 'beak', wMM.M *qoši'ūn* ; cf. WM *qosiγu* 'snout; beak (of birds)'
qo'tʌ	قوتہ	stomach (human)	wMM **qota*
qo'to	قوتو	manger; trough; feeding trough	wMM **qoto*
quŋ'qɒr	قونقار	brown cow; cow with brown/black fur	wMM **qungqar*; cf. WM *qungγur*
qʊ'dʌ	قده	crowd accompanying wedding couple	wMM **quad*
qʊ'ɾiʁ	قورغ	prohibition	wMM **qoriγ/*quriγ* ; cf. WM *qoriγ*
qʊɾub't͡ʃi	قربچی	thimble	wMM.M *qurūbči* [قورروبجی]; cf. Mog. [qu'run] ~ [qu'ru] 'Finger', wMM.I *quru'un* [قُرو وُن] 'finger', wMM.IM *qurγun* [قُرغُن]

qʊ'ɾut	قروت	dried sour milk product	wMM *quru'ut
qʊt'qu kʌ'do	قتقو کدو	mix liquids	wMM.M *qutqu*-; cf. WM *qudqu*- 'to mix'
qʊ't͡ʃʌ	قچه	bark (of a dog); imprudence; shouting loudly	wMM.M *quča*- [قوجا], wMM.I *quča*- [قُچَا], wMM.IM *quča*- [قَجا] 'to bark'
ʁo'jʌ	غویه	thigh	wMM.M *γuya* [غویه]
ʁol	غول	waist; center	wMM.M *γol* [غول]; cf. WM *γoul*
ʁol'd͡ʒi kʌ'do	غولجی کدو	refuse; reject	wMM **γolo-*
ʁol'nʌ	غولنه	central	wMM.M *γol* [غول]; cf. WM *γoul*
ʁoɾ'ʁi	غورغی	hook; ring; link	wMM **γorγi/*γorqi*
ʁun'd͡ʒi	غونجی	cow (young, which newly bears a calf)	wMM **γunaji*
ʁu'ɾi	غوری	dough fallen into the fire (and cooked there)	wMM.I *qulir* [قُلِرْ] 'farine', wMM.AL *γulir* [غُولِيرْ], wMM.IM *qulir* [قُلِير], wMM.M *γulir* [غولير]; cf. WM *γuril* ~ *γulir* '???'; cf. Mog. [ʀu'ʀul] ~ [ʀu'lur] 'Mehl'
sʌb'dʌ kʌ'do	سبده کدو	beat with a stick	wMM **sabda-*
sʌ't͡ʃi kʌ'do	سچی کدو	scatter; strew; sprinkle	wMM **sača-*
so'nʌ	سونه	horsefly	wMM **sona*
su'lʌ	سوله	soft	wMM.M *sula* [سولا]; cf. WM *sula* 'weak', Mog. [su'lɔ] 'dünn'
sun'd͡ʒi	سونجی	stretched out	cf. wMM.M *suni'ā*- : *suni'ā-ba* [سونيابه]
sun'd͡ʒi kʌ'do	سونجی کدو	stretch (oneself)	
ʃɒ'tu	شاتو	ladder	wMM.M *šatu* [شاتو] 'ladder'

ʃiɾ'd͡ʒʌ	شیرجه	impure milk	wMM **širaja*
ʃi'ʁʌj	شیغی	anklebone; ankle	wMM.I *šiγa* [شِغَه] 'cheville de l'homme ou des animaux'
ʃɪɾ'ʁʌ	شرغه	Grey	wMM.M *širγa* [شیرغا]; cf. Mog. [ʃi'rɔ] 'gelb', wMM.M *šira* [شیره] 'yellow'
tɒ'lʌ	تاله	meadow; pasture; strip of grass (land)	wMM **tala*
tʌ	ته	Your	wMM.M *ta* [تا] 'you (pl.)'
tʌw'lʌj	تولی	hare; rabbit	wMM.M *taulai* [تاولای], wMM.I *taulai* [ثاولاي] id.; WM *taulai*
tem	تیم	such; kind	wMM.Ibn *teimi* [ثَیْمی] ~ [تیمی]; cf. wMM.I *tein* 'ainsi, de cette façon'; WM *teyimü*
tem't͡ʃʌ	تیمچه	effort; try; attempt	wMM **temeče-*
te'muɾ	تیمور	iron	wMM.M *timur* [تیمور]; WM *temür* id.
tol'ʁʌ	تولغه	top of the head	wMM **tol(u)γa*
toʁ	توغ	flag; banner; standard	wMM.R *tuγ* [توغ] 'flag, banner', wMM.M *tuq* [تُق] (cf. Old Turkic *tuγ* 'id.')
tʌ'jʌʁ	تیاغ	stick	wMM.M *tayaq* [تاياق]
ʈʌ'kʌ	ٹکه	goat (young male)	wMM **teke*
t͡ʃʌ'bʌl	چبل	dirt; uncleanliness	wMM **čibil*
t͡ʃʌ'bi	چبی	side; body part below ribs (soft)	wMM **čabi*
t͡ʃʌl	چل	trickery; deception	cf. wMM.R *čalitu* [جالیتو] 'quick', wMM.M *jail* [جالی]
t͡ʃʌl't͡ʃʌl	چلچل	loquacious; talkative; wordy	wMM **čalči-*

t͡ʃʌpˈt͡ʃi kʌˈdo	چپچی کدو	slash (kill with a sword)	wMM *čabči-*
t͡ʃʌpˈt͡ʃuɾ	چپچور	adze (for cutting bushes)	wMM **čabči'ur*
t͡ʃeˈd͡ʒin	چیجین	bosom; chest; lap	wMM.M *če'eji*
t͡ʃeˈmʊk	چیمک	joint (of bones); thighbone (femur); upper arm bone (humerus)	wMM **čemük*
t͡ʃemʊkˈlʌ	چیمکله	dislocation of a joint	
t͡ʃɪmˈqo kʌnˈdo	چمقو کندو	pinch	wMM **čimqo(-)*
t͡ʃoˈqu	چوقو	forehead	wMM **čoqu*
t͡ʃol	چول	desert	wMM.M *čöl* [جول]; cf. WM *čöl*
t͡ʃʊˈgul	چگول	calf	wMM.R. *tuqul* [توقول] 'calf', wMM.M *tuγul* [توغول]; cf. WM *tuγul*, Mog. [tʊˈʀul] 'Kalb'
ũˈʁi	اونغی	hole for handle in axe or hammer	wMM **ungγi*
uˈni	اونی	edge of an arrow that joins the bow	wMM.R *huni* [هونی] 'poles of a tent'
ˈʊtqu kʌˈdo	اتقو کدو	mix liquids	(see **[ˈqʊtqu kʌˈdo]** above)
χɒg	خاگ	sweepings; dirt (swept up)	wMM **qaγ* ; cf. WM *qaγ* 'dust, dirt'
χɒˈto	خاتو	wife	wMM.Ibn *qatun* [قاتون] 'знатная дама', wMM.R *qatun* [قاتون] 'queen' ; cf. Mog. [qɔˈtun] 'Frau'

ACKNOWLEDGEMENT

The author thanks his teacher and advisor Dr. György Kara for looking over a previous draft of this paper, and for directing him to Ligeti's important articles.

REFERENCES

Franz Schurmann (1962), *The Mongols of Afghanistan: An Ethnography of the Moghôls and Related Peoples of Afghanistan*, 's-Gravenhage: Mouton.

Gerhard Doerfer (1971), *Khalaj Materials* [= Indiana University Publications, Uralic and Altaic Series, Vol. 115], Bloomington: Indiana University.

Gerhard Doerfer and Semih Tezcan (1981), *Wörterbuch des Chaladsch (Dialekt von Charrab)* [= Bibliotheca Orientalis Hungarica, XXVI], Budapest: Akadémiai Kiadó.

G.K. Dulling (1973), *The Hazaragi Dialect of Persian*, London: The Central Asian Research Centre.

Kuribayashi Hitoshi 栗林均 (2003) *Ka-i yakugo (kōshubon) Mongorugo zen tango, gobi sakuin* 「華夷訳語」(甲種本) モンゴル語全単語・語尾索引, Sendai 仙台: Tōhoku Daigaku Tōhoku Ajia Kenkyū Sentā 東北大学東北アジア研究センター.

Louis Ligeti [= Lajos Ligeti] (1954), "O mongol'skix i tyurskix dialektax Afganistana", *Acta Orientalia Academiae Scientiarum Hungaricae*, Vol. 4, pp. 93-114.

——— (1955), "Le lexique Moghol de R. Leech", *Acta Orientalia Academiae Scientiarum Hungaricae*, Vol. 4, pp. 119-58.

——— (1962), "Un vocabulaire mongol d'Istanboul", *Acta Orientalia Academiae Scientiarum Hungaricae*, Vol. 14, pp. 1-99.

——— (1964*a*), "Les voyelles longues en moghol", *Acta Orientalia Academiae Scientiarum Hungaricae*, Vol. 17, pp. 1-48.

——— (1964*b*), "Mongol'skie elementï v dialektax xazara Afganistana". In: *Kratkie soobščeniya Instituta Narodov Azii*, No. 93 (Mongolovedeniya i tyurkologiya), Moskva, pp. 5-22.

Michael Weiers (1972), *Die Sprache der Moghol der Provinz Herat in Afghanistan: Sprachmaterial, Grammatik, Wortliste*, Opladen: Westdeutscher Verlag.

Nicholas Poppe (1927-8), "Das mongolische Sprachmaterial einer Leidener Handschrift", *Izvestiya Akademii nauk SSSR*, 1927, pp. 1009-40, 1251-74; 1928, pp. 55-80.

——— (1938-9), *Mongol'skij slovar' Mukaddimat al-Adab* [= Trudï Instituta vostokovedeniya, 14], čast' 1-2 (1938), čast' 3 (1939), Moskva: AN SSSR.

Peter B. Golden (2000), *The King's Dictionary: The Rasūlid Hexaglot – Fourteenth Century Vocabularies in Arabic, Persian, Turkic, Greek, Armenian, and Mongol*, Leiden: Brill.

Tariq Malistani (1993), *Farhang-i ibtidā'ī-i millī-i hazārah: bi-inzimām-i tarjamah bih fārsī-i ingilīsī / Hazaragi-Dari/Farsi-English: A Preliminary Glossary*, Quetta.

CHAPTER 5

NATIONALISM AND MONGOLS

Olzvoi Battumur

The two words, nationalism and Mongol, have different meanings and are in usage among different ethnic Mongols in Central Asia. Mongol nationalism can be understood in two dimensions, first in terms of space, where the nationalist ideas are prevalent among which Mongol ethnic group and in which country, and the second dimension is as to who is included and who is excluded by a certain nationalist idea.

Along the way of their long history, Mongols spread all over Inner and Central Asia. Due to this migration, distinction between Mongols of Mongolia and Mongols outside Mongolia is difficult to be made. Thus Mongolian nationalism can cover both the Mongols living in Mongolia and also outside the country. Their nationalist aspirations differ from each other depending on their history, particularly their fight against or collaboration with other nationalities and ethnic groups.

MONGOLIAN NATIONALISM IN THE TWENTIETH CENTURY

Mongolian nationalism in the 20th and early 21st century can be divided into two phases in relation to the social change that occurred in the year 1990. The social change was a result of the end of Soviet regime in Mongolia, after which Mongolia started a democratic state with capitalist market economy. The first phase was during the period prior to 1990, when nationalism was banned and was regarded as something against the state, people and the whole country. The second phase is post-1990, when nationalism was allowed and it became something that is important in the country at different levels.

In the first phase, Mongolian nationalism was a force opposing the Soviet hegemony in Mongolia. The nationalists of that era did not actually mean to threaten the "friendship and brotherhood of the two countries" and the Soviet rule in Mongolia, but yet the Mongolian state under the guidance of Russian authorities regarded nationalism as anti-state. The authorities feared that Mongolian nationalism would lead to the "complete independence" of the country. Mongolian nationalism supported traditional culture, language, Mongolian script, religion, true Mongolian history and all its tangible and intangible cultural heritage. In other words, Mongolian nationalism was proud of everything that was regarded as pure Mongolian and sought to regain it. When they talked of Mongolness, they also intentionally and unintentionally talked of non-Mongolness on the other side. Unlike Mongolness, non-Mongolness was not cherished. State officials and Soviet rulers accused the Mongolian nationalists for loving Mongolness more than the non-Mongolness. Non-Mongolness during the communist era always meant Russian. For the rulers, therefore, Mongolian nationalism meant "anti-social" and more specifically "anti-Soviet Union", even though the so called nationalists did not actually mean to oppose the Soviet Union. Dozens of Mongolian academics and intellectuals were imprisoned on this charge.

After the collapse of the communist regime in 1990, there has been revival of Mongolian nationalism which spread all over the country and manifested itself in various ways in different sects of the society. As compared to the previous era, nationalism this time is regarded in a completely opposite way. Unlike in the communist period, it is not considered to be anti-social behaviour. Instead, nationalism has bocame a symbol of independent nation with its unique culture. Now nationalism in

Mongolia is a valuable treasure that helps to keep its unique culture which distinguishes Mongols from others; protects Mongolia and Mongol culture from any danger of extinction; preserves the genuine Mongolness and further enforces solidarity among the people and independence of Mongolia.

There are different sentiments of nationalism, as regards the content and the impact of nationalism. All those types and sentiments of nationalism share the same essence of keeping Mongolness as "pure" and "genuine" as possible. One of the sentiments in Mongolia was pan-Mongolian nationalism or in other words the "Great Mongol" sentiment which developed in 1920s. This meant a willingness and aspiration to seek possibilities to unite all the Mongols in the world.

Another type of national sentiment among the Mongols in Mongolia is *Khalkh* centred nationalism. *Khalkh* Mongolians form the majority of the population which is 75-80 percent. In Mongolia, people think that *Khalkh* Mongolians are more "pure", "genuine" and "true" Mongols than the other ethnic Mongols. All others are suspected for various reasons, such as Inner Mongolians are Sinicized, Buryats are Russified, Oirat Mongols in the west of the country are ruled by the descendants of Khasar, younger brother of Chinggis Khan and Kazakhs, Dukhas are not Mongols etc. Historically, the conflict can be between the Western and Eastern Mongols, and other Mongols can be traced to the middle ages. As compared to the Western Mongols, *Oirats*, *Khalkh* Mongols were Eastern Mongols. This conflict accentuated in the communist era. Under communism, the conflict turned into conflict between the minority and majority. Since the majority is of the *Khalkh* Mongols, all other minorities were forced to learn *Khalkh* culture, such as language. This put the *Khalkh* Mongols in the upper level above other ethnic Mongols. Thus the idea that the *Khalkh* Mongols are the "true" Mongols while the others are not, and therefore, they must imitate *Khalkh* Mongolism was strengthened. Among the other ethnic groups, Inner Mongolians in China and Buryats in Russia are described as being hybrid and not pure. At the state and government level, *Khalkh* centred nationalism is also not the right policy to be supported, as *Khalkh* centred nationalism destroys solidarity in the civil society and weakens the concept of welfare state.

Lately, Mongolian community has started to have another type of nationalistic sentiment which is xenophobic nationalism. Xenophobic nationalism is directed against foreigners. Mongols with xenophobic nationalism believe that foreigners threaten Mongolian "purity". There are two kinds of threats, firstly, foreigners or foreign culture destroys the "original" Mongol culture and brings in change. Second threat is about due to the foreigners marrying Mongolians and producing not pure but hybrid Mongols. In its early phase, Russians and Chinese were the main target of this nationalistic sentiment, but nowadays it includes many other foreigners such as the Koreans and Japanese and so forth. Xenophobic nationalism is similar to the *Khalkh* centred nationalism by regarding Inner Mongolians and Buryats outsiders, foreigners and non-Mongols. For xenophobic nationalists Inner Mongolians and Buryats are not Mongols but as foreigners, because they are hybrid. This type of nationalism tries to preserve Mongol culture. In the ideology of xenophobic nationalism, Mongol culture is an original indigenous culture and, therefore, it is a valuable world heritage that must be protected from possible damages. Unfortunately, xenophobic nationalists express themselves with neo-Nazist signs such as the flag, and classify and level people according to their nationality, citizenship, race, origin and other identities. They even insult foreigners or resort to physical violence against them. Such a behaviour is unacceptable especially in our generation of humanistic democratic globalisation and anti-racism. In this way, xenophobic nationalism badly damages Mongolia's reputation in its international relations.

The other type of national sentiment is the state centred civic nationalism which is preferable both at the level of state and government and civil society. This national sentiment does not distinguish people with their ethnic diversity, but the important factor is to have Mongolian citizenship. Therefore, even non-Mongols like Kazakhs and Tuvans are Mongols like any other Mongols, because they all share the same identity by being citizens of Mongolian state. Compared to the previous types, this national sentiment does not have any negative effect both at the national level among different Mongol ethnic groups in Mongolia, and at the international level in relation to foreign countries. Therefore, Mongolian state points to this national sentiment as the ideal one that can be employed in the state policy. This type of nationalism also protects Mongol traditional culture. Globalisation threatens traditional cultures by changing them and destroying them. The policy of Mongolian state is neither rejecting globalisation nor losing traditional Mongolness, but to combine old and new and build its own globalized culture with its unique Mongolness.

CHAPTER 6

MONGOLIAN LANGUAGE AND CULTURE IN NATIONAL IDENTITY

B. Uranchimeg

National identity reflects vastly divergent life experiences, perceptions and methods of expression. The essence of our national identity lies in the ability to preserve our heritage, and language which is the most natural symbol of public and private identity. Language with a sense of collective identity has been mobilized as a powerful tool for successful implementation of national identity among populations. By adopting a certain language, a certain population or a certain group in society declares what identity it wants to demonstrate to itself as well as to the rest of the world. Therefore, language as a vehicle of communication plays a key role in the construction of national identity. This paper attempts to explore matters of language, culture and national identity relationships in Mongolia.

There are at least three to five thousand different languages in use in the world leaving aside dialect divisions within languages, and each is quite different from others. Differences are especially pronounced between languages of different families. In so far as all languages share some features in common, whether in pronunciations, grammatical organization, or expressive power, one may speak of human language as an abstract set of characteristics perhaps part of the biologically inherited structure of the human mind. As the cultural anthropologist Wade Davis explains: "A language isn't just a body of vocabulary or a set of grammatical rules. It is a flash of the human spirit, a vehicle through which the soul of a particular culture comes into the material world". Our perception of our own language can become, in varying degrees, a source of pleasure, pride, anxiety, offense, anger, and even violence.

Language is a reflection of culture. While Americans use only a handful of terms to describe snow, including the actual word snow, sleet, freezing rain, and a few others, Eskimos, on the other hand, have many words to describe snow. Snow that is falling, snow on the ground, snow in blocks, and snow that makes wavy patterns each are explained through the use of separate words. Snow is a central feature in Eskimo culture, thus it is essential that sufficient vocabulary exists to specifically describe it. Apart from such differences, more significant are the difficulties involved in trying to translate words relating to custom and habit matters between the languages of communities having different cultures. Such differences arise from the differences in people's way of life. Thus speakers of different languages are said to think in different ways. There are several notions here. One is that languages 'carve up' the reality in different ways. Another is that these language differences are covert or unconscious; we are not consciously aware of the way in which we classify objects. Third, these language differences influence our world view.

Colors may convey different messages to people of different cultures. Due to the respective cultural background and tradition, some phrases containing color words have far surpassed their original meaning, forming different connotations. One could use color vocabulary to gauge the social and mental evolution of a culture. Color naming is related to the forms of cultural categories conventionalized in language and thought. Between 1879 and 1905, scholars classified systems of color naming among people throughout the world. They reported languages that named all colors with only two terms, as if everything were red or black. When a language used additional color terms, red, black, and white were always named; a term for green predicted a term for yellow, while both were predicted by a term for blue. The relations suggested color terms everywhere evolved in one order. If one speaks a language that has only two basic color terms, they will correspond to white and black. One will distinguish between colors on the basis of brightness, from white to black. A light blue sky would be called 'white'; a dark gray sky would be called 'black'. Thus, one's native language determines in some fashion the nature of one's experience and that members of linguistic communities necessarily inhabit different experiential words.

For instance, Mongolian and Russian are completely different languages, while Russian and English being Indo-European languages, unlike English, distinguish lexically between dark blue and light blue. The Mongolians and Russians are not constrained by the use of single words to discuss 'blue', thus literal meaning of the word differs from the English translation. There is no corresponding English color term since English *blue* covers both light and dark blue color fields. Another quite similar to this and also a really interesting example exists in Mongolian: the color *бор* refers to gray when it is a color of horse, while it is light brown when it refers to the color of clothes etc. In Mongolian language golden color symbolizes human life, road, and motherland as being used in the sense of preciousness, respect and majesty. Blue color associates with smoke, haze, cloud, mirror and ash and so on. When blue color associates with one's laugh it shows somebody's arrogant attitude or disgust. English idiom "green with jealousy" means to be very jealous because you want something that someone else has. Mongolian equivalent is also conveyed with color association, but color is yellow here: 'атаархсандаа <u>шар</u> хөдлөх'. Another idiom 'blue streak' which literally means to move very quickly is associated with black in Mongolian '<u>хар</u> хурдаараа гүйх'. Each has additional meanings-certain cultural association-that are hidden behind the word.

The red color is also associated with certain same emotions as in:

- She *turned red* with embarrassment. (*Longman Active Study Dictionary of English*, 1991, p.562)

- At this Gerelt *blushed bright red*, and rather than stay and he laughed at, turned and ran out of the station... (Ts. Ulambayar, *A boy called Gerelt. My belowed swallows*, Ulaanbaatar 1986, p.45)

The former shows one's embarassment while latter refers to the feeling of anger and shame. According to the above comparison and analysis, there is obvious similarities between the senses of color word "red". But Mongolians may not use this color in the meaning that English speakers use and vice versa.

The nature of color is more complicated than just a wavelength. It contains emotional and symbolic components as well as well as purely visual ones. There are lots of different meanings for red in almost every culture. In Asia, red is almost always good luck. In Japan, red ink is a traditional method of writing a letter that ends a relationship. There are more than thirty single characters describing different kinds of red in Chinese: red of wine, red of silk, red of wood, red of meat and so on. And even more phrases are used to describe different levels of red.

In heraldry, before 1930's blue and white were used by Mongolians as the colors of official mourning to signify unforgettable memory. All people who attended funeral processing of the first Prime Minister of Mongolia, wore blue and white cloth around their sleeves. And white represents purity and sincerity while blue is seen as the color of eternal life, peace and heaven. Moreover, there are alternative color names that are more metaphorical, figurative, or poetic, expanding basic color terms. The color liver red in Mongolian usually associates with rocks and cliffs.

The impact of culture is more obvious in use of the alternative, object derived color names, richer in connotation as in literal meaning of water blue, ash blue, cloudy gray /horse/, sea shell white /teeth/, cherry black /eyes/. All these are not just about words, but how the meaning of colors evolves from daily life. On many occasions, it is not the basic meaning of the color that functions, but the profound cultural associations related to the color that functions. It shows that the cultural environment in which people grow up, can have surprising effects on how they interpret the world around them. Color categories, used by Mongolians differ from those used by English speakers. It can be explained in terms of the following motivational factors. Most culture-specific color words in Mongolian language are related to peculiar features of ancient customs, habits and livelihood traditions of nomadic husbandry.

Covering a vast area of over 1.5 million sq kms. in Central Asia, Mongolia has the lowest population densities in the world. The vast pastoral area of nomadic civilization with its own highly developed cultural inheritance and quite sophisticated technology suited to their own living conditions is the source of Mongolian culture. Mongolian people have their own cultural identity based on the speciality and peculiarity of their existence and many historical, social circumstances. Environmental diversity and extreme climate and harsh surrounding habitat imposed the same cognitive (motivation) on the Mongolians. Motivation is part and parcel of perceptions, which in turn, are based on the attitudes, beliefs, values and past experiences.

Mongol pastoral herders are seen to be a reservoir from which industrialized and urbanized Mongolians inherit their linguistic spirit. If being Mongolian meant living in a *ger* in the midst of a sheep herd and being good at riding horses, then the Mongolian identity of those who lived in high-rise apartments, rode buses, and worked at desks or in factories where knowledge of foreign languages was required was problematic. However Mongol language, the cultural trait most obviously shared by all Mongolians, continues to be fostered. Assigning Mongolian identity to a work also makes us feel that we are not only consumers of the language, but contributors as well. It is natural to want a unified set of qualifying cultural elements, and to want these elements expressed beautifully in a national body of literature wherein each text reflects a uniquely Mongolian perspective. Such homogeneity leads to a comfortable sense of cultural identity, and contributes to national pride.

Thus, our national identity reflects the language with rich written tradition in the world and the nomadic culture which was largely shaped by the nomadic pastoral lifestyle and it conjures a romantic image of a steppe land. Nomadism was the main indigenous component of Mongolian civilization, which having stood the test of time, has survived even now.

REFERENCES

1. J.Bayansan, *Culture, Language and National Mentality* [Soyol, Khel, Undestnii Setgelgee] (Ulaànbaatar: Mongolian National University, 2002).
2. Sh. Bira, *Studies in Mongolian History, Culture and Historiography* (Ulaanbatar, 2001).
3. Tsetsenbileg Tseveen, "The Creation of National Identities of Mongols," Central Eurasian Studies Society. Abstracts of Papers Presented at Annual CESS Conference 2003.
4. Steven Pinker, *The Language Instinct* (USA, 1994).
5. Robert Maclaury, *Color and Cognition in Mesoamerica* (USA, 1997).
6. Einar Haugen, *Language Conflict and Language Planning: The Case of Modern Norwegian* (Cambridge, Mass: Harvard University Press, 1966).
7. B.Uranchimeg, Thesis. *Cognitive Study on Color Terms* (Ulaanbaatar: University of Humanity).

CHAPTER 7

CHINGGIS KHAN IN LITERARY MEMORY: IDENTITY FORMATION IN MONGOLIA

Sindhu Rao

Scholars or travellers to Mongolia have remarked on the pervasive use of the name Chinggis Khan in large and small matters pertaining to daily life as well as long-term goals of the nation. There is a certain consciousness of Chinggis Khan in the Mongolian mind that seems to be a part of their selfhood. It is not as a historical figure that he is remembered but his life and exploits have assumed legendary and mythic dimensions over the last eight hundred years. While *The Secret History of the Mongols* is a written record of Chinggis Khan's times and triumphs, literacy was not cultivated by the Mongols for quite some time to come, in fact for several centuries. The memory of their warrior-hero was celebrated in songs and probably bardic recitals. A parallel could be fruitfully drawn with Manas, the hero of the Kyrgyz oral epic, whose exploits and prowess have been sung by bards for a thousand years, and his name is an inspiration to the people of Kyrgyzstan in every matter concerning both the personal and the national. Evidently people who have been under an alien cultural yoke, when they are free of it, look to their roots for an affirmation of their national identity. The idea of a heroic, golden past acts as a fillip to the task of national reconstruction. In the case of both Chinggis Khan and Manas it is folk-memory that has kept the hero as a living presence through the centuries, and mainly by means of rituals and practices that affirm the value they place upon racial memory. In recent times when Mongolians were asked what they would choose to have as a first name in addition to the name they already bear, an overwhelming majority of the male population opted for 'Chinggis'. Newspapers reported this as an instance of the continuing popularity of the 13th century conqueror's image in his homeland.

While Mongolia and China both have an emotional investment in the memory of Chinggis Khan, the rest of the world has a very different perception of the man and his achievements. Jawaharlal Nehru called him the greatest military commander the world has known. The peoples who were conquered by him saw him as a 'scourge'. Whatever the perception may be, Chinggis Khan has captured the imagination of writers and artists, time and again.

Prior to the emergence of the Mongols as an ethnic group under the leadership of Chinggis Khan who established the stupendous Mongol empire in the 13th century, their history is obscure. The earliest attempts at identifying them as an ethnic entity were in the form of oppositional relations to the Chinese, who were geographically one of their near neighbours: the Mongols were a nomadic people with herds and flocks, while the Chinese were largely settled agriculturists. Early Mongol contact with China was mostly in the form of raids on the settled populace. The Great Wall across northern China, which was built to protect the Chinese against invaders from that direction, also serves as a marker of a cultural divide, between the nomadic culture of the Mongols and the sedentary settled culture of the Chinese.[1] Nevertheless it was not an effective defence against the Mongolian invasion of China led by Chinggis Khan in the early thirteenth century. The conquest was completely successful: the heartland of the Mongols,[2] mostly inhabited by warring Mongol tribes, suddenly expanded to a vast territory that stretched from the Pacific ocean in the east to the Adriatic Sea in the west, and from Siberia in the north to South East Asia. In 1280 AD, with the downfall of the Sung dynasty, the whole of China came under the Great Mongol Empire.

Kublai Khan, the grandson of Chinggis, used Peking as the seat of his governance over the whole empire, in preference to the earlier capital Karakorum, which is near present-day Ulaanbaatar. Since Kublai Khan's successors were weak, Mongol control of, and presence in, Chinese territory began to deteriorate. Only with the ascent of Timur (1336-1405 AD) did the Mongol empire once again attempt to reassert its might over Central Asia, Transcaucasia and China. After Timur's death, the Mongol empire lost its former glory and disintegrated into various tribal populations. The Ming dynasty of 16th century China tried to destroy the unity of the Mongol tribes and employed a divide-and-rule policy which effectively set the semi-nomads of southern Mongolia (present-day Inner Mongolia) against the nomadic tribes of northern Mongolia. In the long run, however, throughout the Ming dynasty era, China-Mongolia power relations fluctuated, without either gaining significant victory.

With the establishment of the Manchu dynasty in 17th century China, a new era began in the history of Mongolia, because it was during this period that the Mongols were subjected to a sharp geographical division (Inner and Outer Mongolia), and were brought under the submission of the Manchus. Both Manchu China and Russia followed the Ming policy of divide-and-rule in order to prevent the Mongol tribes from uniting into a power of any political significance. This state of affairs lasted until the fall of the Manchu race (the last dynasty to rule in China), which came about with the Chinese Revolution of 1911. With the help of Tsarist (and later Soviet) Russia, Outer Mongolia declared its independence as the Mongolian People's Republic (MPR) in 1924.

In the coming decades, the MPR was recognized as an independent state by the Kuomintang Government. The relations between the MPR and the People's Republic of China (PRC) fluctuated, since Mongolia was viewed primarily as a Soviet satellite. During the Cold War period, Mongolia continued to reflect the Soviet attitude towards China and it was only in the 1980s that normal diplomatic ties could be resumed between China and the MPR.[3] The disintegration of the Soviet Union in 1991 inevitably had direct repercussions for a country that had modelled its political administration so closely on the socialist ideology. With its emergence from the Soviet sphere of influence, Mongolia had to contend with the challenges of recasting its history, identity and statehood. The nature of this recasting was problematized by ethnic considerations and issues surrounding territory, political ideology and organization, and administrative policy with reference to the global context. In his research on Mongolian territorial identity, Alexander C. Diener has explored "competing trajectories of nationalization."[4] According to him the terms post-communist and post-socialist are problematic because of the retention of power by the Mongolian People's Revolutionary Party. He proposes the term post-Marxist-Leninist as more applicable to Mongolia's current situation, since it implies a more nationalistic socialist approach to governance in independent Mongolia.[5] Diener goes on to explore the complex negotiation of discourses with regard to Mongolia's sense of identity and nationhood. He identifies a distinct polarization that has taken place in the process of identity formation in present-day Mongolia: there are those who support placing nomadism at the centre of the new nationalization process, and those who view this traditional way of life as archaic and incompatible with the country's current need to engage with global trends.[6]

The return to native roots and nomadic culture has at its core the achievements of the historical phenomenon, Chinggis Khan, the 13th century Mongol nomad who united the scattered and warring tribes into a formidable political force, and created one of the largest empires in the world. He has a unique place in Mongol history and in contemporary economic, political and cultural issues. The present need felt by a significant part of Mongolia's intelligentsia for reviving nomadic culture is crystallized in the heroic figure of Chinggis Khan. In this reconstruction, myth and history are blended, to form a modern-day hero who lends momentum to Pan-Mongolism, of which nomadic culture is a part. Pan-Mongolism " represented the desire of indigenous Mongols to have a united state based on the model of the Empire of Chinggis Khan."[7] It was a sentiment that gained currency in the 1990s, after the Soviet structure receded from Mongolia's political atmosphere.

In the context of the debates around present-day nationalism in Mongolia, the depiction of Chinggis Khan in literature (in various genres such as travelogue, fiction and biography) testifies to the appeal he had to the imagination of writers widely separated in time, space and culture. We can look at the work of Ibn Battuta (a 14th century Muslim pilgrim), Vassili Yan (a Russian writer of the Soviet era), Mildred Cable and Fransesca French (lady missionaries who travelled to Central Asia in the early 20th century), and John Man (a British historian writing in the 21st century).

Ibn Battuta (1304 AD–1368 AD) was one of the greatest travellers of the Middle Ages. His travels lasted for nearly thirty years and covered about 75,000 miles across three continents. His account of his travels (*Rihla* in Arabic) is a mine of information about the religious, social, economic and political conditions of the Muslim world in the Middle Ages, when it was just recovering from the European Crusades and the Mongolian invasions and destruction. True to his calling as a devout Muslim pilgrim, he perceives Chinggis Khan as the scourge of Muslim lands, depicting him as the destroyer and enemy of Muslim peoples throughout Central Asia. His account reads like a catalogue of Muslim shrines destroyed by "the accursed Tinkiz".[8] Understandably, nothing else of Chinggis Khan apart from the terrible threat he posed to Islamic peoples finds a mention in Ibn Battuta. One must also remember that these were times when religion pervaded and ruled every aspect of life and provided a world-view for the believer. Ibn Battuta could not have seen Chinggis Khan in any other way than his portrayal suggests.

An entirely different picture emerges from Guillame de Rubruck who travelled to Mongolia in 1254, only twenty seven years after the death of Chinggis Khan. He vividly describes Karakorum, a city with twelve Buddhist temples, two mosques and one church. Khan Mongke (brother and predecessor of Kublai Khan) welcomed all sects of Christians, setting an example of tolerance not found in Europe till about six centuries later. The Russian writer Vassili Yan (pen-name of Vassili Yanchevetsky), born in 1875 in Kiev, had travelled on foot and horseback extensively. In 1901 he crossed the Kara-Kum desert on horseback and visited Khiva and Bukhara, Persia, Baluchistan and finally India. While on these travels, he was inspired by the idea of writing about the "great shadows of Asia"[9] – Alexander, Chinggis Khan, Tamerlane, Babur and other Eastern conquerors. Yan visited Central Asia again after World War I and returned to Russia in 1918. He devoted himself to the writing of fiction based on historical themes from 1923 onwards. The novel *Jenghiz Khan* appeared in 1939 and *Batu*, its sequel, in 1941. The final book of the historical trilogy is called *The Golden Horde and Prince Alexander.*

Yan's portrayal of the Mongol conqueror has a historical perspective, and the novel has for its narrator a dervish who takes his task as a scribe very seriously. He speaks of the duty of a person who has witnessed extraordinary things to record it on paper:

> Will I have enough words and strength to create a trustworthy account of that merciless destroyer of peoples Jenghiz Khan and his ruthless army? Audacious was the invasion of those savages from the northern steppes, when at the head of the army rode their red-bearded leader, when furious warriors sped through the tranquil valleys of Mavera-un-Nahr and Khorezm[2], leaving on the roads behind them thousands of mangled corpses, when every instant gave birth to new horrors and people asked one another, 'Will the heavens, shrouded in the smoke of burning villages, ever shine anew, or is the end of the world upon us ?...[10]

Several specific historic episodes, dealing with the Mongol subjugation of the Khwarezm state, which are dramatized in Yan's novel lend a further dimension to the Mongol Khan's character. When Chinggis Khan initially sent emissaries and merchant groups to Shah Muhammad of Khwarezm, he was looking for the establishment of trade relations, not war. But having conquered such vast areas outside the Mongolian heartland, he now clearly expected the Shah to bow to his sovereignty, and conveyed this expectation by addressing him as his son. The Shah reacted by ordering his governor Inalchik Khan to have the 450 emissaries and merchants slain, and their goods seized. When Chinggis Khan demanded that the governor be handed over for punishment, the Shah refused and killed the Mongol emissaries. Thus Chinggis Khan's campaign against the sultanate of Khwarezm became inevitable, in the words of historian W. Barthold. This particular episode has been chronicled by Yan in another version of history that portrays Chinggis Khan as a human sufferer; he depicts the Mongol emperor as being moved to tears on hearing the news of his emissary's death. The ruthless conqueror is seen grieving alone atop a hillock, smearing his face with dirt in ritual mourning.[11]

The fact that Chinggis Khan was primarily a nomad before he became a conqueror sets him apart from other world-renowned figures. This nomadic culture stayed with him as part of his identity and personality throughout his career of empire-building. In every new region that became part of his domain, he preferred to appoint governors and hold them accountable to him for law and order. He never felt the urge to erect palaces and monuments to commemorate his victories; much less did he feel inclined to set up headquarters and political capitals to live in. At heart, he was a simple nomad, preferring to erect his tent (*ger*) in the open steppe, and living in a characteristically Spartan style, with rough black canvas for clothing, bedding and the simplest of fare suited to a herdsman constantly on the move. In fact, his lifestyle hardly changed from the time he was the young and vulnerable Temuchin, to the time when he became the invincible emperor Chinggis Khan. The only times when he temporarily halted in settled built-up structures were when he besieged the ancient cities of Bokhara and Samarkand. In the former capital, he used the largest mosque as the point from which to address the terrified cowed citizens; in Samarkand, he used the Khwarezm Shah's Green Palace. In every capital that he invaded and conquered, Chinggis Khan would have the population carefully surveyed; the young workers and master craftsmen would be forcibly sent to far away Mongolia, where they formed artisan settlements, while the women were distributed amongst his soldiers. The old and the very young were usually killed. Ruthless as this was, his administrative decisions were those that ultimately led to the enrichment of Mongolia's cultural climate, by bringing to it ethnic elements from the diverse Central Asian

Khanates. As his empire expanded southwards, he and his army could not endure the heat of the plains and were forced to turn back. Yan compares the return of Chinggis Khan's booty-laden army to its native Mongolian steppes to an old tiger returning to its lair with its sagging belly sated and swaying, from having devoured a kill.[12]

This connection to their native land and nomadic culture is a legacy that Chinggis Khan left behind to the Mongol people. Gore Vidal, a 20th century American traveller Mongolia testifies to the strong native sentiments that characterize the Mongol nomads: when required to move into communal apartment blocks under the Soviet influence, they put their animals and belongings in them and stayed in their tents (*yurts*) as usual.[13] A travelogue written in the early 1940s, The Gobi Desert, by two lady missionaries Mildred Cable and Fransesca French, offers an insight into this refusal to change a way of life that had endured for centuries: "The Mongol's home is his tent, and his nomadic life is the expression of a compelling instinct. A house is intolerable to him, and even the restricting sense of an enclosing city wall is unbearable."[14] During the course of their travels in Mongolia, Cable and French observed that the Mongol nomad's culture and identity are greatly influenced and shaped by his way of life – the man of the trade-routes is constantly seeking to settle on a piece of land and raise a family, while in the open steppe spaces the nomads wander in tribes, singing and shouting, "free as the air he breathes, tied to no building and confined by no walls of city or of home."[15] Cable and French have also observed the ecologically balanced relationship between the nomad and his land: "He belongs to the desert and the desert belongs to him."[16] They also comment on the centrality of trade-routes and roads in the outlook of the roadman of Central Asia, for whom the love of the road is in his blood.[17] This generic term applies to the Mongols as well.

John Man, a recent biographer of Chinggis Khan, speculates that if urbanisation and agriculture were to take over the heartland of pastoral nomadism in Mongolia, it would still be a strange irony: ".... for if they do, it will be in the name of Chinggis Khan, the man who made Mongolia part of China. And if Mongols resist this pressure, then they too will do it in the name of Chinggis, the man who made China part of Mongolia."[18] According to Man, Chinggis Khan is not just a symbol of politics and culture for two very different peoples, but he is also a symbol of spirituality, peace and of the unity of opposites for current-day Mongolia.[19] In his research on Chinggis Khan, he attempts to analyse the reasons why the Mongols felt such a compelling need to mythicize a mortal human being and also the forms that these myths and legends assumed. Some of the more prominent myths revolve around the mystery of his birth, death, his funeral rites and his final resting-place. From a very large and bewildering array of Tibetan, Chinese, Buddhist and Mongolian lore, Man deduces that the only information to be had is the enormity of the loss of actual facts. He concludes that over a period of time, people had been unwilling to accept their god-king's death as natural and cast it into the form of a story of revenge and tragedy, with the fall of their hero caused by a woman and a foreigner. He is of the opinion that such stories supplied a psychological need for the Mongols, to explain their loss of power.[20]

Some myths also seek to render Chinggis Khan immortal; they present him in the form of a guardian spirit, who punishes those who do not believe in him and rewards those whose belief is implicit in their actions. In the final analysis, Man opines that Chinggis Khan is not, as he was in life, an avenger, but a power for good.[21] At the time of his supposed illness and death, it had been considered vitally important to conceal the real facts, lest anarchy, internal strifes and power struggles destroy the unity that Chinggis Khan had achieved amongst his peoples. And since the real facts are yet to come to light, the mythicizing of Chinggis Khan serves to fill this gap in history, and caters to the psychological needs of the Mongols through all the changes and conflicts that they have experienced up to the present day. *The Secret History of the Mongols*, which many Mongols regard as the final authority in the documentation of their country's history, contains many of these myths. Reviewing Chinggis Khan's career as conqueror and tyrant, John Man comes to the conclusion that the Mongol emperor remained a hero to the rulers who reigned after him and a monster to his victims – Muslims, Christians, Russians, and finally the Soviets. To the Russians, he remains etched in their psyche as a destroyer of their religious faith and as a scourge of their cultures. To them, Chinggis Khan poses a grim reminder of part of their national heritage – "Scratch a Russian and you'll find a Tartar."[22]

The charisma that Chinggis Khan has in the eyes of Mongolians has been exploited by different kinds of people. In 1920, a rather colourful adventurer, Baron Roman Nicolaus Fyodorovich von Ungern–Sternberg, aided by a motley army composed of White Russians and veterans of World War I, came into prominence. According to Peter Hopkirk,[23] the power-hungry Baron believed himself to be a reincarnation of the legendary Mongol emperor, and in that capacity sought to resist the Bolshevik advance into Mongolia. He was supported by the Japanese for their own reasons. Having converted to Buddhism, he had faith in his *Karma*, and claimed that he would be an even greater conqueror than Chinggis Khan: "He would rule until 'from his subterranean capital shall emerge the King of the World."[24] His attempted coups against Bolshevik rule ended in failure, however, and he was responsible for the deaths of many thousands of innocents who had believed in him. His military bungling only led to Mongolia being "handed to Lenin on a plate."[25] His inglorious career, reincarnation and all, was ended ignominiously by a Red Army firing squad.

In the early years of Sovietization, China had made many attempts to harness Mongol nationalist sentiment (about Chinggis Khan as a symbol of their past culture) in an effort to counter Soviet influence. But their attempts were not very successful because Chinggis Khan was "a villain in Soviet eyes,"[26] and such hero worship was anathema to Soviet ideology. Since Mongolia was a Soviet satellite, it became a risky proposition to recast Chinggis Khan as a hero. In the 1930s, Japan entered the political scene, with a view to conquest of Mongolia, China and Siberia. To this end, the Japanese also played on Mongol sentiments about their hero: they demanded custody of the Lord's Enclosure[27] since they knew that it would be controlled by those who ruled the rest of Mongolia and that part of China. As Man puts it, "Suddenly Chinggis's relics, Chinggis's very soul, had become the key to empire in Asia."[28] At this point they came into conflict with China, because China claimed that Chinggis was a Chinese emperor and the whole Mausoleum a Chinese relic. In the civil war that followed, Mongolia and China were ironically united in competing to praise and recast Chinggis Khan – as a symbol of Chinese resistance to the invader, as the founder of the Mongol empire, and as the founder of the Yuan dynasty in China. The sub-text, of course, was that China claimed Mongolia as part of its Communist empire. John Man speaks of the ritual details (in the 1940s) that accompanied the incorporation of Chinggis Khan into Chinese history and culture as one of their illustrious ancestors.[29]

With Mao's Cultural Revolution in the 1960s, the cult of Chinggis received a blow, since Mao perceived the ancestral leader as a challenge to his own hegemony. In what Man calls a sneering poem, Mao wrote: "The one Heaven is proud of for one generation! What he knew was no more than hunting eagles."[30] Under the wave of xenophobia that Mao released, the Inner Mongolian People's Revolutionary Party (which supported pan-Mongolism) was the main target of political attack, since pan-Mongolism was a threat to Maoist ideology in China.

But in present day Mongolia, the cult of Chinggis Khan is revived, and doing well, ever since Mongolia moved out of the Soviet sphere of influence. While much of the cult's celebration of Chinggis anniversaries and other commemorations is part of the historical and cultural heritage, Chinggis continues to symbolize his land and its people – "the nation as an independent political entity; the nomadic herding lifestyle; the spirit of rugged individuality; the feel of the landscape."[31]

In China, Chinggis symbolizes Chinese unity and imperial grandeur. Oyun, a leading Mongolian scientist, and sister of the slain democrat leader Zorig, has this to say of Chinggis Khan as a symbol:

> These are turbulent times and people need something to hang on to ...what do ordinary Mongolians see? The social fabric torn apart, street children, corruption. People do not see the real fruits of

> democratic change yet. Democracy is supposed to empower people, but we have seen an increase in poverty and unemployment, and an increasing gap between rich and poor, so a lot of people are less powerful, more threatened economically, than they were under communism. Half the population have to struggle to survive. They see the nation threatened by poverty, by weakness. So they look to Chinggis and that part of their history as a symbol of strength.[32]

Oyun goes on to analyse the reasons for Chinggis Khan enduring as a symbol for so many centuries – his strength lay not just in conquest, but in the idea of fair administration rooted in a written legal system. She believes that Mongolia's competitive advantage lies in three things – their countryside, their nomadic ways and their natural resources. Mentioning that Chinggis Khan well knew the strength of the country's pasturelands and the nomadic culture that went with them, Oyun is of the opinion that Mongols today should be "looking back to the rural economy from which (they) came originally, looking back to look forward. And in this Chinggis as a symbol is perfectly valid."[33] Together with a need for keeping in touch with their past is the unanswered question of what Mongolia's identity truly consists of, and to what extent China and its history figure in the formation of this identity.

John Man is of the opinion that the conflicts between eastern and western civilizations that Mongolian society is currently facing might possibly be resolved in the name of Chinggis Khan, because he is not only a symbol of politics and culture for two very different peoples, but a symbol of spirituality, peace and the unity of opposites as well.[34] Speaking with Sharaldai, author of a book entitled *Power of Eternal heaven*,[35] John Man establishes that for present-day Mongols who subscribe to the Cult of Chinggis Khan, the legendary conqueror serves as an intermediary between the common mortal and the Divine, which is symbolized by the Eternal Sky. He interprets Sharaldai's words (*Chinggis Khan is a spirit for all of us*) thus: his life shows his people today that violence, however successful initially, will fail, and that all conflicts can be resolved in peaceful discussion. John Man's final comment upon the enigma of Chinggis Khan is that of all his transformations, this last is the oddest: from a 'louse' on a mountain to a conqueror who terrorized the world; after death, to demi-god; and presently, to a spirit of universal harmony, which might help to sustain his country and his people.[36]

REFERENCES

1. Sharad K. Soni, *Mongolia-China Relations: Modern and Contemporary Times,* New Delhi: Pentagon Press, 2006, p.2.
2. It stretches from the Khingan mountains in the east to the Altai range in the west; from lake Baikal in the north to the southern part of the Gobi desert, up to the Great Wall of China.
3. Soni (2006), pp.10-14.
4. Alexander C. Diener, "Mongols, Kazakhs, and Mongolian Territorial Identity: Competing Trajectories of Nationalization", *Central Eurasian Studies Review*, Vol. 4, No. 1, Winter 2005, p.19.
5. *Ibid*, p.19.
6. *Ibid*, p.21.
7. Sharad K. Soni, "Role of Buryat Intellectuals in Pan-Mongolism," *Himalayan and Central Asian Studies*, Vol. 11, Nos. 3-4, July-December 2007, p.51.
8. H.A.R. Gibb, Trans., *Ibn Battuta: Travels in Asia and Africa 1325-1354.* Selected by H.A.R. Gibb, with Introduction and Notes. New Delhi: A.E.S., 1997 p.175.
9. Cited in Vassili Yan, *Jenghiz Khan,* Moscow: Raduga Publishers,1939, p.8.
10. Vassili Yan, *Jenghiz Khan: A Novel,* Trans. Moscow: Linda Noble Raduga Publishers, 1939, pp.10-11.
11. *Ibid,* p.135.
12. *Ibid,* p.336.
13. Robyn Davidson, ed., *Journeys: An Anthology*, London: Picador, 2001, p.403.
14. Cited in *ibid*, p.403.
15. Mildred Cable and Fransesca French, *The Gobi Desert,* London: Virago Press Ltd., 1984, p.267 .
16. *Ibid*, p.267.
17. *Ibid*, p.206.
18. John Man, *Genghis Khan: Life, Death and Resurrection,* London: Bantam Books, 2005, pp. 402-3.
19. *Ibid*, p.403.
20. *Ibid*, p. 275.
21. *Ibid*, p. 346-7.
22. *Ibid*, p. 312.

23. Peter Hopkirk has written extensively on Central Asia, with several books on various phases of Central Asian history. See his *Setting the East Ablaze*, Oxford: O.U.P., 1986.
24. *Ibid*, p.145.
25. *Ibid*, p.148.
26. Man, *op cit*, p.87.
27. The Mausoleum of Chinggis Khan (Edsen Khoroo in Mongolian), where he "has undergone the final and strangest part of his metamorphosis from barbarian chief to divinity." *Ibid*, p.317.
28. *Ibid*, p.328.
29. *Ibid*, p.330.
30. *Ibid*, p.336.
31. *Ibid*, p.396.
32. *Ibid*, p.398.
33. *Ibid*, p.399.
34. *Ibid*, p.403.
35. The book explains the nature of Chinggis Khan's semi-divinity. See *ibid*, p. 404.
36. *Ibid*, pp.404-6.

CHAPTER 8

MONGOLIA'S NATIONAL SECURITY: PAST, PRESENT AND FUTURE PERSPECTIVES

A. Tuvshintugs

After being under Soviet regime for seven decades Mongolia could return to the mainstream trend of the twentieth century only by the year 1990. The collapse of the Soviet empire and the bankruptcy of the communist ideology created necessary environment for Mongolia's national revival and real independence. In 1990, Mongolia held the first free elections in its twentieth century history and has since taken important steps toward a multiparty, pluralistic and democratic society.

A rapid revival of national culture has accompanied Mongolia's political liberalisation campaign as it sought to reduce the influence of Marxist-Leninist ideology and to foster the idea of ethnic revival. Chinggis Khan, once labelled as tyrant and aggressor during the Soviet period, was reassessed as national hero, and 840 year's anniversary of his birth was widely commemorated in the year 2002. The parliament decided that the traditional script abolished in the 1940s would be eventually restored, taught in the schools, and widely used along with the Cyrillic script. Freedom of religion was proclaimed and Buddhist monasteries were reopened.

Socialist modernization, especially carried out between 1960 and 1990 brought unprecedented level of education and healthcare to traditionally nomadic Mongolians. Almost universal literacy and a very low level of infant mortality by the standard of developing countries were achieved during the decades of hugely subsidized industrialization and urbanization under the guidance of Soviet planners. Economic equality and state- guaranteed social welfare system became the essential elements of Soviet system in Mongolia.

Market economic reforms, vigorously pursued by the successive governments in the 1990s, had enthusiastic support of major international donors and active expansion of domestic private entrepreneurs. After 1990, Mongolia had to overcome "the most serious peacetime economic collapse any nation has faced" during the twentieth century. The national economy has experienced positive growth rates from 1994 onward and some people have certainly become better off. But the number of poor and unemployed remains high, and a regional and social polarization is emerging.

Geography has returned as a decisive factor in Mongolian perspectives. In terms of trade, travel, lifestyle and culture, Mongolia is undeniably drawing closer to the Asian world, following the rapid development of trade with East Asian partners and establishment of diplomatic ties. Cultural contacts are also rapidly extending along this line. Northeast Asia and Central Asia are now the most important immediate interest for Mongolia in the twenty-first century. The developments in these two sub-regions will undoubtedly influence Mongolia's national security and developmental choices in near future.

MONGOLIAN SECURITY WITHIN THE SOVIET BLOCK

During the Cold War, Mongolian People's Republic (MPR) was the first military- political ally of the USSR, the weakest but the most trusted chain in the Soviet military alliance in the Asia Pacific Regional security system. That means that Mongolia's external security policy at that time had only single pillar, i.e., Soviet Union. Soviet economic, political and diplomatic support as well as its conventional and nuclear umbrella were the guarantee of Mongolia's independence and security. Although being real and reliable, this guarantee, on the other hand, forcefully cut Mongolia-China and more broadly Mongolia's international relations.[1] In addition the country had to bear a heavy burden of developing rapidly its armed forces.

The Soviet Union was interested in insuring security and territorial integrity of Outer Mongolia primarily because it was a very important factor of its own security. Prevention of the Japanese aggression against the MPR was considered in Moscow as a major precondition of defense and security and of the Soviet Far Eastern region. In the 1930s Outer Mongolia was a very reliable and loyal partner of the Soviet Union and in fact protected much of its Far Eastern border. It was in the 1930s when a military union between the USSR and the MPR was finally established. This union existed till early 1990s.[2]

Particularly, in 1960-70s, when sharp tension in relations between Soviet Union and China led practically to mutual military confrontation, Mongolia had been involved in "double cold war" situation. Thus, for a quite long period of time the territory of Mongolia, at least a part of it, was a field or front line of possible war or armed conflict between the two of our great neighbors. In general, during the height of the Cold War, Mongolia's foreign policy and security (military) strategy relied on the former USSR and consequently aimed at Europe (socialist camp or Warsaw Pact). Some argue that it was fault of Mongolia itself. But in reality, during that time of hostility between the two rival systems (capitalism and socialism), and, in addition, between the Soviet Union and China, there was not any other optimal option for Mongolia.

The main emphasis in the national security concept throughout the twentieth century was on traditional concepts of defense of the people and land from foreign aggression in alliance with a powerful ally. That was the general picture or state of Mongolia's foreign policy and security strategy of the country during the "socialist era" upto 1990s.

National Security Policy Based on National Interests

The disintegration of the so-called socialist world and of the Soviet Union itself, the end of the cold war, normalization of Sino-Soviet and later of Sino-Russian relations and some other developments in international relations favorably changed Mongolia's geopolitical environment. These changes allowed Mongolia to expand its relations, define its own national interests and priorities, and pursue them.

Mongolia underwent a fundamental change due to radical changes in its external environment and internally. It started a transition from an authoritarian State with a centrally planed economy to a democratic one with market economy. With these external and internal changes, its perception of vital national interests, values and national security have undergone fundamental changes.

In early 1990s, adoption of a national security concept was a necessity and in fact a social order. With the socialist world view and view of itself shattered, Mongolia needed to address the emerging challenges of a new geopolitical and economic realities, including absence of a powerful ally or an alliance system, drying up of external sources of investment and assistance, changing people's attitude towards the state, society, human rights, etc. The first step in this direction was thorough discussion and adoption of a new Constitution that would be the soul as well as the basic law in of the land. The new Constitution was adopted in 1992, which proclaimed, in its fist chapter dealing with the sovereignty of the state that State power would be vested in the people of Mongolia which would be exercised through direct participation in state affairs and through the representative bodies of state power elected by them. It is in this spirit that the second chapter of the new Constitution deals with human rights and freedoms.

According to the Constitution, the Parliament is the highest organ of state power that has the exclusive right to determine the basis of its domestic and foreign policies and, declare state of war or emergency as well as determine the structure, composition and powers of the National Security Council. The National Security Council of Mongolia was established in 1992. One of its first tasks was to organize discussion and eventual adoption of the national security concept of Mongolia. The Council decided at that time that the concept would be more effective if two other policies are addressed in parallel: concept of foreign policy and the fundamentals of the military doctrine. Inter-agency working groups comprising of members of parliament, government as well as experts and scholars representing different political parties and views worked in 1992-93 and were able to present their common draft in 1994 for consideration by the parliament.

The concept addresses national security issues in broad terms, not only in terms of defense of the people and the land from external attack. Though insurance of Mongolia's independence, sovereignty, territorial integrity and inviolability of state frontiers are accorded priority attention, the concept goes beyond them and focuses on such issues as security of the social order and state system, security of citizens' rights and freedoms, economic security, scientific and technological security, security of information, security of Mongolian civilization (meaning Mongolia's identity and way of life), security of the population and its gene pool and ecological security.

This has found reflection in the 1992 Constitution of Mongolia, which proclaimed building a humane, civil and democratic society in the country as its ultimate aim. In 1994 the State Great *Hural* (Parliament) of Mongolia adopted a set of three important documents that define its vital national interests and national security: concept of national security, concept of Mongolia's foreign policy and the fundamentals of the military doctrine. In the past 15 years these broad policy documents served as general guidelines of Mongolia's national security policy.

After the adoption of the New Constitution, Mongolia has been able to define the basic principles of relations and main fields and forms of cooperation with Russia and China, and reflect them in bilateral treaties of friendly relations and cooperation, signed with them in 1993 and 1994 respectively.

The treaty with Russia, unlike the previous treaty with the Soviet Union, does not contain provisions of collective self-defense or automatic collective action in case of perceived threat. Article 4 of the new Treaty stipulates that the parties shall not participate in any military political alliance against each other, nor conclude with third countries any treaties and agreements running counter to the interest of sovereignty and independence of the other party. They have also agreed that neither of them would allow the use of their territory by third states for aggressive or other violent acts against the other party, i.e., for undermining the security interest of the other party.

Furthermore, Russia has pledged to respect Mongolia's policy aimed at nonstationing on its territory or transit through it of foreign troops as well as nuclear and other weapons of mass destruction. The treaty with China also stipulates that the Parties shall not allow countries to use their territory against state sovereignty and security of the other party. Unlike Russia, China has pledged to respect Mongolia's policy of nonstationing on its territory or transit through it of foreign troops as well as nuclear and other weapons of mass destruction in a separate press statement.

Any external threat to Mongolia, whether political, military, terrorist, economic, or other, will somehow be directly or indirectly connected with one or both of our two neighbors. By the same token, it could be said that its security is also one way or the other connected with two neighbors as well as with their mutual relations. Therefore it is logical that relations with the two neighbors constitute the cornerstone of our security policy and thus are accorded top priority in our foreign relations.

Multipillarity, complexity and openness of Mongolia's foreign policy undoubtedly attracted attention of the regional and world community, and the country's position on the international arena has been strengthened substantially. Today, results of this change are tangible.

Understandably, this kind of process is not always run easily and smoothly. Achievements and problems are not always connected with a particular country's activity or an activity of a single ministry. In this sense, the faith of Mongolia's security strategy shall be influenced by developments in our external environment, particularly one in Northeast Asia (NEA).

Nowadays, when even the most powerful nation alone is not capable to provide full guarantee of its own security, not mentioning regional or international ones, importance of initiative and participation of small nations is growing.

In creating a truly global environment for peace and security not only global and regional powers, but small states too, should contribute an important part, as was noted in the UN Secretary-General's address to the Mongolian Parliament during his visit to Mongolia in 2002.[3]

Therefore, as a sovereign member of the international community, Mongolia has been casting hopes on NEA, as the nation strove to gain political and economic support during the past seventeen years of comprehensive reform and transition into a free, democratic society with market economy. As the Foreign Policy Concept of Mongolia states, "... Conditions for joining the regional integration will be created by expanding the bilateral cooperation with countries within the region."[4] Accordingly, the following actions were taken, namely:[5]

- Since joining ARF in 1998 Mongolia has been actively and consistently participating in its activities at all levels, an important step to get closer to the ASEAN countries and strengthen Mongolia's position within Asia;
- In 2004 Mongolia joined the Asian Cooperation Dialogue (ACD);
- In 1991 Mongolia applied for membership in the Pacific Economic Cooperation Council (PECC), and in 1997 created the PECC National Committee, or MonPECC, becoming an auxiliary member in 2000. Now the goal is to upgrade this status into a full membership;
- Actions were taken to join the Northeast Asia Cooperation Dialogue (NEACD), a Track Two arm of the Six Party Talks on Korean Peninsula nuclear issues; however, Mongolia's admission scheduled for April 2005 Seoul Meeting was delayed due to North Korea's suspension of the talks. The American side has notified that as soon as North Korea rejoins the Six Party Talks, Mongolia's admission will be secured;
- Mongolia applied for APEC in 2003 but this bid was

stalled due to temporary moratorium on new membership until 2007;

- In 2005 Mongolia signed the ASEAN Treaty of Amity and Cooperation (TAC)[6] and bilaterally seeks support for joining the ASEAN Plus Three mechanism as a fourth partner;
- At the 6th Asia-Europe Meeting (ASEM) held in Helsinki, Finland in September 2006, Mongolia was invited to participate in the forum's future events, making the country effectively one of its newest members, along with Romania, Bulgaria, India, Pakistan and the ASEAN Secretariat. This event has received an immediate public support domestically and is hailed as one in the series of foreign policy achievements of post-Cold War Mongolia.[7] As described by Ambassador Sodov Onon to the European Union: "... Mongolia considers the ASEM process as an important mechanism that greatly contributes to the enhanced cooperation and mutual understanding between Asia and Europe." Therefore, Mongolia had sought to join this unique dialogue and cooperation process for several years. Mongolia's bid to join ASEM was finally endorsed by the ASEM Leaders at their Summit meeting in Helsinki, in September 2006.[8]
- Mongolia has been part of the UNDP-sponsored Tumen River Project;
- Mongolia takes part in some ESCAP projects, such as the Asian Highway Project.

In addition, active participation exists in various Track Two settings, such as Council for Security Cooperation in Asia Pacific (CSCAP), as well as the annual Conference on NEA economic cooperation held in Niigata, Japan.

Nuclear Weapon-Free Status

In accordance with principles of the National Security Concept of Mongolia and within the framework of the policy of safeguarding the nation's security by political and diplomatic means, in 1992 Mongolia declared itself as a nuclear weapon-free zone (NWFZ). Seventeen years have passed since then, and ten years since this initiative gained full support of the international community and UN General Assembly began to deliberate on this issue.

The General Assembly passed three resolutions recognizing Mongolia's unique NWFZ and pledging further support; the UN Secretary-General also reported to the General Assembly several times on this initiative.

The following are Mongolia's achievements in an effort to gain international support for the declared NWFZ:

1. The 2000 Assurance by five nuclear powers was an important step toward strengthening Mongolia's political security and is recognized so by the UN. To obtain this assurance, the Mongolian Parliament in May 2002 adopted Law on Nuclear Weapon-Free Status;
2. The Non-Aligned Movement has supported Mongolia's NWF status at its 2000 Durban Conference and 2003 Kuala Lumpur Conference respectively, and stipulated that its international recognition and institutionalization would be a major step toward establishing a nuclear non-proliferation regime in Asia Pacific;
3. Mongolia's NWF status was further deliberated at 2001 Sapporo Consultative Meeting involving the experts from five nuclear powers, Mongolia and UN, where the status was given a definition, and issued specific recommendations for obtaining international recognition and institutionalization. These recommendations serve as guidelines for steps to be taken ahead.

Pursuant to Sapporo Recommendations, in early 2002 Mongolia submitted written proposals to Russia and People's Republic of China (PRC), and in April and July of the same year received supporting responses from Moscow and Beijing. The

Mongolian side has been engaging the two neighbors to launch tripartite negotiations.

The UN General Assembly Resolution No. 55/33S has included non-nuclear aspects of Mongolia's security, such as economic and ecological vulnerability, in addition to its NWF status.[9]

Participation in UN Peacekeeping Missions

Mongolia pursues the policy of participating in UN peacekeeping operations (PKOs), which is perceived as a duty of a sovereign member of that organization. At present Mongolia's Armed Forces possess 3 military teams and over 20 trained military observers ready to serve under UN mandate.[10] During the past period, more than 20 observers from our Armed Forces have fulfilled their missions in three PKOs run by the UN, in the Democratic republic of Congo, Sudan and Western Sahara. The Mongolian Government had sent the 3rd military team to UN operation in Sierra Leone. Furthermore, the goal is to broaden the scope of Mongolia's participation in UN PKOs by including police (law enforcement) and civilian observers, besides uniformed military, and thus continue to contribute in the cause of maintaining global security. As Mongolia needs external expertise and financial support in enhancing PKO capacity, it welcomes the U.S. pledge to offer training and technical assistance in this task.

MONGOLIAN SECURITY PERSPECTIVES IN EARLY 21st CENTURY

Mongolia neither has sufficient capability to protect itself nor to threaten others. That means, in case of need, the country would have to apply for international legal and military assistance and protection. Mutual benefit can not be directly understood as equality of core and other interests. On the regional arena every player defends its own national interests and participates in international relations with its own understanding, courses and ideas. In other words, all play their own game.

For instance, interests of our two neighbors towards Mongolia always remain unchangeable -none of them wants to give the other a dominant position over Mongolia nor both of them want increase of a third party influence there, and if such increase would turn into dominance they may join in a common struggle against it. This kind of approach could be against our concept of a third neighbor, but it is not against our core national interests. Understandably, our two neighbors are wary not because they are afraid of Mongolia itself. But they are cautious of someone else might use us or our territory for the actions harmful to their own national interests. In such a case, they will certainly retaliate accordingly. That means Mongolia is not always in winning position, and there is a risk of calling fire to our own heads. Of course, they would be careful in their actions respecting sovereignty of Mongolia and taking into account common interests and international norms and rules. Thus, the cards are in others' hands, and our faith will depend on which card they play with.

Another example is that in case if Washington and Tokyo jointly dominate Northeast Asia, it would hamper realization or even maintaining national interests of Moscow and Beijing in the region. That in turn would lead Russia and China to develop mutual security cooperation and partnership, and create a coalition around them. This kind of approach lays a basis for suspicion that the two countries care more of creating anti-US and Japan coalition rather than the regional security development. In general, attention of great powers and other regional players to strategic stability and regional development does not match the present security requirements and positive possibilities existing in the region. From this point, one can not be sure about the future of the region.

Mongolia's long-term future, i.e., the future of its multilateral policy is indefinite. In today's democratic civilized world, could a small, harmless country like Mongolia have good relations with great and influential countries? Certainly, yes. At the official level, there are not any unsolved serious problems in Mongolia-China and Mongolia-Russia relations. But in recent years, some Chinese scholars have been arguing that the

Mongolia-US defense relations, Mongolia-Taiwan relations and Dalai Lama's visit cause problems for Mongolia's cooperation with China. Also, the Russian academic A.L.Lukin observes that "It is most strange that Mongolia, a country located in the middle of Asian continent, has been orienting to the western political values rather than those of Asia."[11] Mongolia's relations and cooperation with the USA, Japan and Korea may of course reduce a little bit influence and position of Russia and China in Mongolia, but they never would be able to change 100 per cent dependency of Mongolia upon the Russian oil supply or 75 per cent supply of food stuffs from China. Presently, 50 percent of foreign investment in Mongolia comes from China. In other words, in a single polar world, the multi-pillar policy should overcome some uneasy challenges. What will be the future of this policy when, as some scholars insist that the world would gradually turn into multipolar one. Finally, political and economic transition goals will be fulfilled by Mongolia in general. Mongolia will provide its external security not, as previously, by joining military coalitions, but by coordinating its national interests with the interests of neighboring countries as well as other regional nations. This approach receives full support from the world community.

REFERENCES

1. L. Molomjamts, "Security of Mongolia and Northeast Asia", *Regional Security Issues and Mongolia*, vol. 1, no. 32, 2007.
2. A. Yu. Sidorov, "Geopolitics and Ideology in Soviet-Mongolian Relations in the 1930s," *Regional Security Issues and Mongolia*, vol.1, 2005.
3. Kofi Annan, UN Secretary-General, Address to the State Great Khural (Parliament) of Mongolia: "Small States in Era of Globalization", Ulaanbaatar, October 16, 2002.
4. Mongol Ulsyn gadaad bodlogyn uzel barimtlal, *Concept of Mongolia's Foreign Policy*. p. 40.
5. G. Tomorchuluun, Mongol Uls ba Zuun Azi. Paper presented at 2005 Conference of Mongolian, Chinese and Japanese scholars, July 5, 2005, Ulaanbaatar.
6. Gadaad heriin, Said ARF-yn hurald oroltsov. "*Gadaad hariltsaa*", Mongol Ulsyn GHYa-nii medeelliin tovhimol. No.10 (164), 2005 ony 9 dugeer sar. Huudas 8.

7. Dorjjugder Munkh-Ochir, "The Asia-Europe Meeting (ASEM) as Option for a Small State: A Mongolian Perspective." Paper published in the Jorge Marshall Center for European Security Studies. August 2007, Garmish-Partenkerhin, Germany.
8. Sodov Onon and Ishtsog Ochirbal, 2006. "From Chinggis Khaan towards Democracy: Mongolia's Role in Euro-Asian Affairs." Proceedings of the Luncheon Briefing *Mongolia:, From Chinggis Khaan to ASEM*, Co-organised by the European Commission and the Mission of Mongolia to the European Union, http://www.eias.org/luncheons/2006/mongolia2311 06/proceedings.pdf, (accessed July 18,2007), p. 19.
9. UNDP Mongolia, *Economic and Ecological Vulnerabilities and Human Security in Mongolia*, Ulaanbaatar, 2005.
10. Ya. Choijamts, Mongol Uls NUB-yn enhiig sahiulah ajillagaand oroltsoj ehelsen ni. Paper presented at the Conference on 60th Anniversary of the UN, Ulaanbaatar, October 20, 2005.
11. A.L. Lukin, *Journal of Asia-Pacific Region*, No.1, 2006, p.115.

CHAPTER 9

ECONOMIC SECURITY OF MONGOLIA: SOME PERSPECTIVES

J. Gulgou

As a small economy Mongolia is heavily dependant on external factors. Export of the country equals half of its GDP. More than 40 per cent of the national savings is contributed by foreign sources. Obviously these figures are characteristic of national economies having limited capacity and uncompleted infrastructure.

EXTERNAL DEBTS

One of the criteria of economic security or independence of a nation is the overall scope of its external debts and its ability to serve and/or settle these obligations. Fortunately, with regulation of the arrears accumulated during the socialist period (1940-1990) to the former Soviet Union in 2003, Mongolia's position in this regard has improved tremendously. According to the statistics for 2006, external debt of the Mongolian Government is about 1.4 billion US$ of which 38 per cent is borrowed from Asian Development Bank, 21 per cent from World Bank, 18.8 percent from Japan. In the same year, 45 million US dollars were needed for serving these obligations: repayment and interest. It means that 1.7% of GDP is used for this purpose, which can be considered as normal in the contemporary world. The scope of private commercial credit of the nation is negligible.

For a better management of the foreign debt of

Mongolia, following measures are recommended:

(a) To establish by law a ceiling for overall foreign debt related to GDP in per cent as a long term guide for maximum amount for lending abroad. If any Government feels that it may need more credit than fixed by the ceiling, the parliament should amend the law.

(b) The country should encourage foreign direct and portfolio investment in order to replace partially, the need for foreign loans.

(c) The government should target its foreign obligations evenly among foreign nationals, and not create overdependence on one or fewer countries.

FOOD IMPORTS

The other aspect of economic security is the rate of domestic production in relation to the total consumption of food products. Having more than 30 million heads of livestock and enough area of cultivated land, Mongolia should not face food shortage in the long-term perspective. The foreign currency-reserves of the country, equal now to 24 weeks' import needs are enough for securing short-term demands in food supply as well.

For further improvement of food security:

(a) Pattern of food consumption of the Mongolian people should be changed, i.e., share of meat and wheat products should fall. And vegetable and dairy products need to be consumed more.

(b) More efficient use of food products should be encouraged by introducing advanced technology of processing and conservation, besides providing electricity to rural areas.

DEPENDENCE ON FEWER MARKETS

The main point of vulnerability of Mongolia's national economy is connected with the uneven distribution of her international relations. China has a dominant position in Mongolia's foreign economic relations. According to the statistics of 2006, almost half, viz, 47.9 per cent of international trade of the country is with its southern neighbor. People's Republic of China has also been No.1 country in foreign direct investments for the last 8 years providing 40 per cent of its total volume.

Despite China's declaration of "Good Neighborly Policy" as part of its new strategy of "peaceful development" with all neighboring countries, it is important to predict the behaviour of strong China, which would appear after 10 to 15 years. Mongolia needs to keep in mind, as to how long will the present political system survive in that country and what effect would be on Chinese foreign policy if "regime change" happens there?

China consumes now about one fourth of world steel, copper and aluminum. Meanwhile its own production in copper, caters to only 25 per cent of its overall consumption. The prevailing majority of Mongolia's mineral exports are delivered to its southern neighbor- China. Meanwhile more than 50 per cent of Chinese investment in Mongolia has been in mining and geology sector. Mongolia needs to assess the reaction of Chinese buyers, if the supply from Mongolia gets interrupted/reduced by any reason.

(a) Counter measures for reducing the influence of overdependence on one neighbor have multifaceted components: free trade agreements with other countries, countervailing/antidumping duties for imports (allowed by WTO) etc.

(b) Mongolia should prefer to invite prestigious and well-known participants from other countries in exploiting recently discovered big deposits like Tavan tolgoi coal, Oyu tolgoi copper. The other way of handling this issue is to create within the country, capacities for deeper processing of minerals in order to make it easier to transport the final products for distant buyers, and avoiding the two immediate markets.

(c) Mongolia's policy regarding foreign participation in exploiting its natural resources should be transparent and stable and besides being free from any corruption-motivated decision making.

DEMOGRAPHIC EXPANSION

Other point which requires vigilance is, demographic spill-over. According to the researches, as a result of pollution and deserts, 50 million of rural Chinese are going to be displaced within 10 years from now. This demographic shift may affect not only urban and less populated areas within China but also neighboring countries like Russian Far East, Central and South Asia. Mongolia being a sparsely populated country can be affected by this kind of trans-border displacement. Obviously Mongolia needs to be ready for regulating this movement by entering into relevant international conventions etc.

Demographic expansion can be also caused by importing labor force into Mongolia. The number of Chinese workers legally and illegally employed in Mongolia has been growing. The main reason of increase is that the Chinese laborers are cheaper and more productive than their Mongolian colleagues. There is quiet high possibility of brewing tension between Mongolians and Chinese guest workers based on salary-employment disparities and nationalistic mentality. The best way of preventing such clashes is a policy to limit the scope of importing labor force. Determination of Mongolian authorities at every level to handle any developments of such ethnic motivated clashes by peaceful and legal means and to fight every nationalistic action from Mongolian side, are equally important.

PETROLEUM DEPENDENCE

Mongolia is almost 100 per cent dependant on petroleum products. For the last 10 years entire volume and domestic price of their supplies were synchronous with the Russian policy and regulations of oil exports. The efforts to search oil in Mongolia made during the last several years, promise brighter future. It is estimated that within 8 years the country will be able to extract 23 million barrels of oil which will cover significant share of the needs of Mongolia. But this matter again requires wise long term policy: Companies working in this field are mainly Chinese and whole volume of oil to be extracted is projected for being exported as crude. As one can see, the country may be switched from one kind of dependence to other kind.

(a) Obviously, Mongolia should seek possibility of conditional/linked supply with its two neighbors in energy sector as per common international practice. Supplies of third countries should also be a permanent source of Mongolian petroleum products needs.
(b) Introduction of alternative technologies like gasification of coal, lignite based liquid fuel should be the other priority of Mongolian Government.

TRANSIT TRANSPORTATION

Another weak point of the Mongolian economy is its dependence on transit transportation. Threat of technical or political de-functioning of the trans-Mongolian railway connecting with two immediate neighbors at any moment by different motivation does exist, particularly of political nature.

The country should try to secure international legal guarantee of goodwill function of the railway. The other options include additional tracts of connectivity by railway and paved road. Mongolia should also try that these transport corridors function under international surveillance or management.

CHAPTER 10

WOMEN AND DEVELOPMENT IN CONTEMPORARY MONGOLIA

Maqsooda Shitoni

Women of Mongolia have been the sustaining force of their nation throughout centuries of statehood, living and raising livestock in the mountains, deserts and the steppes of the country. While they share many opportunities as well as constraints usually faced by women everywhere else, they also experience particular advantages and disadvantages based on the traditions of Mongolian life style, which combines a nomadic and sedentary life style with influence of the Asian and European cultural manifestations.[1]

POSITION OF WOMEN BEFORE 1921 REVOLUTION

The position of women in the Manchu period was almost identical to those of the traditional societies elsewhere. Gender discrimination was the order of the day and women were considered and treated as an article of perishable commodity. Women's position was that of a chattel. Religion, which in case of Mongolia was yellow sect of Buddhism, and scornful chauvinistic attitude of the men folk towards the weaker section of the society had deprived women of their freedom of thought and their rights. Just as their freedom and rights were curbed, for them to read and write was a sin. They were treated like domestic slaves and were sold in order to pay the debts. If the husband was punished for some crime; they were also punished without committing anything wrong. Religious prejudice weighed them down, and they were forcibly married and seldom respected. Such state of affairs continued throughout the Manchu era. Howorth rightly observes:[2]

> She was middle aged at 30 old and wrinkled at 40, and at 50 or when she became a widow, she shaves her head and sets up as a family monk. A woman works hard and is harshly treated. Her place is next to the door and the felt she sleeps on is the thinnest and poorest. She takes little care of herself and little care is bestowed on her. She is born, married, bears some children, does her work and dies.

Position of Women after 1921 Revolution

The socio-economic exploitation and family oppression were brought to an end by the Revolution of 1921. Women were given the opportunity to receive primary, secondary and higher education along with men on equal basis in all sectors of society. They started participating in political social and economic life of the country. The first constitution of Mongolian People's Republic adopted in 1924 established women's equal rights with men in education and employment. She became a full-fledged and active member of the society. In 1924, the women's organization committee was founded, which promoted the wide participation of women in political, social and labor activity while the Constitution granted them the right to participate in elections. Since then, many women were elected as deputies and it was made clear that those women as leaders should be on the top level position. During the 1930s enormous gains were made by and for women: 16 women ministers, deputy minister and agency heads, 35 per cent of judges were women, 40 women headed cooperatives and 14 women out of 35 were in the *Khural* (legislative body) by 1940. The Party and State devoted particular attention to making education and culture accessible to women.[3]

Educational achievements were impressive for both boys and girls. In 1923, Mongolia's first secondary school had only five female students; however, five years later it had 558 of them.

Education for women was emphasized and their participation in politics and decision making was encouraged. Co-education became normal practice and the pedagogical principles for both boys and girls were the same from the kindergarten up. In 1931, about 40 per cent of school enrollment was female and out of 600 people elected to local bodies, 30 per cent were women: two of these being Aimag Governors. By 1969, 76 per cent of all women were literate and by 1989 the literacy rate for the entire population, male and female, had risen to 86 per cent. As a result, in the field of higher education, the enrolment of women constitutes more than three quarters and they comprise 67.2 to 80.2 per cent of school teachers.

With the expansion of industry and science sector, more jobs became available, many of which were taken by women. In seeking work they were partly driven by material considerations and partly by the fact that in socialist society labor was a main criterion for a person's worth. All this made women independent, enhanced their self assuredness and increased their role in the society. Participation in social life greatly changed their outlook, their way of life and thinking. Professionally, they became more politically aware. Their role in the society and in the family changed. Mother and child protection laws ensured that women are not disrupted in their work as deputies in the ministries, doctors, engineers, writers and industrial workers.

Government took many measures to build a large work force. Between 1960-70 emphasis was on social welfare, health condition, pension benefits and establishment of professional training centers where women could get training. By 1925 the custom of forcibly marrying off women was abolished by law. Abortion was illegal although not uncommon and contraceptives were mostly unavailable. Total fertility rate reached 7.53 in early 1970 and population growth rate peaked in a few years. Efforts were made to provide many maternity homes with qualified medical personnel, free medical care and meals. Large families were recommended and mothers of such large families were awarded the "Order of Mothers Glory," which entitled them to annual cash or free stay in a rest house for a period of 14-21 days.[4]

Working mothers also had the right to take holidays of six months after childbirth. This act was enforced since 1977. The upbringing of the children was the common task for both the parents. All the family members shared the household chores. More than half of the population engaged in national productive labor was women. The establishment of cooperative movements in rural areas helped women and freed them from the burden of much work. In urban areas also many kindergartens looked after the interests of mother and child thereby giving women further chance to utilize her time in useful work comfortably.[5] Rights of women to work, to rest, to educate and equal pay were guaranteed.

One finds majority of women working on an equal footing with men as herds, in factories, State farms, Agricultural Associations and in other enterprises. With the development of economy and culture, women have acquired higher merit in all fields of society. However, the emancipation in the socio-economic sphere was at the cost of freedom of expression.

Collapse of Socialist Structure and Position of Women

The transition period was a painful period for both men and women as it had negative impact on the situation despite the positive impact it brought in the coming years. As everywhere in the world, women, children and the elderly suffered the most. In case of Mongolian women they were hit hard and were put in the most difficult situation. Although the new constitution which was formed after the collapse of the socialist regime gave women equal rights, these laws were not yet implemented.

In contrast to the socialist period where many women in the political sphere held posts such as Ministers, Chairperson, Secretary of the Party Organization and Deputies of Great Peoples *Khural* (legislature), there were only three women parliamentarians among the 76 male members of the great *khural* after the transition. This represents an eight fold decline in the representation of women in the legislative body as compared with the pervious system.

According to the report of NSO (Women and Men in Mongolia) in 1998, "Women's political, social and economic participation is much lower than men's in that women constitute only 10.5 per cent of current parliament members, 11per cent of government (Cabinet) members, 0 percent of Aimag and capital city governors, 2.4 percent of Sum and district governors, 6-13 percent of citizens, representatives *Khurals* (local legislatures) at all levels, 0 percent of the heads of the citizens, representatives, *Khurals* and 3-8 percent of Presidium members. Even in the judicial branch, despite women constituting about 70 percent of all legal professionals, only 23.5 percent of the Supreme Court members are women."

The women who once dominated various fields of economy have no say in the decision making of the country. During the socialist period, they had some power in decision making, they accounted for just under half of Mongolia's work force, dominated in banking, health and educational sectors. They also predominated in several sub-sectors notably communication, trade, technology, utility services, public canteens and insurance. Thus the professional gap between men and women narrowed significantly. However, as the socialist system collapsed, so did the rights and voices of women in Mongolia. In the educational, health and banking sectors they also lost their jobs and they have been pushed away from the political and social life of the country through early retirement. In 1990 subsidies were withdrawn and many economic entities had to manage without it, hence a lot people preferred to survive by reducing the number of staff. As a result, number of pensioners increased by four fold. No pension is given to the single women and widows if the husband dies outside their place of work. Even when pension is granted, it is often not enough to feed the family and there is no adequate support to provide education to the children. Widows are not in a position to buy daily commodities and they could not work full time. Women between the ages of 38 to 55 with more than four children were forced into early retirement.Women who were rewarded for having many children and were called the "glorious mothers" during the socialist period, were now reduced to poverty. Consequently, these same women who constituted over half of the labor productivity, have been almost ignored in various spheres of country's life and are relegated to very ordinary status.

Between 1990 and 1994 several measures were introduced to change the basic pension scale, but due to the increase in prices and tariffs on consumer commodities, basic goods and all types of public service, the condition remained as before. In 1995, about one quarter of the population was estimated to be living in poverty and over 20 per cent of poor households were headed by women. The rise in the number of female headed households inevitably increased unemployment among women with low levels of education and skills, while low wages for those in employment were the major cause for the prevailing trend towards the feminization of poverty.

To address these issues, the government of Mongolia approved in 1994 a poverty alleviation programme and was implemented with international assistance. Subsequently, in 1995 another resolution was passed under which pension was increased. However, it was applied to veterans over 70 years old, creating unfavorable conditions for old women who retired on privileged terms because they were mother of many children. Retired people, both men and women, were not even able to pay the apartment rents as the pension was less than the cost for the rent, which, under the socialist period, was almost free just as good work meant a good apartment. With the collapse of the socialist period, neither the salaries nor pension was enough to settle the bills, henceforth forcing a large movement of women towards the countryside where they felt they could survive. There was nobody to look after the children as day care centers, child care and school system had collapsed, while the few available institutions were of no use to poor families. In 1995, there were 5,12,000 households in Mongolia with an average family size of 4.4 with the number of female headed households and children born out of marriage increasing annually. While female headed families constituted 4.4 per cent of households in 1980, this number increased to 7.2 per cent by 1995.

Health condition also deteriorated due to the lack of routine health care, absence of medicine and healthy diet. In the socialist period, agricultural farms and cooperatives were responsible for the health check-ups and they were looking after the maternity hostels and such institutions. But 50 per cent of these hostels are closed down and remaining some are in the hands of local administration who complain of having no resources to maintain them. The maternal mortality also increased due to the lack of medical staff and transportation. Between 1985 and 1995, the maternal mortality rate especially among the school drop outs, low literacy and unemployed mothers increased to 185 per 100,000 births and infant mortality rate was 44.8 per 1000 live births. The percentage of unattended births in rural areas is also increasing and incidence of abortion has given rise to maternal mortality. Furthermore, due to the lack of contraceptives, there has been an increase in the prevalence of sexually transmitted infections. Abortion was legalized in 1989, which stepped up the incidence. In 1991, the number of abortions reached its peak with 31,217 and so did the number of divorce; in 1986-92 the rate increased by one third but is now back to the level in 1985. There were 2,243 cases of divorce in 1990 and about 6000 in the first quarter of 1993. This number also increased as a consequence of limited utilization of family planning methods. The quality and care of the doctors became below standard as many good doctors left and took jobs in business fields instead.

VIOLENCE AGAINST WOMEN

Official studies and data on violence against women are limited. Common forms of violence against women such as physical violence and emotional abuse within the family are taken as something private. There are some laws. However, these were established by people who have less knowledge on these issues, thus making the newly passed family laws less effective even if these were implemented. The laws on beating, insulting, verbal abuse leading to suicide is sometimes addressed, but not taken seriously. No action is taken to protect or defend the victim.

Sexual harassment by persons in position of authority, the

rape of girl children and women within and outside the family along with prostitution have become a critical concern. Similarly, alcoholism in domestic life has also increased to such an extent that domestic violence has become another big concern especially for children and women. In the effort to increase the population during the socialist period, children born outside matrimony were accepted. However, these created problems after the transition period as these children in one family belonged to different fathers and were often abused by the new father. Consequently, not merely the mothers but the children along with their moms were the victims of violence, forcing many of them to leave the house and start a street life. In the socialist system state supported these families, but now there is no adequate support except the relatives who help them sometimes. These factors have a negative impact on child development while it also limits women's participation in social and educational field.

Recently in 2008, a research entitled "Country Gender Assessment-2008 Study," was conducted by the National Network of Mongolian Women Organization and the Asian Development Bank. The research report has been published in the *UB Post* which states that there has been no decline in violence against women. The report concludes:[6]

> Violence against women seems to be growing in terms not only of its forms, but also its severity. Trafficking in women and girls, forced prostitution, pornography, incest, date and marital rape, and sexual harassment continue to render women's lives insecure at home, at work and in public spaces. In addition, the rising nationalism with its strongly anti-women's rights rhetoric, a religious revival with strong conservative overtones, and increase in traditionalist attitudes have been strengthening patriarchal and anti-democratic discourses according to researchers. These discourses advocate for a hierarchically governed cohesive nation, supported by clear hierarchies within the society (citizen vis-a-vis the state, the younger vis-a-vis the older) and within the family (women vis-a-vis men, the younger vis-a-vis the older). A common feature of the nationalist, religious and traditionalist discourses is the stated need to control women's rights and freedoms, especially their sexual and reproductive rights: women's autonomy and

power are seen as a threat to the 'unified' nation. This stance has increased levels of symbolic/rhetorical violence against women in the public sphere and served to legitimate different types of violence against women and girls, and the preclusion of women's political participation. The nationalist discourse is not only broadly supported by the population, but has significant influence at policy-making levels. It is rather indicative that the draft Comprehensive National Development Strategy contained a clause on 'maintaining the purity of the national gene pool.' Legal and policy framework improved only slightly with the passage of the law against domestic violence, a program designed to combat domestic violence, and the revision of the Criminal Code to include a clear provision on trafficking and signing of the Palermo protocol. Whilst these improvements open significant avenues for citizens and NGOs to advance women's rights, the overall state policy towards women remains inadequate, researchers said. One of the key causes is the official pro-natalist stance, which views and values women primarily in their reproductive capacity. Hence, the labor code, social welfare code and many other laws maintain a protective stance, which results in discrimination against women and denies them the right to partake fully in social, cultural, political and economic processes and advance their livelihoods. It is telling as well as disturbing that the draft Comprehensive National Development Strategy contained a section on 'encouraging women, while they are young or youngish, to give birth to four or more children; take care of their children until the youngest is six years old and breastfeed until the child is six years old.

DISCRIMINATION AGAINST WOMEN

Discrimination on gender basis is quite acute, and male oriented and headed institutions deny the deserving female job seekers any place in their establishments. If they get employed, it is more likely to be in unskilled, manual, and low-wage jobs. They work under less favorable occupational health and safety conditions. They also tend to be laid off more frequently than men. Additional social security requirements for women create an obstacle to their employment. With the result, unemployment among women has increased since 1992 and they constituted 49.3 per cent of the labor force. Among economically active women, unemployment has increased to 9.6 per cent, pushing many of them into flesh trade. On inquiry, it was revealing to know that most of the sex workers enjoyed the trade as a source to quick buck without any hard labor and investment; however, it also raises a concern as those being fresh in the trade are most likely not aware of their state of affairs when customers lose interest in them due to old age or infirmity. Infections of STI, UTT and above all HIV/Aids are very frequent among the sex workers.

This type of business was altogether missing during the socialist period, and it has come as a legacy of free market economy and globalization. External forces are instrumental in the growth of flesh trade and pornography. The five-star hotels in general have call girls to serve the clients and mostly the foreigners. Some prestigious hotels have become havens for street girls, seeking richer foreign customers from whom they can earn 80-200 US dollars a night. Transparency, open society and ascendance of prostitution that increase the demand for under age boys and girls is posing a threat to the health of nation as reported cases of Aids and other STIs continue to rise quite alarmingly.

In 1990, thousands of professional women lost their jobs in agriculture and animal husbandry due to the privatization of this sector. In pre- revolutionary period *Khot Ail* (a group of three to four families) used to share the tending of livestock turn by turn and made daily products together, so that there was not much load of work. During the socialist period, agricultural *Negdels* (farm lands) were responsible for the livestock. With the transition to market economy, privatization of agriculture sector enabled the rural population, including women to own property leading to an improvement in living standard. The rural population has free and equal access to land, common pastures and water resources and benefits from traditional form of mutual assistance and support. However, this transition also had negative impact on the status of rural women by increasing their work load. At present, 45.1 per cent of Mongolian women live in rural areas. As Barbar Skapa mentions in her article, "in the rural areas prior to privatization, women worked primarily in single species collective units as dairy maids or as herders. But privatized herds which are always mixed need more tending and processing of animals products, hence requires additional family labor. These rural women have to spend considerable time in producing the dairy products without any vacation, level of wages or limit of working hours. For this reason, it is estimated that rural women now labor several hours more per day than men. They still have to take charge of the cooking, cleaning and looking after the children, the elderly and the infirm.

The diversified herds demand much labor with herding, attending weak and sick animals, milking, collecting water and dung or wood for fuel, making felt for *ger* (tent), trading goods and traveling to bag *sum* or *aimag* centers. The single headed families keep small number of herds due to the lack of manpower. While all the herders face the risk of severe winter or other conditions that may wipe out many animals, female single headed households are more vulnerable to such conditions and may have to sell off their indispensable stock in order to buy goods which they cannot make by themselves. When they deplete their animal resources they may eventually have to move back to their natal house. But if they prefer to stay back in their own *gers*, they have to work for the richer families or sink into poverty.

There has been increase in migration from rural to urban areas due to the decline of social, cultural and communal services, leading to lack of favorable living and working conditions in rural areas and consequently forcing people to move to urban areas. The primary areas of concern are the deteriorating access of rural women to health service or to educational opportunities, their limited access to information or loans for income generating activities such as the processing of animal products, and to marketing facilities and their limited capacity to cooperate or to participate in social life.

Nutrition system is also getting worse day by day. Under the socialist system, food security was provided by the agricultural and herder collectives; hence, nutrition problem was not of a concern. However, after the transition the condition has changed enormously especially in rural areas and most affected are children, old people and pregnant women. Anemia (caused by iron deficiency,) in pregnant women is considered to be as high as 40 per cent. The number of mothers with poor nutrition who give birth to low weight is also increasing from 1988-92; i.e., from 3.4 per cent of all births to 4.5 per cent in 1990 and 6 per cent in 1992. According to the United Nations Food and Agricultural Organization, a third of the Mongolian population now lives below the nutritional starvation levels. Although in urban areas stores are full of commodities, they are very expensive and the purchasing power of the society has decreased. Daily commodities have become very expensive, thus turning single women's life more difficult.

Nevertheless, it appears to be a transitional phase and the market economy demands capital, entrepreneurship and above all, expertise in financial institutions. Obviously, the main casualty is the women folk in such circumstances. But the Mongol women folk have left behind the hibernation period and are now again actively engaged in economic activities.

Mongolia and Women NGOs

Democratic Revolution of 1990 changed the scenario of Mongolian political, social and economic life. Under the economic and social crises, Mongolian women also brunt the burden of these changes, but did courageously overcome the hurdles and participated in these changes. In 1992, women started mobilizing together for their political, social, and economic status.

During these past 19 years, women overcame the hurdle and emerged with many ideas and activities. They have created a network which helps to promote their interests. Many came into existence in Ulaanbaatar and are registered with Ministry of Justice. Besides the registered groups, there are more emerging associations, but these could not compete in the market force and as such did not develop. Prior to 1990 Mongolia had one effective Association, Mongolian Women's Federation with Ms. Gerelsuren as its President. During the socialist period this Organization was a State organization and exercised both government and non-government functions. But now it is working as an NGO with diminished state resources and with the support of foreign donor countries.

Apart from these organizations, there are many others such as the Federation of Mongolian Democratic Women's Association, Mongolian Business Women's Federation, Women for Social Progress, Lawyer women's Association, Liberal women's Brain Pool, Mongolian Consultative Committee, Women Information and Research Centre and Women Against Violence which are active in the field. These organization have a broad agenda including equal rights, access to work, housing and credit, women legal issues, employment generation and vocational crisis intervention, health care for mothers and infants, promotion of the women's movements and establishment of an independent database. These issues are sources of the deterioration of status of women in Mongolia during the economic crisis. In addition, the indifference of government towards the elevation of the economic status of the women has been alarming. *Mongol Messenger*, an English Newspaper, quoted Mrs. Ider, the Chancellor of the Supreme Court who is also working for the eradication of discrimination against women as saying that "women in political sphere need to be enhanced. Despite the fact that there were a lot of educated, intelligent and talented women working for the advancement to management, the other strong sex was not interested in sharing the power, the women is a great power which could be used in the development of the country." The deterioration of women's status has economic, social, and political dimension in the absence of a clear government policy or machinery for the women. These NGO's have demanded the active participation in the political, social and economic life of the country. Seeing politics as an effective way to solve their problems, women across the country united to form a coalition of women's organization in preparation for the 2008 parliamentary elections. There were 26 candidates on the list of 313 competing for office. The oldest organization, the Mongolian Women's Federation, appealed to the public to support female candidates.

According to the research of LEOS in 1998, there were 21

political parties which had four seats in parliament. Mongolian National Democratic Party also took some steps to appoint some women as senior advisor. As per the report, "An important progress in the political life of Mongolia is the fact that over the last few years these parties that had been concentrated in the capital city only, have reached out into rural areas establishing local branches and intensifying party work in the country side."

As mentioned above, these NGO's with the assistance of different international women's Organization and with the financial assistance of Australia have established a centre for the victims of different kinds of violence, which has been operational for quite some time where they provide medical as well as moral support to such destitute people. Violence in the family on women and children has become order of the day, and mostly people prefer to hide such shameful acts sometimes for the sake of their reputation and sometimes simply not thinking it as a crime. Hence, priority should be given to the women's problems and their basic civil rights. A service to support single mothers was formed in Ulaanbaatar at the initiative of the women's democracy movement and the single mother society. The Centre aims to help youth and single mothers in securing employment.

International NGOs in association with the local NGOs have stepped in to alleviate the status of women folk and bring them back on the pedestal that they were standing upon. They are making use of their expertise in their new endeavors mainly in small scale trade and commerce. The structure of female employment also underwent a considerable change. Mongolian business women federation was established in 1992, under whose guidancc many women enterprises have emerged and they utilized their experience in various fields of business. And some of them have succeeded in establishing their own business.

This author has observed that the women who worked previously in state run canteens became at first street peddlers of baked items. There are many *Mukhlag* (small convenience store) run by men, women and even children in Ulaanbaatar. Many women also entered the private sectors as canteen operators and restaurant owners. For instance, a lady who was an interpreter in the Academy of Sciences, started her own restaurant serving Indian food, and has 6 other members as staff. Another woman who was working as a kindergarten teacher established her garment business and is now exporting to USA. She has more than 20 staff members who are all young women. A dentist opened a private dental clinic with the help of a small loan from special credit line for women. Former state truck mechanic when out of work, received a loan and put herself and her brother to work on repairing trucks and now she has registered business and is supplying tyres and has a larger workshop. Another woman along with her husband started business of used cars from Japan. Some outstanding women did wonderful jobs of not merely getting themselves a job, but employed other women co-workers in their business, which was established with a small loan under a UNIFEM Credit Scheme Project. One lady started her business at home by making sausages to peddle in the street, as she had the experience of making sausages in her meat factory where she was working during the socialist period. Within six months, she obtained loan and soon repaid it with an additional contribution to the fund so that more women could profit. A year later, she leased production space and hired 14 more employees from the factory where she once worked and imported quality equipment from Germany, which she financed through another loan.

The UNIFEM project is used for women in isolated areas where outreach and monitoring cost are high. The personal commitment of the banking staff, the NGO staff and the volunteers all act as invisible power behind women's cooperation and consciousness. There has been an extraordinary effort to encourage women of Mongolia as seen by the NGOs that visit clients in their *gers* (Tent) or apartments who go on foot or by bus and contact elderly women to start their own manufacturing units and make use of new varieties of raw materials. To implement the laws on National Program of Action, Ministry of Health and Social Policy from 1997-1999 provided a budget of 30 million *tugruks* but not the whole amount was spent for the program.

The funds are also provided by the donor organizations like

the World Bank, Asian Development Bank, United Nations Development Program, TACIS, World Health Organization, United Nations Population Fund and the Japanese government. Such financial assistance provided by the above organizations helps to achieve the goals of the National Action Program such as poverty alleviation program, projects for improving the access to health and education for the vulnerable groups. However, there is no adequate monitoring of the use of these funds.

UNICEF and NGOs from United States, Japan and Australia also implemented 6 projects and thousands of women in rural and urban areas receive soft loans, grant aid and free machines and technology to enable them produce garments and grow vegetables which can help alleviate poverty and address some of the problems confronting women. Likewise, the government of Mongolia is also trying to solve the problems of women with the help and assistance of different international organizations. A national program on women's issues for the period up to 2020 was discussed by the congress Labor Minister, E. Gombojav, who stated that "the government will make every effort to decrease the poverty and the death rate of the mother, and by 2000-10, priority will be given to the economic and social development of women by creating employment schemes. By 2010-20, foreign and domestic financial fund will be used for poverty alleviation program to assist poor and female headed families with low income. Rural women with few animals will be provided part time jobs through income generating projects. Besides, they will be provided land for cultivation and restocking, low cost housing, priority health care and vocational education for their children." To accomplish these objectives, NGOs and local networks need to raise awareness among rural women. They should be provided information on gender issues, family relations and participation in the society. For this *Aimag* and *Sum* committees should be given power to decide and identify the projects to be funded as well as implemented.

According to the statistics, women make up 50.4 per cent of the country's population and represent 43 per cent of all highly educated people; 70 per cent of lawyers and 36.8per cent of state employees in education, health trade and financial sectors. Of the female population, 43.2 per cent are below the age of 16; 47.4 per cent are aged 16-54 and 9.4 per cent are 55 years old and above. By the year 2020, the female population is expected to number 1730600, out of whom 33.9 per cent will be under 16; 54.1 per cent will be working age and12 per cent will be aged 55 and over.

To conclude, the transition has been heavily weighing upon the women folk and children especially. The interest shown by the women with the help of other international agencies is quite gratifying, and with the stabilization, the women folk are bound to play a positive role in the political and economic activities more effectively than during the days of regimentation. The national poverty alleviation programme along with the donor countries and UN, Asian Development Bank and Japanese TASMS are trying to create jobs. Priority is given to the *Aimags* and these *Aimag* governments along with the *Sum* need to show the ability to generate employment for women by using credit productivity. They need to start credit funds and involve the local financial community, local women's networks and NGOs. By doing so, visibility of such groups will increase and so will the status of women.

REFERENCES

1. *The National Program of Action for the Advancement of Women*, Ulaanbaatar, 1996, p.4. The National Program of Action for the Advancement of Women was created by the Mongolian Government in Ulaanbaatar.
2. Henry H. Howorth, *History of the Mongols,* Pt.1-1V, London, 1876-88, Moscow: Central Department of Oriental Literature, 1973, p.42 (revised edition).
3. *Mongolia*, no. 2, Ulaanbaatar, 1977.
4. *The 60th Anniversary of People's Mongolia*, Moscow: Novosti Press Publishing House, 1981, p. 101.
5. *Mongolia,* no. 2, Ulaanbaatar, 1977.
6. B. Bulgamaa, "Male Population Declining, Along with Women's Rights: Study", *The UB Post*, 8 January 2009 at http://ubpost.mongolnews.mn/index.php?option=com_content&task=view&id=25 16&Itemid=36

CHAPTER 11

INDIA AND MONGOLIA

Gauri Shankar Gupta

> "India and Mongolia are ancient lands of the ancient people of Asia. The historic and cultural collaboration between India and the Mongol is most fascinating and unique and is as old as the history of the spread of Indian culture and ideas into Central Asia and Siberia. We in India consider the Mongol veneration of Sanskrit, a matter of special privilege. We hold the people of Mongolia in high esteem for preserving in translation as well as in manuscripts, the vast collection of our precious Sanskrit text on our philosophy, poetry, logic and astronomy lost by us over the centuries. In modern times, too many Mongols visited India – the land of Buddhism."
>
> *Atal Bihari Vajpayee*, Foreign Minister of India.
> February 9, 1978

India and Mongolia are two ancient civilizations of Asia. Though geographically far apart, the two countries have had civilizational links spanning over a period of 2500 years, perhaps even more. These links are fascinating, intense and inseparable; transcending all human activities, from language, literature, religion, medicine, folklore, to culture and traditions. There is a common thread that runs through the people of our two countries. That is why Mongolians and Indians easily identify with each other and immediately feel at home. Since the contemporary edifice rests on the solid foundation of these historic and rich exchanges, this paper delves upon them.

YESTER-YEARS

In the 3rd century BC following the invasion by the Huns, some parts of northern India were briefly under the rule of the Hun Empire. The Huns were a mixed tribe and the present day Khalkha Mongols formed part of them. Origin of Mongoloid people in Northern and North-Eastern parts of India has been attributed to this conquest of the Huns. Similarity in cultural and social traditions of some of the tribes in North-Eastern India and Mongolian nomads is yet another fascinating aspect of this interaction. There are historical writings confirming that Buddhism first traveled to Mongolia in 3rd century BC during the Hun period. During the Nirun State (402 AD-555 AD), Buddhism was widely accepted in the territory which now forms Mongolia. Mongolian Monks used to study at Nalanda University in India during 5-8th centuries AD.

Rise of Temujin or Chinggis Khan in the late 12th and early 13th century is yet another significant link in our historic ties. According to an old Mongolian chronicle, when Chinggis Khan was on his way to India chasing Jalal-ad-Din, son of Khorezm ruler Muhammad, he saw a Bodhi deer on the banks of Sindhu River. The deer bowed before the Mongol king. (Deer is a sacred animal for the Mongols.) Touched by the gesture, Chinggis Khan was convinced that India was a sacred land and could not be conquered. He, therefore, not only retraced his steps but also brought with him two Buddhist monks to Karakorum, the ancient capital of the Mongol Empire.

Since then, contacts between the Mongol rulers and Indian Buddhist scholars have been regular and intense. Several Buddhist stupas and monasteries were constructed in Mongolia during this period and several Indian and Tibetan scholars traveled to Mongolia. Babar, the founder of Mughal dynasty which ruled India between 1562 and 1857 is supposed be the descendant of Timur and Chinggis Khan. Kublai Khan, the grandson of Chinggis, who ruled over one of the largest land empires in the world and who had moved the capital of Mongol empire to present day Beijing from Karakorum was first to declare Buddhism as state religion of the Yuan Dynasty. Lama

Phagspa (1235-1280) made a profound impression on Kublai Khan and was considered by him as *guru* (teacher) and used to consult him for every important decision. He was given the title 'Teacher of the Realm' and was later conferred with the status of 'Imperial Tutor'. He also developed a new script called *Phagspa* script based on *Nagari* system of India. By this time the influence of Buddhism on Mongolia was so strong that the two great Mongolian Khans – Chinggis and Kublai were considered incarnations of Bodhisttavas; Vajrapani and Manjusri.

Even after the disintegration of the Mongol empire in 1368 AD, Buddhism continued to remain most popular religion in this region. Altan Khan who succeeded in reuniting the Mongol tribes in the 15th and the 16th century spearheaded the revival of Buddhism in a big way. In 1578 he invited Sonam Gyatso, head of the Yellow Sect in Tibetan Buddhism to visit Mongolia. On this occasion Altan Khan bestowed on him the title 'Dalai' meaning 'as immense as the ocean'. Later on Sonam Gyatso came to be known as the Third Dalai Lama and his predecessors were posthumously designated as the first and the second Dalai Lamas. Thus the Dalai Lama owes his title to Mongolian ruler Altan Khan.

Undur Gegen Zanabazar – the first Bogd Khan (religious king) of Mongolia – remains the single most important link in Indo-Mongolian historic ties. Born in 1635, Zanabazar was a genius from his childhood. According to one of the chronicles, at the age of three he was able to recite Buddhist sutras and make replicas of Buddhist temples. Over the time he emerged as a great spiritual leader, an excellent sculptor, a prolific writer and an outstanding linguist. At a very early age he traveled to Tibet and acquired profound knowledge of Buddhist and Sanskrit literature. In 1686, he invented a new set of alphabets known as *Soyombo* script which was based on Indo-Tibetan scripts and languages. The very word *Soyombo* is of Sanskrit origin, (from *svayambhu*) which means 'self-generated' or the one 'that creates itself'. Though the script died after a while, the first alphabet *Soyombo* to which the script owes its name became the national symbol of Mongolia signifying its independence and sovereignty. According to many scholars the symbol of *Soyombo* is based on Vedic thoughts. During his period the Mongolian language and literature borrowed heavily from Indo-Tibetan literature including the Vedic philosophy.

Given the intense interaction between our two civilizations over millennia, the literary links between India and Mongolia are not only vast but historic and fascinating. 109 volumes of Mongolian *Kanjur* and 224 volumes of *Tanjur*, now being preserved in the State Public Library in Ulaanbaatar, are symbolic of rich literary and religious exchanges between the two countries since 3rd century BC starting with the Hun Empire. The 109 volume *Kanjur* which embodies the most sacred Buddhist literature coming from the mouth of Lord Buddha himself and other Buddhist scholars such as Nagarjuna, Aryadeva, Asanga, Dharmakirti, Vasubandhu and Dignaga is the Mongolian version of a vast collection of over 1200 works from India and Tibet. The 224 volume *Tanjur* contains the translation of Indian texts ranging from profane literature, to medicine, to poetry, to philosophy, to grammar, to astrology. *Meghduta* of Kalidasa, *Kavyadarsa* of Dandin and innumerable precious literary works of Indian scholars forms an integral part of Mongolian *Tanjur*. Prof. Bira has aptly described them as "great monuments of the history of Indo-Mongolian cultural contacts". Mongolians consider these two collections so sacred that parts of *Kanjur* and *Tanjur* have been written with ink made of nine precious stones. Recently these collections have been digitalized with the help of Indian Government so that these historic and sacred books could be preserved for posterity.

In addition to these epoch making works, stories of King Bhoja, Vikramaditya, Lord Krishna, *Ramayana* and *Mahabharata* form part of Mongolian literature and folklore. Over the centuries Mongolian scholars have translated innumerable other literary works from India and Tibet which form part of our common heritage. Given these intense, profound and wide-ranging literary and religious contacts and exchanges, the two countries are aptly described as "spiritual neighbours" or "brothers of dharma".

During the course of these literary exchanges, the Mongolian language has borrowed and assimilated hundreds of Sanskrit words – ranging from *ger* (ghar/grih), *kar* (kar), *sansar* (sansar), *buyan* (punya), os (os), *shuleg* (sloka), *radna* (ratna), *avyas* (abhyas), *joti* (jyoti), *baksh* (bhikshu) and so on. Sanskrit words relating to diverse branches of science, cosmology, astronomy, medicine and so on have been adopted and modernized in Mongolian terminology. Surely several of these words must have come to Mongolian language during the pre-Buddhist period because basic words like *kar* and *ger* have no direct relation with religion. Mongolians also have a long tradition of having Sanskrit names such as *Ganga, Zandan, Radna, Indra, Badma, Raccha, Naran, Davaa, Anand, Amaraa* and so on.

Though the river Ganga flows several thousand kilometers away from Mongolia, it is considered sacred both in India and Mongolia. One of the sacred lakes in Mongolia has been named as Ganga Lake. According to some chronicles, water of river Ganga from India was brought and poured into this lake several thousand years ago and since then it has been named as Ganga Lake. Similarly the three national sports of Mongolia, archery, wrestling and horse riding were also the most important sports of India in the ancient times. Horse riding and archery were the most essential part of the education of the warrior class-kshatriya. Wars were won and lost based on these two skills.

These are just a few illustrations of our rich historic exchanges and contacts. Historians have documented numerous such exchanges between our two people and civilizations spanning over thousands of years.

MODERN TIMES

Given such a rich legacy of interaction, assimilation and exchanges by our ancestors, it is but natural that the two countries have established very close and friendly relations in modern times. Around the time of India's independence, a Mongolian delegation came to New Delhi to attend the first Asian Relations Conference held in March 1947 at the initiative of Jawaharlal Nehru. Since then the leadership of the two countries have been in constant contact with each other. This led to establishment of diplomatic relations between our two countries on December 24, 1955. India was the first country outside the then Soviet block to establish full diplomatic ties with Mongolia.

Given our close ties, India strongly advocated Mongolia's case for UN membership. At the 10th United Nations General Assembly (UNGA), the Indian Permanent Representative Krishna Menon said, "Mongolia was founded neither yesterday nor today, but has been existing as an independent State over many centuries. Hence, similarly like any other country, the Mongolian Peoples Republic has full rights to become a member of United Nations Organization". Pandit Nehru in his address to the 15th UNGA making a very convincing and strong case for Mongolia's admission to the United Nations said, "If they received so many countries in the United Nations then why should Mongolia stay outside it? What had she done wrong? What kind of error did she commit with the Charter? The people of Mongolia are tranquil and her peace-loving toilers are firmly striving for progress, and it seems absolutely wrong, from the principle point of view, not to allow her to the great organization."

Nehru had a special place in the hearts and minds of Mongolians. He was the first world leader who described Chinggis Khan as a great son of Asia and a world leader. Western historians had always described him as invader, and a barbarous murderer because he was the first Asian who challenged western supremacy and defeated many European rulers expanding his empire right up to Moscow. Nehru also gave diplomatic and political support to Mongolia at a time when Mongolia was considered 'untouchable' in the comity of nations. Nehru was also instrumental in establishing diplomatic ties between India and Mongolia in 1955. All these initial gestures from Indian side laid a solid foundation of Indo-Mongolian ties in the modern era.

Eminent Indian philosopher and politician, the then Vice President of India, Dr. S. Radhakrishnan paid a historic visit to Mongolia in 1957, which laid down the foundation of regular exchange of high level visits between our two countries. Since then three Vice Presidents of India Dr. Shankar Dayal Sharma (April 1992), K. R. Narayanan (September 1996) and Krishan

Kant (August 1999) have visited Mongolia. The President of India R. Venkataraman paid a State visit to Mongolia in July 1988. From Mongolian side, Prime Minister Tsendenbal (1973), Chairman of the Presidium Bathmunkh (March 1989), President P. Ochirbaat (February 1994), President N. Bagabandi (January 2001), and Prime Minister N. Enkhbayar (January 2004) visited India.

These regular high-level exchanges have played a significant role in promoting bilateral cooperation between our two countries in modern times. Indo-Mongolian relations have been considerably strengthened in recent times. State visits of President N. Bagabandi in January 2001 and Prime Minister N. Enkhbayar in January 2004 provided a new impetus to Indo-Mongolian ties. During the visit of Prime Minister Enkhbayar bilateral relations between the two countries were elevated to the level of partnership encompassing all possible areas of cooperation. Over the years, the two countries have signed 28 agreements on bilateral cooperation, which provide a comprehensive legal framework for cooperation in all areas of human activities.

These high level exchanges have been duly supplemented by ministerial level visits and regular exchanges between the two parliaments. The two countries organized a year long celebration to mark the 50th anniversary of establishment of diplomatic relations during 2005. During this period a series of events were organised. These included, reciprocal naming of streets in Ulaanbaatar and New Delhi, release of a special commemorative stamp, a conference on Indo-Mongolian relations, a special publication dedicated to Indo-Mongolian ties, a photographic exhibition spanning 50 years of diplomatic ties, several cultural events and a visit by Mongolian Foreign Minister to India precisely coinciding with the date of establishment of diplomatic relations in 1955. In addition to the bilateral visits, the leaders of the two countries have also been meeting regularly on the sidelines of major international and regional conferences and gatherings. The two countries have a long tradition of closely coordinating their positions at international and regional fora. Mongolia has unequivocally supported India's candidature to permanent membership of an expanded UN Security Council.

India on its part has extended modest development assistance to Mongolia over the years. Brief details of India's development assistance are as follows:

(i) **Scholarships**: Over the years India has been extending scholarships to Mongolian students to pursue their higher education in Indian Institutions. Presently Indian government awards about 40 scholarships every year to Mongolian students. These scholarships are considerably popular among the student community in Mongolia. Several Indian educated Mongolians occupy high positions in Mongolian Government as also in the private sector. These include the incumbent Minister of Home and Justice, Legal and Economic Policy Advisors to the President and former Foreign Policy Advisor to the Prime minister.

(ii) **Training Programmes**: In addition to the scholarship scheme, under India's Technical and Economic Cooperation Programme (ITEC), 50 training slots are being allocated every year for Mongolian nationals for training in variety of fields, such as agriculture, small scale industry, information technology, banking, management, rural development, and so on. These training programmes have considerably helped Mongolia in development of its human resources.

(iii) **Education**: Under an Agreement signed between the two Governments, the Government of India set up the Indo-Mongolia Joint Higher Secondary School in Ulaanbaatar in September 2003. At present five Indian teachers are based in this School teaching English, Mathematics and Information Technology. India has also offered its assistance to Mongolia in updating and modernization of its school curricula.

(iv) **Vocational Training**: In 1996, under India's Technical and Economic Cooperation Programme (ITEC), Rajiv Gandhi Vocational Training Center with eight faculties was set up in Ulaanbaatar. These faculties are: Machine Shop; Auto Mechanics;

Plumbing; Electrical work; Radio & TV repairing; Computer Programming; Gemstone cutting and Polishing and Printing. A total of about 450 students receive their vocational training in these faculties at the Center every year. There is a proposal to add some new faculties to this Center.

(v) **Economic Assistance**: A mini cement plant has been set up in Khovd province under a soft loan extended by India. During the visit of Prime Minister N. Enkhbayar to India, the Government of India extended an additional soft loan of 10 million US dollars to enable the Mongolian authorities to import goods, services and projects from India. It has been proposed to expand this loan to 20 million US dollars.

(vi) **Information Technology**: In IT sector, with a grant of 1 million US dollars, the Government of India set up the Atal Bihari Vajpayee Centre for Excellence in Information and Communication Technology in October 2002. The Center is equipped with sophisticated computer labs and the only Video Conferencing facility in Mongolia. Subsequently in 2005, the Government of India also set up ten Community Information Centres in 10-Aimag capitals in Mongolia. Now all these centres are connected to the Video Conferencing facility in Ulaanbaatar. This facilitates introduction of distance education and telemedicine programmes to remote areas of Mongolia. A separate tele-education and tele-medicine project is also under consideration.

(vii) **Digitalization**: Mongolia is home to several precious manuscripts, which are a cultural and literary heritage of mankind and a symbol of our rich cultural and literary exchanges. These manuscripts were digitalized during 2005-06 with the help of Government of India. This will help in preserving these precious historic writings for the posterity.

(viii) **e-Governance**: In the area of e-governance, the Government of India has agreed to provide appropriate softwares and expertise to Mongolia to introduce e-governance in the country.

(ix) **Agriculture**: In 1998, under the agreement for cooperation in agriculture, Indo-Mongolian Friendship Farm was set up near Darkhan. Since then some research work has also been undertaken in the research lab in Darkhan for developing appropriate varieties of wheat and potato seeds suitable for Mongolian climatic conditions, which are characterized by low precipitation, short summer and harsh winter. It has now been decided to develop this Friendship Farm into a Model Agricultural Farm. Indian experts would also be deputed to Mongolia to help Mongolian authorities in evolving appropriate policy framework in the field of agriculture and dairy development. The two countries are also cooperating in Yak research projects.

(x) **Solar Electrification**: A pilot project to provide solar electrification to Dadal *Soum*- birth place of the legendary Chinggis Khan- was completed successfully in 2006, coinciding with the 800th anniversary of the Mongol empire. Considering the significance of this place this was considered an important symbolic gesture by India towards Mongolian people and its leadership. Similar projects are expected to be undertaken in some other *Soums*.

(xi) **Trade and Economic Ties**: Trade and economic exchanges remain the weakest link in Indo-Mongolian relations. To promote this link the first ever exclusive India Trade Exhibition in Mongolia was held from August 30 to September 3, 2004 in Ulaanbaatar. Conferences in the areas of IT, biotechnology, pharmaceuticals and agriculture and dairy development were also held coinciding with this exhibition to promote cooperation in these areas. Bilateral trade which was about 1.2 million US dollars in 2003 was more than 10 million US dollars in 2006. India has emerged as major supplier of animal vaccines to Mongolia. An Indian company has also invested in Mongolia in telecom sector. In hospitality sector there are five Indian restaurants in Ulaanbaatar and one of the hotels is managed by an Indian group. Export of handicrafts has also picked up in the recent years. Cooperation in IT sector has also picked up considerably. Mongolia is also keen to have Indian investments in mining sector. Mongolia exports wool and cashmere to India.

(xii) **Defence**: During the visit of President N. Bagabandi to India in January 2001, an agreement for cooperation in defence areas was signed. Under the agreement the two countries are taking steps to intensify cooperation in some basic areas such as training, maintenance of equipment and joint exercises. First joint military exercise- Nomadic Elephant- between the two countries took place in 2005

(xiii) **Spiritual Ties**: Given the ancient spiritual and religious ties between our two countries, the Government of India allocated a plot of land for construction of a Mongolian Monastery at Bodh Gaya during President Bagabandi's visit to India in January 2001. During the visit of Prime Minister N. Enkhbayar, payment for the plot at Bodh Gaya was waived. This will enable the Mongolian Buddhist community to construct a Mongolian Monastery in the holiest place of Buddhism. Mongolian studies has been one of the main areas of focus of the Central Asian Studies Programme at School of International Studies, Jawaharlal Nehru University in Delhi.

(xiv) **Emergency Assistance**: From time to time, as a good friend, India has provided food and medical supplies as emergency assistance to Mongolia during the time of crisis such as juud and drought.

In addition to the Government-to-Government interaction, in the recent past, several new steps have been initiated to promote exchanges between the business communities of the two countries. Prime Minister Enkhbayar's interaction with the

Indian business community in January 2004 was also instrumental in invigorating these links. As a result, some joint ventures are under negotiations in the areas of Information Technology, education, juice manufacturing, cultural tourism and so on. These private initiatives would further accelerate this process of economic exchanges between the two countries. In the field of education several educational institutions are now collaborating on institutional basis. Since 2004 a large number of Mongolian students have been coming to India to pursue their studies in Indian universities at their own expense. As of now more than 500 Mongolian students are studying in India. Medical tourism to India is also on the increase, particularly for eye surgery. In view of the above, the historic Indo-Mongolian ties would acquire a new dynamism in the near future, which will bring the two ancient civilizations even closer.

Appendix I

Exchange of Visits between Indian and Mongolian Parliaments

From India

- Dr. G.S. Dhillon, Lok Sabha Speaker – July 1974
- Dr. Balram Jhakhar, Lok Sabha Speaker – October 1985
- Shivraj Patil, Lok Sabha Speaker – July 1995
- P.A.Sangma, Lok Sabha Speaker – October 1997
- GMC Balayogi, Lok Sabha Speaker – July 2001
- Najma Heptullah, Deputy Chairperson of Rajya Sabha – July 1999.

From Mongolia

- Yu. Tsedenbal, Chairman of Great Ih Hural – 1959.
- Yu. Tsedenbal, Chairman of the Presidum of the Great Ih Hural – 1973.
- T. Batmunkh, Chairman of the Presidum of the Great Ih Hural – 1989.
- N. Bagabandi, Chairman of the State Great Hural – 1996.
- R. Gonchigdorj, Chairman of the State Great Rural – November 1998.
- J. Byambadorj, Deputy Speaker of State Great Hural led a Mongolian Parliamentary delegation from 7 to 9 May 2002.
- S. Timur-Ochir, Speaker of the State Great Hural visited India on 22-26 January, 2003 on the occasion of the Golden Jubilee of the Indian Parliament.

Appendix II

Exchange of other Important Visits between India and Mongolia

From India

- Indira Gandhi, Minister for Information and Broadcasting – 1965
- Y.B. Chavan, External Affairs Minister – July 1976
- B. Shankaranand, Minister for Health – 1983
- Pranab Mukherjee, Commerce Minister – September 1994
- Dr. Balram Jhakhar, Agriculture Minister – April 1994
- Sonia Gandhi – July 1995
- Pramod Mahajan, Minister for IT and Communication – September 2001
- V. Kapoor, Lieutenant Governor of Delhi in December 2001 at the invitation of the Governor of Ulaanbaatar
- Dr. Murli Manohar Joshi, H.R.D. Minister – July 2002
- Dr. Sanjay Paswan, Minister of State for Communications and IT – October 2002
- Vinod Khanna, Minister of State for External Affairs – September 8-9, 2003.
- E. Ahamed, June 2005
- M.M. Pallamraju, Raksha Rajya Mantri, May 2006
- Shiela Dixit, Chief Minister of Delhi, July 2006

From Mongolia

- L.M. Rinchi, Minister for Foreign Affairs – 1975
- Dugersuren, Foreign Minister – February 1978 & 1982
- Tsogt, Trade and Industry Minister – February 1996

- J. Amarsanaa, Justice Minister – April 1998
- N. Enkhbayar, Leader of Opposition for medical treatment of spouse and self (September 1999)
- Sodnomtseren, Minister for Agriculture and Industry – January 2000
- A. Battur, Minister for Enlightenment – March-April 2000
- B. Jigjid, Minister for Infrastructure – February-March 2002
- A. Tsanjid, Minister for Education, Culture and Science – March 2002
- Mr. Enkhbold, Mayor of Ulaanbaatar led a five-member delegation to India from 23 to 27 May 2002 at the invitation of Lt. Governor of Delhi.
- J. Gurragchaa, Defence Minister – November 11-18, 2003
- B.Jigjid, Infrastructure Minister – from January 11-19, 2004
- Ts. Sharabdorj, Minister of Defence, December 2005
- Ts. Munkh Orgil, Foreign Minister, December 2005

Appendix III

List of Operational Agreements /MoUs between India and Mongolia since the establishment of Parliamentary Democracy in 1990

Sl No.	Date	Agreement / MoU
1.	April 1992	Agreement on Economic and Technical Cooperation
2.	February 1994	Agreement between India and Mongolia for the Establishment of a Joint Committee on Cooperation (1994)
3.	February 1994	Agreement on Avoidance of Double Taxation.
4.	February 1994	Treaty on Friendly relations and Cooperation.
5.	April 1994	Agreement between India and Mongolia on Cooperation in the field of Agriculture.
6.	September 1994	Agreement on Cooperation between Planning Commission of India and National Development Board of Mongolia.
7.	September 1994	MoU on Establishment of a Joint Trade Sub-Committee.
8.	July 1995	Protocol on Cooperation between the Parliaments.
9.	September 1996	Agreement on Trade and Economic Cooperation.
10.	October 1997	Protocol on Cooperation between the Secretariats of Indian Lok Sabha and Mongolian State Great Hural.
11.	December '98	Agreement on Tourism Cooperation.
12.	November 1998	Air Service Agreement
13.	March 1999	Agreement between the Comptroller & Auditor General of the Republic of India and the Auditor General of Mongolia.
14.	January 2001	Agreement for the Promotion and Protection of Investments.
15.	January 2001	Extradition Treaty.

16.	January 2001	Treaty on Legal Assistance on Civil and Commercial Matters.
17.	January 2001	Treaty on Mutual Legal Assistance in Criminal Matters.
18.	January 2001	MoU on Cooperation in Information Technology.
19.	January 2001	Agreement on Cooperation in Defence Matters between the Government of India and Mongolia.
20.	September 2001	Agreement on Cooperation in Information and Communication Technology.
21.	September 2001	Protocol of the First Meeting of India-Mongolia JWG on IT.
22.	July 2002	MoU on Cooperation in the field of Education [Establishment of Joint School].
23.	October 2002	MoU on Cooperation in the field of Telecommunications.
24.	September 2003	Cultural Exchange Programme for the period 2003-05 between the Government of India and Mongolia.
25.	January 2004	Protocol Cooperation between the Republic of India and Mongolia in the field of Biotechnology.
26.	January 2004	Agreement on Cooperation in the field of Animal Health and Dairy between the Republic of India and Mongolia.
27.	January 2004	Agreement for Cooperation in Space Science, Technology and Applications between the Republic of India and Mongolia.
28.	December 2005	Agreement on Visa-free Travel for holders of Diplomatic and Official Passports.

CHAPTER 12

THE MONGOLS AND PROF. RAGHUVIRA

Lokesh Chandra

The journey of my father Prof. Raghuvira in several states of the Mongolian people, is a long and tortuous path transiting dreams of identity, the richness of life throbbing deep in the unconscious, the vision of a future freed from the serfdom of imperialism, and a renaissance wherein science is endowed with values, and all are enshrined in a supra-scriptural transcendence.

Raghuvira lost his mother before he had seen two springs of childhood. When he went to the People's Republic of Mongolia in the winter of 1955 to secure microfilms of Mongolian Buddhist texts, his stray musings, in the early hours of the morning of the New Year of 1956 in the heavily curtained hotel of Ulaanbaatar were:

My bed is cold,
Cold my hands and feet,
Heart aches for my mother's lap.
No lullabies, no caressing hands,
No cradle shall swing for me.

Absence of the mother was compensated in his adolescent years by the clarion call of *Vande Mataram* (Salutation to Mother India), the hymn of India's freedom struggle. The counterpart of *Vande Mataram* is the ancient Russian slogan *Zhivyot rodina mat* (Long Live the Motherland), the powerful rallying cry that Stalin had to resurrect from the deeps of Slavic consciousness to defeat the fascist aggression of the armies of Hitler. It changed the course of the Second World War and led to the defeat of fascist forces. Likewise, *Vande Mataram* was the mighty flame, the hectic dance, that shook the foundations of the British Empire, an empire on which the sun never set. Though committed to anti-imperialism, Prof. Raghuvira admired the immense learning and dedicated devotion of European scholarship to understand the various facets of the art, history, philosophy, literature and other domains of India and other Asian countries. To study at the roots of the flux and chaos of the political and intellectual destiny of India of his times, he wanted to take a journey to London the home of the British Lion, and to see their well of life. He studied Historical Linguistics at the School of Oriental Studies of the University of London, to comprehend the common course of our languages and those of Europe, and to find a creative discourse inherent in this shared heritage of speech. He studied Greek the divine mind of the West Lithuanian with its unique proximity to Sanskrit, Old Church Slavonic again alive with Sanskrit inflections, and so on. He glimpsed an entirely new order of culture. To him it was an insight into a reality beyond time. He fell in love with Chinese ideograms in the Japanese language and studied Japanese with Chamberlain. His guide for the Ph.D was the great historian of New Indo-Aryan languages Prof. R.L. Turner. Prof. Turner was mesmerised by the immensity of the interests of my father. The in-breathings and out-breathings of different civilisations reflected in languages were extraordinary insight of Raghuvira into human endeavour moving into eternity, and eternity moving into human life. He has summed it up in the words of the *Atharva Veda*: "The unbounded ocean am I". Prof. Turner was a member of the commission that chose mandarins for the Indian Civil Service, the most coveted position in the British Empire. He offered him to join this prized service to enrich India with his image of wonder and his indefatigable dedication. Any Indian would have grabbed the offer, but Raghuvira was a son of the Revolution, of *Vande Mataram*, and he politely said: "I do not want to serve the Empire, I want to serve my Country". Prof. Turner saw in him 'a great Indian' and encouraged him till his last days for the unswerving sincerity of his love for India and a constant striving to substitute actuals for abstractions.

Prof. Raghuvira envisioned a future India alive with energy, action and transformation. The sculptural stillness of time flashed before him Platonic ideal forms. The nationalism of Ireland was reflected in her greatest of poets, Yeats. The words of the poet gave him a quest: "Nations, cultures, schools of thought may have their Daemons". Daemon in the Platonic sense is the indwelling power or spirit, the original genius that endows humans with supernatural or divine energy to dynamise their lives and fortunes. My father asked himself: "have any Asian people ever governed Europe". There came to his mind the empire of the Mongolian tribes of the Huns ruling over Europe from 370 to 455. They overran the pastoral Alani who occupied the plains between the Volga and the Don, overthrew the empire of the Ostrogoths, whose aged Gothic King Ermanaric committed suicide, they defeated the Visigoths and arrived at the Danube. They inspired unparalleled fear throughout Europe. Attila received 6,000 pounds of gold in 443, and the tribute was further raised by 2,100 pounds of gold per annum. Influx of wealth altered their character and brought about decline. They continued to exist till the middle of the sixth century. Again, my father Prof. Raghuvira saw the Golden Horde that ruled the whole of Russia (including Ukraine and Belorussia) for three centuries (1223-1502), longer than the British governed India. Batu the grandson of Chinggis Khan expanded the western frontiers of the Mongol Empire from the Urals to the Carpathians, comprising most of European Russia and tide in the 16th century.

Prof. Raghuvira found a new mental continent in Empire of the Mongols. He became keen to know the cults and culture, language and literature, their centuries and their dismantled world, the essence of what the Mongols have been and may be again. He wanted to gain an insight into the heart of Mongol life, the sacred core of their arrows, their howling and rumbling icy winds, their galloping horses, under a blue sky that was their imprint of eternal beauty, the divine Tengri. He brought a German grammar of Mongolian from Luzac and Co. London in 1928 and started studying the language. It was an entirely new vocabulary that belonged to the Altaic family. 'Altan' means gold and my father discovered that Mongolia's spiritual and literary heritage was the golden light, the *Altan Gerel* or the *Suvarna-prabhasa-sutra*, or the irreducible diamond in the rock (*Vajra-chhedika*). He read the history of Buddhism by Tshemphel Gushi translated into German by George Huth in 1896 under the title *Geschichte des Buddhismus in der Mongolei*. The trilogy of the tales of Bhoja, Vikramaditya, Krishna, alongside the *Pancatantra* and the *Vetalapancavimsati* were a sacred pattern, leaping from time's loom. To Raghuvira, Indians and Mongolians were brothers and sisters in *Dharma*. The popular image of the barbaric ferocity of the Mongols was totally altered in his mind. Transfigured by the tremendous of their literary activity over the last thirteen centuries, the Mongolian persona was filled with a new blossom and bough in his perceptions. In years to come he exercised a deep impact on the mind of Pandit Jawaharlal Nehru about his perceptions of Mongolian history and culture, who made a strong plea for the admission of Mongolia into the United Nations.

The history of Herodotus says that *Skythe* (English Scythian) is *sk* = saka with the plural suffix *uth*. The plural suffix clearly identifies them as Mongolians. The suffix *uth* is *ud* in Classical Mongolian (*Enedkeg bicig-ud* 'Indian books' in the Mongolian *Kanjur*). Herodotus lived about 485-425 BC. He speaks of the kingdom of Scythia which comprised parts of Europe. Herodotus believes that the Scythians were of Asian origin. Thucydides (about 462-395 BC) regards them as irresistible if they should ever unite in one common purpose. Scythian bowmen were recruited to serve as policemen in Athens. Thus Mongolian presence as a ruling class in Europe goes back to the fifth century BC.

Coins of Saka rulers of the first century BC have been found in Mathura (India). A coin has the name Qagan Hagamasa. Haga is the Mongolian word *qaga* 'to attack from all sides, to besiege' and *masi* 'extremely, very much'. In Buddhist texts *masi* is used to translate the prefixes *pra-vi-ati-*. Thus Hagamasa can correspond to Sanskrit *Pravira*, the name of the son of Puru in the Mahabharata. This is the earliest dated occurrence of the Mongolian word *qagan*. Thus India has preserved an important word of Mongolian history.

In 1936, the Government of Japan sent two students to study Sanskrit with Prof. Raghuvira. One of them brought an ancient Mongolian xylograph dated 1662 AD on the writing and pronunciation of Sanskrit mantras used in Mongolia. Its title is *Egesig kiged geigulugci-usug uol orusiba* "herein are contained vowel and consonant letters". The introduction by the Mongolian scholar Gombojab details the phonetics of Sanskrit. The Mongols studied the traditions of Panini centuries before the Europeans. Prof. Raghuvira was proud to own and study the first Mongolian xylograph in India and spoke about it to Jawaharlal Nehru at a meeting of the Indian National Congress at the Wardha Ashram of Mahatma Gandhi in 1934. He related to Nehru how Chos.kyi.hod.zer had written the earliest Mongol grammar *Jiruken-u tolta* inspired by the tradition of Panini in 1308-11, during the reign of the Yuan Emperor Khaisan Kulug. The Mongols had studied the system of Sanskrit grammar five centuries earlier than European scholars. Nehru was taken by surprise that Mongolian scholars studied Panini centuries before the Europeans. He reflected for a moment and said "We have to study history in the wider contexts of social, spiritual and literary developments". Raghuvira had given a new image of the Mongols to Nehru. The Mongols were great conquerors, but had also reached a level of refinement and erudition that was outside time. When the question of the admission of Mongolia to the UN came up before the 10th General Assembly, India's permanent Representative Krishna Menon said: "Mongolia was founded neither yesterday nor today, but has been existing as an independent state over many centuries. Hence, similarly like any other country, the Mongolian Peoples Republic has full rights to become a member of the United Nations Organisation".

Prime Minister Tsedenbal gave to Prof. Raghuvira the Mongolian stories of King Bhoja, known to the Mongols as *Arji Burji Qan*. It is one of the trilogy of stories of "thirtytwo wooden men" woven around King Bhoja, Vikramaditya and Krishna. Prof. Rahu Vira showed it to the then President of the Republic of India, Dr. Rajendra Prasad. He was enthralled by the word *Arji Burji Qan*. The Mongols had put intrinsic beauty of pronunciation which identified the stories with them. The poetry of words lies in the depth of identity, in their poetic imperfection, by coming into their own. He requested Prof. Raghuvira to translate these stories. Prof. Raghuvira transliterated the Mongolian text, gave word to word meanings, and a running translation of the stories. President Rajendra Prasad said that these stories of King Bhoja lend depth to our relationship with Mongolia. The powerful cultural images of the Mongols created by Rahuvira in the corridors of power were the innate order of the spiritual fraternity of India and Mongolia: the age-long memoried self, the rustle of vestments of centuries.

Prof. Rinchen visited India for four weeks in December of 1957 at the invitation of Prof. Raghuvira. He narrated the harrowing sufferings of the Mongolian people, the genocide of their age-old culture, the replacement of the national script by the Cyrillic, thousands of monks shot, around eight hundred monasteries destroyed down to the foundations and so on. Raghuvira arranged his interview with Jawaharlal Nehru. The noble and typically Mongol physiognomy of Rinchen fascinated Nehru. Prof. Rinchen related the destruction of art and literature, the annihilation of the intelligentsia and men of culture, the ongoing Sino-Soviet conflicts and so on. Rinchen spoke in English, but he would drift into French every now and then, and when he spoke of the inhuman tortures inflicted by the ideological Czars, he would resort to German. Raghuvira interpreted his French and German. The multi-lingual genius of Rinchen and Raghuvira left a deep impression on Nehru and gave a poignancy to the political role of the Mongols, wedged between two super powers. Raghuvira had in his hand the Mongolian translation of the *Meghaduta* wrapped in brocade. Nehru was curious all the while as to what it was. After an hour as the meeting was coming to a close, Raghuvira showed the long folios and told Nehru that the Mongols had translated the *Meghaduta* of Kalidasa long before the Europeans. Nehru stood surprised. Rinchen added: "*Meghaduta* is the classical lyric of our people, a pearl of our literature". The Mongols were continually acquiring a new image and meaning in the mind of Nehru, a people who had participated in the highest excellence in the economy of the universe. Their history was an epiphany of values besides cosmocratic victories of Chinggis Khan. From his reflection and pondering Nehru said: "we have a special relationship with Mongolia". The Mongolian translation of Kalidasa had struck new chords of surprise and admiration for the Mongols and gave a new grounding of warm vistas. From this interior landscape came the impassioned plea of Nehru at the 15th United Nations General Assembly for Mongolia's admission: "If they received so many countries in the United Nations then why should Mongolia stay outside it? What had she done wrong? What kind of error did she commit with the Charter? The people of Mongolia are tranquil and her peace-loving toilers are firmly striving for progress, and it seems absolutely wrong, from the principle point of view, not to allow her to the great organisation".

Prof. Raghuvira envisioned the publication of the 108 volumes of the Mongolian *Kanjur*, which symbolizes the cultural interflow between India and Mongolia over the centuries, embodying the Mongolian versions of 1161 Sanskrit works, most of which have perished in India. His life was cut short by a car accident in 1963 and it is after constant perseverance for a decade that in 1973 I could commence to fulfil his dream of bringing to light the immense corpus (100,000 pages) of the Mongolian *Kanjur* to make it accessible to the world of learning as a foremost *oeuvre* of Mongolia's literary legacy.

The development of the Mongolian *Kanjur* can be traced back to the Yuan dynasty when under the reign of the Yuan Emperor Khaisan Kulug (1308-1311), Chos.kyi.hod.zer started the translation of Buddhist sutras into Mongolian. During the reign of Altan Khan of Tumed (1507-1582) major part of the *Kanjur* was translated. In 1628-29 Ligdan Khan (1604-1634) commissioned the Lotus-Gold *Kanjur* (*Badam Altan Ganjur*) written in gold and silver in 113 volumes. Under the orders of Emperor Kang-his the Imperial Red edition of the Mongol *Kanjur* was xylographed in 1717-20. It represents the literary riches of the great people of Mongolia and at the same time a monument to the admiration of Prof. Raghuvira for their spirituality across the centuries, along side the epic of their conquests.

Prof. Raghuvira was no less enthralled by the endless forests, the invariable presence of minor lakes, and the vast solitariness of the grasslands of Mongolia. These three ingredients -vastness, forests and water- make up the fascination of the Mongolian landscape. Falling in love with Mongolia the Land is a creeping passion, a gentle and barely perceptible enthrallment. Its beauty is not of a kind that takes eyes and senses by storm. It practises that subtle invasion of the spirit which is the mark of all true beauty. It sets the heart and soul on fire. Parting it leaves one's memories and experiences tinged with a delicate and persistent melancholy.

Prof. Raghuvira spelt out the many-sided genius of the Mongols who helped in the evolution of a new world by four historic inventions. They have bequeathed gun-powder that modernized warfare, and their conquests opened up the East and West from which evolved colonialism and now we advance to a shared glocalism. The paper currency invented by the Mongols freed the economy from crude cowrie, copper, silver and gold currency and prepared the way to a more convenient currency program. The Mongols gave steam to Europe in the 16th century. There were thousands of Mongol slaves in every major Italian city, which reached its climax in the middle of the 15th century. Genoese merchants secured them from slave traders wholesaling in the Black Sea ports (*Del traffico e delle condizione degli shiavi in Venezia nel tempi di mezzo*, by Lazari 1862:1.470). They were using hot air turbines for turning prayer wheels of *Om Mani-padme hum*. Thus the ancient Buddhist prayer from the Karanda-vyuha gave rise to steam screw propellers of ships. Steam jet blowers in the shape of birds are datable to 1579 (G.B. Isaachi, *Inventioni*, Parma 1579). The Mongols benefited mankind by opening up the East and West, paper currency, gun-powder and steam.

Mongolia is a land of enchanting fantasies: spaces and silence, meadows and minds, shivering cold and shimmering logic, depth of Buddhist thought and the breath of statues, a subtle invasion of the spirit in the vast void (*shunyata*) of the sprawling land. The new aesthetic of young poets sings of the national cultural tradition focused on the future. The quote of Ts.

Bavuudorj in the English rendering of Simon Wickham-Smith, wherein mantras are the ornaments of sound:

Times of loud noise inside the ger
Of the fire's smell...
The Lion protects our heritage in the moonlight.
Father's dreams underfoot,
Mother's fingers on her rosary,
Only Buddha in their minds...
Their calm clear eyes are heavy,
Their mantras flying, as ornaments of sound...

CHAPTER 13

LINKS BETWEEN INDIAN AND MONGOLIAN LITERATURE: SOME PERSPECTIVES

Yü. Mönkh-Amgalan* and *G. Galbayar

Mongolian people have an ancient tradition of intellectual and cultural wealth. Ever since Mongolians appeared on the Central Asian plateau, a bridge between East and West, they have been producing their own unique oral and written literature. During the historic development of creating independent literature, related closely to nomadic culture and civilization, Mongolians not only preserved their own traditions but also grew acquainted with the classical literature of ancient civilisations of the West and the East. Although the development of Mongolian literature is related to the classical literature of neighboring peoples, it is even more closely related to the rich art and literature of India. Many Mongolian and foreign researchers, such as Ts. Damdinsüren, D. Yondon, D. Tserensodnom, L. Khürelbaatar, J. Gendendarma, and Yü. Mönkh-Amgalan in Mongolia; W. Heissig in Germany; and B. Ya. Vladimirtsov in Russia have noted the ancient literary ties between India and Mongolia.

This paper addresses the issues of the spread of Buddhism as well as relations between Indian and Mongolian literature from early times till the twentieth century onwards.

Benedictions and songs are very common among Mongolians and hold a special place in Mongolian literature. Benedictions are words said by older people to youths and successors wishing goodness and happiness. One commonly uttered benediction in Mongolia is the following: "Be like the Ganges River, gushing forth from its floor; Be like a Kalpavriksha sandalwood tree, blossoming from the tips of its branches" (*Ganga moron shig, yoroolоosoo undarch; Galbar zandan shig, üzüüreesee delgerch yaw*), pointing to the obvious Indian influence.

The words in benedictions such as the Ganges is an Indian famous river, and Kalpavriksha sandalwood is a wishing tree with an aromatic smell in the Indian tales and legends. In the Mongolian mindset, the Ganges is the biggest river, and the most aromatic-smelling wood is that of Indian Kalpavriksha sandalwood in India because the Buddhist religion spread deeply several times in Mongolia since ancient times. Mongolia has worshipped India as the most sacred country of the world and the birthplace of the Buddhism.

People sing folk songs to express their feelings when being joyful or sad. Among the folksongs of the Mongols we have lines such as the following:

Ganga l mörnii gurgaldai
Gadaa ireed dongodno
Only the nightingales of the Ganges
Come and sing outside

Or lines such as "The sun of the Jambudvipa is an ornament in the sky" (*Zambutiwiin nar ni ogtorguidaa chimeg*...) or "the gentle sun of the Jambudvipa" (*Uyakhan Zambutiwiin naran*...).

In these songs, Mongolians believe that the bird with most lyrical sound lives on the Ganges river and the sun which shines over the whole world also depends on great India.

Many documents about India in ancient Mongolian folklore and culture show that Indian art and literature was disseminated among Mongolians since ancient times. Besides, Vedic historical writings, which first spread orally and which were later written down in the Old Indic language, the most ancient resource of Indian literature, have many similarities to Mongolian fire sacrifice, sacrifice to heaven, and the eulogy of local deities, mountains, and hunting. This shows that Indian and Mongolian oral culture and traditions had an ancient relationship, or that their lifestyle, culture, way of thinking, and historic paths have been similar to each other. It is, therefore, necessary to do a comparative study of Vedic historical writings with various types of Mongolian folklore.

Some rare sources of Indian classic literature such as epics *Rāmāyana* and *Mahābhārata*; tales *Pañcatantra*, Saga of King Vikramāditya (*Bigarmigid*), *Biography of King Kesene* and *The Tale of the Thirty-Two Wooden Men*; didactic poems such as Nāgārjuna's *Drops of Nectar* (*Rasiyan-u dusul*); some Buddhist biographies like *Biography of a Rabbit*, *Kavyadarsha* written by Dandin, an ancient Indian theorist; and others not only came into Mongolian literature via Buddhism but also completely changed their nature.

Both India and Mongolia have borrowed many tales and epics from each other, because they have such wealthy sources of folklore. It becomes clear from the great epic *Rāmāyana* studied by academician Ts. Damdinsuren in his article "How the Rāmāyana disseminated in Mongolia". The above mentioned tales such as *Pañcatantra* and *The Tale of the Thirty-Two Wooden Men* were narrated among Mongolians for several hundreds of years and as a result, were adapted to Mongol culture. For example, kings and noblemen with elephants, beautiful palaces decorated with many types of patterns and toys are represented commonly in the Indian versions, while brave men with good horses instead of kings and noblemen with elephants, Mongolian *gers*, *teepees*, and huts instead of beautiful palaces, and Mongolian national games such as chess, puzzles, and shuttlecocks are represented in the Mongolian versions of the tales.

How these works became part of Mongolian literature and their interrelationships have been thoroughly studied by Mongolian researchers such as Ts. Damdinsüren, D. Yondon, D.Tserensodnom, L. Khürelbaatar, J. Gendendarma and Yü. Mönkh-Amgalan. We, therefore, focus here on the *Pañcatantra* in Mongolia. In ancient times Mongolians had their own historic tradition of reading, analyzing and translating the world-famous work known as the *Pañcatantra*, which is written as a poem connected by short tales and stories about good and bad things that happen commonly in human life into their native language. The Russian Mongolist B. Ya. Vladimirtsov noted in his book *A Collection of Mongolian Short Stories from the Pañcatantra* that in the 13th century *Kalila wa Dimna*, one version of the *Pañcatantra,* was translated from Persian into Mongolian, and Möngke Khan, grandson of Chinggis Khan, was reading the tale. Unfortunately, that particular translation to this day has not been found, and may have disappeared over the years. During the 17th and 18th centuries, however, some popular works such as the *Jewel Ornament* (*Chandmany chimeg*) and the *Precious Ornament* (*Erdeniin chimeg*), were translated into Mongolian from Tibetan and spread throughout Mongolia. Some researchers consider that this type of writing was widely disseminated in Mongolia. So these can be considered as variants of tales from the *Pañcatantra* or tales based on or inspired by tales in the *Pañcatantra*, rather than calling them exact versions of tales in the Indian *Pañcatantra*. These collections, which spread throughout Mongolia, are associated with the name of Nāgārjuna (*Nagarjunai* in Mongolian), an ancient Indian poet and writer. There are some works written in Mongolian which are similar to the tales in Nāgārjuna's book *Drops of Nectar to Nourish the People* (In Mongolian, *Arad-i tejiyekü rasiyan-u dusul*). More than ten out of thirty tales in these collections are the same as the tales in *Pañcatantra*. However, these were Indian collections translated from Tibetan, Mongolians wrote the similar version as folklore and the original tales and poems have changed completely and finally they assimilated into Mongolian culture and thinking.

Some tales and teaching poems, which spread in India and Mongolia, are correlated to each other. For instance, although, the main idea of the *Pañcatantra*, spread in India and Mongolia, valued the truth, the tale's idea is not only to prefer the truth but also the end results. In some cases, the untrue things might be promoted to achieve the goal. Mongolians are not only reading the version of *Pañcatantra* (translated by J. Gendendaram, scholar and translator, in 1972) until now but have also handed it on to the next generation. This work which was written as a guidebook to govern the state, has deep and multiple meanings. This shows that Indian and Mongolian culture and literature have had an ancient and deep relationship

During the twentieth century, Mongolians were actively introduced to modern world education, art, and culture, and over 100 great works written by such important Indian writers as Tagore, Prem Chand, and Chandar were translated from Indic languages into Mongolian in the second half of the twentieth century. This had a significant influence on Mongolian literature and Mongolian readers. Besides, Mongolians read and translated ancient Indian and Chinese classics into Mongolian and made great progress in the advancement of intellectual culture. Almost 70 to 80 per cent of the world classics were translated into Mongolian, including those contained in the "world literary dictionaries" written in popular world languages, and Indian works account for a significant percentage of them. In recent days, we have not only been translating and reading Indian classics but have also been writing literature in modern style. For instance, following the "ten methods of good stylistics" of *Kavyadarsha* written by Dandin, the famous modern Mongolian poet, B. Yawuukhulan wrote his poem called "The Reeds of Black Water Lake" (*Khar us nuuryn shagshuurga*):

Khar us nuuryn shagshuurga
Namryn salkhind isgerne
Kharakhad neg l uitgartai
Nams nams bökhölzönö

The reeds of Black Water Lake
Whistlc in thc autumn wind.
So sad to look at,
As they sway back and forth.

J. Badaraa, another modern Mongolian poet, also followed the same style in writing his poem "Autumn Night" (*Namryn shönö*):

Meltelzsen süü shig sarny tuyaand

Gyaltalzsan ***shüüder*** *suwdan öngötei*
S*ugsalzan naigakh* ***ö****w****s****nii tolgoid*
S*uwdalsan* ***shüüder*** *namryn sürtei*

In the brimmed milk-like moonlight,
The sparkling dew has the color of a pearl;
On a hill of quivering, swaying grass,
The beads of dew have the splendor of autumn.

In both these poems, we see abundant use of the Mongolian sibilant ("noisy") consonants *s* and *sh*, following the precedent set by *Kavyadarsha*.

In the 1990s, the education system was reformed, many thousands of young people had possibilities to study abroad, many public and private schools and universities were established, and students began acquiring worldwide education. In the twentieth century, many foreign classics including Indian ones, were translated through the Russian language depending on the social system. But now these are read and translated into native languages.

To conclude, Indian and Mongolian literature have close linkages since early times. The development of Buddhism and its dissemination have had a widespread influence on the relationship between Indian and Mongolian literature. Some books about Buddhist philosophy and theory were translated into Mongolian and Mongolized over the years, finally becoming Mongolian. Most of these works emerged from among the ordinary people. The imageries and ideas in Indian and Mongolian literature are very similar. The fact that Mongols succeeded in absorbing Indian literature and making it Mongol, has been a significant contribution to Mongolian literature. It is clear that the ancient cultural and historical relationship between Mongolian and Indian literature will continue well into the future, and will develop even more deeply.

REFERENCES

1. Ts. Damdinsüren, *Ramayaana Mongold delgersen ni*, Ulaanbaatar, 1979.
2. *Mongol uran zohioliin toim*, 2 vols., Ulaanbaatar, 1976.

3. D. Yondon, "Mongolia and India", in Sh. Bira, ed., *Indological Studies in Mongolia*, Ulaanbaatar, 1989.
4. L. Khürelbaatar, *Songodog ulamjlal, mongol yaruu nairag*, Ulaanbaatar, 1989.
5. L. Khürelbaatar, *Duun utgyn yaruu zokhist*, Ulaanbaatar, 2005.
6. O. Nyamdavaa, *Mongolia and India: Spiritual Neighbours*, New Delhi, 2000.
7. R.C. Sharma, ed., *Perspectives on Mongolia*, New Delhi: Seema Publishers, 1988.
8. K. Warikoo and S.K. Soni, "Mongolia-India Relations in Contemporary Times", in R.C. Sharma and Others, eds., *Mongolia: Culture, Economy and Politics,* New Delhi: Khama Publishers, 1992.

CHAPTER 14

LANDLOCKED MONGOLIA AND ITS TRADE AND ECONOMIC COOPERATION WITH INDIA

O. Nyamdawaa

LANDLOCKED MONGOLIA

There are 31 landlocked developing countries in the world. Most of them including Mongolia are situated in Asia. The share of transit transport expenses in export earnings of landlocked developing countries is much bigger than that of coastal countries. Transit transport costs through Russia and China, paid by Mongolian businesses, including insurance, amount to about 8 per cent of GDP. This is double the cost of other developing countries and triple of the developed countries. According to the World Bank, the transportation and other related costs of exporting goods from Mongolia in a container equals to 3000 US dollars, which is 2-3 times higher as compared to the transportation costs of other countries at the same development level, but with access to the sea.

In April 2005, Mongolia ratified the Intergovernmental Agreement on Asian Highway Network, connecting Mongolia to the international road network through 3 routes. These projects are being implemented with the financial assistance from bilateral, as well as international donors such as Japan, Asian Development Bank and World Bank.

For the landlocked countries it is very important to have friendly relations and cooperation with neighboring countries besides having transit agreements with them. Mongolia has transit agreements with People's Republic of China (signed on 26 August 1991), Russian Federation (29 October 1992), Republic of Kazakhstan (22 October1993) and Democratic Republic of Korea (10 May 1996).

AGREEMENT WITH CHINA

Transportation Agreement between Governments of Mongolia and People's Republic of China was signed on 26 August 1991. This agreement provides for:

- Use of sea port (Tianjin port - nearest port to Mongolia) and freedom of transit to and back to sea port, besides transit of ships under Mongolian flag through internal water and territorial sea of China;
- Road Transportation of goods of landlocked country by vehicles of the transit country. When necessary, appropriate agencies of Contracting Parties should consult in the use of vehicles of landlocked country;
- Transit Transportation of goods of landlocked country by railway shall be made through OSJD Agreement of Freight Transportation relation;
- Using ships under the Mongolian flag for sea transportation of goods;
- Facilitating transportation and customs procedure and exemption from export, import and other tax and any deposit for transit goods of landlocked country;
- Freedom of using customs warehouse, terminals in seaport for goods of landlocked country.

AGREEMENT WITH RUSSIA

Transit Transportation Agreement with Russian Federation was signed on 19 October 1992. It provides for:

- Freedom of transit traffic for landlocked country to and back from sea port of transit country;
- Using of sea port for goods of landlocked country;
- Freedom of transit of ships under Mongolian flag through internal water and territorial sea of transit country;

- Using local transportation tariff or other conditions that are agreed upon through bilateral agreements among countries or better tariffs and conditions should be applied;
- Taking needed measures in facilitating smooth transit of goods and reduction of technical barriers to trade;
- Applying domestic laws of the transit country with regard to the regulation of transit of goods both at the border and other custom procedures;
- For levying no other extra charges except the customs clearance;
- Russian Federation took upon the obligation to set special customs warehouse or terminal zones for the purpose of storage, transit, grouping, and other operations of landlocked developing countries goods that are in transit.

"Transit-Mongolia" National Development Programme

This programme is aimed at conducting an integrated policy to develop transport logistics frame work for access to neighboring regional markets and creating Trans-Asian transit transport link and increase of domestic exports and economic benefits. This National program will cover the following areas.

1. To improve legal environment for foreign trade, international transportation and logistics services and join necessary international conventions and agreements in doing so, improve and update domestic laws and regulations, regulate and improve institutional interaction and cooperation.
2. Carry out actions of facilitating trade and logistics and update foreign trade documents to meet international standards, establish cargo terminals, facilities and logistics centers, economic and trade centers and transport networks connecting these centers.
3. To extend the domestic road and transport networks and eventually connecting them to international highway

networks, build secondary parallel rail line, electrify, extend and improve carriage and locomotive fleet, increase transfer capacity and build new rail lines.

4. To make Zamiin-Uud-Ulaanbaatar-Altanbulag transport route as a main international transit transport corridor and build service infrastructure along the route, introduce traffic safety monitoring system, support private sector transport activities on Trans-Asian transport route and respectively create realistic exits to sea ports through the territory of neighboring countries.
5. Measurement of trade and trade facilitation will be implemented and in the course of improving an efficiency and facilitating border and customs inspection, introduce latest advancement of techniques and technologies as well as not reducing the efficiency of border and customs inspection,improve facilitation and qualification of human resource/experts, and to get facilitation of laboratories, techniques and technologies met with international standards.
6. To introduce "Single window service" system using latest information and communication technologies to aid in facilitating trade, transport, and logistical service, simplify data and information included in the foreign trade and transport documents and to synchronize and convert them into single electronic format and make documentation requirements from different authorities more simple and unified and establish a system that provides up-to-date and prompt delivery of information about foreign trade and transport to customers.

Mongolia is looking forward to closely cooperate with international organizations and donor countries in elaborating this "Transit-Mongolia" national program and its implementation with increased involvement of private sector and further developing the use of public private dialogue and partnership mechanism. These activities will also create convenient legal environment for foreign investors and businessmen. With the establishment of trade and transport facilitation infrastructure

Mongolia will freely enter other world markets and provide its population with steady and better supply of goods and services. It is believed that with creation of freight terminals and logistics centers connecting air, railway and road transport network and becoming an international transit transport route, Mongolia will become a transiting country itself fulfilling its objective to create a new transport and logistics service market.

This "Transit Mongolia Programme" has been created due to increase of transit goods between China and EU and China and Russia through Mongolia by railway. So every year service facilities are needed for eight million transit containers on the Mongolian territory. Foreign technical and financial assistance and close cooperation from international organizations and donor countries will be of great importance to Mongolia.

"Transit-Mongolia" National Development Programme aims at:

1. Improving a legal environment of foreign trade, international transport and logistics;
2. Developing and facilitating trade and logistic services;
3. Extending the national transport networks eventually connecting them to international transport corridors;
4. Promoting a transit transportation;
5. Easing border, customs and specialized inspection control;
6. Introducing latest ICT to aid in facilitating trade and transport;
7. Creating freight terminals and logistics centers connecting air, railway and road transport network and becoming an international transit transport route.

MONGOLIA-INDIA TRADE AND ECONOMIC COOPERATION

Both Mongolia and India can emerge as significant development partners in areas, where India excels in technical development and scientific expertise. Mongolia offers great potential for sustainable partnership in the following areas:

(a) Mining of important minerals; cooking coal and natural gas;
(b) Road development technology;
(c) Information technology and space;
(d) Bio-technology.

Despite the fairly close political relations between India and Mongolia, present trade and economic relations do not amount too much. As Table 1 shows, India's exports to Mongolia accounted for less than 0.1 per cent of India's exports throughout the decade of the 1980s. India's imports from Mongolia have been nil throughout this decade. In absolute terms, the level of India's exports to Mongolia show a great deal of fluctuation.

Table 1: India's Exports to Mongolia (in Rupees)

Year	Absolute Value	As Percentage of India's Total Exports
1980-81	129,228	0.02
1981-82	564,853	0.07
1982-83	69,813	0.01
1983-84	195,624	0.02
1984-85	156,910	0.01
1985-86	227,471	0.02
1986-87	406,430	0.03

Table 2: Commodity Composition of India's Exports to Mongolia

(Percentage shares)

1980	1981	1982	1983	1984	1985	1986
81	82	83	84	85	86	87

Table 3: Identified Potential Items for Increasing Trade Turnover

India's Exports	India's Imports
1. Tea	1. Wheat
2. Coffee	2. Raw wool
3. Spices	3. Crude minerals
4. Cashew	4. Metalliferous ores
5. HPS ground nut	5. Coal, coke, briquettes
6. Oil meals	6. Textile yam, fabrics, madeups
7. Sugar and molasses	7. Cement
8. Fruits and vegetables	8. Non-ferrous metals
9. Marine products	9. Cashmere yarn

10. Iron ore	10. Skin and hides
11. Mica	11. Fertilizer
12. Sports goods	
13. Basic chemicals	
14. Plastic and linoleum	
15. Engineering goods	
16. Cotton yam, fabrics, Made ups	
17. Manmade yarn, fabrics, madeups	
18. RMG cotton	
19. RMG manmade fibres	
20. Project goods	
21. Medicines	
22. Feature films	
23. Printed books	
24 Leather uppers	

Table 4: Mongolia's Trade with India (2000-07)

(In thousand US$)

Year	Export	Export Percent-age	Import	Import Percent-age	Total Trade	Total Trade Percent-age
2000	421.0	0.08	1,767.7	0.29	2,188.7	0.2
2001	18810.0	0.01	1379.1	0.22	1430.8	0.1
2002	39298.0	0.00	1045.8	0.15	1054.2	0.1
2003	31199.0	0.01	854.2	0.11	939.8	0.1
2004	644.7	0.07	625.7	0.06	1270.3	0.1
2005	20271.0	0.01	1518.2	0.13	1573.8	0.1
2006	1535.8	0.10	2395.4	0.16	3931.2	0.1
2007	599.6	0.07	1684.7	0.19	2284.3	0.1

Since Mongolia has entered into market economy and introduced the private sector as the primary basis of the development of its national economy, the Government attaches great importance to develop good friendly political and comprehensive economic and trade co-operation with India. Taking into consideration the poor and unsatisfactory economic cooperation, both India and Mongolia have evolved a legal basis for successful economic cooperation. These are as follows:

1. Agreement between the Government of Mongolia and the Government of India on trade and economic cooperation was signed on September 16, 1996, which

not only encourages and develops trade and economic cooperation but also accords to each other the most-favoured-nation treatment in respect of customs duties and all other taxes on imports and exports and the methods of levying such duties and taxes. Second paragraph of Article 2 of this agreement states, "Either of the Contracting Parties, if it prescribes imports and exports licences or permissions, shall grant the other Contracting Party treatment no less favourable than that granted to a third country in respect of such licences or permissions." This agreement encourages the cooperation of cottage, small, medium and large size enterprises between the two countries.

2. The Agreement between Mongolia and India for the avoidance of double taxation and the prevention of fiscal evasion with respect to taxes on income and on capital, was signed on February 22, 1994, which applies to persons who are resident of one or both of the two countries. Article 7 of this Agreement states, "The profit of an enterprise of a Contracting State shall be taxable only in that Sate unless the enterprise carries on business in the other Contacting State through a permanent establishment situated therein". Article 10 of this Agreement states, "Dividends, paid by a company, which is a resident of a Contracting Sate to a resident of the other Contracting State may be taxed in that other state." The article 24 of he Agreement says "Where a resident of India derives income or owns capital which, in accordance with the provisions of this Agreement, may be taxed in Mongolia, India shall allow as a deduction from the tax on the income of that resident an amount equal to the income tax paid in Mongolia, whether directly or by deduction: and as a deduction from the tax on the capital of that resident an amount equal to the capital tax paid in Mongolia".
3. The Agreement between Mongolia and India for the promotion and protection of investments, was signed

on January 3, 2001 which creates conditions favourable for fostering greater investment in trade, economic, industrial, scientific and technological cooperation by investors of one Contracting Party in the territory of the other Contracting Party. The Agreement also recognizes that the encouragement and reciprocal protection under international agreement of such investment will be conducive to the stimulation of individual business initiative and will increase prosperity in both Contracting parties. The Agreement states that investments and returns of investors of each Contracting Party shall at all times be accorded fair and equitable treatment in the territory of the other Contracting Party. Article 7 of this Agreement states, "Each Contracting Party shall permit all funds of an investor of the other Contracting Party related to an investment in its territory to be freely transferred, without unreasonable delay and on a non-discriminatory basis."[16]

4. Agreement on Air service, signed in 1998 in New Delhi, expresses the intention of the Contracting Parties to promote their mutual relations in the field of civil aviation and to conclude an agreement for the purpose of establishing air service between and beyond their respective territories. Direct links are essential part of boosting the exchange of passengers and trade between the two sides. The immediate task between the two countries is to start a charter flight between Ulaanbaatar and New Delhi.
5. Agreement on Tourism signed in 1998 in New Delhi, expresses the desire of both sides to widen existing links of friendship between the two countries and foster a deep understanding in the establishment of wide co-operation in tourism, specially in human resources development for tourism and travel management.
6. The Ministry of Energy, Geology and Mining and Ministry of Infrastructure of Mongolia signed an

agreement in 1996 for assistance in establishing Joint Venture Company in Ulaanbaatar, Mongolia.

After the favourable legal framework has been created between Mongolia and India, 3 Indian restaurants and one trading company on cosmetics-"Dal mal", one Joint venture, one franchise office of the Indian company and one monastery were set up in Ulaanbaatar. Also some Indian companies are successfully taking part in the Millennium road construction activities. Efforts are also being made for setting up Honorary Consulate offices in the main metropolitan cities of Mumbai, Kolkata and Chennai in India.

The inauguration ceremony of a Joint Venture Company was performed by K.R. Narayanan, the then Vice-President and former President of India, on September 16, 1996 during his official visit to Mongolia. Subsequently in 1997, Electra (India) Limited sent raw material for manufacturing transformers of the following capacity: 63 KVA-10Nos.; 100 KVA-5Nos; 250 KVA-5Nos.

The two countries are agricultural countries. India has great experience in farming and Mongolians are the masters of animal husbandry. These fields are very beneficial and there is scope for Indian farmers to come to Mongolia for developing joint farms in the years to come. The Mongolian agricultural delegation with a representative of its Foreign Ministry visited India in 1997 which led to the setting up of the Mongolian-Indian friendship: "Nairamdal" farm in Darkhan ul province, Khongor farm. The Indian government supplied 1000 kgs. of different cold resistance and early maturity wheat seeds and onions seeds for this farm.

The government of India under ITEC programme decided to set up nine faculties in Mongolia where Mongolian children can get technical training. The machines and equipments have been supplied by NSIC (National Small Industries Cooperation). In the same way the two countries can also cooperate in setting up small and medium size industries in Mongolia.

Trade and economic delegation accompanied the President of Mongolia, N. Bagabandi to India and had separate business meetings with CII chamber of commerce and PHD Chamber of

Commerce and Industries in 2001. Telecommunication and IT delegation accompanied the Minister for Infrastructure of Mongolia in March 2002 and had separate meeting with NIIT and APTECH and members of NASSCOM. An Indian Exhibition was organized in Ulaanbaatar in September 2002. These activities provide more possibilities to know each other's opportunity to develop trade and economic cooperation between the two countries.

There is potential for developing economic cooperation in the field of telecommunication and IT. The Telecommunication and IT Institute named after A.B. Vajpayee was inaugurated in September 2002. For Indian entrepreneur and business houses, there are great possibilities to take part in different tenders and bids sponsored by World Bank and ADB and other international organizations. Indian companies have participated in more than 20 tenders and got successfully 15 projects in the different range of cost. The President, Petroleum Authority of Mongolia visited India on January 23, 2002 and signed MoU with ONGC Videsh Limited, thus opening a new opportunity for India to commence new area of cooperation in the exploration of oil in Mongolia. According to this MoU, the two sides will be engaged in petroleum exploration and production.

The stumbling block for developing trade and economic cooperation is long distance and poor infrastructure development. Commencing direct flights between New Delhi and Beijing gives an opportunity to send cargos to each other's countries via China. But sending goods through cargo flights becomes very expensive which is not profitable for trade. There is another opportunity to send goods from India to China and from China through railway to Mongolia. It is comparatively cheaper than the cargo flights as 20 feet container costs 2,700 US dollars plus custom duties of the receiving side of the goods which is 20-30 per cent.

Indian Consortium to build Mongolian Highway

An Indian consortium of engineering consultants and financiers has been awarded the construction of the prestigious

East-West Highway, known as the Millennium road, in Mongolia. The Consortium, led by Intercontinental Consultants and Technocrats Pvt. Ltd. (ICT) and KMC Construction Ltd. is investing US$ 40 million in the construction of the first phase of the Millennium Road, consisting of a 212 km stretch. An MoU to this effect was signed recently with the Mongolian Ministry of Infrastructure at the Mongolian capital of Ulaanbaatar by K.K.Kapila, Chairman and Managing Director of ICT and Director of KMC Gautam Reddy on behalf of the Indian Consortium. This MoU is a sequel to the pre-feasibility study of the entire 2,600 kms Millennium Road carried out by ICT, without any charge, as a gesture of goodwill. This study has now paved the way for international participation in the construction of the millennium Road, which is expected to contribute immensely to the economic development of Mongolia.

ICT has been a pioneer in road consultancy projects in Mongolia and has successfully completed eight projects since 1993 and is currently working on two more projects. All these projects have been funded by international funding agencies, including Asian Development Bank (ADB), International Development Agency (IDA) and Kuwait Fund for Arab Economic Development (KFAED).

The Ministry of Infrastructure, Government of Mongolia is desirous of getting a part of Millennium Road (2600 kms. Long East-West Road Link) to be built through international funding. The Government of Mongolia has invited private entrepreneurs to come forward with their offers to help build the Millennium road. In response to this invitation an Indian International Consortium consisting of M/s. Intercontinental Consultants and Technocrats Limited, Hong Kong (ICT) and KMC Construction Limited, India (KMC) besides others (including financiers) came forward to build a part of the Millennium Road on deferred payment basis.

The Government of Mongolia gratefully acknowledged this offer from the Consortium that intends to invest to the tune of US$ 40 million. To start with, the Consortium would like to execute the road section Orkhon river-Dashinchilen-Lun (W09). The terms and conditions of the proposed project are as follows:

1. The selected road section is about 212 kms (including the Orkhon bridge and its approaches) and costs about 28.6 million US dollars according to Pre-Feasibility Study estimates. This cost may undergo changes based on detailed engineering.
2. Out of US$ 28.6 million, 70 per cent of it (US$ 20 million) will be the loan by the Consortium against sovereign bank guarantee by the Government of Mongolia. Remaining 30 per cent (US$ 8.6 million) shall be counterpart funding by the Government of Mongolia.
3. Payments related to the project are completely exempted from all taxes, duties and levies. The Consortium will also be allowed to duty free import of all equipment and associated items in connection with the project with the condition that the same will re-exported or alternatively disposed off as per the rules in force.
4. About 12 per cent (5 per cent design and 7 per cent supervision) of it (3.43 million US dollars) will be the Consultancy Service charges for detailed engineering and construction supervision, by the Consortium.
5. The repayment of loan, at an interest rate of 3.5 per cent per annum with additional 0.5 per cent processing fee (i.e. a cumulative all inclusive rate of 4.0 per cent per annum) will commence from 2007 and the entire accrued amount will be completely paid off in 14 equated bi-annual payments.

The "Millennium Road" project for construction of horizontal and lateral road network in Mongolia offers a great opportunity for Indian participation as well. Road directions are: Ulaanbaatar-Lun-Dashinchilen-Bridge over the Ugii Lake-Battsengel-Bridge over the Khanui river-Tariat-Tsakhir-Zagastai hill-Ider-Zavkhanmandal-Durgun-Ulgii-Tsagaannuur-Ulaanbaishint, Ulaanbaatar-Undurkhaan-sumber roads (Location: Tuv, Bulgan, Arkhangai, Zavkhan, Khovd, Bayan-Ulgii, Khentii, Dornod aimags).

Mongolia changed a lot in the nineties, and there has been

great improvement in the lifestyle of Mongolians during this period. Onc would believe that Mongolian economy has made a smooth transition from centrally planned economy to market driven economy, and the negative social impact of this change has not been so significant as compared to other comparable economies. Mongolia has truly made its currency fully convertible, and widely privatized land and state property. The overall privatization process of state enterprises is being conducted progressively. Moreover, the principles of democracy have been truly implemented in Mongolia.

To conclude, geographical barrier has led to a very subdued economic relations and marginal partnership between India and Mongolia. However, this geographical determinism is being overcome and economic partnership is emerging in many fields of common interests. Mongolia and India are two developing nations but with varying economic situations. Mongolia is rich in resources but short of man-power, while India with its abundant manpower has rich experience of economic transformation. In the given situation, both countries have definite geographical compulsions but they have the political will and understanding for cooperation. There are good prospects for experienced and hard working Punjabi farmers for bringing agricultural boom, even in the hard climatic and weather environment in Mongolia. Besides, rich mineral resources of Mongolia could be gainfully exploited with the Indian technology. In sum, there is scope for mutually beneficial cooperation and there are specific areas such as information and space technology and bio-technology, where prospects for future development are assured. Some other areas where there are excellent opportunities to collaborate include energy, road development for industrial complexes, education and health management. Indian firms can take advantage of tender announcements by ADB, World Bank and other international agencies which are substantially participating in the development process of Mongolia. Further, India can take advantage of development in the area of petroleum and cooking coal in the southern part of Mongolia, where several foreign countries are actively participating.

Traders/business houses of both sides face the following

problems, which need to be resolved:

1. The containers take long period of time to reach Mongolia. Containers should take 40-45 days theoretically, but in practice it takes from 50 days to 65 days. Some of them pay for goods in advance before manufacturing. Manufacturing takes 1-2 months. Then the custom processing takes 14 days, and to reach Mumbai port 7 days. The buyers pay their money 3-4 months in advance, and business people do not like their money to be left for 4 months for one container.
2. Traders claim that goods are damaged on the way, sometimes to the extent of 40 per cent
3. There are custom duties amounting to 10-20 per cent in each country on an average.
4. Transport charges are high- 3000-4000 US dollars for 20 feet container between India and Mongolia. Road transport and railway have become more expensive. From Delhi to Mumbai goods are transported by train or trucks and from Tianjing to Ulaanbaatar by railway.
5. There is no active encouragement from the governments for developing trade relations between the two countries
6. There is no direct air linkage between Mongolia and India. DHL and EMS are very costly to send sample goods. Cargo is too expensive between the two countries. They use only Thai international and Air China, as there are no direct flights between India and Mongolia

Considering excellent political relations between the two countries, Mongolia needs to develop good economic and trade relations with India. Though such relations are currently at low level, trade relations between private sectors of the two countries have increased during the last ten years. Economic relations are at the stage of learning each other's potential and willingness. But there has always been a growing interest in mutual economic cooperation between the two countries.

CHAPTER 15

TRADE AND INVESTMENT COOPERATION BETWEEN INDIA AND MONGOLIA

Nawal K. Paswan

It was a coincidence that when India launched its market-oriented economic reforms (movement from a socialist closed economy to a pro-market open economy[1]), Mongolia began its transformation from a centrally planned economy to a market-based economy in 1991. International institutions, consulting firms and national government have pushed liberalization in India by advocating policy measures such as privatization,[2] dis-investment,[3] commercialization, deregulation and international integration. In its seventeen years (1991 to 2008) of economic transition, Mongolia's policies towards foreign trade have shifted drastically from limiting trade outside the Soviet-dominated economies to encouraging and promoting trade with all nations.

Throughout the transition, successive Mongolian governments have pursued various trade liberalization policies in the hope of strengthening and expanding international trade. The enhanced role of the private sector in the Mongolian economy is being supported by a number of measures aimed at liberalizing the economy. These measures include reduction of price controls, opening up of foreign trade, floating exchange rates, and the privatization of state-owned enterprises and joining the WTO in 1997. New edition of Taxation laws, which are in force from January 1, 2007 would result extension of international trade. As a result the foreign trade turn over is increasing and approaching the volume over GDP.[4]

One of the world's largest landlocked countries,[5] Mongolia previously depended heavily on both the Former Soviet Union (FSU) and the Council for Mutual Economic Assistance (COMECON, now known as 'CMEA') for trade. This organization was active between 1956 and 1991 and coordinated economic policy among the nations that were under Communist domination. These states, Bulgaria, Cuba, Czechoslovakia, East Germany, Hungary, Mongolia, Poland, Romania, and the Soviet Union accounted for over 90 per cent of Mongolia's external trade.[6] The fall of the FSU and subsequent dissolution of CMEA forced Mongolia to reassess and diversify its trading strategies. Mongolia has diversified her geographical dependence on CMEA partners and trade with non-CMEA countries has been significantly increasing. Trade played an important role during the transition.[7] More favorable terms of trade and an impressive reorientation of the trade pattern helped absorb the shock left by the collapse of the former Soviet Union and the Council for Mutual Economic Assistance. In the mid-1990s, trade with new export markets (China, USA, Japan, and Korea) and rising copper prices boosted exports and normalized imports. Nevertheless, the trade balance has remained negative throughout the period underscoring the vulnerability of the external sector to international prices volatility of the three key exports: copper, gold, and cashmere.

Currently Mongolia heavily relies on international trade, but its export base is narrow and commodity-based. Mongolia's overall trade policy objectives are to support economic growth through an active trade policy, promote the industrial, agricultural, and services sectors, and increase exports.[8] The Action Programme of the Government of Mongolia for 2004-08, also aims to change Mongolia's export structure by diversifying export products and markets, and to work towards the establishment of free-trade agreements with Russia, China, and the United States.[9] Mongolia has not signed any regional or bilateral free-trade agreements. It has been involved in various bilateral trade-related arrangements, which do not involve preferential treatment.[10]

Mongolia has not concluded any regional trade agreements.[11]

Nor is it a member of the Asia Pacific Economic Cooperation (APEC). The authorities consider that joining the Bangkok Agreement would offer concrete advantages to Mongolia.[12] Mongolia is negotiating a Transit Transport Framework Agreement with China and Russia to aid the transit of Mongolian products through its neighbouring countries to third countries. The authorities expect that this would help to make the transit of Mongolian exports in the North-East Asian region more efficient, which would improve the international competitiveness of Mongolian products destined for third countries.[13] Due to its small size and weak potential, for Mongolia, economic, trade and investment integration into a larger regional cooperation structure is not the best but perhaps the only way to accelerate its economic growth and long-term sustainable development.[14]

The objective of this paper is to explore the definite and specific possibilities of trade in goods (and services as also trade cum investment related areas of economic cooperation) with a few case studies for forging synergetic partnerships between India and Mongolia. This paper also investigates the possibilities of deeper integration and cooperation between India and Mongolia in trade and investment based on combination of empirical approaches. This paper is organized under following five major sections beside introduction.

Section I deals with the genesis of India-Mongolia economic relations and examines the changing nature and composition of bilateral trade between India and Mongolia and it also estimates the export and import intensities indices between both countries to measure the degree of representation in bilateral trade. **Section II** discusses the foreign direct investment in Mongolia and identifies the potential products or sector in which India can establish joint-venture *(or vice-versa)* with the help of Intra-Industry Trade (IIT) index at 6-digit HS classification. It also examines nature and extent of IIT at the 6-digit HS classification using UN Trade Statistics available in PC-TAS database. This exercise will help in setting-up a joint marketing strategy in the identified products and establishing bilateral potential joint ventures (investment linkages). It also examines the extent of trade potential between India and Mongolia at the 6-Digit HS classification. **Section III** discusses the nature of foreign direct investment (FDI) and investment linkages between India and Mongolia and promotion of FDI. **Section IV** examines and identifies the nature and extent of degree of complementarities (at overall products and sectoral products levels) in the bilateral trade structure at 2-digit HS classification. It also supplements with product level analysis matching the products between India's exports to and import from Mongolia and *vice-versa.* This exercise will identify the products for fast track liberalization. **Finally**, last section is devoted to examine the overall assessment of the present status of India-Mongolia trade and investment cooperation and future prospects for mutual cooperation with identification of areas which are needed to be prioritized and also draw some conclusions for policy implications.

I. BILATERAL ECONOMIC AND TRADE RELATIONS

Genesis of India-Mongolia Economic Relations

This section glances through the present status of India-Mongolia relations or engagement on the basis of information available with the head of the Indian Mission in Mongolia.[15] It also takes into account various agreements and Memorandum of Understanding (MoU) in the different focused fields or areas which has been signed between India and Mongolia to promote stronger economic relations between both countries.

An India-Mongolia Joint Declaration was issued following the visit of Premier Yu. Tsendenbal in February 1973. The Declaration provided general principles to guide bilateral relations. In February 1994, a Treaty of Friendly Relations and Co-operation was signed during the visit of President Ochirbat to India, providing *inter alia*, for: (a) Developing equal and mutually beneficial co-operation in various spheres including political, economic, trade, science and technology, health, agriculture, ecology, culture, education, communications and tourism; (b) Development of links between the two Parliaments, Governments and NGOs on both sides; (c) Co-operation, bilateral and multilateral, in combating international crimes including terrorism; and (d) Closely co-operating within the framework of the UN, NAM and other international organizations, with a view to furthering the cause of peace and international security, globally and in Asia.

The India-Mongolia Joint Declaration of January 2001 *inter alia* states: (a) Mongolia would fully support India's endeavour to become a permanent member as the expansion of the UN Security Council takes place; (b) Mongolian side reaffirmed its support for Indian efforts to normalize relations with Pakistan on the basis of the Simla Agreement; (c) Both the countries recognize the serious threat posed to nation states and international peace and security by terrorist groups; (d) Both the countries condemn terrorism in all its forms and also condemn the States that aid, abet and directly support cross border and international terrorism; (e) Both India and Mongolia reiterated their resolve to work for strengthening international consensus and legal regimes against terrorism; and (f) The visit of Mongolian President provided an important road map for further development of bilateral relations in the 21st century.

During the visit of the then Minister for Commerce Pranab Mukherjee, in 1994 two MOUs pertaining to the establishment of a Joint Trade Sub-Committee and Co-operation between the Planning Commission of India and the National Development Board of Mongolia were signed. The Commerce Minister offered Indian assistance for conducting a survey of geological mines by the GSI and assist Mongolia in training specialists in the mining sector. As a follow up to this, an agreement for co-operation in the field of geology and mineral resources was signed in September 1996. However not much has taken place in this area, primarily because of privatization process in Mongolia. In September 1996, during the visit of the then Vice President, K.R. Narayanan to Mongolia, an Agreement on Trade and Economic Cooperation between India and Mongolia was signed. The Agreement provides for MFN status to each other in respect of customs duties and all other taxes on imports and exports. During the visit of President Bagabandi to India in January 2001, both sides signed an Investment Promotion and Protection Agreement.

Mongolia is keen to develop industrial co-operation with India in textiles, cement, cashmere, leather, IT, pharmaceuticals and other small-scale industries. However considering the size of the market, the response from Indian companies has not been encouraging. The main items of Indian exports to Mongolia include medicines, animal vaccines, silk, jute, yarn, dyeing chemicals, etc. Imports from Mongolia include raw wool, hides and skins and fluorspar. Bilateral trade has not developed much due to the problems of trans-shipment through Chinese ports, high freight rates and delayed delivery schedule.

Pattern of India-Mongolia Trade

The magnitude of value between India's trade with Mongolia is computed and presented on the basis of two comparable sources, i.e., national sources (DGCI&S) and international source (DOTS/IMF). DGCI&S provides the data on financial year while DOTS/IMF gives data on calendar year. National data is computed from Directorate General of Commercial Intelligence and Statistics (DGCI&S) published by the Ministry of Commerce, Government of India and international sources data is computed from the Direction of Trade Statistics Year Book (database) published by the International Monetary Fund, Washington DC.

India's trade with Mongolia is computed from DGCI&S and presented in **Table 1**. In the last five years, India-Mongolia trade has increased more than ten times from US$ 1.55 million in 2003-04 to USD 16.88 million in 2007-08. In fact the bilateral trade was stagnant during 2003-04 and 2004-05 but it increased further in 2005-06 and reached at USD 2.79 million in 2005-06 and USD 16.88 million in 2007-08. However, India's bilateral trade with Mongolia is just a miniscule of its global trade, being no more than 0.004 per cent as can be seen in **Table 1**. Another feature of India's bilateral trade with Mongolia is characterized by fluctuating trends and observed that it has been maintaining a surplus position with this country during 2003-04 to 2004-05 and 2006-07 but deficit position in two years 2005-06 and 2007-08.

Table 1: India-Mongolia Bilateral Trade (Value in US Million Dollar)

Year	2003-04	2004-05	2005-06	2006-07	2007-08
India's Export to Mongolia	0.81	1.35	1.17	2.36	7.58
% Growth		66.82	-13.51	102.07	221.85
India's Total Export	63,842.55	83,535.95	103,090.5	126,262.67	162,983.9
% Growth		30.85	23.41	22.48	29.08
% Share	0.00	0.00	0.00	0.00	0.00
India's Imports from Mongolia	0.74	0.21	1.62	2.24	9.30
% Growth		-72.38	688.02	38.43	314.59
India's Total Import	78,149.11	111,517.44	149,165.7	185,604.10	251,562.2
% Growth		42.7	33.76	24.43	35.54
% Share	0.00	0.00	0.00	0.00	0.00
India's Trade with Mongolia	1.55	1.56	2.79	4.6	16.88
% Growth		0.07	79.34	65.06	267.09
India's Total Trade	141,991.6	195,053.38	252,256.2	311,866.78	414,546.1
% Growth		37.37	29.33	23.63	32.92
% Share	0.00	0.00	0.00	0.00	0.00
India's Trade Balance with Mongolia	0.06	1.14	-0.45	0.11	-1.72
India's Trade Balance	-14306.56	-27981.49	-46075.20	-59341.43	-88578.36

Note: This figure of trade values doesn't include the part of the Indian products entering Mongolia through third countries exports.

Source: Directorate General of Commercial Intelligence & Statistics (DGCI&S), Ministry of Commerce, Government of India (online database).

India's Trade with Mongolia

India's trade with the world and Mongolia is computed from Direction of Trade Statistics Year Book (IMF) and presented in Table 2. It can be observed from this table that India's exports to Mongolia was US$ 0.07 million in 1990 which suddenly increased to US$ 0.86 in 1991 and further reached US$ 1.15 million in 2005. This reflects the fluctuating trend in trade between India and Mongolia. India's imports from Mongolia also registered fluctuating trends during the period 1990 to 2005. In 1990, India's imports from Mongolia was US$ 1.69 million which decreased to US$ 0.02 million in 1991 and since then it maintained fluctuating trend reaching the highest ever point of

US$ 1.27 in 2005. The level of trade between India and Mongolia is very low as compared to India's world trade. The justification of low level of trade between both countries can be examined with the help of trade intensity index. Thus, an attempt has been made in the next section to identify the reasons of low level of trade between these two countries through this trade intensity index.

Table 2: India's Trade with Mongolia and World (Value in US$ Million)

Year	India's Exports to World	India's Exports to Mongolia (%)	India's Imports from World	India's Imports from Mongolia (%)
1990	17813.00	0.07	23991.40	1.69
1991	17873.50	0.86	19509.40	0.02
1992	19232.60	2.28	23196.60	0.00
1993	20989.80	0.98	21268.80	0.05
1994	24196.20	0.73	25485.80	0.00
1995	30538.00	0.73	34486.50	0.02
1996	32325.60	2.29	36054.80	0.09
1997	34622.10	0.93	40896.40	0.18
1998	33665.20	1.53	42162.10	0.20
1999	35921.60	2.15	47900.50	0.28
2000	42625.80	1.63	50336.10	0.15
2001	45227.10	1.25	59036.30	0.06
2002	50496.30	0.67	58912.40	0.42
2003	61118.50	0.78	74070.00	0.69
2004	75385.20	1.36	99835.30	0.34
2005	97918.10	1.15	134690.00	1.27

Source: Estimated from International Monetary Fund (IMF); *Direction of Trade Statistics Year Book*, database, Washington DC.

Trade Intensity between India and Mongolia

An implicit statistical indicator of the growing complementarities in trade between India and Mongolia is provided by the growing (export and import) intensities. This index provides additional insight into changes in India's trade with Mongolia flows. In an attempt to explore the potential of India-Mongolia trade expansion, we have computed export and import intensities of both countries. This index was first used by K. Kojima[16] (1964).

It measures the share of one country's trade with other country as a proportion of the latter's share of world.

Export Intensity Index (xij) = *{ (Xij / Xi) / [Mj / (Mw - Mi)] }*

where: **xij** is EII of trade (Exports) of country i with country j; **Xij** is Exports of country i to trading partner j; **Xi** is Total exports of country I; **j** is Total imports of country j; **Mw** is Total world imports and **Mi** is Total imports of country i

It is defined for country **i**'s exports to country j as the share of its exports going to **j** (**Xij**/Xi) relative to the share of **j**'s import to (M**j**) in world imports net of i's import (Mw-Mi). The equality of these two terms would lead to the value of this country **i**'s export in the same proportion as country **i**'s share in total (net) world imports. Value of this index which is greater than unity would imply over-representation of country **j** in country **i**'s exports, while a value less than unity would imply under representation. Similarly,

Import Intensity Index (mij) = *{(Mij /MXi) / [Xj / (Xw - Xi)]}*

where: m**ij denotes** III of trade (Imports) of country **i** with country **j; Mij** is Imports of country **i** to trading partner **j; Mi is** Total Imports of country **I;** X**j** is Total Exports of country **j; Xw is** Total world exports; and **Xi** is Total exports of country **i**

Similarly, it is defined for county **i**'s imports from country j as the share of **i**'s imports coming from **j** (M**ij**/Mj) relative to the share of **j**'s exports (X**j**) in world exports net of i's exports (Xw-X**i**). When these two terms are equal, this would imply that country i accounts for the proportion of country **j**'s exports identical to country **j**'s importance in total (net) world exports. If this index is numerically greater than unity this would imply over-representation of country **j** in the country **i**'s imports; on the other hand, if a value of less than unity of this index would imply under-representation.

India's export and import intensities with Mongolia and

Mongolia's export and import intensities with India have been computed from DOTS/IMF from 1992 to 2005 and presented in **Table 3.** It can be observed that from **Table 3** that the index value of India's export and import intensity with Mongolia maintained less than unity[17] showing that Mongolia has always been under-represented in India's trade.

Table 3: Trade (Export and Import) Intensity Index Value between India and Mongolia (1992 to 2005)

Years	India		Mongolia	
	Export Intensity With Mongolia	Import Intensity with Mongolia	Export Intensity with India	Import Intensity with India
1992	1.097	0.000	0.000	0.932
1993	0.465	0.023	0.592	0.837
1994	0.501	0.000	0.952	0.000
1995	0.294	0.006	0.006	0.548
1996	0.841	0.031	0.099	0.138
1997	0.319	0.054	0.079	0.242
1998	0.495	0.074	0.049	0.487
1999	0.674	0.092	0.214	0.556
2000	0.407	0.035	0.103	0.431
2001	0.274	0.012	0.010	0.293
2002	0.126	0.087	0.002	0.193
2003	0.122	0.113	0.015	0.130
2004	0.167	0.036	0.071	0.074
2005	0.107	0.092	0.005	0.135

Source: Estimated by Author from International Monetary Fund (IMF); *Direction of Trade Statistics Year Book*, database, Washington DC.

When we examine Mongolia's export and import intensities with India, we find that the same trends less than unity index value, which itself shows that India has also been under-represented in Mongolia's trade. Hence, we can say that both countries are under-representing each other in export and import intensities and due to under-representation in each other trade the existing level of trade is very low. Therefore, both countries need to try to make over-representation in trade to enhance the level of bilateral trade.

Both countries have signed MoU pertaining to the establishment of a Joint Trade Sub-Committee and Co-operation between the Planning Commission of India and the National Development Board of Mongolia. In September 1996, during the visit of the then Vice President, K.R. Narayanan to Mongolia, an Agreement on Trade and Economic Cooperation between India and Mongolia was signed. The Agreement provides for most favoured nation (*MFN*) status to each other in respect of customs duties and all other taxes on imports and exports. During the visit of President Bagabandi in January 2001, both sides signed an Investment Promotion and Protection Agreement. There is an urgent need to follow up these developments and try to implement the same.

India's Exports to Mongolia: Product-wise Analysis

The composition and magnitude of India's trade with Mongolia has been computed on the basis of products-wise. For this purpose, we have classified the products structure at four levels (i) HS-2 Digit; (ii) HS-4 Digit; (iii) HS-6 Digit; and (iv) HS-8 Digit classifications. Data is obtained from the Directorate General of Commercial Intelligence and Statistics (DGCI&S) database which is published by the Ministry of Commerce, Government of India. To examine the magnitude in trade, we have taken 2006-07 and 2007-08 data and tried to examine the potential product which can enhance the level of trade between both countries. An attempt has been summarize the features of products which is being exported by India to Mongolia and classified at the HS-2, HS-4, HS-6 and HS-8 digit products level with the help of DGCI&S database and presented in **Table 4** which is self-explanatory.

Table 4. Summary of India's Bilateral Trade with Mongolia: Product-wise Analysis (2006-07 and 2007-08)

HS-Levels	Total Products	Growth-wise (+)	Common	New	Old
Export Structure					
HS-2 Digit	49	13	21	42	28
HS-4 Digit	117	18	30	86	60
HS-6 Digit	161	18	30	121	70
HS-8 Digit	100	12	21	72	49
Import Structure					
HS-2 Digit	10	2	2	5	7
HS-4 Digit	15	2	2	8	9
HS-6 Digit	18	1	1	9	10
HS-8 Digit	18	1	1	9	10

Note: Total Products denotes the numbers of products trading between both countries. Growth-wise includes only positive growth as percentage change over previous period; Common = exported in both years i.e. 2006-07 and 2007-08; New = exported only in 2007-08 and Old = exported only in 2006-07.

Source: Estimated from *Directorate General of Commercial Intelligence and Statistics* (DGCI&S), Ministry of Commerce, Government of India (online database).

India's Exports to Mongolia at HS-2 Digit

India's exports to Mongolia (at HS-2 digit) was US$ 2.36 million in 2006-07 which increased three-times higher and reached at US$ 7.58 million in 2007-08. The list of the products in this category shows the highest (positive and negative) percentage change over previous period in India's exports to Mongolia. These products include: (i) Electrical machinery and equipment and parts thereof; sound recorders and reproducers, television image and sound recorders and reproducers, and parts. (85); (ii) Man-made filaments. (54); (iii) Silk (50); (iv) Furniture; bedding, mattresses, mattress supports, cushions and similar stuffed furnishing; lamps and lighting fittings not elsewhere specified or inc (94); (v) Miscellaneous chemical products. (38); (vi) Essential oils and resinoids; perfumery, cosmetic or toilet preparations. (33); (vii) Printed books, newspapers, pictures and other products of the printing industry; manuscripts, typescripts and plans. (49); (viii) Aluminium and articles thereof. (76); (ix) Works of art collectors' pieces and antiques. (97); (x) Articles of apparel and clothing accessories, not knitted or crocheted. (62); (xi) Coffee, tea, mate and spices. (09); (xii) Copper and articles thereof. (74); and (xiii) Nuclear reactors, boilers, machinery and mechanical appliances; parts thereof. (84).

India's Exports to Mongolia at HS-4 Digit

India's exports to Mongolia at level of HS-4 digit classification products (brief description) showing the highest (positive) percentage change over previous period (years 2006-07 and 2007-08) include: (i) Glands & other orgns, drd, w/n pwdrd & extrctsthrof/of thr scrtnc for orgnotherpeutc use e.g. heparin & its salts etc. (3001); (ii) Woven fabrics of silk or silk waste (5007); (iii) Prts & accssrs (excl covers,carryng cases etc) usd wth mchns of hdg no.8469 to 8472 (8473); (iv) Dignostc/labortory reagnt on a bckng & prprd diagnstc/labrtry reagnts wh/not on backng, excl of hdng 3002/3006 (3822); (v) Shaving/pre & after shave prpns bath prpn depilatrs & othr perfmry cosmtc/toilt prpnprpn nes;prpd room deodorisers w/n prfmd (3307); (vi) Woven fabrics of artfcs filament yarn,inclfbrcs obtnd from materials of hdg no.5405 (5408); (vii) Prisms, mirrors & othr optcl elmnts,unmntd being prts or fttngs for instrmnts/apprts othr thn such elmnts of gls,nt optcly wrkd (9002); (viii) Preparations for use on the hair (3305); Women/grls' blouses, shrts & shrt-blouses (6206); (ix) Medicaments (excl goods hdg no 3002 3005 or 3006) cnsistnc of two/more constunts mxd together for hmn medcne nt fr rtl sale (3003; (x) Other articles of aluminium (7616); (xi) Hnd pantngs drwngs & pastels, excl drwngs of hdg 4906 & excl hndprntd/hnd dcrtd artcls; collages & smlr decorative plaques (9701); (xii) Other furniture & parts thereof (9403); (xiii) Compnd optcl microscopes, incl those frmcrophotogrphy, mcrocenmtgrphy/

microprjctn; (9011); (xiv) Pumps for liquids; w/n ftted with a measuring device; liquid elevators (8413); (xv) Women's/girls' suits, ensembles, jackets, dresses, skirts, trousers, bib & brace ovrals, brechs & shorts etc. (except swimwear) (6204); (xvi) Other articles of copper (7419); and (xvii) Other woven fabrics of cotton (5212).

India's Exports to Mongolia at HS-6 Digit

India's exports to Mongolia at level of HS-6 digit classification (brief description) showing the highest (positive) percentage change over previous period (years 2006-07 and 2007-08) include: (i) Glnds & other orgns dried w/n pwdrded (300110); (ii) Prts & accssrs of mchns of hdg no.8471 (847330; (iii) Compst diagnostic/labrtry reagnts excl goods of hdg. No. 3002/3006 (382200); (iv) "Agarbatti" & other odoriferous prpns which operate by burning (330741); (v) Other woven fabrics cntng by wt>=85% of artificial filament/strip/like,dyed (540822); (vi) Other objective lenses (900219); (vii) Medicaments containing other antibiotics and put up for retail sale (300420); (viii) Othr prpns for use on hair (330590); (ix) Others articles of aluminium (others). (761699); (x) Blouses, shirts & shirts-blouses of cotton (620630); (xi) Other hand-decorated mnfctrd artcls (970190); (xii) Frntr of othr matrls, incl cane, osier, bamboo/smlr matrls (940380); (xiii) Suits of cotton (620412); (xiv) Othr printd books etc of hd no. 4901 (490199); (xv) Other mdcmnts cntng vitamins/other products of heading no 2936 put up for retail sale (300450); (xvi) Other articles of heading 7419 (741999); (xvii) Othr dyed woven fbrcs wghng <=200 g/m2 (521213); and (xviii) Medicaments containing insulin (300431).

India's Exports to Mongolia at HS-8 Digit

India's exports to Mongolia at level of HS-4 digit classification (brief description) showing the highest (positive) percentage change over previous period (years 2006-07 and 2007-08) include: (i) "Agarbatti" & other odoriferous prpns which operate by burning (33074100); (ii) Other for medical diagnosis (38220019); (iii) Norfloxacin (30042031); (iv)

Blouses, shirts & shirts-blouses of cotton (62063000); (v) Hair dyes (natural, herbal 0r synthetic) (33059040); (vi) Other hand-decorated mnfctrd artcls (97019099); (vii) Heamatinics and erythropoietin (30045010); (viii) Other anthelmintics drugs; antiamoebic and other. antiprotozoal/antifungal drugs (30049029); (ix) Other antihypertensive drugs (30049079); (x) Other medicaments containing insulin.(30043190); and (xi) Articles of brass (74199930).

India's Imports from Mongolia: Product-wise

India's imports from Mongolia at level of HS-2 digit, HS-4 digit, HS-6 Digit and HS-8 digit classification has been taken from DGCI&S[18] on the basis of growth rates for the years 2006-07 and 2007-08. India's import from Mongolia was US$ 2.24 million in 2006-07 which increased to US$ 9.3 million in 2007-08. The products which registered highest percentage change over previous period in India's exports to Mongolia at HS 2 digit are Wool, fine or coarse animal hair, horsehair Yarn and woven fabric (51) and Ores, slag and ash (26). At HS 6 digit classification products are Molybdnum ores & concentrates (2613) and Wool not carded or combed (5101); and at HS 8 digit classification product is Molybdnum ores & concentrates roasted (26131000) registered highest growth during 2006-07 and 2007-08.

Mongolia is trying to diversify its exports in order to be less dependent on fluctuating prices for the main export commodities (copper concentrate, raw cashmere, gold, fluorspar, coal). In 2006 the value of Mongolia's external trade soared by 34 per cent to over US$ 3 billion, with exports rising by 43 per cent to US$ 1529 million and imports up by 26 per cent to US$ 1489 million. After the SARS crisis in 2003 the tourism sector came back strongly with over 300,000 visitors per year and substantial earnings. Some of the Mongolian export items enjoy preferential tariffs under the General System of Preferences (GSP) schemes of the USA, the EU, Canada and Japan. Mongolia does not receive 'Everything but arms' (EBA) treatment (since it is not recognized as a least-developed country); nor is it included in any regional trade agreements.[19]

Mongolia applies a 5.0 per cent flat rate import duty to

which there are few exceptions. This relatively liberal trade regime was commended in the WTO Trade Policy Review in March 2005.[20] EU exports to Mongolia (machinery, chemicals, food) originate mainly from Germany-Mongolia consistently maintains a trade deficit with the EU. Russia is still the main exporter to Mongolia, supplying energy, cars and spare parts.

The gravity model results assess this potential less favorably. Mineral exports, such as copper and molybdenum, appear to lie above the level predicted by the model. The same applies for all other raw materials based on livestock production. In contrast, the model predicts a high untapped potential for the sector 'metal and metal products', which in this case concerns gold. This coincides with the strong positive value of the indicative trade potential. For the agricultural sector, that is 'edible nuts', current exports are well in-line with the predicted values within the gravity setup.[21]

Mongolia's export structure however remains concentrated, in terms of composition. Over nine-tenths of Mongolia's exports are primary-sector (agricultural and mining) base, with minerals representing over half of total exports. Gold, copper concentrate and other minerals, cashmere and cashmere products and textiles accounted for 93% of Mongolia's exports in 2004. Tourism is also emerging as a foreign exchange earner, although Mongolia is yet to tap its potential as a tourist destination. Mongolia's main imports in 2003 included food, manufactured products (including non-electrical machinery, transport equipment and other semi-manufactures).[22]

India is having dynamic comparative advantage in so many products[23] at 3-digit HS classification which include: 1. marine products (preserved); 2. wheat (unmilled and milled/wheat floue); 3. rice; 4. vegetables (fresh and processed): 5. sugar and honey; 6. coffees and substitutes; 7. feeding stuff for animals; 8. tobacco (unmanufactured and refuse); 9. stone and granite etc; 10. iron ore and steel; 11. crude vegetable materials; 12. organic and inorganic chemicals; 13. synthetic dyes; 14. pharmaceuticals and herbal medicines; 15. rubber tyres and tubes; 16. textile yarn; 17. floor coverings; 18. lime and Stone; 19. aluminium; 20. zinc; 21. Handtools; 22. machine tools; 23. rotating electric plant; 24. bicycles; 25. leather goods including Travel goods, hand bags; 26. footwear; 27. textiles and readymade garments and 28. gem and Jewellary products. Therefore, India should export all these products to Mongolia to enhance trade relations between both countries. Mongolia should also make some efforts to generate demand of these products which would increase trade between both countries.

II. Foreign Direct Investment (FDI) in Mongolia

This section is devoted to analyze the state of Mongolian foreign direct investment (FDI) over the last fifteen years. FDI was not permitted while Mongolia was under the FSU's control but since it gained its independence, the government of Mongolia has enacted a series of laws to attract investors. Mongolia took initial steps in 1993 and then again in 1997 to overcome its many legal and political obstacles and create a favorable environment for prospective investors. It has developed from a nation limited to joint ventures between Mongolian state-owned enterprises (SOEs) and those of other COMECON nations into a very liberal FDI regime, "strongly committed to the improvement of the overall investment environment"[24] FDI is a valuable source of private external finance for developing countries as it helps to transfer capital, technology, skills, innovations and often, greater global access to international markets.

Since the Mongolian economy was opened up to the outside world in the early 1990s, foreign investment in Mongolia has been increasing steadily. This increase has been assisted by amendments to and enforcement of the Foreign Investment Law of Mongolia, as well as other measures taken by the Mongolian government to create a legal environment favorable to foreign direct investment. Despite worldwide decreases in FDI amounts, foreign investors' interest in Mongolia has grown in recent years. Especially noteworthy has been investment in mining, textile, trade and services—by investors from East Asia and North America. Mongolia has performed well in terms of attracting FDI, and has great potential to do even better in the future.

According to a UNCTAD survey, Mongolia moved to the "high potential FDI category" in 1999-2001, having been in the lowest FDI potential and performance category from 1993 to 1995. The UNCTAD ranks Mongolia 78 out of 141 nations in its Inward Potential Performance Index for 2003-2005. The index measures the attractiveness of a nation to FDI based upon several criteria including per capita income, GDP growth over the previous ten years, research and development spending as a percent of GDP and the ratio of tertiary students in the population. From 1990 to the end of 2003, 3042 foreign investment companies from 73 countries were registered with the government of Mongolia, implementing total direct investments of about US$ 1 billion.

The main law governing foreign investment in Mongolia is the Foreign Investment Law.[25] Under this law, wholly foreign-owned business entities are allowed; inward foreign direct investment (FDI) receives national treatment. No restriction is imposed on the size and content of FDI into Mongolia, except that the production of weapons is prohibited. Foreign nationals or companies are not allowed to own land in Mongolia; they can lease land for up to 60 years. FDI into Mongolia cannot be legally expropriated. Foreign investors can remit income, profits and payments out of Mongolia without any barriers; they are subject to a 20% withholding tax. The Foreign Investment and Foreign Trade Agency (FIFTA) is responsible for foreign investment policy formulation and implementation.[26] Mongolia has concluded agreements on avoidance of double taxation with 31 countries.[27] It has also signed agreements on Mutual Protection and Promotion of Investments with 34 countries.[28] Mongolia is a signatory of the Multilateral Investment Guarantee Agency.

Chart 1 presents the FDI inflows in Mongolia during 1990 to 2007.[29] At the end of 2007, since 1990, over 7700 foreign invested companies (including the oil sector) have been registered from 93 countries with total direct investment of US$ 2.3 billion and 80 per cent of total investment volume has been made during the period 2000-07. And in the year 2007 foreign direct investment reached US$ 499 million in 1609 companies.

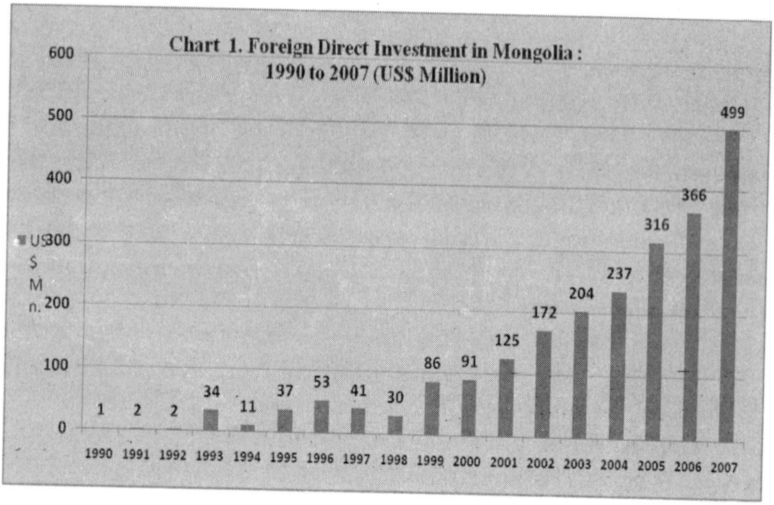

Companies from Belgium, Canada, Cayman Islands, People's Republic of China, Germany, Japan, Republic of Korea, Russian Federation, Switzerland, United Kingdom, United States, Viet Nam, Virgin Islands, accounted for 98.8 per cent of the total investment. **Chart 1** presents the value of total foreign direct investment in Mongolia during the period 1990-2005. It can be observed from this Chart 1 that Mongolia's total FDI was merely US$ 1 million which recorded significant increase and reached at US$ 312 million in 2005. Further FDI data from the UNCTAD indicates that foreign direct investment inflows (FDI) in 2006 were $167 million. This was slightly below the $182 million level in 2005 and represented 26.7 percent of gross fixed capital formation. The total stock of FDI (book value) at the end of 2006 was $876 million, which was equal to 31.2 percent of GDP.

Distribution of FDI Inflows by Source Country

China is the main investor in Mongolia both by amount of investment and number of companies during 2001. Chinese FDI flows are growing in such sectors such as geology-mining ($US 153.8 million); trade and catering services ($US 92.5million); engineering construction, construction materials ($US 30million); and light industry ($US 22.9million).

Canadian investors are very active in the geological survey and mining sectors: 17 of a total of 23 Canadian investors in Mongolia are engaged in this sector and FDI increased from US$ 6million in 2002 to US$ 120 million in 2003. This enhanced Canada's position amongst investor countries from 15th place to second. American investors have concentrated investment in the following sectors: geology-mining and oil ($US 94.3million), processing of animal-origin raw materials (US$ 6.9million), light industry ($US 4.0million), construction and construction materials (US$ 2.6million).

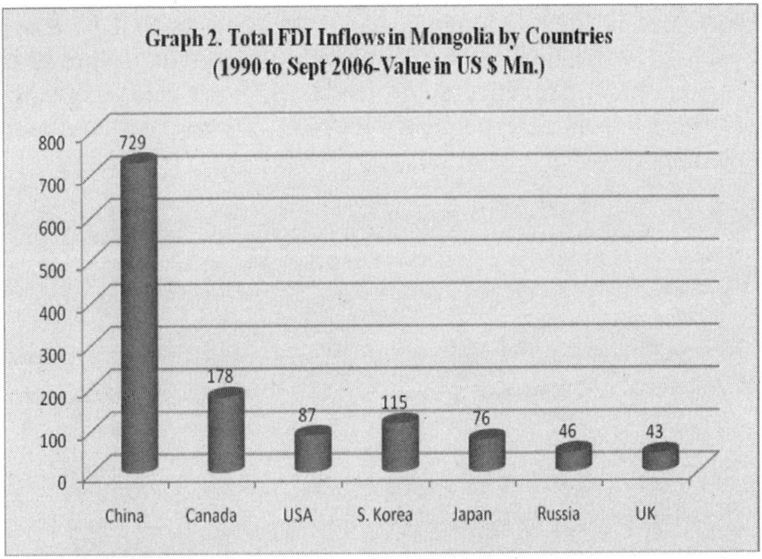

Graph 2 shows the total FDI inflows in Mongolia during 1990 to September 2006. China is the main investor in Mongolia in terms of FDI inflows value US$ 729 million and is ranking top, followed by Canada (US$ 178 million), South Korea (US$ 115 million), USA (US$ 87 million), Japan (US$ 76 million), Russia (US$ 46) and United Kingdom (US$ 43 million). FDI from South Korea is increasing. South Koreans have mainly invested in geology and mining (US$ 12.8 million), light industry (US$ 6.7 million), transportation (US$ 5.6 million) and telecommunications (US$ 5.3 million). Japanese investors'

interest in Mongolia also is on the rise. To date, Japanese investors have preferred light industry (US$ 28 million), telecommunications (US$ 8 million), trade and catering services (US$ 3.1 million) and the processing of raw materials of animal origin (US$ 1.8 million).

Chart 3 represents the percentage share of country-wise distribution of total FDI inflows in Mongolia during 1990 to September 2006. China is the main investor in Mongolia in terms of FDI inflows with 46 per cent followed by Canada (22 per cent), United Kingdom (11 per cent), Russia (7 per cent), South Korea (6 per cent), Japan (5 per cent) and USA (3 per cent). But in 2008, Mongolia has diversified its FDI by major countries with China (46.64 per cent) at top ranking followed by Canada (13.74 per cent), South Korea (6.69 per cent), USA (4.9 per cent), Japan (4.26 per cent), Russia (3.12 per cent) and other countries (20.65 per cent)

Chart 3. Country-wise Distribution of Total FDI Inflows in Mongolia (1990 to Sept 2006)

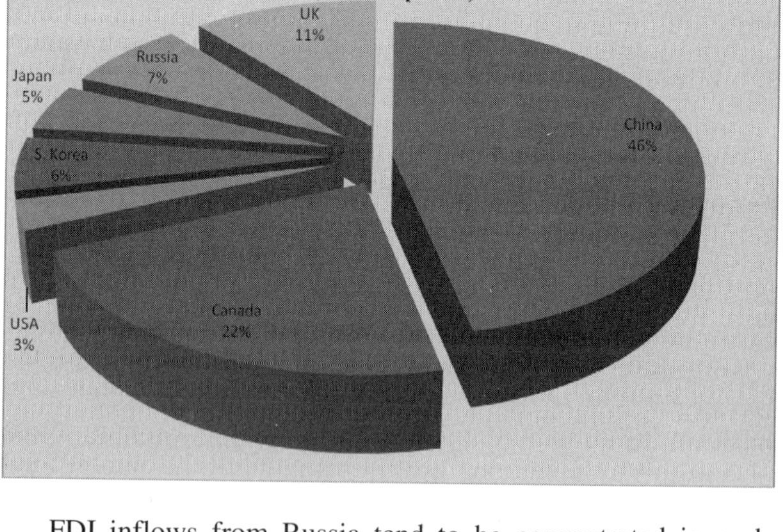

FDI inflows from Russia tend to be concentrated in such sectors as geology and mining (US$ 7.8 million), construction and construction materials (US$ 5.2 million), banking and financial services (US$ 4 million) and the food industry (US$

3.1 million). Ivanhoe Mines of Canada and Rio Tinto are involved in developing Oyu Tolgoi, which will be one of the world's largest copper and gold projects. It is located in the Gobi desert, 50 miles north of the Chinese border. When the mine is fully developed, it is expected to produce 440,000 tons of copper and 320,000 ounces of gold a year. The two companies have indicated that they will spend $3 billion to develop the project. But production has been held up for several years by prolonged negotiations with the government over the terms of taxation, government ownership and royalty payments.

Chart 4. Sectoral Distribution of Total FDI Inflows (1990 to Sept 2006)

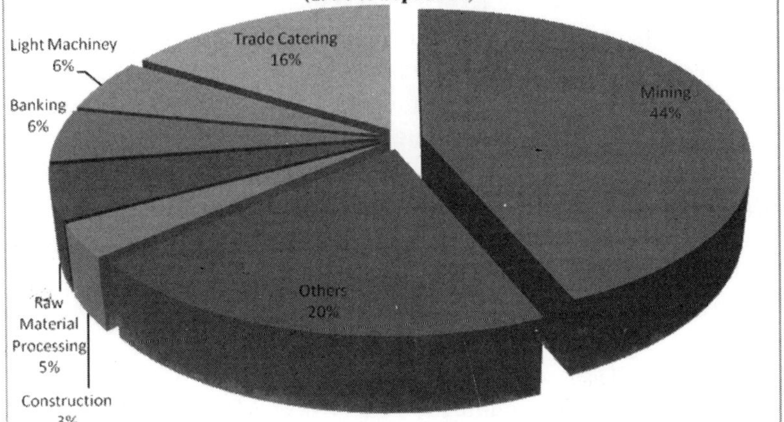

Distribution of FDI Inflows by Sector

Mongolia has an internationally-recognized comparative advantage for attracting FDI into key domestic development sectors. As can be observed in **Chart 4** that the major sectors which attracted highest FDI is mining with 44 per cent followed by trade catering (16 per cent), light machinery (6 per cent), banking (6 per cent), raw material processing (5 per cent) and construction (3 per cent) during 1990 to September 2006. But in 2008, there was little diversification in sectors with mining and extraction attracting highest share of FDI (48.4 per cent) ranking top followed by trade and catering (17.7 per cent), light machinery (4.9 per cent), banking (4.9 per cent), construction (3.2 per cent), raw material processing (3.0 per cent) and others (10.7 per cent).

The Tourism Law of Mongolia was enacted on May 5, 2000 for the first time since Mongolia shifted to the market oriented economy. Its purpose is to regulate all relationships raised between state, private citizens and economic entities engaged in tourism business. In the 2000-2005 period, FDI flows into the tourism sector increased to US $ 5.6 million. Today, FDI in the tourism sector comprises around 1.1 percent of total FDI and 10 percent of the country`s GDP. Currently over 250 travel companies invested by 32 countries. Korea ranks top with 82 companies followed by Korea (82), Japan (31), China (63), USA (13), Russia (17), USA (13) UK (6) and Germany (5).[30]

There has been considerable increase in the number of companies investing in Mongolia, going up from merely two by the end of 1990 to three hundred in 1995. Since 1996, the number of foreign enterprises in Mongolia has skyrocketed to 1803 in 2001. The Foreign Investment and Foreign Trade Agency announced the list of top invested companies in Mongolia for the second time. Companies are listed according to their business success. Top 20 invested companies in Mongolia include:[31] 1. Oil: SOCO Tamsag (USA); 2. Mining: Ivanhoe Mines Ltd., (Canada); 3. Trade and Services: Monhua Qiang (China); 4. Telecommunication Network: Mobicom (Japan); 5. Mining: Boroo Gold (Offshore); 6. Cashmere: Buyan Holding (Japan); 7. Banking: Chinggis Khaan Bank (Offshore); 8. Cashmere & Camel Wool: Mongol-Amicale (USA); 9. Mining: Tumurtei Huder (China); 10. Mining: Zolotoi Vostok (Russia); 11. Textile: Mongol Hung Hua (Hong Kong); 12. Mining GL-Monpolimet (USA); 13. Cashmere: Gobital (Italy); 14. Construction: Zuilun (China); 15. Construction: Huanchan (China); 16. Banking: "Menatep—Sankt Peterburg"; 17. Textile: Temujin Mench (Hong Kong); 18. Oil: Rock Oil (USA, China); 19. Banking: Trade & Development Bank (Luxemburg); and 20. Trade and Services: 4x4 Parts Mongolia (Australia).

List of the major foreign direct investment with company name, nation of origin, sectors, and estimated value in US$ in

Mongolia is presented in Table 5.

Table 5. List of the Major Foreign Direct Investments in Mongolia: Value in US$

Company	Nation of Origin	Sector	Estimated FDI
Ivanhoe Mines Mongolia	Canada	Mining	100,000,000 +
SOCO Tamsag	USA	Petroleum	90,000,000 +
Boroo Gold	Canada	Mining	70,000,000 +
Trade and Development Bank	USA/ Switzerland	Banking and Finance	25,000,000 +
Marubeni	Japan	Cashmere Production	20,000,000 +
Wagner Asia Mongolia	USA	Equipment/CAT, Ford, Ingersoll-Rand	12,000,000 +
Dongsheng Petroleum	China	Petroleum	n/a
Komatsu	Japan	Equipment	n/a
MobiCom	Japan/ Mongolian	Telecommunications	n/a
Itochu	Japan	Equipment	n/a
Siemans	Germany	ICT	n/a
Sugura Mongolia	Japan	Construction	n/a
Seoul Company	Korea	Construction/Hospitality	n/a
United Apparel	Fiji	Apparel	n/a
Coca Cola Mongolia	US/Mongolia	Bottler	8,000,000 +
MSM Co.	US/Mongol/ German	Fast Moving Consumer Goods, Tools and Equipment, Daimler-Chrysler	5,000,000 +
Anglo-American Gold Mongolia	South Africa	Mining	n/a
CVRD	Brazil	Mining	n/a

Source: The Foreign Investment and Foreign Trade Agency, Government of Mongolia.

In 2007, the Government of India offered its expertise in the field of healthcare and education and agreed to implement "Tele-education and Tele-medicine Project" with the Ministry of Health and ICTA with an investment of US$ 3 million for a period of three years. Under the frame work of cooperation with the Government of India, the above mentioned projects are being implemented. Mongolian Government is adhering to a policy in order to strengthen cooperation between the both countries even further in ITC sector.[32]

The Foreign Investment Law of Mongolia (FILM) has transformed the anti-business environment of Soviet era into today's investor-friendly regime. Under the old system everything not provided for in law was illegal. Because such economic activities as franchising, leasing, joint venture companies were not mentioned in earlier Mongolian statutes, they were technically illegal. In 1993 the government enacted FILM to legalize all manners of foreign investment in Mongolia (amended in 2002 to allow for representative offices and franchises). This law defines broad ranges of activity that would otherwise have no validity under Mongolian law. It also defines the meaning of foreign investment under the civil code without limiting activities that foreign investors can conduct. The definition is largely for tax incentives, as only foreign investments over 10,000 USD qualify for tax breaks under the law. FILM also establishes registration procedures for foreign companies. It creates a supervisory agency, the Foreign Investment and Foreign Trade Agency (FIFTA), to run the registration process, liaise between businesses and the Mongolian government, and promote in- and out-bound investments. Now, FIFTA a reasonably fair and efficient agency in promoting FDI in Mongolia and providing investor-friendly environment for investors.

III. INTRA-INDUSTY TRADE (IIT) BETWEEN INDIA AND MONGOLIA

The intra-industry trade (IIT) index reflects the extent of both export-orientation (EO) and import penetration (IP) within the given sector (or products). A high value indicates that there is both export and import trade within the sector (or products). A low level indicates that trade is mainly one way, i.e. the industry sector is either export oriented or mainly import focused. A value for IIT is indicative of the growing tendency of firms, or branches of multinational firms, to specialize in particular products within an industrial sector, possibly due to economies of scale, product differentiation or geographic product specialization. This results in growth in trade which can occur even when factors of production are similar between the countries, i.e., when conditions would normally result in low levels of trade.

The intra-industry trade index is defined as the proportion of total trade remaining after subtracting the absolute value of net exports or net imports. If exports and imports are equal then the IIT index is 100, i.e. whatever the level of trade it flows in both directions in about equal amounts. The index gets smaller if the net difference between imports and exports makes up a larger proportion of total trade, i.e. either as the net difference between imports and exports increases indicating a larger trade in one direction, or this net difference makes up a larger proportion of the total trade indicating that trade is only in one direction. In either case the trade is increasingly one-directional.

It is generally believed that greater the level of intra-industry trade within a region, the more attractive is the prospect for effective intra-regional cooperation. The level (between 0 and 100) of the IIT indices and the trend in IIT over time in terms of these values provides a measure of the degree and changes in complementarity in production between two countries or region. The higher the index level, the greater is the complementarity and extent of IIT.

To increase the economic relations between India and Mongolia it would require alliances and cooperation scheme at production and marketing levels among the companies of both countries. One way to approach the current state of entrepreneurial relations is through the analysis of IIT between India and Mongolia.

One measure of the level of IIT was proposed by Balassa in 1996 but the most widely used measure is the *Grubel-Lloyd* index. The problem with the Grublel-Lloyd index is associated with biases created by trade imbalances at the multilateral level (Grubel and Lloyd 1975).[33] Some economists have attempted to correct this, but a widely acceptable method of correction has yet to be found. As argued by Helpman (1987),[34] attempts to modify the Grubel-Lloyd index to correct for trade imbalance bias are inappropriate since the nature of bias is not known. In particular, we do not know whether the imbalance is caused by homogeneous or differentiated products and whether the trade structure is in equilibrium or not. This explains why in general, bilateral IIT is more interesting than overall IIT.

IIT creates closer links between two countries by providing more positive gains to each other. This is valid in the context of reform and internationalisation of manufacturing activities, which enhance assembly production from imported parts and components in different countries.[35] Under these circumstances, political opposition to such market-driven economic cooperation induced by trade liberalisation will be less disturbing if structural adjustment takes the form of intra-industry rather than inter-industry characteristics.[36] Thus, the prospects for closer economic cooperation can be examined by analysing the nature of IIT within the concerned group of countries.

It is hypothesised that the greater the level of IIT within a region, the more attractive is the prospects for effective bilateral cooperation. Examining this proposition necessitates the estimation of Grubel-Lloyd IIT index. The following methods are used for the estimation of IIT:

Global IIT in commodity ***k*** for country ***i*** at aggregate level:

$$\mathbf{IIT}_{iwk} = [(X_{iwk}+M_{iwk})-|X_{iwk}-M_{iwk}| \,/\, (X_{iwk}+M_{iwk})] * 100$$

Where **X*iwk*** denotes country ***i***'s global export of commodity ***k*** and **M*iwk*** denotes country ***i***'s global import of commodity ***k***. This index of IIT measures the amount of total trade within a commodity. Usually it will be calculated for all or a group of commodities at 3-Digit SITC level.

Bilateral IIT in commodity ***k*** of country ***i*** with country ***j*** at aggregate level:

$$\mathbf{IIT}_{ijk} = [\, \Sigma(X_{ijk}+M_{ijk})- \Sigma\, |X_{ijk}-M_{ijk}| \,/\, \Sigma\, (X_{ijk}+M_{ijk})] * 100$$

This index of IIT measure gives the amount of total trade within an industry (commodity group). It is calculated by partner and ***summed*** (or aggregated of low segment products) over all 8-

digit commodities at the 2 and 4-Digit level. But here, we only present the global IIT at 6-digit for India and Mongolia to examine the potential products which both countries have specialization. This Index of IIT also gives the amount of trade within a product in both countries.

Table 6 presents the Intra-Industry index value between India's exports to the world and Mongolia's imports from the world in two points of time, 2000 and 2005 at the 6-digit HS Classification.[37] This exercise will identify the industries where potential for investment exists. It may be observed that the firms involved in these industries, may benefit from joint ventures with firms that are major importer (Mongolia) of the particular products. Further it can be extended to foreign direct investment promotion between India and Mongolia.

The nature of India's IIT with Mongolia at global level in 6-digit HS classification points the possibility of India's setting up joint ventures in Mongolia in those products or sectors having higher IIT index value are presented in this Table 6 which is self explanatory.

Table 6. Intra-Industry Index Value of Top 50 Products between India's Exports to World and Mongolia's Imports from World (2005): (Value in US$ Thousand)

Top Major Products Shorted out on the basis of IIT Index Value

HS-6 Digit	Product Description	India's Export to World	Mongolia's Import from World	Total Trade	IIT Index Value
844312	Sheet fed, office type (sheet size not exc-22x36 cm	82	81	163	99.387
790112	Zinc not alloyed unwrought containg by weight less	61	62	123	99.187
842121	Filtering or purifying machinery and apparatus for	5085	5175	10260	99.123
960610	Press-fasteners, snap-fasteners and press-studs an	163	159	322	98.758
511190	Woven fabrics of carded wool/fine animal hair,>/=	1054	1083	2137	98.643
252220	Slaked lime	60	62	122	98.361

281121	Carbon dioxide	160	166	326	98.160
830150	Clasps and frames with clasps, incorporating locks	48	50	98	97.959
210390	Sauces and preparations nes and mixed condiments	1739	1664	3403	97.796
842220	Machinery for cleaning or drying bottles or contai	908	959	1867	97.268
560129	Waddg of oth textile materials & articles thereof/	131	124	255	97.255
283711	Cyanides and cyanide oxides of sodium	742	700	1442	97.087
200520	Potatoes prepard or preserved, o/t by vinegar or ac	137	129	266	96.992
870590	Special purpose motor vehicles nes	2291	2157	4448	96.987
220900	Vinegar and substitutes for vinegar obtained from	158	171	329	96.049
842930	Scrapers, self-propelled	47	51	98	95.918
200950	Tomato juice unfermented & not spirited, whether	53	58	111	95.495
820719	Rock drilling/earth boring tools, nes, parts	413	374	787	95.044
853080	Electrical signalling, safety or traffic control	142	128	270	94.815
290110	Saturated acyclic hydrocarbons	102	91	193	94.301
520839	Woven fabrics of cotton, >/=85%, not more than 200	7678	6791	14469	93.870
732611	Balls,grindg&similar articles of i or s,forged or	7972	7050	15022	93.862
180690	Chocolate and other food preparations containing c	3070	2710	5780	93.772
481420	Wallpaper,coatd/coverd on the face side w a decora	82	72	154	93.506
290519	Saturated monohydric acyclic alcohols nes	620	716	1336	92.814
851721	Facsimiles machines	58	67	125	92.800
854459	Electric conductors, for a voltage >80V but not ex	3002	2596	5598	92.747
080711	Watermelons, fresh	432	500	932	92.704
846591	Sawing machines for working wood/cork/ bone/hard	191	164	355	92.394
392210	Baths, shower-baths and wash basins, of plastics	203	173	376	92.021

850820	Saws, hand-held, with self-contained electric moto	63	53	116	91.379
630900	Worn clothing and other worn articles	4837	4060	8897	91.267
080810	Apples, fresh	2832	3422	6254	90.566
841382	Liquid elevators	252	208	460	90.435
841830	Freezers of the chest type, not exceeding 800 l ca	502	414	916	90.393
560122	Wadding of man-made fibres and articles thereof	26	32	58	89.655
470610	Cotton linters pulp	64	52	116	89.655
847420	Crushing/grindg machines for earth/ stone/ores	5168	4144	9312	89.003
720291	Ferro-titanium and ferro-silico-titanium	28	35	63	88.889
680800	Panels,board etc of veg fib,straw etc agglomeratd	31	39	70	88.571
850790	Parts of electric accumulators, including separato	2627	3330	5957	88.199
200710	Homo prep (jams,fruit jellies etc) ckd prep whethe	306	240	546	87.912
840820	Engines, diesel, for the vehicles of Chapter 87	1925	1506	3431	87.788
640291	Footwear,outer soles/uppers of rubber or plastics,	159	124	283	87.633
151329	Palm kernel/babassu oil their fract,refind but not	60	46	106	86.792
852540	Still image and other video cameras	216	165	381	86.614
481820	Handkerchiefs, cleansing or facial tissues and tow	61	80	141	86.525
902580	Hydrometers, pyrometers, hygrometers & psychro-meters	319	241	560	86.071
731449	Grill, netting, fencing, iron or steel, nes	118	157	275	85.818
842833	Cont-action elevators/ conveyors for goods/mat, bel	112	150	262	85.496

Source: Estimated by Author from PC-TAS Database.

Table 7 presents the IIT index value between Mongolia's export to world and India's import from the world for the years 2000 and 2005. Similar computation has been done for

Mongolia's exports to the world and India's imports from the world at global level in 6-digit HS classification which points the possibility of Mongolia's setting up joint ventures in India in those products or sectors having higher IIT index value are presented in this **Table 7** which is self explanatory.

Table 7. Intra-Industry Index Value of Top 50 Products between Mongolia's Exports to World and India's Imports from World (2005): (Value in US$ Thousand)
Top Major Products Shorted out on the basis of IIT Index Value

HS-6 Digit	Product Description	Mongolia's Export to World	India's Import from World	Total Trade	IIT Index Value
551419	Woven fabrics of oth syn staple fib,<85%,mixed w/c	815	812	1627	99.816
071230	Mushrooms and truffles dried but not further prepa	103	104	207	99.517
610333	Mens/boys jackets and blazers, of synthetic fibres	71	82	153	92.810
620452	Womens/girls skirts, of cotton, not knitted	530	451	981	91.947
610432	Womens/girls jackets, of cotton, knitted	85	71	156	91.026
261100	Tungsten ores and concentrates	358	432	790	90.633
610819	Womens/girls slips and petticoats, of other textil	54	72	126	85.714
620331	Mens/boys jackets and blazers,of wool or fine anim	139	194	333	83.483
620432	Womens/girls jackets, of cotton, not knitted	460	325	785	82.803
060499	Foliage,branch,etc w/o flowers/ buds&grass for bouq	48	70	118	81.356
510121	Degreased shorn wool, not carded, combed or carbon	4655	6829	11484	81.069

620343	Mens/boys trousers and shorts, of synthetic fibres	1773	1123	2896	77.555
510130	Carbonised wool, not carded or combed	578	361	939	76.890
610520	Mens/boys shirts, of man-made fibres, knitted	265	159	424	75.000
620342	Mens/boys trousers and shorts, of cotton, not knit	2680	4643	7323	73.194
610343	Mens/boys trousers and shorts, of synthetic fibres	95	168	263	72.243
441900	Tableware and kitchenware, of wood	734	410	1144	71.678
620821	Womens/girls nightdresses and pyjamas, of cotton,	205	107	312	68.590
620469	Womens/girls trousers & shorts,of other textile ma	963	496	1459	67.992
620719	Mens/boys under-pants and briefs,of other textile m	133	64	197	64.975
410512	Sheep or lamb skin leather, otherwise pre-tanned	16398	36215	52613	62.334
570110	Carpets of wool or fine animal hair, knotted	1057	464	1521	61.012
620443	Womens/girls dresses, of synthetic fibres, not kni	49	115	164	59.756
510820	Yarn of combed fine animal hair, not put up for re	230	552	782	58.824
611710	Shawls, scarves, veils and the like, of textile ma	392	948	1340	58.507
620520	Mens/boys shirts, of cotton, not knitted	8600	3396	11996	56.619
261390	Molybdenum ores and concentrates nes	46677	18214	64891	56.137

620630	Womens/girls blouses and shirts, of cotton, not kn	288	743	1031	55.868
610463	Womens/girls trousers and shorts, of synthetic fib	59	155	214	55.140
170219	Lactose and lactose syrup, <99% lactose on dry mat	763	2087	2850	53.544
610620	Womens/girls blouses and shirts, of man-made fibre	891	321	1212	52.970
620311	Mens/boys suits, of wool or fine animal hair, not	329	936	1265	52.016
620442	Womens/girls dresses, of cotton, not knitted	185	65	250	52.000
620312	Mens/boys suits, of synthetic fibres, not knitted	117	41	158	51.899
230230	Wheat bran, sharps and other residues, pelleted or	223	651	874	51.030
260800	Zinc ores and concentrates	10219	30162	40381	50.613
620422	Womens/girls ensembles, of cotton, not knitted	200	65	265	49.057
510320	Waste (other than noils) of wool/of fine animal ha	565	1847	2412	46.849
620711	Mens/boys underpants and briefs, of cotton, not kn	18	62	80	45.000
410110	Bovine skins, whole, raw	4022	14348	18370	43.789
740311	Copper cathodes and sections of cathodes unwrought	8057	28811	36868	43.707
260300	Copper ores and concentrates	326217	1178812	1505029	43.350
610910	T-shirts, singlets and other vests, of cotton, kni	8907	2445	11352	43.076

610711	Mens/boys under-pants and briefs, of cotton, knitte	64	240	304	42.105
010600	Animals, live nes	1656	438	2094	41.834
610510	Mens/boys shirts, of cotton, knitted	3628	958	4586	41.779
252910	Felspar	161	625	786	40.967
250100	Salt (includg table salt&denaturd salt) pure sodiu	147	581	728	40.385
050790	Whalebone,horns,etc unworkd or simply prepard,unsh	239	60	299	40.134
620319	Mens/boys suits, of other textile materials, not k	1152	288	1440	40.000

Source: Estimated by Author from PC-TAS Database.

There are 225 matched products (at 6 Digit HS Category) in India's exports basket and Mongolia's Import basket having more than 50 IIT index value and 975 products with range of 1 to less than 50 IIT index value. Therefore, India has potential to establish trade generating joint ventures in all these identified products (having high IIT Index Values) with Mongolia and scope for IIT specialization in several products. Thus, India and Mongolia *(vice-versa)* could set up a ***joint marketing strategy*** in those matched products which have the ***potential of joint ventures*** which intern, enhance the India-Mongolia trade. The products negotiated for fast track liberalization and concessions under preferential trade should relate to high potential/intra-industry trade.

There are a number of industries or products where potential for investment exists between both countries. It may be observed that the firms involved in these industries, may benefit from joint ventures with firms in that are major importers of the particular products countries. Further it can be extended to foreign direct investment promotion between both countries. Mongolia has performed superbly in terms of attracting FDI, and has great potential to do even better in the future. According to a UNCTAD Survey, Mongolia moved to the "high potential FDI category" in 1999-2001, having been in the lowest FDI potential and performance category from 1993 to 1995.

Investment Linkages and Promotion of Foreign Direct Investment

It is well known fact that the extent of low level of bilateral trade between India and Mongolia is constrained by the limited export capabilities. In this context importance needs to be assigned to promote bilateral investment flows between both countries. For this reason, the flow of intra-industry trade of India and Mongolia provides some direction for investment flows. This is because India, instead of exporting and importing the same products (at 6-digit) from Mongolia could choose to invest in Mongolia to manufacture such a product for either for domestic market, or for export to third countries or to further buyback the same in the investing countries. In the latter case this would also contribute to better balancing bilateral trade between India and Mongolia. Such a decision to invest in partner country also depends on the investment climate prevailing in that country.

The trade data of bilateral export and import at product level is very less, that's why an attempt has been made here to consider the matched products of India's exports to the world and Mongolia's import from the world in the same products and *vice-versa* to compute intra-industry trade (IIT) in this matched product. There are large number of products which are matched in India's exports to world and Mongolia's imports from the world. Top 50 products have been presented in Table 6 and 7 in the previous section. All those products having higher degree of index value may be considered for promoting investment and setting up joint venture between India and Mongolia. These products should also be identified as potential products and could similarly be put under fast track liberalization by India and Mongolia. It is also desirable for both countries to start moving towards concluding India-Mongolia Free Trade Agreement (IM-FTA).

Since the transition to free market economy starting in 1990 about 2,300 business entities representing 70 countries and with more than US$ 800 million of paid-in capital were created. About one third of them are operating in mining industry and 20 percent in the light industry. Such increase in investment helps to accelerate economic growth, to develop export industry, to introduce new equipment and technology, to strengthen human resource capacity and thus to increase competitiveness of Mongolian goods and products. Several measures were taken during the last two years in order to attract and encourage foreign investment, to create favorable environment as well as to sustain macroeconomic stability Technological equipment and machinery imported by foreign investors who will run export oriented production are relieved from import and custom duties. Also the Law on Foreign Investment was amended in 2002 by creating legal grounds for business entities with foreign investment to conclude sustainability agreements.

The strategy to increase foreign investment in the longer term is aimed at accelerating economic growth and its capacity increasing income of the population and speeding up the development of the country. In the near future the focus is being put on creating an environment that will help in increasing foreign investment. Measures are being taken to prepare skilled workers with technical knowledge who will be able to work at the business entities with foreign investment. Through simplifying licensing system with respect to different products and services related to foreign investment, support is being rendered to both export industry and business owners in rural areas. Foreign direct investment is thus being attracted effectively to all areas of processing and services, however, investment in the mining sector is the priority. The FDI support is one of ways to improve living standards through creation of new work places, increase of the citizen's income and thus will contribute to reduction of poverty. The Government of Mongolia particularly encourages foreign investment in mining, agriculture, infrastructure, tourism, banking and financing, information, communication technology and construction.[38]

IV. Trade Complementarities Between India And Mongolia

It is observed that two countries would have potential trade cooperation if they have extensive trade complementarities.[39] One of the simplest ways of measuring the degree of complementarity between two countries is to examine the extent of similarity or dissimilarity in their export and import structures. If the export structure of one country has high degree of similarity with the import structure of the other country and vice-versa, then one can infer that there is potential complementarity for trade between the two countries.

One measure or index designed to estimate complementarity of trade between pairs of countries is known as *"COSINE measure"* (COS) of trade complementarity developed by Linnemann[40] (1966). The COSINE index is a measure that reflects the intensity of bilateral trade between pairs of countries. In other words, it gives an idea of the extent to which the export structure of one country matches with the import structure of another and vice-versa. The formula of index is:

Cosine Measure of Trade Complementarity[41]

Cosine Measure of Trade Complementarity between Exports of Country i with imports of country j:

$$Cos\ Xi\ and\ Mj = \Sigma_k X_{ik} * M_{jk} / \sqrt{}\ (X_{ik}2 * M_{jk}2)$$

Where E is exports, M imports, subscripts j, k exporting country, importing country and commodity and I class respectively.

Cosine Measure of Trade Complementarity between Exports of Country j with imports of country i:

$$Cos\ Xj\ and\ Mi = \Sigma_k X_{jk} * M_{ik} / \sqrt{}\ (X_{jk}2 * M_{ik}2)$$

Where E is exports, M imports, subscripts j, i, and k are exporting country, importing country and commodity class respectively. The value of the measure lies between 0 and 1.[42] In the absence of any complementarity and in the presence of perfect complementarity, the measure takes the extreme value of zero and one. The movement from 0 to 1 is an indication of the increasing trade complementarity between the two countries. The cosine measure could also be considered as an indicator of the extent of competitiveness between the two countries. Lower value of the cosine measure would indicate that the two countries have potential competitiveness rather than potential complementarity.

Overall Product Complementarities between India and Mongolia

In this section, India's trade complementarities with Mongolia, with India as a supplier (exporter) and Mongolia as a market (importer) and *vice-versa* for the period 2000 and 2005 taking all products at 6-digit classification under the harmonized system (HS) is analysed. The results of computation are summarized in **Table 8** and **Table 9** and these tables are self-explanatory. The results show that the number of matched products between India as a supplier and Mongolia as a market are higher as compared to Mongolia as supplier and India as a market. Total number of matched products between India as a supplier and Mongolia as a market was 1270 in 2000 which increased to 1504 in 2005 while the number of matched products in case of Mongolia as supplier and India as a market was 163 in 2000 which increased to 185 in 2005.

Table 8. Overall Trade Complementarity Index Value between India and Mongolia

	2000	2003	2005
India's Exports and Mongolia's Imports	0.1614	0.1107	0.0309
India's Imports and Mongolia's Exports	0.8307	0.7845	0.7136

Source: Estimated from PC-TAS Database.

The degree of trade complementarities (index value) is moderate in India as a supplier and Mongolia as a market and poor in Mongolia as supplier and India as a market. The index value of trade complementarities in India as a supplier and Mongolia as a market was 0.1614 in 2000 which decreased to 0.0309 in 2005. Reversing the trade complementarities between Mongolia as supplier and India as a market, the degree of trade complementarities was moderate with value of 0.8307 in 2000 and 0.7136 in 2005. Generally products are offered concessions at 6-digit HS classification. In this context, it will be useful to identify those products that have good or moderate trade complementarities at the product level.

Table 9. Number of Matched Products between India and Mongolia's Global Trade

	2000	2003	2005
India's Exports and Mongolia's Imports	1270	1459	1504
India's Imports and Mongolia's Exports	163	339	185

Source: Estimated from PC-TAS Database.

Though the overall trade complementarities is high between India's imports and Mongolia's exports while low trade complementarities exist between India's exports and Mongolia's imports but there are large number of products demonstrating high or moderate trade complementarity at 2-digit HS sectoral/ products level between both countries.[43] The results of top 10 Products (at 2-digit HS Classification) having high or moderate trade complementarities between India's Exports and Mongolia's Imports (and vice-versa) are presented below and detailed in **Tables 10** and **11**.

Sectoral Trade Complementarities between Mongolia's Exports and India's Imports

At the sectoral level, 6-digit HS products under each chapters (2-digit HS) are grouped and then work out their trade complementarities. This is to find out whether India's trading partner Mongolia has good or moderate complementarity at the sectoral level independently of such complementarity at the product level and *vice-versa*. India's export-import complementarity (2005) ranked in terms of top value and defined in terms of chapters (HS-2 digit) with Mongolia include: (i). 03-

Fish & Crustaceans (0.998); (ii) 64-Footwear, Gaiters, & The Like (0.995); (iii) 26-Ores Slag & Ash (0.992); (iv) 71-Pearls, Stones, Prec. Metals, Imitation Jewelry, (0.990); (v) 40-Rubbers & Articles Thereof (0.897); (vi) 73-aticles of Iron or Steel (0.859); (vii) 78-Lead & Articles Thereof (0.725); (viii) 84-Nuclear Reactors, Boilers, Machinery & Mechanical (0.657); (ix) 62-Articles of Apparel & Clothing Accessories-Not Kni (0.653) and (x) 94-Furniture, Bedding, Cushions, Lamps & Lighting Fit (0.619). Comprehensive list of products at the 2-digit products are presented in **Table 10.**

Table 10. Trade Complementarities Index Value between India's Exports and Mongolia's Import (2000 and 2005)

HS-2 Digit	Chapter & Description	2000	2005
	All Commodities:	*0.714*	*0.831*
02	Meat & Edible Meat Offal	1.000	1.000
04	Dairy, Eggs, Honey, & Ed. Products	0.711	0.665
05	Products of Animal Origin	1.000	1.000
07	Edible Vegetables	0.284	0.229
08	Ed. Fruits & Nuts, Peel of Citrus/Melons	0.068	0.154
09	Coffee, Tea, Mate & Spices	0.273	0.596
10	Cereals	0.428	0.792
11	Milling Industry Products	1.000	0.997
12	Oil Seeds/Misc. Grains/Med. Plants/Straw	0.027	0.037
15	Animal or Vegetable Fats, Oils & Waxes	0.213	0.960
17	Sugars & Sugar Confectionery	0.066	0.646
18	Cocoa & Cocoa Preparations	0.476	0.768
19	Preps. of Cereals, Flour, Starch or Milk	0.330	0.642
20	Preps of Vegs, Fruits, Nuts, Etc.	0.316	0.725
21	Misc. Edible Preparations	0.060	0.289
22	Beverages, Spirits & Vinegar	0.431	0.510
23	Residues From Food Industries, Animal Feed	1.000	0.649
24	Tobacco & Manuf. Tobacco Substitutes	0.155	0.438
25	Salt, Sulphur, Earth & Stone, Lime & Cement	0.266	0.556

26	Ores Slag & Ash	n/a	1.000
27	Mineral Fuels, Oils, Waxes & Bituminous Sub	0.999	1.000
28	Inorganic Chem, Org/Inorg Compounds of Precious Me	0.053	0.048
29	Organic Chemicals	0.233	0.109
30	Pharmaceutical Products	0.914	0.970
31	Fertilizers	1.000	0.250
32	Tanning or Dyeing Extracts, Dyes, Pigments, Paints	0.204	0.200
33	Oils & Resinoids, Perfumery, Cosmetic or Toilet Pr	0.672	0.656
34	Soaps, Waxes, Scouring Products, Candles, Modeling	0.600	0.581
35	Albuminoidal Sub, Starches, Glues, Enzymes	0.441	0.733
36	Explosives, Matches, Pyrotechnic Products	0.498	0.649
37	Photographic or Cinematographic Goods	0.818	0.452
38	Miscellaneous Chemical Products	0.033	0.301
39	Plastics & Articles Thereof	0.342	0.385
40	Rubbers & Articles Thereof	0.714	0.885
42	Articles of Leather, Saddlery & Harness, Travel Go	0.234	0.676
44	Wood & Articles of Wood, Wood Charcoal	0.488	0.322
47	Pulp of Wood, Waste & Scrap of Paper	n/a	1.000
48	Paper & Paperboard, Articles of Paper Pulp	0.473	0.379
49	Printed Books, Newspapers, Pictures, Manuscripts,	0.158	0.026
50	Silk, Inc. Yarns & Woven Fabrics Thereof	n/a	1.000
51	Wool & Fine or Coarse Animal Hair, Inc. Yarns & Wo	0.034	0.171
52	Cotton, Inc. Yarns & Woven Fabrics Thereof	0.040	0.096
53	Veg. Textile Fibers Nesoi, Yarns & Woven Etc.	0.686	0.818
54	Man-Made Filaments, Inc. Yarns & Woven Etc.	0.818	0.852
55	Man-Made Staple Fibers, Inc. Yarns Etc.	0.823	0.908

56	Wadding, Felt & Nonwovens, Special Yarns, Twine, C	0.158	0.173
57	Carpets & Other Textile Floor Coverings	0.209	0.414
58	Special Woven Fabrics, Tufted Textiles, Lace	0.597	0.174
59	Impregnated, Coated, Covered, or Laminated Textile	0.836	0.764
60	Knitted or Crocheted Fabrics	0.148	0.032
61	Articles of Apparel & Clothing Accessories-Knitted	0.004	0.599
62	Articles of Apparel & Clothing Accessories-Not Kni	0.017	0.478
63	Made-Up Textile Articles Nesoi, Needlecraft Sets,	0.020	0.028
64	Footwear, Gaiters, & The Like	0.282	0.435
65	Headgear & Other Parts	1.000	1.000
68	Articles of Stone, Plaster, Cement, Asbestos, Mica	0.011	0.081
69	Ceramic Products	0.629	0.715
70	Glass & Glassware	0.224	0.876
71	Pearls, Stones, Prec. Metals, Imitation Jewelry, C	1.000	0.988
72	Iron & Steel	0.242	0.258
73	Rticles of Iron or Steel	0.064	0.212
74	Copper & Articles Thereof	0.999	0.682
75	Nickel & Articles Thereof	1.000	0.951
76	Aluminum & Articles Thereof	0.166	0.297
78	Lead & Articles Thereof	n/a	1.000
79	Zinc & Articles Thereof	1.000	0.453
82	Tools, Spoons & Forks of Base Metal	0.648	0.444
83	Miscellaneous Articles of Base Metal	0.862	0.442
84	Nuclear Reactors, Boilers, Machinery & Mechanical	0.157	0.218
85	Electrical Machinery & Equip. & Parts, Telecommuni	0.091	0.263
86	Railway or Tramway Locomotives, Rolling Stock, Tra	0.663	0.303
87	Vehicles Other Than Railway or Tramway Rolling Sto	0.208	0.315
88	Aircraft, Spacecraft, & Parts Thereof	1.000	0.997

90	Optical, Photographic, Cinematographic, Measuring,	0.473	0.354
91	Clocks & Watches & Parts Thereof	0.050	0.957
92	Musical Instruments, Parts & Accessories	n/a	1.000
93	Arms & Ammunition, Parts & Accessories	0.997	0.999
94	Furniture, Bedding, Cushions, Lamps & Lighting Fit	0.785	0.631
95	Toys, Games & Sports Equip, Parts & Acces.	0.865	0.491
96	Miscellaneous Manufactured Articles	0.135	0.087

Source: Estimated by Author from PC-TAS Database.

Sectoral Trade Complementarities between India's Imports and Mongolia's Exports

Comprehensive list of products at the 2-digit products of trade complementarity between India's imports and Mongolia's exports for 2000 and 2005 are presented in **Table 11.** Mongolia's export-import complementarity (2005) ranked in terms of top value and defined in terms of chapters (HS-2 digit) with India include: (i) 93-Arms & Ammunition, Parts & Accessories (0.999); (ii) 11-Milling Industry Products (0.997); (iii) 88-Aircraft, Spacecraft, & Parts Thereof (0.997); (iv) 71-Pearls, Stones, Prec. Metals, Imitation Jewelry (0.988); (v) 30-Pharmaceutical Products (0.970); (vi) 15-Animal or Vegetable Fats, Oils & Waxes (0.960); (vii) 91-Clocks & Watches & Parts Thereof (0.957); (viii) 75-Nickel & Articles Thereof (0.951); (ix) 55-Man-Made Staple Fibers, Inc. Yarns Etc. (0.908); and (x) 40-Rubbers & Articles thereof (0.885).

Table 11. Trade Complementarities Index Value between India's Imports and Mongolia's Exports (2000 and 2005)

HS-2 Digit	Chapter & Description	2000	2005
	All Commodities:	*0.031*	*0.161*
01	Live Animals	n/a	1.000
03	Fish & Crustaceans	0.990	0.998
05	Products of Animal Origin	0.349	0.589
06	Live Trees & Other Plants	n/a	1.000
07	Edible Vegetables	n/a	1.000

08	Ed. Fruits & Nuts, Peel of Citrus/Melons	1.000	1.000
12	Oil Seeds/Misc. Grains/Med. Plants/Straw	1.000	1.000.
17	Sugars & Sugar Confectionery	n/a	1.000
22	Beverages, Spirits & Vinegar	1.000	1.000
23	Residues From Food Industries, Animal Feed	1.000	1.000
24	Tobacco & Manuf. Tobacco Substitutes	1.000	1.000
25	Salt, Sulphur, Earth & Stone, Lime & Cement	0.014	0.234
26	Ores Slag & Ash	1.000	0.992
27	Mineral Fuels, Oils, Waxes & Bituminous Sub	0.988	0.419
28	Inorganic Chem, Org/Inorg Compounds of Precious Me	1.000	n/a
30	Pharmaceutical Products	1.000	1.000
38	Miscellaneous Chemical Products	n/a	n/a
39	Plastics & Articles Thereof	1.000	1.000
40	Rubbers & Articles Thereof	n/a	0.897
41	Raw Hides & Skins & Leather	0.318	0.412
42	Articles of Leather, Saddlery & Harness, Travel Go	n/a	1.000
43	Furskins & Artificial Fur, Manufactures	0.096	0.450
44	Wood & Articles of Wood, Wood Charcoal	0.712	0.176
47	Pulp of Wood, Waste & Scrap of Paper	n/a	0.578
49	Printed Books, Newspapers, Pictures, Manuscripts,	1.000	1.000
51	Wool & Fine or Coarse Animal Hair, Inc. Yarns & Wo	0.034	0.024
52	Cotton, Inc. Yarns & Woven Fabrics Thereof	n/a	1.000
55	Man-Made Staple Fibers, Inc. Yarns etc.	n/a	1.000
56	Wadding, Felt & Nonwovens, Special Yarns, Twine, C	n/a	1.000
57	Carpets & Other Textile Floor Coverings	0.963	0.408
60	Knitted or Crocheted Fabrics	n/a	1.000
61	Articles of Apparel & Clothing Accessories-Knitted	0.079	0.557
62	Articles of Apparel & Clothing Accessories-Not Kni	0.499	0.653
63	Made-Up Textile Articles Nesoi, Needlecraft Sets,	1.000	1.000
64	Footwear, Gaiters, & The Like	n/a	0.995

68	Articles of Stone, Plaster, Cement, Asbestos, Mica	0.847	n/a
71	Pearls, Stones, Prec. Metals, Imitation Jewelry, C	0.998	0.990
72	Iron & Steel	0.166	0.125
73	Rticles of Iron or Steel	0.956	0.859
74	Copper & Articles Thereof	0.438	0.102
76	Aluminum & Articles Thereof	0.995	1.000
78	Lead & Articles Thereof	1.000	0.725
79	Zinc & Articles Thereof	n/a	1.000
81	Base Metals Nesoi, Cermets, Articles Etc.	n/a	1.000
84	Nuclear Reactors, Boilers, Machinery & Mechanical	0.527	0.657
85	Electrical Machinery & Equip. & Parts, Telecommuni	0.886	0.140
86	Railway or Tramway Locomotives, Rolling Stock, Tra	n/a	n/a
87	Vehicles Other Than Railway or Tramway Rolling Sto	0.048	0.303
88	Aircraft, Spacecraft, & Parts Thereof	n/a	1.000
89	Ships, Boats, & Floating Structures	n/a	n/a
90	Optical, Photographic, Cinematographic, Measuring,	1.000	n/a
94	Furniture, Bedding, Cushions, Lamps & Lighting Fit	1.000	0.619
95	Toys, Games & Sports Equip, Parts & Acces.	n/a	1.000
97	Works of Art. Collectors' Pieces, Antiques	n/a	1.000

Source: Estimated by Author from PC-TAS Database.

Trade support network in Mongolia is weakly developed and the number of trade support institutions is very limited. The trade promotion services are provided mainly by trade representatives attached at overseas Embassies and the Chamber of Commerce and Industry of Mongolia and Foreign Investment and Foreign Trade Agency. They provide services in few areas, mostly organizing overseas and domestic trade fairs, business missions, seminars, contacts, trainings, registration, documentation, providing with economic, trade and legal information etc. Many important services such as targeted market research, trade intelligence, product design, quality management, trade financing are still missing or under supplied. Current network is not effective enough, due to lack of suitable legal regulations and clear operating guidelines, lack of qualified and skilled human resources, accumulated experiences and fair competitions. Most of the recently formed non-governmental business and product associations are lacking both in trade promotion skills and financial resources and are working mainly for doing business and for their own survival. Establishing more effective trade support network is of vital importance for Mongolia.

As regards economic and trade cooperation between Mongolia and India, both the countries can emerge as significant development partner in the areas, where India excels in technical development and scientific expertise. On its part Mongolia offers great potential for sustainable partnership in the (a) mining of important minerals, cooking coal and natural gas, (b) road development technology, (c) information technology and space and (d) bio-technology. For Indian entrepreneur and business houses, there are great possibilities to take part in Mongolia in various tenders and bids sponsored by World Bank and Asian Development Bank (ADB) and other international organizations. So far the Indian companies have participated in more than 20 tenders and successfully secured 15 projects in different cost range. The President of the Petroleum Authority of Mongolia visited India on January 23, 2002 and signed a MoU with ONGC Videsh Limited. This has given a new opportunity for the Indians to commence new area of cooperation in the exploration of oil in Mongolia. According to this MoU, the two sides will be engaged in petroleum exploration and production.

V. Conclusion: Policy Recommendations

In this section, an attempt has been made to conclude and provide some tentative ideas for policy recommendations based on available data and information related to Mongolia's global and bilateral trade and investment cooperation with India with the help of computed various trade indices. It is observed that the low level of bilateral trade between India and Mongolia is due to the low level of trade intensity which demonstrates that both countries are under-representing in their bilateral trade.

Both countries have signed MoU pertaining to the establishment of a Joint Trade Sub-Committee and Co-operation between the Planning Commission of India and the National Development Board of Mongolia. In September 1996, during the visit of the then Vice-President, K.R. Narayanan to Mongolia, an Agreement on Trade and Economic Cooperation between India and Mongolia was signed. The Agreement provides for most favoured nation (MFN) status to each other in respect of customs duties and all other taxes on imports and exports. During the visit of President Bagabandi in January 2001, both sides signed an Investment Promotion and Protection Agreement. There is an urgent need to follow up these developments and try to put it in practice. If both governments could have taken these developments seriously, the level of economic relations would have been different especially in terms of trade and investment value.

Despite having low level of India-Mongolia trade during 1990 to 2007, the potential is high between both countries to increase the level of trade and investment. Mongolia is keen to develop industrial co-operation with India in textiles, cement, cashmere, leather, IT, pharmaceuticals and other small-scale industries. However considering the size of the market, the response from Indian companies has not been encouraging. The main items of exports to Mongolia include medicines, silk, jute, yarn, dyeing chemicals, etc. Imports from Mongolia include raw wool, hides and skin and fluorspar. Bilateral trade has not developed much due to the problems of trans-shipment through Chinese ports, high freight rates and delayed delivery schedule. There is an urgent need to lower down the tariff rate on import, reduce the freight charges and increase the efficiency in delivery system.

India's trade with Mongolia registered very significant growth during last five financial years (2003-04 to 2007-08) and reached around US$ 16.9 million in 2007-08. India's exports to Mongolia are little lower in terms of value (US$ 7.5 million) as compared to India's imports from Mongolia (US$ 9.30 million) in 2007-08. But it can be improved further if some bottlenecks in trade between both countries are removed. The business is not peaking up between both the countries due to inadequate information about available business opportunities and also lack of direct and regular interaction between the business houses. Though some modest progress has been made in liberalization and privatization but still banking facilities are inadequate. Both countries are also facing language barrier in augmenting the business.

India has comparative advantage in some product and specialization in producing these products. The focus group of product includes (i) plantation crops; (ii) Rmg of various textile material; (iii) drugs & pharmaceuticals; (iv) machinery and instruments; (v) leather and its products; (vi) cotton yarn, fabrics, and other textile items; (vii) agriculture products; (viii) plastic & linoleum products; (ix) cosmetics/toiletries; (x) ayurvedic/herbal products; and (xi) Packaged edibles. In the category of technology and service sector, India has prioritized on the basis of specialization and comparative advantage which include: (i) telecom and information technology; (ii) food processing; (iii) oil and gas sector; (iv) professional services; (v) construction and related engineering services; (vi) educational services; (vii) environmental services; (viii) health related and social services; (ix) tourism and travel related services; (x) recreational, cultural and sporting services; and (xi) other business generating services.

Despite having so much potential and prioritized sector or focus industries in both countries, economic relation is trade and investment oriented. Though trade between India and Mongolia is increasing but it is below the existing potential. India-Mongolia trade and investment even though advancing, are much below their potential. There is large number of products/sectors having high potential to establish trade generating joint ventures (TGJVs) between India and Mongolia. Hence there is need to enhance cooperation at production level and establish joint marketing strategy and network to boost trade and investment cooperation. There is need for synergizing partnership especially at the level of business enterprises for forging trade and investment linkages to realize existing potential between both countries.

India has the potential to establish trade generating joint ventures in all these identified products (having high IIT Index Values) with Mongolia and scope for IIT specialization in several products. Thus, India and Mongolia *(vice-versa)* could set up a *joint production and marketing strategy* in those matched products which have the *potential of joint ventures* which intern, enhance the India-Mongolia trade. The products negotiated for fast track liberalization and concessions under preferential trade should relate to high potential/intra-industry trade.

The degree of trade complementarities (index value) is moderate in India as a supplier and Mongolia as a market and poor in Mongolia as supplier and India as a market. The index value of trade complementarities in India as a supplier and Mongolia as a market was 0.1614 in 2000 which decreased to 0.0309 in 2005. Reversing the trade complementarities between Mongolia as supplier and India as a market, the degree of trade complementarities was moderate with value of 0.8307 in 2000 and 0.7136 in 2005. Generally products are offered concessions at 6-digit HS classification. In this context, it will be useful to identify those products that have good or moderate trade complementarities at the product level. These products can play major role in promoting and enhancing bilateral trade between both the countries.

Some priority areas for tapping the untapped potentials between both countries are: (a) abolish/reduce the existing information gap; (b) reduce the still existing high tariff and non-tariff barriers at least on selected products of export interest to both countries; (c) prevailing logistical infrastructure for serving the needs of the expansion bilateral trade and investment is highly inadequate; (d) business-to-business (B2B) contact between both countries are at low and erratic level; and (e) Mongolia's willingness to join Asia-Pacific Trade Agreement (APTA) will further enhance trade and investment relationship between both countries. Finally, there is a need to develop comprehensive database for comparative analysis.

REFERENCES

1. External trade liberalization which marked a departure from the import substitution strategy began in the mid 1980s, but received a major impetus with the launch of the neoliberal "economic reform" strategy in 1991. Since 1991, India has undertaken a major economic reforms programme i.e. imports liberalization, reduction in tariff rates and removal or relaxation of quantity restrictions on imports. Mongolia restricts the import and export of certain items viz. (a) Uranium and uranium concentrates; (b) Poisonous chemicals; (c) Human blood, organs and blood products; (d) Firearms and ammunition; (e) Artifacts and cultural property, including historical, cultural, fossils, archeological and similar items; (f) Breeding animals, rare species of animals, animal offspring; (g) Precious metals, precious and semi-precious stones, ore, minerals and rare elements and (h) Alcohol.
2. Privatization is defined as the exit of the government as a producer in a given market, and complete transfer of the government ownership to the private player.
3. Disinvestment is defined as the reduction in government equity in public sector enterprises.
4. Dashnyam Nachin (2007), Country note on Trade and Investment Policy Coordination Country: Mongolia, *ARTNeT Consultative Meeting on Trade and Investment Policy Coordination,* 16-17 July, Bangkok, Thailand.
5. Lack of territorial access to the sea, isolation, remoteness from world markets, and high transport and transit costs experienced by landlocked developing countries (LLDCs) impose serious constraints on their overall socio-economic development, including their trade competitiveness. As a result, landlocked developing countries are among the poorest countries in the world: out of 31 such countries, 16 are classified as least developed and half of the LLDCs are in Africa. The 31 landlocked developing countries are Afghanistan, Armenia, Azerbaijan, Bhutan, Bolivia, Botswana, Burkina Faso, Burundi, Central African Republic, Chad, Ethiopia, Kazakhstan, Kyrgyzstan, Lao People's Democratic Republic, Lesotho, Malawi, Mali, Moldova, Republic of Mongolia, Nepal, Niger, Paraguay, Rwanda, Swaziland, Tajikistan, The Former Yugoslav Republic of Macedonia, Turkmenistan, Uganda, Uzbekistan, Zambia and Zimbabwe.
6. Nixon, et al. (2000), *The Mongolian Economy: A Manual of Applied Economics for a Country in Transition.* Edward Elgar Publishing Ltd. Northampton, MA.
7. It is important to note that Mongolian statistical data varies widely depending on the source. In some cases, there are as much as US $100 million discrepancies between private, national and international statistical offices. Even in some cases, there are wide difference in national data and international data sources in trade and

its difficult for researcher to decide which data is appropriate while dealing with policy related issues. For example, according to the *State Statistical Bulletin*, total foreign trade turnover in 1999 was at US $761.4 million whereas the *Mongolian Statistical Yearbook* (MSY) reported a turnover of US $871.1 million (Nixon 2000, National 2000). These statistical discrepancies are common to many transition economies but in the case of Mongolia they result mostly from imprecise reporting mechanisms within the government and statistical bodies as observed in Nixon, et al. 2000. *The Mongolian Economy: A Manual of applied Economics for a Country in Transition*, Edward Elgar Publishing Ltd. Northampton, MA.

8. *Action Programme of the Government of Mongolia for 2004-08.*
9. World Trade organization (WTO), *Mongolia Trade Policy Review*, WT/TPR/S/145.
10. World Trade Organisation (WTO) *Trade Policy Review of Mongolia* (Report by the Secretariat), WT/TPR/G/145, 15 February 2005.
11. Mongolia is planning to join Bangkok Agreement now known as Asia Pacific Trade Agreement (APTA) and enjoying observer status in Shanghai Cooperation Organisation (SCO).
12. The Bangkok Agreement (now Asia Pacific Trade Agreement) involves a preferential tariff arrangement among members; current members are Bangladesh, China, India, Republic of Korea, Lao People's Democratic Republic, and Sri Lanka. The ESCAP functions as the secretariat for the Agreement. Also see a presentation made by the Executive Secretary UNESCAP, Kim Kak-su entitled *"Potential and Future Direction of the Asia Pacific Agreement"* in APTA Ministerial Council Meeting in Beijing on 2nd November 2005. Detailed analysis of potential benefit for Mongolia in joining APTA can be seen in a report prepared by Indra Nath Mukherji (2006) *"Asia Pacific Trade Agreement: Implications of Exchange of Trade Preferences for Member and Prospective Member Countries of ESCAP"* Study Commissioned by United Nations Economic and Social Commission for Asia and the Pacific, Bangkok.
13. World Trade organization (WTO), *Mongolia Trade Policy Review*, WT/TPR/S/145.
14. A presentation made by Vangansuren Ulziibaya on *"Integration of Mongolia into Asian Economic Community"*, National University of Mongolia, 2007, Slide No. 6.
15. Information in this section is extracted from Head of the Indian Mission in Mongolia Report.
16. K. Kojima, (1964), "The Pattern of International Trade among Advanced Countries", *Hitotsuboshi Journal of Economics*, Vol.5, No.1.
17. Except 1992 India's export intensity with Mongolia was 1.097 which is above the unity.
18. Estimated from *Directorate General of Commercial Intelligence and Statistics* (DGCI&S), Ministry of Commerce, Government of India (online database).

19. Mongolia-European Community, Strategy Paper 2007-13 (23 February 2007)
20. See http://www.wto.int/english/tratop_e/tpr_e/tp245_e.htm Mongolia is a WTO member since 1997.
21. Helmers Christian (2006), *Options for Mongolia for the Formation of Bilateral Free Trade Agreements – Options in Merchandise Trade: An Overview*, Ministry of Industry and Trade (Trade Analysis and Negotiations Unit), November, Ulaanbaatar, Mongolia.
22. World Bank (2007), *Mongolia Promoting Investment and Job Creation An Investment Climate Assessment and Trade Integration Study*, Poverty Reduction and Economic Management, Department East Asia and Pacific Region, Document of the World Bank Report No. 41036-MN.
23. Nawal K. Paswan, (2003), *Agricultural Trade in South Asia: Potential and Policy Options,* APH Publishing Corporation: New Delhi. Complete set of products having dynamic revealed comparative advantage is available with the author.
24. Hari D. Goyal (1999) *"A Development Perspective on Mongolia*" The Regents of the University of California.
25. The Foreign Investment Law was adopted in 1991. Subsequently, the minimum amount for foreign investment was set at US$10,000. FDI in the banking sector is covered under the Banking Law.
26. World Trade organization (WTO), *Mongolia Trade Policy Review*, WT/TPR/S/145.
27. These are: Belarus, Belgium, Bulgaria, Canada, China, Czech Republic, Egypt, France, Germany, Hungary, India, Indonesia, Italy, Kazakhstan, Kuwait, Kyrgyz Republic, Luxembourg, Korea, Malaysia, Netherlands, Poland, Romania, Russian Federation, Singapore, Switzerland, Turkey, Ukraine, United Arab Emirates, United Kingdom, Uzbekistan, and Viet Nam.
28. These are: Austria, Belarus, Belgium, Bulgaria, China, Czech Republic, Cuba, Denmark, France, Germany, Hungary, India, Indonesia, Italy, Japan, Kazakhstan, Korea, Kuwait, Kyrgyz Republic, Lao People's Democratic Republic, Malaysia, Netherlands, Philippines, Poland, Romania, Russian Federation, Singapore, Switzerland, Turkey, Ukraine, United Arab Emirates, United Kingdom, United States, and Viet Nam.
29. Data is taken from the Foreign Investment and Foreign Trade Agency *(FIFTA)* of Mongolia.
30. Ministry of Road, Transport and Tourism (2006), Mongolia.
31. Dashnyam Nachin (2007), *A note on Trade and Investment Policy Coordination Country: Mongolia for ARTNeT,* Consultative Meeting on Trade and Investment Policy Coordination 16-17 July, Bangkok, Thailand.
32. Abstract of paper on *"ICT Cooperation between India and Mongolia"* by Ch. Saikhanbileg in this volume.

33. H.G. Grubel, and P.J. Lloyd, *"IIT: The Theory and Measurement of International Trade in Differentiated Products*", London: Macmillan, 1975.
34. E. Helpman, "Imperfect Competition and International Trade: Evidence from Fourteen Industrial Countries", *Journal of Japanese and International Economics*, No. 1, 1987, pp. 62-81.
35. A.K. Dixit, and G.M. Grossman, "Trade and Protection with Multistage Production," *Review of Economic Studies*, No.5, 1982, pp. 361-92.
36. K. Fukasaku, "Economic Regionalisation and Intra-Industry Trade: Pacific-Asian Perspectives", *OECD Development Centre Technical Paper* No.53, 1992.
37. Estimated intra-industry index value (more than unity) between India's exports to the world and Mongolia's imports from the world in the same products at HS-6 digit level are 147.
38. Traders' Manual for Landlocked Countries: Mongolia (Part IV): Investing in Mongolia (2006).
39. Nawal K. Paswan, (2003), *Agricultural Trade in South Asia: Potential & Policy Options,* APH Publishing Corporation: New Delhi.
40. H. Linnemann, *An Econometric Study of International Trade Flows*, North Holland, Amsterdam, 1996.
41. Thus, for identifying the different levels of trade potential on the basis of computed EIS and IES measures, we have applied three cut-off points which lie between zero to one. (a) *Low Potential* (LP) falls under the range of more than 0.001 but less than 0.250; (b) *Moderate Potential* (MP) falls under the range of more than 0.250 but less than 0.550; and (c) *High Potential* (HP) falls under the range between 0.550 to 1.000. Low Potential indicates Poor Complementarity; Moderate Potential indicates Partial Complementarity; and High Potential indicates Perfect Trade Complementarity. Since not much of difference was noticed in these cut-off points in 2000, the same were retained for 2005.
42. In the case of India's export-import complementarity and Mongolia's export-import complementarity, the index value of HS-2 digit found unity (1) value in few products which denotes the quite few number of HS-6 and HS-8 products involved in trade between both the countries and hence reveal unity (1) index value. Because computation takes care of each and every products at the HS-6 or HS-8 (and summed) while generating results at HS-2 level. Therefore, it is not necessary to generalize the proposition of higher degree of index value shows moderate trade complementarity between both countries. But in few cases, it is correct and should be verified and supplemented with the bilateral trade value at product-wise.
43. Complete set of matched products and trade complementarities (product-wise) of India's exports to the world and Mongolia's imports from the world *(vice-versa)* in same products at HS-6 digit level is available with the author.

CHAPTER 16

STABILISING BORDERS: SINO-MONGOLIAN RELATIONS

Srikanth Kondapalli

China's relations with Mongolia are expanding in political, economic, cultural and strategic spheres in the recent past. This is in contrast to the at times acrimonious relations between two neighbours in Asia who share the largest borders of more than 4,000 kilometres. Mongolia is juxtaposed between two major countries- Russia and China, and is considered to have a significant impact on China's northern areas security.[1] While China-Mongolia relations are rooted in history, current upswing in bilateral relations is relatively broad-based. Termed currently as part of "comprehensive cooperation", bilateral relations underwent a chequered history from acrimony after China's relations soured with the then Soviet Union in 1960 to turbulent days of May 1983 to diplomatic normalisation of late 1980s and subsequently to the formulation of "good-neighbourly partnership of mutual trust" agreed to in 2003.

This paper explores the increasing interactions between China and Mongolia, specifically looking at the broader determinants of China's foreign policy objectives and goals towards Mongolia, key provisions and policy prescriptions during the mutual high level political visits between the two, briefly enlisting the economic cooperative measures and finally reflecting on the bilateral relations. It is argued in this paper that China has followed a long-term policy of stabilising borders with Mongolia (as with several other countries) in the recent period as a part of its revived policy of "good neighbourliness" with the objectives of not only ushering peace and stability in these areas but also transforming these borders from sterile entities to creating significant stakes in each other by expanding border trade, economic cooperation, connectivity while at the same time guaranteeing measures against any fissiparous tendencies, specifically in the Inner Mongolian region. These policies are expected to serve China in its comprehensive rise in Asia and beyond in the near future.

DETERMINANTS

Although recent Chinese official foreign policy discourse discounts any hidden national ambition to "recover" lost territories specifically in Mongolia after the Qing dynasty collapsed in 1911, several Mongolians are still concerned with such prospects given the rise of China in the recent period.[2] For, while Russia (and then the Soviet Union) supported Mongolia, the disintegration of the USSR in 1991 created uncertainties for Mongolia.[3] In this context, China and Mongolia cite the treaty of 1994 in re-defining the new momentum in bilateral relations.[4] Bilateral relations between the two has shown improvement from the 1980s after one of the Chinese conditions, viz., no to Soviet troops deployment in Mongolia was met. Subsequently, after Mongolia conceded to the Chinese minimalist foreign and security objectives on border issues- Inner Mongolia, Tibet and Taiwan, bilateral relations flowered to become "friendly." As Annexure 1 below indicates, high level political visits between the two countries increased from the 1980s but more substantially in the recent period with "state visits" [*guoshi fangwen*] showing an upward trend when compared to only "friendly visits" [*youhao fangwen*] of the 1950s.[5] During the period of socialism, the fraternal party-led states in China and Mongolia termed their visits "friendly" or "unofficial friendly visits", while the 1970s were bereft of major political interactions between the two countries. In the late 1980s and 1990s till the time of the 1998 summit meeting, bilateral visits were termed "unofficial" indicating to the relative tensions between the two countries. "State visits", rather than "friendly visits", provide for more legal guarantees and are beneficial to China.

Foreign Policy Considerations

Behind the above mentioned qualitative improvement in relations between China and Mongolia in the 1990s lay several considerations. Foremost, from the Chinese point of view is the minimalist and maximalist positions which appeared to be in transition to that of the latter. China's considerations on Mongolia include securing Mongolian support to its minimalist foreign policy positions on Inner Mongolia, Tibet and Taiwan, maintaining regional security by advancing nuclear weapon free zone over the region, building long-term stakes between the two countries by expanding gradually the envelope of exchanges and cooperation in economic, trade and connectivity. At a maximum, China intends to enhance its influence in the region for its rise while keeping at bay major powers'– specifically the United States- influence in Mongolia.

One of the main drivers in improving relations with Mongolia in the recent decades is the post-Mao Chinese leadership's objective of creating a peaceful and stable external environment and ward off challenges to its security and thereby promote trade and commerce for the subsequent rise of China.[6] For these China needs to work out a strategy that guarantees stability on borders while at the same time convert Mongolia to the Chinese positions and interests. Some of these include Chinese concerns on peace and security of its borders in Inner Mongolia, on Tibet and Taiwan given the inter-linkages of Mongolia to these issues given its predominant Buddhist population and historical factors respectively.[7] These also include Chinese efforts to keep at bay major powers hold over Mongolia.[8] Indeed, vis-à-vis Russia, through increased interactions with Mongolia at several layers, China has been able to replace Russia in several parameters. At the same time there has been a Mongolian "southward drift" towards China that poses concerns for Russia.[9]

Border issue

The two countries now share a long border of about 4,676 kms. On December 26, 1962 both countries signed an agreement to solve the border issues.[10] Premier Zhou Enlai, during his conversation with Mongolian Chairman of the Council of Ministers of the Mongolian People's Republic J. Zedenbal in December 1962 and a month after the Sino-Indian border clashes, underlined the need for "legally defin[ing] the borders between our friendly lands". Zhou outlined the principles of Sino-Mongolian border settlement as based on "principles of friendship, equality, mutual understanding and mutual concessions". While Zedenbal disagreed with the Chinese actions in the Sino-Indian clash by suggesting that this is "regrettable", during this conversation he also raised the issue with Zhou that Mongolian inhabitants of Hurimt village in Balgan-Ulgiisk district in western Mongolia have constructed buildings and have started using forest resources nearby in areas claimed by China. Zedenbal suggested that China look into this matter to find a "reasonable solution", which appeared to have been accepted by the Chinese officials, although such gestures (like providing cattle-feed, etc) were made when bilateral relations were comfortable.[11]

In addition, on July 19, 1984 both sides signed an agreement for joint border inspection and on November 28, 1988 another agreement was signed on border control to stabilise these areas. On June 24, 1991, border posts trade management system was signed. On April 29, 1994 both sides agreed to take measures to protect border movements.[12] Subsequently, during the July 2004 visit of Mongolian President Nachagyn Bagabandi, both sides signed a document on border management.[13] These agreements have provided for legal guarantees for stabilising borders and measures to efficiently conduct border management, while also providing necessary tools for China to regulate traffic on both sides.

One more relevant issue here is that both sides have been interested in tackling the spread of desertification in Mongolia and Inner Mongolia. This phenomenon has reached near alarming levels with the negative fallout on pastures, cultivation, etc. Joint survey teams were formed recently to control desertification and work out measures for the transformation of the desert. A "Sand Prevention and Control Association" was formed in Inner Mongolia for the purposes of joint research on control of sand storms and annual meetings.[14]

Securing Inner Mongolia

One main consideration behind Chinese efforts to secure and stabilise borders with Mongolia is to avoid any suspicions and tensions between the two sides given the historical nature of their relations. Specifically, given the equations between Inner Mongolia and Mongolia over a period of time, the security of Inner Mongolia is uppermost for the Chinese leadership. Cross-border movements suffered as both sides entered into a cold war following the Soviet skirmishes with China in the 1960s through 80s. While Mongolia is sparsely populated (with less than 3 million), Inner Mongolia, on the other hand has more than 20 million inhabitants. Any generation of identities between the two could pose concerns for the Chinese leadership.[15] China is wary of the Mongolian Democratic Party's stance on "Greater Mongolian" agenda of "Uniting the Three Mongolias" [of Mongols in Mongolia, Inner Mongolia (in China) and Mongolian Buryatskaya (in Russia)]. When a call for forming *Inner Mongolian People's Party* was made at Princeton University in March 1997, China's concerns increased. According to Wang Wei-fang about 17 per cent of Inner Mongolians reportedly adhere to this party's appeal. To curb such pan-Mongolian nationalist movements, China is said to have followed a policy of expanding economic contacts with Mongolia, in addition to tying down the latter with legal guarantees and multilateral processes and counter-terrorism efforts.[16]

As a part of this strategy, China has insisted that Mongolia denounce "three evils" [viz., separatism, extremism and splittism]. This is a legal strategy that China started following in coincidence with the September 11 events. This is a strategy to counter challenges to China from groups in Taiwan, Xinjiang, Tibet and Inner Mongolia. The Mongolian leaders today have announced their support to the Chinese position on "splittist" phenomenon and oppose Inner Mongolian splinter groups position on nationalism.

To create more concrete stakes and bring about stability between the two regions, China has initiated annual economic cooperation meetings between Inner Mongolia and Mongolia, of which eight such meetings took place by November 2007. Specific areas of cooperation were identified in these meetings and both sides resolved to focus on mining, ports and transportation networks with a majority of such work initiated by the Chinese side.[17] Baotou Steel, for instance has plans for extensive mining operations in Mongolia. As a part of this effort, railway networks are also being strengthened. On connectivity, China launched several programmes of road and railways. One such project was launched in 2007 to connect Mongolia to the sea port in China. Three phases of railway lines have commenced between Inner Mongolia, Mongolia and Russia. These include:

1. 487 kms. from Xinqiu (Fuxin City in Liaoning Province), to Bayan Ul in northern Inner Mongolia at a cost of $790 million and to be completed by 2010. This line is to handle 12 million tonnes of coal in three to five years and 25 million tonnes in five to ten years and 35 million tonnes in 15 years
2. 230 kms. long line from Bayan Ul northward to Zhuengadabuqi Port, on the border of Mongolia.
3. The third section would stretch northward to Choibalsan City in Mongolia, where it would join the railway to Russia's Borzya.[18]

Tibet and Taiwan Issues

Interlinked to the above are Chinese concerns on any emerging linkages between Mongolia and Tibet or Taiwan. The Dalai Lama's visits (to Mongolia's largest monastery Gandantegchinlen) were termed as private by the Mongolian leadership, although the Buddhist community and the emerging civil society in Mongolia support the Tibetan leader.[19] Nevertheless, during the visit of the Dalai Lama, China expressed its discomfort and even utilised coercive diplomatic measures such as restricting movements between the two countries.

Through the joint statements and communiqués mentioned above, China extracted Mongolian acknowledgement that the latter adheres to the "one China" policy and, in addition, does not support Taiwanese independence movement and stated that Taiwan is an "inalienable" portion of China. More over, Chinese official accounts also interpret that Mongolia has supported the Chinese position on the March 2005 "anti-secession" legislation whereby China could explore "non-peaceful means" to resolve the Taiwan issue. These are major legal concessions that China extracted from Mongolia. However, in reality, several in Mongolia argue that their country should explore mutually beneficial contacts with Taiwan. This is not acceptable to China.

On the part of Taiwan, the issue of exploring relations with Mongolia are complicated because of the Republic of China's (ROC) stance on Mongolia. The Kuomintang government from 1924 (and after the 1949 shift to Taiwan) eyed Mongolia. The ruling Democratic Progressive Party – which is independent-minded and in its stride to re-interpret identities across Straits wish to move away from all things Chinese- has revised this position and it is officially disbanded in 2006. Mongolians detest the ROC's Mongolian and Tibetan Affairs Commission which is the successor to Qing dynasty's *Li Fan Yuan*. This institution evokes fears in Mongolia about the Chinese intentions towards Mongolia.[20]

With an eye on Taiwanese investments (which form the second largest such reserves in the world today after Japan), Mongolia established reciprocal trade offices with Taiwan to increase trade and investments in September 2002. In August 2003 trade officials of both countries held a forum. By this period, bilateral trade reached about $5 million (with Mongolian exports touching $92,341). Ten Taiwanese companies have invested in Mongolia whose total investment reached $9 million-mostly in the textile industries. Tourism and other related aspects are being explored currently.[21] Also, in the security field, during the Mongolian military operations with the United States against terrorism, Taiwan wished to join forces in June 2006.[22]

Reform and Opening up

As mentioned above, a China on its rise needs enormous resources to feed its industrialisation process. Also, in its rise to global power, China needs allies and friends to provide support. With these twin objectives and in the backdrop of the reform and opening up policies, China has now extensive engagement with several countries including with Mongolia. It has launched a Western Development Campaign of developing the interior western regions (about 16 provinces and regions) with extensive infrastructure and investment projects from the tenth Five year Plan period in 2000 onwards.

The need for raw materials, markets and avenues for investment is a major concern for China today as it graduates from relatively low to medium technologies and economically developed nature. The near double digit growth figures that China posted from the 1990s demands resources from every other corner of the globe including from the resource rich Mongolia.

Mineral-rich Mongolia is a useful destination for the Chinese companies to scour away iron, copper, oil and other resources in order to feed Chinese industrialisation and growth rates. Some of the Mongolian ores are considered to be largest in the world and could be tapped at least till the medium term. For instance, Dashdorj area has an estimated 200 million tonnes iron ore deposits, some of the Mongolian coal deposits are estimated to contain $500 billion of the fuel reserves, while some western companies like that of Canada – Ivanhoe Mines – has contracts to extract 21.3 billion kilograms of copper and 23 million ounces of gold.[23] China Shenhua, the largest Chinese coal producer, has several projects to transport coal from Mongolia to China by railways.[24] These are precious for China's rise.

BILATERAL RELATIONS

China and Mongolia have a long history of interactions, some of which proved to be long-lasting specifically in economic, cultural and demographic patterns, while at a subterranean level both are concerned over each other's intentions specifically on the status of their respective nationhood.[25]

Recent improvements in bilateral relations are traced to the 1990s, when in 1994 both sides signed a "treaty on friendly and cooperative relations" which in effect led to comfort levels in interactions by mutually guaranteeing to each other on their respective minimalist foreign policy objectives and goals.[26] 1998 joint statement, 1999, 2003 and 2006 high-level political interactions are also said to have nurtured further these relations and diversified them into other areas of mutual concern.[27]

China's President Jiang Zemin visited Mongolia in July 1999. The discussions between the two leaders and officials was so intense that a reporter suggested that the scheduled news conference was cancelled due to difference of opinion on how to utilise the Chinese free grant of Yuan 30 million.[28] Subsequently the joint communiqué issued during the visit of Mongolian Prime Minister Enkhbayar in January 2002 both sides reiterated that "it is of strategic importance to continue to develop a long-term, stable and healthy good-neighborly cooperative relationship of mutual trust between the two countries".[29] Both premiers suggested that they look forward to establish "enduringly stable, healthy, and mutually trusting relationship of good neighborliness, friendship, and cooperation and expand their mutually beneficial cooperation."[30]

Hu Jintao, after being elevated to the President post, chose to make Mongolia as his first state visit abroad in 2003.[31] Hu suggested a four-point strategy to improve relations with Mongolia. These were:

1. To establish China-Mongolia partnership of good-neighborliness and mutual trust be established and that the two countries will forever be good neighbors, good friends, and good partners;
2. To maintain the frequent exchange of top-level visits should be maintained in the interest of further expanding bilateral relations;
3. To make efforts to promote mutually beneficial trade and economic links and to launch multi-channel, multi-area, and multi-category cooperation;

4. That the two sides should strengthen their cooperation in international and regional affairs in joint efforts to maintain peace and stability in the region.[32]

Eventually, the 2003 joint declaration announced the formation of "good-neighborly and mutual-trust partnership [*mulin huxin huoban guanxi*]" and that both "will be good neighbors, good partners, and good friends forever". China expressed its support to the Mongolian candidature in the APEC, ASEM and Asia Cooperation Dialogue processes, observer status in SCO, while Mongolia declared that it will adhere to the "one China" principle.[33] Hu offered $300 million in aid to Mongolia, which was to be utilised by Chinese workers in building roads and other infrastructure projects in Mongolia-mostly connecting mineral resources of the country.

In November 2006, during the visit of the Mongolian Prime Minister Miegombyn Enkhbold to Beijing, the two countries agreed to pursue their bilateral cooperation in five main fields, viz.,

1. Maintaining the good momentum of growth of visits and exchanges to increase the mutual understanding and trust and consolidating and developing the bilateral partnership.
2. The promotion of economic and trade cooperation in the key areas of infrastructure and energy exploration, with cooperation on the construction of power stations, roads and railways in Mongolia, and the formulation of medium and long-term plans for economic and trade relations.
3. The expansion of collaboration on natural resources, disaster prevention and relief, and the prevention and control of contagious diseases.
4. Fostering cultural and humanitarian exchanges and cooperation, raising the number of student exchanges, and hosting activities of a "nation day".
5. Intensifying communication and coordination within the Shanghai Cooperation Organization (SCO), strengthening the consultation mechanism between

> China, Mongolia and Russia with joint efforts to safeguard regional stability and to promote regional cooperation, and to combat drugs trafficking.[34]

These statements indicated to not only expanding contacts at the highest levels of decision-making in both capitals, which is necessary not only for avoiding any gaps in perceptions but also for building long-term stable relations between the two countries. More importantly, these statements also indicate the transition from Chinese minimalist to maximalist foreign policy objectives. That is, after the Chinese side is relatively satisfied after securing official Mongolian guarantees on core issues of borders, Inner Mongolia, Tibet and Taiwan, it appeared that both are moving towards higher levels of interactions in several fields.

MILITARY COOPERATION

China is in an advantageous position in the strategic and military spheres in Mongolia, specifically after the Soviet disintegration. Russian troops deployment in Mongolia – a major contention between China and Soviet Union- were withdrawn by Russia in the 1990s. In 1990 the Soviet Union agreed to withdraw troops positioned in Mongolia.[35] This has relieved Chinese security. By advocating a nuclear weapon free zone, China was able to ward off any nuclear-capable ballistic missile presence in Mongolia (despite Soviet deployments previously).

Military relations between China and Mongolia improved with mutual visits of higher level military commanders and cooperation in several areas of concern.[36] China today is extending assistance to the Mongolian military personnel in training, supply of uniforms, etc. In addition, Mongolian officers are participating as observers in Chinese-conducted multilateral counter-terrorism operations.

ECONOMIC RELATIONS

From relative isolation, bilateral economic relations are increasingly exhibiting integration. China became Mongolia's largest trading partner and its investments in Mongolia are considered to be the highest, although in overall terms few, in Mongolia. The official discourse in China insists that such economic cooperation should be "centered around resource exploitation and infrastructure development."[37] In addition, recently China formulated a policy of "guidance by the government, businesses' participation and market operation" in this regard.[38] This provides for stronger Chinese state-level interference in economic affairs as well.

Although significant economic relations commenced between the two countries in the 1990s, these proved to be more productive from the late 1990s, as Annexure 2 indicates.[39] In 2001, during the visit of the Mongolian Prime Minister Enkhbayar both countries decided to expand such relations. Subsequently, Chinese minister for foreign trade and commerce Shi Guangsheng visited Mongolia in mid-2003 to boost such ties.[40] Today, bilateral economic relations have expanded between the two countries so much that the lines of national territory, in some sectors, appear to blur. For, according to Sedbazar Otgonbat, Vice Chairman of Mongolia's foreign investment and foreign trade agency as cited by James Brook, Mongolia is on the path to become "China's Canada" with trans-border interactions and connectivity increasing day by day.[41]

Trade galloped between the two countries from a mere $24 million in 1989 to about a billion recently. While Mongolian exports increased, specifically with its export basket consisting of raw materials, overall these trade figures with China pointed to the emerging dependency relationship. Although Mongolia has a fovurable balance of trade position, trade figures from 2000-2001 indicate that Chinese exports to Mongolia are also increasing substantially. Today Mongolian products overwhelmingly are destined to the Chinese market rather than to any other major market in the world. Mongolian leaders also visit Chinese port city of Tianjin to urge for more passage of these goods abroad.[42] Thus Mongolian exports to China constitute more than 60 percent of its total exports. In addition, the Chinese currency is one of the most circulated currencies in the Mongolian market.[43] However, if we include rampant smuggling and illegal trade across porous borders these further add up to the trade figures between the two countries.[44]

Nearly one-third of joint ventures in Mongolia are traced to China. In addition, nearly one-fourth of investments in Mongolia originate from China. These relate to not only Chinese funded infrastructure projects like roads, railways, bridges, telecommunications, etc but also in joint venture companies. In addition, energy pipelines are being planned to be constructed with Chinese support to pump out oil and gas from Mongolia, although Russia still dominates this aspect. Economic dependency relationship, according to Morris Rossabi, is emerging between China and Mongolia, with the latter exporting raw materials (copper, iron, zinc, oil, raw cashmere, animal products and others) while importing Chinese finished products at greater costs to its nascent economy.[45] China also made use of Mongolian abolishment of tariffs and was said to have displaced Mongolian products.[46]

Another area of economic interactions is the setting up of facilities on the border areas to enhance trade, investments, production and exports. At Erenhot, which was an important business passage between Europe and Asia during the 10th Century, China has set up a special economic zone to further expand economic relations with Mongolia in the fields of bio-engineering and food processing.[47]

CONCLUSIONS

China's relations with Mongolia appear to be arriving at a balance in the last one decade with consensus emerging among the two ruling elites that expansion in bilateral relations is beneficial to both. As compared to the previous period, last one decade exhibited stable political relations between the two. Today, China is poised to replace Russia – the traditional actor in Mongolia for the last seven decades – in the political, economic, cultural and strategic spheres. As Russia receded into the backdrop in the decade in Mongolia following the disintegration of the Soviet Union, that of the Chinese stock enhanced in the recent period.

One of the overwhelming concerns of China vis-à-vis

Mongolia is how, firstly, to stabilise vast swathes of borders between the two countries. While this has been the major consideration of successive leaderships in Beijing, recently reform process has added a new dimension. That is, in addition to securing for itself peace and stability on borders and warding off fissiparous tendencies in Inner Mongolia and redeployment of military forces from the Mongolian borders to coastal regions (opposite to Taiwan), China recently expanded trade and commerce with this region. One of the main considerations here is to secure raw materials like copper and other resources for its burgeoning industrialisation process and rise. Additionally, an economically dependent Mongolia tied up in legal formulations and Chinese-led multilateral initiative of SCO could as well provide China with cushions in its rise. A rising China also needs allies and friends in the international system.

To a large extent, events in bilateral relations between China and Mongolia indicated to forward momentum in this direction. It is not without reason that recent official foreign ministry yearbooks term China's relations with Mongolia as "friendly". While economic dependency of Mongolia is secured by China through extensive infrastructure and industrial projects, it appears that Mongolia is headed towards political dependency as well. Despite following independent foreign and multilateral policies in the recent period, Mongolia appeared to be conceding to several political conditions from Beijing. For Mongolian concessions on border issues, Inner Mongolia, Tibet, Taiwan and other "internal issues" of China appear to be unilateral with no report available on reciprocal "concessions", if any, to Mongolia. Although economic aid and other related aspects could be mentioned here as providing mutual benefit, even these maximise Chinese gains.

It needs to be seen then how such interactions would be pursued in future. Nevertheless, several incidents in Mongolia involving attacks on Chinese citizens or their properties indicate to the growing public animosity to the Chinese inroads into Mongolia- in contrast to the elitist consensus being arrived at in both capitals. As with such incidents in Kazakhstan, Afghanistan and Pakistan, anti-Chinese sentiment in these states is a new phenomenon unheard of in Chinese interactions with others in the last more than five decades.

REFERENCES

1. See Lu Junyuan, "*Menggu guo diyuan dexing jiqi guoji guanxi*" [Mongolia's geo-political features and International relations] *Renwen Dili* [Human Geography], Issue 4, 2000.
2. In general, the Chinese official accounts on bilateral relations with Mongolia start with such historical links. See Li Xiangyang, "*Zhongguo renmin gongheguo yu Menggu guanxi*" [People's Republic of China and Mongolia Relations] in Tang Jiaxuan ed. *Zhongguo Waijiao Cidian* [Dictionary of China's Diplomacy] (Beijing: World Knowledge Publications, 2000) pp. 624-26. For a Mongolian concern in this regard, see Bayar Batzorig, "New environment of military ethics" at <http://nsa.nps.navy.mil/Publications/Micewski/Batzorig.htm >
3. On the overall relations see Sharad K Soni, *Mongolia-China Relations: Modern and Contemporary Times,* New Delhi: Pentagon Press, 2006 and Shakti Madhok, *Sino-Mongolian Relations 1949-2004* , New Delhi: Reliance Publishing House, 2005.
4. See "Chinese, Mongolian Presidents Hold Talks" *People's Daily* July 16, 1999 at <http://english.peopledaily.com.cn/199907/16/enc_19990716001001_HomeNews.html>
5. See Li Xiangyang, "*Zhongguo renmin gongheguo yu Menggu guanxi*" p. 625
6. Migeddorj Batchimeg, "Future challenges for the PRC and Mongolia: A Mongolian Perspective" *China Brief* , Vol. 5, Issue 10 (May 05, 2005) at <http://www.jamestown.org/publications_details.php?volume_id=408&issue_id=3322&article_id=2369704 > accessed on June 2, 2005
7. See Zhang Xiujie, "*Mengu de guojia anquan zhanlue ji ZhongMeng anquan guanxi*" [Mongolia's National Security Strategy and China-Mongolia Relations] *Dangdai Yatai* [Contemporary Asia-Pacific] (Beijing) Issue 11, 2005.
8. Fang Hua, "*Menggu yu daguo guanxi de bianhua*" [Transformation in Mongolian relations with major powers] *Xiandai Guoji Guanxi* [Contemporary International Relations] (Beijing) Issue 7, 2006.
9. Sergei Blagov, "Mongolia drifts away from Russia toward China" *China Brief,* Vol. 5, Issue 10, May 05, 2005 at <http://www.jamestown.org/publications_details.php?volume_id=408&issue_id=3322&article_id=2369706 > accessed on June 2, 2005
10. Of the 17,000 square kilometers of border dispute, China gained 5,000 sq. km. See Soni, 2006, pp. 159 and 250-74 on the border agreement. The thalweg and Pamir principles became the principles of border dispute resolution.
11. See "Record of Conversation (from East German archives) between Chinese Premier Zhou Enlai and Mongolian leader J. Zedenbal, Beijing,

26 December 1962" [translation by Wolff, O. Corff, and C. Ostermann] at <http://cwihp.si.edu/cwihplib.nsf/16c6b2fc83775317852564a400054b28/99988aba1841996a8525692100551 0e3?OpenDocument&Highlight=0,China>

12. This is based on Li Xiangyang, "*Zhongguo renmin gongheguo yu Menggu guanxi*" [People's Republic of China and Mongolia Relations] in Tang Jiaxuan ed. *Zhongguo Waijiao Cidian* [Dictionary of China's Diplomacy], Beijing: World Knowledge Publications, 2000, p. 626
13. "Chinese, Mongolian Presidents Meet" *Xinhua,* July 6, 2004 at <http://service.china.org.cn/link/wcm/Show_Text?info_id=100356&p_qry=Pakistan > accessed on August 18, 2004
14. "China Seeks Cooperation with Mongolia in Sand Control" *Xinhua*, April 6, 2004 at <http://www.china.org.cn/english/international/92233.htm > accessed on May 15, 2006
15. See Christopher P. Atwood "National Questions and National Answers in the Chinese Revolution; Or, How Do You Say Minzu in Mongolian?" at < http://www.easc.indiana.edu/>
16. Wang Wei-fang, "'Pan-Mongolism" and U.S.-China-Mongolia relations" *China Brief*, Vol. 5, Issue 10 (May 05, 2005) cited at <http://www.asianresearch. org/articles/2644.html > accessed on July 20, 2005
17. See "Chinese Inner Mongolia to enhance cooperation with Mongolia" *Xinhua*, November 15, 2007 at <http://english.people.com.cn/90001/90776/6303523.html >
18. This is based on "Construction starts on railroad linking China, Mongolia, Russia" *Xinhua*, November 11, 2007 at <http://english.people.com.cn/90001/90776/90882/6300314.html >
19. See "Dalai Lama's travel plans to Mongolia kept secret" *International Herald Tribune*, August 20, 2006 at <http://www.iht.com/articles/2006/08/20/news/mongolia.php >
20. Alicia Campi, "Sino-Mongolian relations from Beijing's viewpoint" *China Brief*, Vol. 5, Issue 10 (May 05, 2005) at <http://www.jamestown.org/publications_details.php?volume_id=408&issue_id=3322&article_id=2369705> accessed on June 2, 2005
21. Jessie Ho, "Taiwan, Mongolia Trade Officials Hold Forum to Strengthen Economic Relations" *Taipei Times*, August 14, 2003
22. See "Taiwan wants to join US anti-terror drill in Mongolia" *Taipei Times*, November 23, 2005 at <http://www.taipeitimes.com/News/taiwan/archives/2005/11/23/2003281355 > accessed on April 17, 2006
23. This is based on Rob Delaney, "Tapping Mongolia's iron wealth: Global resources companies jockey to meet Chinese demand" January 11, 2005 at <http://www.iht.com/articles/2005/01/10/bloomberg/sxore.php> accessed on November 8, 2007
24. See Winnie Zhu, "China Shenhua energy may build coal rail link from Mongolia" August 14, 2007 at <http://www.iht.com/articles/2007/08/14/business/sxshenhua.php >

25. See Sharad K. Soni, "Mongolia-China Relations in Historical Perspective (1691-1911)" *Azad Institute Paper 23*, Kolkata: Maulana Abul Kalam Azad Institute of Asian Studies, 2004.
26. For extensive coverage of such interactions see Department of Policy Planning, Ministry of Foreign Affairs, People's Republic of China ed. *Zhongguo Waijiao* [China's Foreign Affairs], Beijing: World Affairs Press, various years.
27. See Tsedendamba Batbayar, "Mongolian-Chinese Bilateral Relations: New Decade and New Agenda" in K. Santhanam and Srikanth Kondapalli eds. *Asian Security and China 2000-2010*, New Delhi: Shipra Publications, 2004, pp. 226-37
28. Aleksandr Denisovich, "Chinese, Mongolian Leaders Sign Cooperation Agreements" *ITAR-TASS,* July 16, 1999 *FBIS-CHI-1999-0716* July 19, 1999
29. "China, Mongolia Issue Joint Communique on Continuing 'Stable, Cooperative' Ties" *Xinhua,* January 11, 2002 *FBIS-CHI-2002-0111* January 11, 2002
30. "Text of Sino-Mongolian Joint Communique" *Xinhua Domestic Service,* January 11, 2002 *FBIS-CHI-2002-0111* January 14, 2002
31. "Chinese President Hu Jintao Held Talks with Mongolia President Stresses Further Understanding and Expanding Cooperation" June 5, 2003 at <http://www.sina.com.cn > accessed on June 8, 2005
32. These were cited by Lu Guodong and Li Jian, "Hu Jintao Holds Talks With Mongolian President Bagabandy" *Xinhua Domestic Service,* June 4, 2003 *FBIS-CHI-2003-0604* June 5, 2003
33. See the joint declaration at "China and Mongolia Issue Joint Declaration" *Xinhua Domestic Service,* June 5, 2003 *FBIS-CHI-2003-0605* June 10, 2003
34. These five points are cited at "China, Mongolia reach five-point consensus to further ties" *Xinhua,* November 23, 2006 at <http://english.people.com.cn/200611/22/eng20061122_324199.html> accessed on April 9, 2007
35. See Sharad K. Soni, "Mongolia between Russia and China: Changing Equations" *Azad Institute Paper 22,* Kolkata: Maulana Abul Kalam Azad Institute of Asian Studies, 2003.
36. See Department of Policy Planning, Ministry of Foreign Affairs, People's Republic of China ed. *Zhongguo Waijiao* [China's Foreign Affairs], Beijing: World Affairs Press, various years; "Chinese Defense Minister Visits Mongolia" *Xinhua*, January 24, 2000 at <http://english.peopledaily.com.cn/200001/24/eng20000124W104.html> and "Chinese, Mongolian Defense Ministers Hold Talks " *Xinhua,* June 11, 2001 *FBIS-CHI-2001-0611* June 6, 2001
37. See Department of Policy Planning, Ministry of Foreign Affairs, People's Republic of China ed. "Mongolia" in *China's Foreign Affairs 2005* (Beijing: World Affairs Press, 2005) p.235. This is re-iterated in the 2006 yearbook. See *China's Foreign Affairs 2006* , Beijing: World Affairs Press, 2006, p.244

38. Yang Jiechi, during his first visit abroad after becoming the foreign minister, stated in Ulan Bator in June 2007 this policy. See "Mongolian Leaders Meet with Yang Jiechi" July 2, 2007 at <http://www.fmprc.gov.cn/eng/wjb/zzjg/yzs/gjlb/2742/2744/t336596.htm>
39. See the studies of Zhang Lijun, "*Dui Zhong Meng jingmao guanxi de huigu yu sikao*" [Retrospect and reflection on China-Mongolian trade relations] *Nei Mengu Shifan Daxue Xuebao* (*Zhexue Shehui Kexue ban*) [Inner Mongolia Normal University Journal (Philosophy & social sciences) Issue 6 (1997) and Xing Yan, "ZongMeng jingmao guanxi xianzhuang yu qianjing" [Reality and expectations of Sino-Mongolian trade] *Heping yu Fazhan* [Peace & Development] Issue 4 (2003)
40. See "Sino-Mongolian Relations: A Backgrounder" March 2004 at <http://accessasia.co.uk/press.asp?PressId=247> accessed on July 30, 2004. This article suggested that Mongolian domestic economic troubles in post-Soviet days led to economic deals with China.
41. James Brook, "Mongolia's Shifting Ties: More China, Less Russia" *New York Times,* July 9, 2004 at <http://www.nytimes.com/2004/07/09/business/worldbusiness/09mongolia.html> [accessed on July 14, 2004]
42. See "Mongolian PM Visits Tianjin" *Xinhua,* November 08, 1999 at <http://english.peopledaily.com.cn/199911/08/eng19991108N104.html> Nearly nine Sino-Mongolian ventures were established at Tianjin.
43. See "Sino-Mongolian Relations: A Backgrounder" March 2004 at <http://accessasia.co.uk/press.asp?PressId=247> accessed on July 30, 2004.
44. See Morris Rossabi, "Beijing's growing politico-economic leverage over Ulaanbaatar" *China Brief* at <http://www.jamestown.org/publications_details.php?volume_id=408&issue_id=3322&article_id=2369703> accessed on June 2, 2005
45. Several Chinese firms like Baotou, Shaogang and Jiuquan have invested in Mongolia for scouring through the iron ore deposits. For instance at the Dashdorj iron ore deposits (estimated to have 250 million tonnes) in Mongolia, Chinese steel giants like Shaogang have contracted for producing 1.5 million tonnes of steel annually from 2006. See Rob Delaney, "Tapping Mongolia's iron wealth: Global resources companies jockey to meet Chinese demand" January 11, 2005 at <http://www.iht.com/articles/2005/01/10/bloomberg/sxore.php> accessed on November 8, 2007
46. Morris Rossabi, "China Seeks to Bolster Its Economic Profile in Central Asia" August 14, 2000 at <http://www.eurasianet.org/departments/business/articles/eav081400.shtml>
47. See "China to Build Special Economic Zones Along Northern Border" *People's Daily,* October 9, 2000 at <http://english.peopledaily.com.cn/200010/09/eng20001009_52136.html>. Mongolia also is promoting other free economic zones with one established at Zamiin Uud about 350 miles northwest of Beijing and involving a US firm Winwheel Bullion in 2006. See "Mongolia to open free trade zone, near Chinese border " April 27, 2006 at <http://www.mongolia-web.com/content/view/438/2/> accessed on May 15, 2006.

ANNEXURE 1
High level Political visits between China and Mongolia

Time	Visiting Leader	Remarks
September 28-October 17, 1952	Prime Minister Tsedenbal	"friendship visit" [*youhao fangwen*]
July 31- August 1, 1954	Premier Zhou Enlai	"friendship visit"
September 27-October 5, 1959	PM Tsedenbal	"friendship visit"
May 27- June 1, 1960	Premier Zhou Enlai	"friendship visit"
December 25-27, 1962	PM Tsedenbal	"friendship visit"
March 30-April 3, 1989	Mongolian Foreign Minister	"unofficial friendly visit" [*zhengwu youhao fangwen*]
August 31-September 4, 1989	Foreign Minister Qian Qichen	"unofficial friendly visit"
August 26-19, 1991	President Yang Shangkun	"unofficial friendly visit"
May 7-11, 1992	PM Byambasuren	"unofficial visit"
April 6-11, 1994	Mongolian Foreign Minister	"unofficial visit"
April 28-29, 1994	Premier Li Peng	"unofficial visit" [*zhengwu fangwen*]
March 27-30, 1996	PM P. Jasrai	"unofficial visit"
January 27-February 1, 1997	Mongolian Foreign Minister	"unofficial visit"
August 19-22, 1997	Foreign Minister Qian Qichen	"unofficial visit"
December 10-15, 1998	President N Bagabandi	"State visit" [*guoshi fangwen*]. Joint declaration on "establishing a long-term stable, healthy, and good-neighborly relations of mutual trust and cooperation oriented towards the 21st century"
1999	PM R. Amargajal	50th anniversary of the establishment of relations celebrated

Time	Visiting Leader	Remarks
July 1999	President Jiang Zemin	"state visit"
January 7-12, 2002	PM Nambaryn Enkhbayar	"official visit"
June 2003	President Hu Jintao	"state visit"
July 1-6, 2004	President Bagabandi Natsagiin	"state visit"
November 2005	President Nambaryn Enkhbayar	"state visit"
November 2006	PM Miegombyn Enkhbold	
June 30- July 2, 2007	Foreign Minister Yang Jiechi	First foreign visit by Yang after taking over from Li Zhaoxing
March 24-26, 2008	Foreign Minister S.Oyun	"official visit"
June 2008	Vice President Xi Jinping	"official visit"

Sources: Compiled from Li Xiangyang, "*Zhongguo renmin gongheguo yu Menggu guanxi*" [People's Republic of China and Mongolia Relations] in Tang Jiaxuan, ed. *Zhongguo Waijiao Cidian* [Dictionary of China's Diplomacy] (Beijing: World Knowledge Publications, 2000) pp. 624-26; Department of Policy Planning, Ministry of Foreign Affairs, People's Republic of China, ed., *Zhongguo Waijiao* [China's Foreign Affairs] (Beijing: World Affairs Press, various years) and others.

Annexure 2

China's Trade with Mongolia (US$ million)

Year	Exports	Imports	Total
1994	42.7	76.11	118.8
1995	62.9	99.0	161.9
1996	72.3	126.4	198.7
1997	63.6	188.0	252.0
1998	62.5	181.0	243.0
1999	68.8	194.2	263.1
2000	110.5	212.0	322.6
2001	123.0	239.0	362.0
2002	140.0	223.4	363.0
2003	155.0	283.9	439.8
2004	233.3	460.3	693.7
2005	318.9	540.9	859.9
2006	433.5	1147.4	1580.9

Source: Department of Policy Planning, Ministry of Foreign Affairs, People's Republic of China ed. *Zhongguo Waijiao* [China's Foreign Affairs] (Beijing: World Affairs Press, various years)

CHAPTER 17

CONTEMPORARY MONGOLIA-RUSSIA RELATIONS

Luvsan Khaisandai

Mongolia is located in the North-East Asia region, which is distinguished by its favourable environment for investment and industrial location, and good prospects for becoming one of the world's active political and economic centers. Researchers have recognized that geopolitical orientation of "peripheral countries", for instance Mongolia, has played an important role in securing regional balance. Indeed, the peculiar geopolitical situation of Mongolia has a significant impact on regional affairs.

Therefore, by choosing Asia as third direction of its foreign policy, Mongolia set the goal of participation in political and economic integration of North-East Asian region. Since Mongolia's traditional foreign relations are characterized by good neighbourly relations for many centuries, this paper seeks to analyse Mongolia-Russia relations in the contemporary period in the context of Mongolia's position in North-East Asian region. People of both countries share a rich historical experience in mutual contacts and cooperation in all spheres of social life. It is also important to note here that Mongolian and Russian diaspora communities live in each other's countries. All these create a favourable environment for further development of both countries' relations in the new millennium.

Mongolia and Russian Federation established formal diplomatic relations on November 5, 1921. Pending Soviet Union restructuring in 1980s and democracy building in Mongolia in 1990s and former USSR's disintegration, Mongolia-

Russia relationship relied on adherence to the proletarian internationalism ideology and guidance to two systems peaceful co-existence policy. Being fully dependent on Moscow Mongolia was described as a USSR satellite state. Later the disintegration of former USSR and succession of Russian Federation to world politics ushered a new history-making era in Mongolia-Russia bilateral relationship. The new treaty on friendly relations and cooperation was concluded in 1993 and Ulaanbaatar Declaration signed in 2000 constructed a solid foundation under the bilateral relationship structure.

Once one-way highest-level visits until the year 2000 began reciprocated by series of top ranking officials and high level visits such as led by the Russian Federation President, Chairman of the Federal Council, Chairman of the Government and Russian Foreign Minister to Mongolia. Then Mongolian President N. Bagabandi met Russian leadership in Moscow on the commemoration of 60th anniversary of World War II. Later President N. Enkhbayar and President V.V. Putin conferred at the Shanghai Cooperation Organization Summit to further foster bilateral cooperation. Chairman of the State Great Khural paid official visit to Moskow. Russian Federation Chairman of the Federal Council attended the oath-taking ceremony of the Mongolian President. Russian Foreign Minister made working visit to Ulaanbaatar in March 2006 and negotiated wide ranging economic cooperation. President N.Enkhbayar paid official visit to Russian Federation in December 2006, and Moscow Declaration was signed during this visit. Mongolia-Russia cooperation is expected to increase its horizons in the new millennium.

Although defence and military cooperation has been discontinued at present, two sides signed bilateral agreement in 2004 on military and defence technology grant under which Russia would supply 5 million US $ military technology to Mongolia. Since 1990s Russian Federation foreign trade and economic investment notably decreased even though its predecessor USSR was a leading trade partner and economic actor. In 2006, the total amount of trade turnover between Russia and Mongolia reached at 592.9 million US $, imports being 547.8 million US $ and exports being 45.1 million US $

respectively. Nowadays, bilateral trade is almost entirely border trade. During the past few years, Russian investment in Mongolia basically stopped. However, there are nearly 300 economic ventures with 100 percent Russian investment, notably "Zarubejstroy", "Burvodstroy", "Golden Orient Mongolia" and joint ventures such as "Inckon" and "Erdenetsroi".

Settlement of "grand debt" became a historical landmark that broke ground for future improved and increased Mongolian-Russian cooperation. The two sides agreed to set up Task Force for discussing trade, economic and commercial cooperation program under the existing Intergovernmental Joint Commission. Numerous consultative working organs, such as 10 commissions and focal points, Sub-Commission on local administration and border cooperation, trade liberalization, transportation and energy, working group on real estate were set up to manage bilateral cooperation.. It is essential to improve efficiency and effectiveness of their work.

Since early 1990s cultural and educational exchanges stagnated. The Russian Government, however, came forward with its decision to receive 60 Mongolian graduate students and 30 post graduate Ph.D and MA eligible students annually since 1996. The fellowship and scholarship program gradually increased and in the year 2000 reached the level of 200 graduate students and 50 post graduate Ph.D and MA eligible students annually.

With a view to improve legally binding environment for bilateral cooperative programs, the two sides have negotiated about 10 new cooperation agreements. Mongolia seeks further promotion of cooperation with the Russian Federation's administrative member territories. All border crossing ports are governed under the 1994 Bilateral Agreement on the "Simplification of border-crossing and travel regime for Mongolian and Russian nationals". Despite these and other positive changes in the development of Mongolia-Russian affairs there are number of outstanding issues, particularly liberalization of bilateral trade, improving efficiency of the major Mongolia-Russia joint ventures such as "Mongolrostsevtmet" and "Ulaanbaatar railway" as well as sustainable supply of fuel and energy from Russia.

Simplification of access for reciprocal visits of two countries' nationals issuance of visas on substantially reduced price or exempted fee await solution. The Russian side stated that it could accept Mongolia's proposal for non-visa treatment for its nationals on reciprocity during the Moscow bilateral consular affairs consultative meeting in 2005. The two sides also examined the possibility of nominating Honorary Consuls in several districts of the Russian Federation and establishing Consular Missions elsewhere. They also discussed future co-ordination between their law enforcement and border management as well as customs and special service administrations for the enforcement of rules and regulations on Mongolian-Russian borders to prevent illegal livestock trafficking.

Nowadays, there exists a favorable political climate for having balanced relations with the two neighbors. Mutually beneficial cooperation in political, economic, commercial, business, investment, education, culture, sciences, and environment and defense areas developed dynamically. There are increased direct links at all levels of state or government institutions, namely border local districts, provinces, local republics, cities as well as NGOs.

To conclude, Mongolia's external environment greatly depends on the state of affairs between its two neighbors-Russian Federation and People's Republic of China; and building strategic partnership and mutual confidence between them will certainly create a most favorable surrounding for Mongolia's security and survival. Friendly bilateral relationship between Russia and China and normalcy between South and North Korea as well as amity among nations in South East Asia and Central Asia mostly determine Mongolia's external existence. Also foreign trade revenues including world market prices on copper, gold, oil and wool will continue to determine Mongolia's future development and prosperity. Existing multilateral cooperation structures in Asia-Pacific region will play a challenging role to architecture of regional security and stability all over Asia.

Today, in Mongolia-Russia relations, there are no such political issues that cannot be resolved. This factor is key to the ongoing good neighbourly relations between Mongolia and Russia, which indicates that multilateral cooperation based on equal partnership, remains to be the peculiarity of the new generation. In the 21st century, Mongolia-Russia relations are not only expected to develop intensively but the cooperation between the two countries may also become a trendsetter in regional and multilateral activities.

CHAPTER 18

RUSSIA-MONGOLIA RELATIONS IN THE 21st CENTURY

Elena Boykova

For more than 70 years Mongolia developed its relations with the Soviet Union based on the commonality of ideological tasks—the construction of communism and the struggle against capitalism. The geopolitical importance of Russia and Mongolia formed the characteristic features of the Mongolian foreign policy in the 19th-20th centuries. Due to its geographical position Mongolia did not have much choices of developing its external contacts. Actually the only choice it had, was to prefer either China or Russia, and the choice finally went in favour of Russia.

In the beginning of the 1990s, after ideological component of the Soviet-Mongolian relations disappeared, the two sides seemed to have reached such a level from where there would be no return i.e., the relations between the two countries became stagnant. Such a situation lasted rather long which resulted in Mongolia managing to find new economic and political partners. While the disintegration of the USSR resulted in the real collapse of economic relations between Russia and Mongolia, simultaneously it gave a strong impulse to the development of Mongolia's economic relations with both the western countries as well as China.

For quite a long time Russia continued to have a stereotype notion about the former Soviet-Mongolian relations, which were characterized as "eternal and indestructible friendship", but it did almost nothing to support and develop such relations. It was only in 2006 during his official visit to Mongolia that the former Prime Minister of Russia M. Fradkov declared that Russia "feels disposed to expand and deepen economic relations with Mongolia." It took Russian authorities rather long to bring such feelings to the forefront. In fact, not so long ago Russia finally realized that the period of inertia in the bilateral relations with Mongolia should be abolished and that it is now high time to build these relations according to the principles of contemporary international relations.

Russia's adaptation to the new political realities in Mongolia has been very slow. But now Russia and Mongolia are gradually moving towards a new stage of their relations so that the future the two countries could become strategic partners and allies. Russia and Mongolia are tied by their historical past i.e., mutual sympathies, which are passed on to new generations. However, at the beginning of the 1990s, it was also believed that bilateral relations cannot just drift away. It took about 10 years that the relations between Russia and Mongolia were normalized and that both countries realized that they still are necessary to each other. Russia finally realized that it would never be "an elder brother" to Mongolia. However, Russia has not yet formulated its new geopolitical role in Mongolia and, therefore, bilateral relations have still not been stable. Russia should precisely formulate its long-term economic and political interests in this country.

Probably, the real estimation of the potentials, prospects and risks of the joint projects can become a pragmatic approach to the relations between the two countries. Only recently Russian business elite realized that its own desire is just not enough for the development of its interests in Mongolia; rather attractiveness of investment projects, persistence in progress of these interests and the ability to come to an understanding with Mongolian partners are far more important.

In December 2006, during his meeting with President V. Putin in Russia, the President of Mongolia N. Enkhbayar discussed all complex issues of the bilateral relations, including the development of economic and trade relations. As a result of this visit, some documents, including the Moscow Declaration were signed. In this document both the parties stated their mutual aspiration to achieve an increase in efficiency in bilateral interaction in the spirit of strategic partnership. The process of political and military rapprochement of the two countries started coming on the right track as became evident from the visits of the Minister of Foreign Relations and the Commander of the General Headquarters of the Armed Forces of the Russian Federation to Ulaanbaatar. But the position of Russia in Mongolia is now noticeably weaker than the positions of the USA and China there.

Mongolia has occupied an appreciable place in Central Asia and in the world in general. The country has attracted attention of foreign partners and has become a prospective partner. It does not have to choose, as before, from the two variants. It can take itself a decision, with whom and what sort of relations it has to develop. Now Mongolia, apart from its two geographical neighbours—Russia and China, has some more important strategic "neighbours": the USA, Japan and the countries of EU. All these neighbours have their own interests in this country.

Mongolia's role in Central Asia is constantly growing. But in what degree? The answer to this question will depend on Mongolia itself and, first of all, on the level of political and economic stability in the country as well as on the stability of its foreign policy and foreign economic line. Unlike the Central Asian countries – the members of the CIS, where political leaders are more circumspect in signing long-term documents, mainly due to still rather unstable geopolitical situation both in the world and in the region, Mongolia, despite certain internal political problems, is a more politically stable country, which could actively partake in the working out of multilateral measures concerning such urgent problems as regional security.

One of the effective forms of interaction of Mongolia with Russia, the USA, EU and China could be elaboration of plans of joint actions, for example, in the social and humanitarian spheres, in the intermediate and long-term perspective. Just extended temporary frameworks could become a parameter of interest of all participating countries in the realization of such projects and a factor of stability.

Now, it is just not enough to state that Russia and Mongolia remain friends. It is necessary to fill the vacuum in relations with new contents, in order to resolve the problems. A systematic approach to the bilateral relations suited to the new situation in the world and in the region is necessary, otherwise these relations will not move forward. Russia and Mongolia can and should become strategic partners—they have good reasons and opportunity for it. For Russia the task of the prime importance is the forming of new information policy with respect to Mongolia, because now in Russia the interest to know about Chinggis Khan is very high, but unfortunately the Russians know very little about modern Mongolia.

The Presidential elections of 2008 in Russia have resulted in continuation of Putin's policy. The role of Russia in Central Asia seems to be growing, and it is unreal to break this process. How quickly it will reach its height can't be predicted. It will be faster, if Russia carries out vigorous, systematic and weighed policy appropriate to its rank of a great power. But in any case without the participation of Russia the problems of regional security, struggle against international terrorism, illegal migration and drugs trafficking cannot be resolved. It is hoped that Russia will return as the leader functioning in Central Asia, though it will not be the sole leader in this region any more. For the successful realization of the foreign policy line in the long-term perspective, Russia should precisely formulate its economic, military, cultural and geopolitical interests that concern both Mongolia and the whole of Central Asia. The objective of Russia should be to transform itself into a favourable and attractive international partner—in economic, military, political and other areas.

CHAPTER 19

MONGOLIA-RUSSIA RELATIONS: SOME PERSPECTIVES

Ilyas Kamalov

Russians perceived the Mongolian invasion that occurred at the beginning of 13th century as a punishment of God. However, they never thought that this "punishment" would last for nearly three centuries. As a matter of fact, together with the defeat of Russians by the Mongolians in the war of Kalka that took place in 1223 AD, the domination of Mongolians over Russian *knez* (prince) continued until the end of 15th century.[1] Russians treat this era as a "black" chapter in their own history and they even shut their eyes on this issue completely. Whereas, Russians owe the foundation of Tsarist Russia and the governmental and military structure of the state to Mongolians and also to the Golden Horde State that was founded by Mongolians but subsequently Turkicized and Islamized afterwards. One can also see the influence of Mongols on Russia in social life, economy, law, language, culture and arts. On the other hand, after the Russian *knezs* were freed from the dominance of Golden Horde State and they founded the Russian State by uniting around Moscow, the relationship between Russians and Mongolians continued. In early 16th century, the process of Russian expansion began and Mongolian societies were not immune from this process. In fact a number of ethnic groups originating from Mongols, exist within the Russian Federation today.

Besides, Russia played an important role in the independence of Mongolia since the beginning of 20th century. Some groups within Mongolia that were disturbed by the policy of China in 1911 got into touch with Russia and sought to obtain the support of Russia in their struggle for independence.[2] Thus, the treaty of amity that was signed between Russians and Mongolians in 1912 became crucially important for Mongolia. This treaty became a diplomatic step through which Mongolia established communication with one of the most major powers of the era and demonstrated itself on the international stage. However, the said treaty didn't recognize the independence of Mongolia. Russia and later the Soviet Union acknowledged Mongolia as an autonomous republic dependant on China until the end of 1946. Though, the political and economic support of Russia to Mongolia dates back to earlier. Even though Soviet Russia was struggling with its own economic problems at that time, Russian government contributed to the economy of Mongolia.[3] Moscow played a crucial role in the determination of the position of Mongolia on the international stage and Mongolia became a member of United Nations with the support of Russia after the Second World War. Moreover, Mongolia, who had tense relations with China in 1966, asked Russia to position its troops in Mongolia and these troops remained in Mongolia until the beginning of 1990 playing important role in the protection of the integrity of Mongolia.

The Soviet political and economic support undoubtedly helped Mongolia to develop. The contribution of Russians is unquestionable in the emergence of new cities in steppes and in the construction of industrial establishments in these cities. For instance, the companies such as Ulan-Bator Railways, Mongolsotsvetmetal and Erdenet that were founded in the Soviet period, still continue to operate and represent approximately 30 per cent of the income source of Mongolia.[4] Besides the setting up of joint companies and delivery of economic assistance, Moscow also sent its own experts to Mongolia to study there. In 1985, more than 15,000 Russian experts were studying in Mongolia.

However, dependence of Mongolia on Moscow was not so good in respect of its politics and economy. For, the economic crisis experienced by the former Soviet Union in 1980s affected both Russian and Mongolian communities and Mongolia faced an economic crisis too. Soviet troops retreated from Mongolia and Russian experts left the country. Without foreigners it was impossible for the local industry to improve. Besides, due to the change in international politics after the fall of the former Soviet Union, Mongolia too had to review its foreign policy just like other countries that followed Moscow-based foreign policy, and tried to develop cooperation with other Asian countries and also the USA in addition to Russia and China.[5]

Even though Russia and Mongolia signed a new treaty for cooperation in 1993, Mongolia was ignored by Yeltsin, who gave priority to West in Russia's foreign policy and also because the country itself was reeling through an economic crisis. One of the results of these developments was that China established closer relationships with Mongolia, particularly in trade and economy. Most of Mongolian goods are exported to the world through China, and Chinese investors carry out intense activities in Mongolia. There are three thousand registered Chinese companies in Mongolia, which are still active. Similarly, Japan also contributed to Mongolia especially in respect of economy. Japan granted 1 billion 300 million US dollars of credit and irrevocable aid to Mongolia between 1991 and 2004.[6]

Trade Partners of Mongolia[7]

Trade Volume %	**1999**	**2000**	**2001**	**2002**	**2003**	**2004**
China	29.5	34.8	32.3	32.1	34.2	35.5
Russia	**20.5**	**21.8**	**23.4**	**23.5**	**21.2**	**19.1**
USA	11.3	13.8	13.7	15.6	11.7	10.7
Korea	3.9	5.9	6.7	8.8	5.3	6.0
Japan	12.9	7.1	6.2	4.1	5.1	5.8
Germany	2.7	2.7	2.8	2.8	3.1	2.4
Others	25.6	22.5	14.9	13.6	19.4	22.8

These figures show that Russia has been left in the background as compared to its rivals. The factors that caused Russia to lag behind in the competition in economic sphere are:

1. Russia has not been able to attain the previous levels in its commercial relationship that existed till 1990s. As a matter of fact, the trade between these two countries mainly comprises of Russian energy resources today. While Mongolia sold 37 commodities to Russia until the beginning of 1990s, today this figure has fallen by 10 times. The share of Russia in the foreign trade of Mongolia is 20 per cent, and the fall in the share of Russia is due to the intense activities of new trade partners of Mongolia, mainly China, USA, Japan and Korea.
2. The scarcity of population and the low productivity in the regions that are situated on the Russia-Mongolia border.
3. Commercial relationship between the two countries is handicapped by the problem of transportation in the border areas.
4. Russia has imposed very high taxes on the Mongolian commodities.

However, Moscow has begun to see the negative impact of these developments and has now given a place to Mongolia in the multi-directional foreign policy that was initiated by Vladimir Putin. New era of the relationship between Russia and Mongolia started with the visit of Vladimir Putin to Mongolia in the year 2000. After this visit, Moscow waived 97 per cent of the debts of Mongolia that the country owed to Russia. After this debt problem was resolved, the relationship between these two countries started to develop rapidly. Now there is no problem that remains unsolved between Russia and Mongolia. Eleven of the sixteen regions in Siberia region of Russia carry out their economic relationship with Mongolia.[8] The kinship of the communities of Buryat and Tuva within the Russian Federation with the Mongolians facilitates this cooperation. Thus, 70 per cent of the trade volume between Russia and Mongolia pertains to these regions of Russia.

During the visit of Mongolian President Nambarin Enkhbayar to Russia on December 4, 2006, the two parties reached agreement on the subjects of exploiting the underground resources of Mongolia, training the Mongol soldiers by Russian experts, selling military technology to Mongolia and developing cooperation in agriculture and animal husbandry. Furthermore, the two sides stated that they would like to increase the trade volume between the two countries up to 1 billion US dollars level.[9] Russia, by conducting multi-directional cooperation with Mongolia seeks to halt the increase of Chinese influence in Mongolia and also to banish USA from this region.

USA attempts to increase its influence not only in Central Asia but also in Mongolia. President Bush of the USA declared during his visit to Mongolia in 2005 that Mongolia could describe the USA as their "third neighbor."[10] Mongolia desires to develop cooperation in military and technology fields with the USA within the framework of operations by UN Peace Forces and other international organizations. In the economic sphere too, USA has begun its cooperation with Mongolia recently. USA announced its readiness to invest 120 million US dollars for the restoration of Mongolian railways and commercial railway ports. In addition, an American company titled "Pibodi Energy" is ready to cooperate with Mongolia for operating the coal reserves.

The recent increase in the interest of global and regional powers in Mongolia is mainly due to its possession of great underground resources. Besides, Mongolia's move towards market economy will facilitate the harnessing of mineral deposits by the foreign investors. Coal, copper and other mineral deposits have attracted the attention of Japan, USA, China, Russia and Australia. Russia and China are also interested in Mongolia becoming a full member of the Shanghai Cooperation Organization. On the other hand, USA and Japan have been cooperating in order to influence its role in the Shanghai Cooperation Organization.[11]

Renewed interest in Mongolia also stems from the huge and empty lands of the country. In this context, Mongolia is cautious in its approach towards China and Japan. The presence of Inner Mongolia within China and also the presence of some opinions proposing the need for Mongolia's union with China undoubtedly disturbs the Mongolian government and also the nationalist groups in Mongolia leading to a more cautious policy towards China. That is why Mongolia has been eager to develop its relationship with Russia which doesn't pose any danger. As such Mongolia follows a policy of balancing between the global and regional powers. While Mongolia approaches Russia in order to protect its integrity, it also tries to develop good relationship with Japan, USA, South Korea and EU countries. Being concious of the importance of its own territory Mongolia seeks to draw optimum benefit from its geography.

Interest in Mongolia is not limited to political and economic fields, but has also extended to cultural relations. Interest in Russian language and literature has never declined in Mongolia. Russian universities opened faculties in Mongolia and a number of Mongol students went to the colleges of Russia. Russia allocates largest scholarship quota for Mongol students.[12] Besides, USA and China have also opened many schools in Mongolia. Russia considers India and Turkey its competitors in the domains of culture and education. Although India and Mongolia are geographically distant, Buddhist connection brings these two countries closer culturally. And these two countries are called "spiritual neighbors" due to this connection. These traditional connections based on the same Asian heritage and Buddhist culture facilitates the development of economic and cultural relations. India even conducted some military exercises, and participated in the military trainings hosted by the USA and Mongolia.[13] Thus, Mongolia, which follows a multi-directional foreign policy, tries to strengthen its relationships with India as well.

Another competitor of Russia in Mongolia in respect of culture and education is Turkey. And Turkey is considered to be a bigger threat to Russia due to its Pan-Turkic ideas. For, Turkey tops the list of countries that have set up a number of schools in Mongolia. Even though these schools don't belong to the state, they play important role in strengthening the solidarity between these two countries. Turkey, just like Russia, opened its doors for Mongol students in its own universities. Similarly, some of the state institutions, such as Turkish Cooperation and Development Administration Presidency (TIKA), carry out restoration of historical sites and other projects in Mongolia. Activities of Turkey are received with great interest especially by the Mongolian society. But the interest of Turkey in Mongolia is limited to the borders of this country, in contrast to other countries, which try to increase their influence in the Asia-Pacific region. One can assume that the rivalry between the near and distant neighbors of Mongolia shall increase in the years to come.

Whereas Russia is placed in a more advantageous position in Mongolia as compared to other countries, Russia needs to address the following issues in order to maintain this advantage and improve its relations with Mongolia:

1. Today, even the Russian proverb "There is a Tatar ancestor in every Russian's breed", implies that "Tatar" is the nation of Turks-Mongols. So the fact of Mongol domination, which is a part of Russian history, and that these two societies once lived together, should not be ignored by Russia in its approach towards Mongolia.
2. Moscow should take notice of Mongol societies living in Russia. It shall also be to the advantage of Russia, if Mongol republics of Buryatia and Kalmykia open their commercial agencies in Mongolia independently of Moscow.
3. While Russia improves its relationship with the Central Asian countries, it has also been trying to develop its relations with the organizations in which China is not a party except SCO.
4. There is need to immediately implement the agreement for eliminating visa conditions between Russia and Mongolia, for freer movement of people.
5. Russia should reduce the customs tax on the commodities that it imports from Mongolia.
6. Since the Mongolian society considers Russia to be the best friend of Mongolia, Russia should built upon this social capital. The USA, Japan and China follow Russia in this list.[14]
7. Russia should increase its investments in Mongolia and give long term credits to Mongolia. Russians can play

active role in projects related to mining and operation of energy resources in Mongolia. As Mongolia has huge underground resources, especially coal, Russia can use its potential in this field for improving the relationship between these two countries. Geographical proximity, past experience in running joint projects, language convenience and good neighborly relations place the Russian businessmen in a more advantageous position than the businessmen from other countries.

CONCLUSION

Even though Mongolia faced a huge crisis after the disintegration of the former Soviet Union, as it lost its most important supporter, the country pulled itself upright very fast and became the focus of interest of both regional and global powers. Its geopolitical situation and resources put Mongolia in a good position. Today, Mongolia has good relationship with all the regional and global powers and tries to maintain a balanced policy with USA, Russia, China, Japan and other countries. Although Moscow couldn't keep up its interest in Mongolia soon after the demise of the USSR as it struggled with its own problems, today Russia is recovering its lost ground developing closer relationship with Mongolia day by day.

REFERENCES

1. Ilyas Kamalov, *Otnoseniya Zolotoy Orsı s Hulaguidami*, Kazan, 2007, p. 25.
2. Sharad K. Soni, *Mongolia-China Relations. Modern and Contemporary Times,* New Delhi: Pentagon Press, 2006, pp. 30-36.
3. Tsedendambyn Batbayar and Sharad K. Soni, *Modern Mongolia A Concise History*, New Delhi: Pentagon Press, 2007, pp. 69-78.
4. See http://www.mongolia.mid.ru
5. Ilyas Kamalov, "Rusya'nın Asya-Pasifik Seferberligi", *Stratejik Analiz*, No. 87, July 2007, pp. 77-84.
6. Nuraniye Hidayet Ekrem, "Japonya ile Cin'in Mogolistan Mucadelesi," at http://www.tusam.net/makaleler.asp?id=624&sayfa=22

7. M.B. Meşaninov, "Torgovo-Ekonomiçeskiye Otnoşeniya Rossiyi i Mongoliyi Na Prigraniçnıh Territoriyah: Problemı i Perspektivı (1992-2004)", at http://www.ivran.ru/library/view_edition.php?edition_id=59
8. Ilyas Kamalov, "Rusya'nın Asya-Pasifik Seferberligi", *Stratejik Analiz*, No. 87, July 2007, pp. 77-84.
9. Lida Gariya, "Rossiya i Mongoliya: Sosedi Naveki", *Kommersant,* 4 December 2006.
10. *Ibid.*
11. Ilyas Kamalov, "Shangay Ekseni, NATO'yu Dengeleyebilir mi?", *Stratejik Analiz,* No. 69, January 2006, pp. 12-13.
12. "Liderı Rossiyi i Mongoliyi Hotyat Vıvesti Otnoseniya na Novıy Uroveny", 9 December 2006, at http://www.epochtimes.ru/ content/view/ 8057/3/
13. R. Bedi, "India Quietly Expands ties With Mongolia," at http://www.newkerala.com/july.php?action=fullnews&id=52661
14. James Brooke, "Mongolia's Shifting Ties: More China, Less Russia", *The New York Times*, 9 July 2004.

CHAPTER 20

U.S. POLICY TOWARDS MONGOLIA SINCE DIPLOMATIC RECOGNITION IN 1987

Alicia Campi

The year 2007 was the twentieth anniversary of the establishment of U.S.-Mongolian official diplomatic relations on January 27, 1987. There has been a seismic change not only in Mongolia's diplomatic and foreign policy during these two decades, but concurrently in its trade patterns. Mongolia in its transition from a command socialist economy to that of a democratic free market has expanded its economic ties with Western Europe, the U.S., Northeast Asia-particularly Japan and Korea, and especially its southern neighbor, China.

This paper explores the many positives and some negatives in the United States' political and economic relations with Mongolia in the past two decades. The U.S. Government established its first embassy in Ulaanbaatar in April 1988, but the first U.S. ambassador, Richard L. Williams, was not resident. In the early years, the United States valued Mongolia only as a window on the Sino-Soviet relationship, and on the new *glastnost* and *perostroika* policies spreading from Moscow to a loyal Soviet satellite. For Mongolia, the new official relationship with the United States gave its political independence and sovereignty greater status, and expanded its foreign policy options. The United States at that time had no real trade volume with, nor serious trade expectations for Mongolia. In 1990 total trade turnover between the two countries was a mere $900,000 according to Mongolian statistics and $2 million according to the

Americans,[1] which were exports of mainly animal hair and animal by-products. There were almost no American imports reaching Mongolia.

When relations commenced, the American Government had no real economic development strategy for Mongolia, and only slowly expanded relations in the cultural and economic fields. In 1989 and 1990, a cultural accord, Peace Corps accord, consular convention, and Overseas Private Investment Corporation (OPIC) agreement were signed. In the spring of 1990, when Mongolia peacefully abandoned communism and embarked on its economic transition and democratization, the United States seriously modified its goals for its relationship with Mongolia, yet even then the momentum for changing the nature of the relationship came from the Mongol side.

U.S. officials in testimony in front of Congress proclaimed that the developing relations with Mongolia was "… in large part an outgrowth of Mongolia's new open foreign and economic policies." They especially credited the early economic reform policies of the Mongolian People's Revolutionary Party (MPRP) dating back to 1987 for implementing Mongolia's own version of *glastnost* and *perestroika* to accelerate the country's economic and political reforms. Deputy Assistant Secretary of State Desaix Anderson proclaimed: "We should be clear on this: the Mongolian leadership has actively sought our cooperation in their reform effort." The Americans noted that Mongolia wanted to learn more about the democratic system and sought to increase the number of Mongolian exchange students in U.S. business schools and were interested in the Peace Corps program.[2]

The United States intensified its official dialogue on issues related to the bilateral relationship with Mongol leaders in Ulaanbaatar in March 1990. One month later, First Deputy Prime Minister Byambasuren visited Washington for discussion with the U.S. Vice President, the Secretary of State, Secretary of Commerce, Peace Corps Director, officials in the Department of Agriculture, and members of Congress. From the beginning, the Mongols expressed strong interest in a trade agreement and acquiring most-favored-nation status. The U.S. response to these ideas was positive but measured. The U.S. Department of State felt the prospect for steady expansion of U.S.-Mongolia relations was good. Policymakers from both the U.S. and Mongolia saw strategic advantages in strengthening the bilateral relationship, especially political ties. During the early 1990s many Mongols, including the first democratically elected President, P. Ochirbat, believed it was very important to quickly establish a strong working relationship with the United States. Ochirbat visited the United States in January 1991 and met with President George H.W. Bush. Upon his return home, President Ochirbat told his nation that "the U.S. public highly valued Mongolia's democratic revolution of 1990 as an excellent example of reform and transition in a peaceful way."[3]

U.S. strategy sought to help Mongolia create a stable free market and democratic society that would be a model for other former socialist nations making the same difficult transition from communism. This momentum from the American side was symbolized immediately by the fact that the new ambassador, Joseph E. Lake, arrived in July 1990 to permanently reside in the country, and within one month, Secretary of State James Baker III visited Mongolia, and then again in July 1991. On the Mongolian side, Mongolian government leaders began a pattern over the years of visiting Washington after making their annual trips each fall to participate in the opening of the United Nations General Assembly in New York.

Baker's early visits initiated a peculiar but potent infatuation with Mongolia by the U.S. Congress and successive American administrations. As a result, many American officials happily made the trek to Mongolia. Although President Bill Clinton and President Ochirbat met in New York in 1995, and Secretary of State Madeleine Albright and Hillary Rodham Clinton visited Mongolia in 1998, the Mongols sought a state visit from a sitting U.S. President. Mongolian President Bagabandi met President Bush in Washington in 2004. Finally, in 2005 the Mongols were successful in attracting highly publicized visits of Secretary of Defense Donald Rumsfield, Secretary of State Condoleezza Rice, and even President George W. Bush.

All these high-ranking visits have really advanced the closeness of U.S.-Mongolian political and military ties. This was exemplified by the state visit of Mongolian President Enkhbayar to Washington during October 22-23, 2007, when he signed a $285 million Millenium Challenge Compact agreement that would dramatically change the bilateral economic relationship. Under this special account in the next five years the U.S. will assist in the modernization of Mongolia's railroad infrastructure, healthcare system, land registration, and vocational education.

In the field of military cooperation, the U.S. began to provide military training to the Mongolian armed forces in the mid-1990s and special food relief during the 1999-2002 *dzuds* (winter disasters). The nature of U.S.-Mongolian military relations changed fundamentally after September 11, 2001, when Mongolia became the first country to offer condolences to the U.S. after it was attacked. Mongolia's strong support of the U.S. in the international area was established in a concrete way by quickly sending Mongol troops as part of coalition forces both to Iraq and then Afghanistan and by welcoming American military advisers to teach elements of Mongolia's military in-country. Mongolia's tenth rotation of troops in Iraq came to an end in September 2008, and it is not yet clear if Poland's withdrawal from the coalition (Mongol forces served under the Polish) will mean that Mongolia's contribution also will terminate.

Additional indication of U.S.-Mongolian military cooperation is reflected by the fact that Mongolia has participated since 2003 in peacekeeping training exercises called Khaan Quest with U.S. Marines from the III Marine Expeditionary Force.[4] In the fifteen-day August 2007 exercise, co-financed by the Government of Mongolia and the Global Peace Operations Initiative (GPOI) of the U.S. Department of State, Mongolia with the U.S. Pacific Naval Command hosted a 20-nation military exercise with Russia, Japan, and China as observers.[5]

On the economic side, the U.S. Government's donor policies and the activities of the early American investors in the 1990s established a foundation of practices and an overall business perception which is the legacy governing today's Mongolian investment climate for American entrepreneurs. For the United States, economic ties with Mongolia in the 1990s overwhelmingly meant donor assistance, rather than joint ventures and private investment. However, from the beginning of the new relationship and throughout the 1990s, the U.S. was only the third largest provider of foreign donor assistance to Mongolia, after Japan and Germany. Aid was dispensed at the rate of about $12-17 million a year through USAID and food aid. Yet, there was the perception by Mongolia and other foreign donors that the U.S., as well as the International Monetary Fund (IMF), set the development aid agenda for Mongolia during the decade, even though the planning sessions took place in Tokyo.

It was the United States in its role as winner of the Cold War that took the lead in devising and implementing programs both to accelerate Mongolia's political reforms and its transition to a free market economy. This strategy was called "shock therapy" and was quite controversial at the time.[6] It involved removing as fast as possible the command economy controls and regulations on prices and trade to shift to a private market economy by introducing a floating currency exchange rate and strict wage and credit controls with abolition of state subsidies. Concurrently, structural changes such as privatization of government assets, financial and banking reforms, encouragement of foreign investment, and educational and healthcare restructuring were implemented. The results were uneven, and in the first half of the 1990s economic dislocation and contraction increased Mongolian poverty and unemployment.

Early in the 1990s political scientists became nervous about China's potential for monopolizing Mongolia's economy, as its northern neighbor, Russia had done in the communist period. As a result, a new foreign policy concept called the 'Third Neighbor Policy' was first proposed for Mongolia as early as 1990 by U.S. Secretary of State James Baker. This strategic concept, which had political, military, cultural and economic components, meant that another large power, such as the U.S., Germany, India, or Japan, would act as a 'Third Neighbor' for Mongolia to counterbalance the traditional roles played by Mongolia's immediate neighbors. Mongolian policymakers quickly were enamored by the concept and in the 1990s embarked on the task of "searching for the Third Neighbor."

One result was that Mongolian political scientists and economists supported Mongolian integration into the Northeast Asian region as the best chance for the country to develop and prosper, as well as to balance China's economic and political influence. Northeast Asia was called Mongolia's natural economic territory, as a "regional Third Neighbor."[7] Many Mongolian policymakers enthusiastically embraced this concept, because it seemed a way to become part of the success of the Asia-Pacific economies. Mongolian leaders did not believe the effects of the Cold War could be swept from the region in only a few years, but some predicted that Mongolia quickly would come strategically under the economic umbrella of the U.S., as well as of Japan and South Korea. They expected that cultural and religious ties would be strengthened especially with India.

Unfortunately, in the second half of the 1990s the Asian economic crisis dashed hopes of this special role for Japan or South Korea. Germany was self-absorbed in its own reunification problems, so for Mongolia the only realistic choice was the United States. At first, American officials in the Clinton Administration dismissed Baker's Third Neighbor concept, because they viewed Mongolia as a friendly, but minor nation wedged between significant American rivals, Russia and China. However, with September 11, 2001 and the rise of international terrorism, the U.S. under President George W. Bush recalculated its strategic interests and gradually embraced the Third Neighbor relationship. Today the U.S. Government and American political scientists do not shy away from this term when describing the U.S. relationship with Mongolia.

In the middle of the 1990s U.S. developmental assistance policies in Mongolia changed in response to the victory of the democratic coalition parties in the 1996 election. There was recognition that the rural-urban divide in Mongolia was not, in fact, being narrowed by American assistance policies, but actually being widened. The major U.S. focal points during the second half of that decade were to provide technical assistance in designing and implementing reform in the financial and energy sectors, in completing privatization of state enterprises, and in implementing agriculture and trade policy modernization. Mongolian-made textiles found a big export market in the U.S. when Mongolia was granted free-trade status in 1999. Exports to the U.S. skyrocketed to $92.9 million in 2000, second only to China's $274.3 million. U.S. imported goods rose from zero in 1990 to $28.4 million by 2000 (ranked 6th).

It was expected that Mongolia's acquisition of free trade status in the U.S. market would help Mongol herders to get better prices for their animal hairs. From 1999 Mongolia's apparel and textile related exports, mostly destined for the United States, increased significantly, so that by 2002 they accounted for 45 per cent of Mongolia's total exports. It was true that cashmere goods marked 'Made in Mongolia' were visible in the United States. Yet, Mongolian wool and animal hair products from 1999-2002 actually lost 8 per cent of the world market share, as these unprocessed materials moved illegally more and more to China for processing. Furthermore, American companies that had invested in cashmere and camel hair procurement, after years of insufficient support from the American Government, finally dropped out of the Mongolian market altogether, when they became embroiled in continuous legal suits. So in the end, U.S.-Mongolian trade in products originating in the herding economy did not increase as expected.

To some extent the 1990s were the heyday for American-Mongolian economic ties. The United States at one point in the 1990s was Mongolia's largest foreign investor, because of the presence of SOCO Tamsag in the petroleum sector, which was sold in 2004 to the Chinese, and Mongol Amicale in cashmere and camel wool procurement.[8] In comparison, in 2006 United States' investment had slipped to 5th place. In the new century large American investments increasingly fled Mongolia, to be replaced by smaller investors. The U.S. Embassy itself suspended disbursement of $3 million in aid in 2002 over a disputed judicial process considering the theft of donated American wheat. This experience left the U.S. Government more wary and unwilling to work directly with Mongol ministries and companies on development projects. Rather it favored using more non-profit intermediaries as monitoring agencies-which increased administrative costs for aid programs.

U.S. momentum in the new decade continued its slowdown to the point where the Mongolian Ambassador to the U.S., Ravdangiin Bold, in August 2004 told a Mongolian reporter that American investment was stubbornly stagnant. Recently, the acceleration of interest in Mongolia's mineral sector, despite the contentious nature of foreign development projects, once again has excited American mineral interests as they have watched America's northern neighbor, Canada, became more and more active. U.S. Ambassador Mark Minton (appointed in 2006) in a newspaper interview cited the U.S. commercial relationship built around Mongolia's mineral resource position and the opportunities this presents for U.S. companies as the "centerpiece of the bilateral relationship."[9] He believes the conclusion of agreements regarding Oyu Tolgoi's copper and gold and Tavan Tolgoi's coal as a "watershed" for Mongolian democracy and the economy. In 2008 it is hoped that the interest of Peabody Energy out of St. Louis, Missouri in entering the Mongolian market will give a big boost to new U.S. investment, but continuing concern over the legal and tax regimes for mineral investors has negatively impacted on this goal. Other new major stimulators to American investor confidence are the growing interest of Merrill Lynch in Mongolia's financial sector and the long-awaited opening of a Hilton Hotel in Ulaanbaatar in 2008.

For the future, one major question impacting the U.S. relationship with Mongolia is whether or not the U.S. should accept the rapidly expanding Chinese economic influence in Mongolia or devise a new bilateral economic strategy for Mongolia to counteract China's growing economic control of the Mongolian market? In today's environment of mineral and oil exploration, demand for high tech consumer goods, and projected energy development, American companies rightly see themselves as the middlemen to the Chinese market. Only textile sector investors in Mongolia look to sell goods into the U.S. market, but increasingly these investors are Chinese-owned entities not American. It appears that past and present American economic development policies in fact may be adverse to U.S.

and Mongolian political interests in building a democratic, transparent, monopoly-free, free market for Mongolia. A final, continuing irritant to the growth of bilateral ties is the high visa refusal rate (over 60 per cent) for Mongolians seeking a U.S. visa and the large percentage of Mongolian "overstays" in the United States who are in illegal status-as many as 20,000 people. This problem affects both educational and business exchanges in many ways and constantly generates negative press towards the United States.

Mongolia is a strategically placed Eurasian nation with only 2.5 million in population. For the United States it often is seen as a relatively successful posterchild among former communist countries for simultaneously and enthusiastically transitioning to democratic governance and free market economic principles. U.S.-Mongolian bilateral trade over the last twenty years has been very limited, despite Mongolia having most favored nation status. U.S. investment is only slowly growing, although political and military relations are closer year by year. The U.S. Government is devoting more resources to rural training to alleviate poverty and spur job creation. For example, the monetized proceeds of food aid ($3.7 million in 2005) currently are used to support programs bolstering entrepreneurship, herder diversification, better veterinary services, and disaster relief. In 2006 USAID claimed to have created or helped 1250 small businesses and assisted 2500 people (including 1500 women) find jobs.[10] The present trends suggest that relations between Mongolia and the United States will continue to strengthen, although it is not likely that the U.S. will become Mongolia's most important economic partner.

REFERENCES

1. Statement of Deputy Assistant Secretary Desaix Anderson before the U.S. House of Representatives' Foreign Affairs Committee, May 1990.
2. *Ibid.*
3. Tsedendamba Batbayar, *Mongolia's Foreign Policy in the 1990's: New Identity and New Challenges*, Ulaanbaatar: Institute for Strategic Studies, 2002, p. 184.

4. Lt. Col. Mark W. Gillette, "Mongolian Soldiers and U.S. Marines Train in Peacekeeping in Exercise KhaanQuest," *Asia Pacific Defense Forum,* Winter 2004.
5. "Khaan Quest 2007 Multi-national Military Exercise Starts in Mongolia," *UB Post,* 30 July 2007.
6. Keith Griffin, ed., *Poverty Reduction in Mongolia*, Australia: Asia Pacific Press, 2003.
7. Comment by Dr. Robert Scalapino when presenting "The Political Process in Northeast Asia and Mongolia's Challenge," unpublished paper presented at Mongolia-U.S. Bilateral Conference, *Mongolia-U.S. Comprehensive Partnership in the Context of North East Asia: Challenges and Opportunities,* Washington, 28 February 2005.
8. FIFTA, "Steppes in the Right Direction," Ulaanbaatar, 2006, p. 2.
9. "United States-the Third Neighbor," *The Washington Times*, 22 September, 2007.
10. See USAID website on Mongolia: www.usaid.gov/location/asia_near_east/countries/mongolia/

CHAPTER 21

BRIDGING THE GAP IN SINO-MONGOLIAN TIES: ROLE OF INNER MONGOLIA

Sharad K. Soni

As the new millennium set off, China and Mongolia, formerly known as Outer Mongolia, witnessed a new high in their post-Cold War normalized relations, mainly due to economic reasons. The year 2000 turned out to be a landmark in Sino-Mongolian relations as China became Mongolia's largest trading partner besides being the largest direct foreign investor. This is a manifestation of what the two sides are now doing to bridge the gap in their relationship which has been "a legacy of at least two thousand years of mistrust and intermittent confrontations and hostilities between the two societies."[1] Perhaps Inner Mongolia Autonomous Region (IMAR) of the People's Republic of China has played the most significant role in the ever growing Sino-Mongolian ties, which bore the brunt of Sino-Soviet Cold War. Over the years, Inner Mongolia has come a long way and now enjoys significant status in the Chinese government policy towards the development of the region on the socio-economic front, especially after the launch of China's "Western Development Programme" in the late 1990s.[2] In the recent years, due to improvement in Sino-Russian as well as Sino-Mongolian relations, Inner Mongolia has been witnessing even greater progress with flourishing border trade, a reality that also signifies the importance of IMAR as a political-geographical unit. But the history of Inner Mongolia as a political-geographical unit begins only with the Manchu occupation of China that gave way to the establishment of Qing dynastic rule (1644-1911).

It is in this context that this paper seeks to trace the origin of Inner Mongolia, which owes much to the Mongol fragmentation following the fall of the Mongol Yuan dynasty in China. It also highlights subjugation of Mongols by the Manchus who made a specific distinction between Outer Mongols and Inner Mongols, besides examining the policies of various regimes in China towards Inner Mongolia right from the Qing dynasty to the People's Republic of China. While dealing with the role of Inner Mongolia in Sino-Mongolian relations in contemporary times, the paper seeks to analyse the following two key points:

(a) Since China shares its longest land border with Mongolia, maintaining cordial relationship with Ulaanbaatar is of paramount importance for the security and stability of northern China, including Xinjiang, Inner Mongolia and the northeastern provinces.

(b) Given the fact that Inner Mongolia acts as a sort of bridge between China and Mongolia, its role becomes vital for cementing the Sino-Mongolian ties, not only in economic and trade spheres but also in political, cultural and strategic realms.

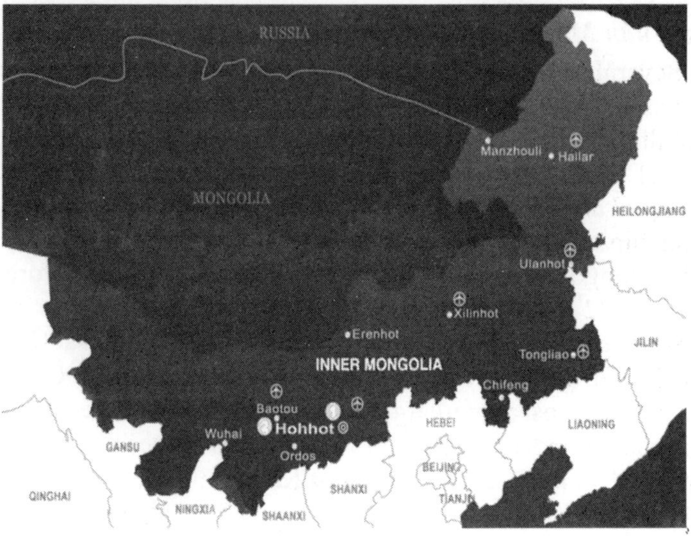

Map: *Inner Mongolia Autonomous Region*

Inner Mongolia: Historical Background

Historical records suggest that the existence of Mongols was known to the rulers of China as far back as the Tang dynasty (618 AD-907 AD) which was considered to be a golden era of Chinese civilization. According to *The Secret History of Mongols*, the Mongol people were first found in the dense forests on the south bank of the Ergun River in Inner Mongolia's Hulun Buir League during the Tang dynasty.[3] It is also evident from the Chinese chronicles in which the name "Mongol" is recorded that under Tang China, the Mongols were known as the *Hui-ho-chieh-chia-su* (Mohammedan Turki-Mongols).[4] During the period beginning from the Southern Sung dynasty up to the ascendancy of the Manchus in China i.e. from 1127 AD to 1644 AD, the Mongols were called by yet another name as the *Mêng-Ku*. But the Manchus were more specific in making the distinction between Northern and Southern Mongols who came to be called as *Wei Mêng-Ku* (Outer Mongols) and *Nei Mêng-Ku* (Inner Mongols) respectively.[5] However, the emergence of Inner Mongolia dates back to the pre-Manchu period as a result of the Mongol fragmentation following the fall of the Yuan dynasty.

Post-Yuan Mongol Fragmentation

Several historians have revealed that Inner Mongolia formed the base for the virile nomadic Mongols to descend and raid agricultural Chinese until Chinggis Khan united all the nomadic Mongol tribes and established his Great Mongol Empire (*yeke mongghol ulus*) in the thirteenth century.[6] Having a commanding leadership quality Chinggis Khan's contribution to the expansion of the Mongol empire can be gauged from the fact that before his death in 1227AD he had already formed "the basis of a far-flung Eurasian empire by conquering its inner zone across Central Asia."[7] Yet, the legacy of Mongol conquest vis-à-vis China is perhaps the most remarkable because not only whole of China was brought under the Mongol rule but also it became the seat to govern the empire since the days of Khubilai Khan, the grandson of Chinggis Khan.[8] It was in 1280 AD that all of China was brought under the Great Mongol Empire when southern China was added to Khubilai's Yuan dynasty following the downfall of the Sung dynasty. Khubilai's Yuan China went down in the history as an extraordinary period during which one people, the Mongols, played a decisive domineering role in the Eurasian continent.

But Khubilai's death in 1294 AD can be considered as the turning point in the history of Mongol rule in China. His successors lacked the ability to govern such a large territory as Yuan China had in its possession and so Mongol rule in China got weakened to give way to the establishment of the Ming rule in 1368 AD. In the post-Yuan period, relations between Ming China and the Mongols can be described in terms of policy pursued by the Ming rulers, which focussed on "not to subjugate the whole of Mongolia but rather to destroy the unity of the tribes, which gave them their striking power."[9] In fact, it was a "divide-and-rule" policy of the Mings that the Chinese could be able to manage the semi-nomads of southern Mongolia (present day Inner Mongolian autonomous region) as border allies against the fully nomadic and mobile tribes of northern Mongolian region (today's independent State of Mongolia).[10]

After some time, when the Ming rulers shed their anti-Mongol animosities, some Mongol people who could not go back to their native land when the Mings ousted their ruler were permitted to stay at their places of residence in China. Consequently, while some Mongols lodged themselves into Chinese mode of life or at least into Chinese system of governance, pacification of a major chunk especially those living outside the Chinese border remained a difficult issue. The reason, as Rossabi examines, was that "...[Since] the Mongols were scattered and divided into so many different tribes that pacification of all these groups was impractical. Moreover, the Mongols during the Ming, scarcely engaged the Chinese forces in full-scale battles. Small bands usually met the Ming troops and mostly encountered them on hit-and-run raids or what might be referred to as guerrilla warfare...."[11] This kind of warfare involving the Mongols reflects the prevailing state of their political organisation which unlike in the past was now unable to be led by a unified Mongol leadership. Rise of a new Mongol empire, therefore, remained a dream for the Mongols who had to pay a heavy price due to their own fratricidal wars. This once again resulted into division among various Mongol tribes who towards the beginning of fifteenth century split into two distinct branches – Eastern and Western or Oirats. The eastern Mongols included Khalkhas, Buryats, Chahars and Tumets, while the western Mongols were a group of Derbets, Oirats and Olets.

Later on, in the seventeenth century, the eastern branch too got divided into northern Mongols (Khalkhas, Buryats) living north of the Gobi desert and southern Mongols (Chahars, Tumets) occupying the area south of the desert.[12] Such divisions among the Mongols resulted in the step-by-step conquest of their respective areas by both the Manchus and the Russians who began to dominate the geopolitics of the Inner Asian region. So far as northern Mongols are concerned Khalkhas were brought into submission to the Manchu rule in China towards the end of the seventeenth century, whereas Buryats were conquered by the Russians and politically separated from the Khalkhas. Since then the Khalkhas of northern Mongolia also began to be referred to as Outer Mongols, the inhabitants of present day Mongolia and the southern Mongols as the Inner Mongols, the inhabitants of today's Inner Mongolia Autonomous Region of China. It has also been revealed that it was because of Southern Mongol nobles' greater cooperation that the Manchu rulers treated them as Inner Circle, while Northern Mongol nobles were treated as Outer Circle due to their comparatively longer resistance.[13]

While coming back to the Ming period one may notice that after division among the Mongols the Ming rulers began to follow the strategy of playing off both the eastern and western Mongols against each other, though the latter were favoured most to counteract the former. But it did not work out properly and the Oirats (western Mongols) who played a major role in Mongolian political developments especially between 1423 AD and 1530 AD even went to the extent of advancing against the Ming power.[14] For example, Batu Möngke (1470 AD-1544 AD), a descendant of the royal family, who is widely known as Dayan Khan made the first attempt and united the Mongol tribes – both the eastern and the western (Oirats) under his leadership. He is said to be so ambitious that like his predecessors he wished to "re-establish Mongol rule in China".[15] But again disunity as well as constant internecine warfare brought the Mongols down which proved to be advantageous for the Chinese to the extent that Dayan Khan "no longer threatened the survival of the Ming empire in the last three decades of his reign".[16] From that time onwards the Mongol areas became more or less independent princedoms with their own names, whose rulers adopted the title of 'Khan'.[17]

The last of the Khans of all Mongolia was Dayan Khan's grandson Altan Khan (1532 AD-1582 AD) of the Tumet Mongols who is credited with having founded the city of Höhhot, the capital of modern Inner Mongolia. Altan Khan also made one last attempt to unite the Mongols during the Ming Period,[18] and was able to exert far greater pressure on the Chinese border areas. Under Altan Khan the reason for Mongol raids on the Chinese territory was again the dispute concerning tribute and trade privileges. When he was denied the terms and conditions he put before the Ming ruler to accept, a series of devastating raids followed since 1551 AD onwards. And it was only after almost twenty years that the Mongol raids culminated in a peace settlement in 1571 AD.[19] With this peace settlement which was aimed at bringing peace in the Mongol-Ming stalemate, the Mongols in western part of Inner Mongolia were now quiescent for a while so that the Chinese could turn their attention to the eastern part of the region (the western part of Manchuria). But in this part the Mongol nobles continued to be intransigent so much so that Altan Khan's death in 1582 AD made the situation further worse. The Mongols eventually became a loose collection of disorganized roaming tribes, warring among themselves and occasionally raiding China, until the rise of the Manchus who finally subjugated the Mongols.

Notwithstanding the above mentioned situation, Ligden Khan of Chahar tribe (1592 AD-1634 AD), who also claimed to be the last of the Mongol Khans, tried unsuccessfully to reunite the Mongols. It was so because right after the death of Altan Khan the control of Mongol power along the Great Wall shifted from the Tumets to the Chahars, and so Ligden Khan considered himself as belonging to the imperial line of Chinggis Khan. By then the Manchus were quite clear that without defeating Ligden Khan and subjugating eastern Mongolia, there was no way out to reach China proper. Thus the beginning of the seventeenth century witnessed Manchu diplomacy at work in creating a network of alliances with eastern Mongols who could be used against Ligden Khan as well as China. By that time already Mongols were a divided lot into several Khanates and princedoms and none of these groups was willing to recognise another's leadership, nor could any provide the kind of leadership required to keep the Mongol unity intact.

Due to internal squabbles and lack of unity the eastern Mongols once again saw a further split: Southern or Inner Mongols and Northern or Outer Mongols. It were the Inner Mongols against whom the Manchus campaigned, while Outer Mongols by and large remained neutral and stayed away from involving themselves in the struggle of Inner Mongols against Manchu conquest. Finally in 1632 AD, the Manchu forces under the leadership of Abahai launched a massive attack against the Inner Mongols. The comparatively weak forces of Ligdan Khan could not match the much stronger forces of the Manchus and at the end in 1634 faced a crushing defeat.[20] However, Ligden with his 100,000 people fled in the direction of Höh Nuur [Kukunor] and although he managed to reach there, on the way itself he had already lost about 80 per cent of his subjects.[21] Shortly afterwards he died at Kukunor, thus came to an end of the imperial line of reigning Mongol Khans dating back to Chinggis Khan. Since then the title "Khan" began to be adopted by numerous Mongol princes, while earlier it was limited in use only to the rulers of the four major Mongol Khanates of Eurasia, i.e., Yuan, Chaghadai, Persia and Kipchak (Golden Horde).[22] With the subjugation of Inner Mongolia a major hurdle in the Manchu conquest of China was now eliminated, and before Peking fell into hands of the Manchus Inner Mongolia had already been placed well under their control.

In the history of both the Manchus as well as Inner Mongols, the year 1636 AD marked a turning point because of two reasons- firstly, Abahai proclaimed himself as emperor of his new dynasty of Qing ("pure") and secondly, at his enthronement ceremony forty-nine princes of sixteen banners of Inner Mongolia elevated him as their great Khan (Mongoian: *Deed Erdemt*; Chinese: *T'ien Ts'ung*).[23] All this along with military and administrative capacities made him a strong contender for the Peking throne and he became more determined in his mission to overthrow the Ming dynasty. But he died in 1643 AD and succession passed on to his son Fu-lin who ascended the Peking throne on 30 October 1644 AD as Emperor Shun chih, the first Manchu-Qing emperor of China. The "divide and rule" policy, which the Manchu rulers inherited from their predecessors, worked properly in order to keep their overlordship intact on both the Inner as well as Outer Mongols. As regards Inner Mongolia, the Manchus organised it as part of their military reserve and brought it under their protection exercising strict control over its government. This organisation was the origin of the institutional and administrative concept of "Inner" Mongolia, resulting in two Mongolias markedly different from each other, Inner Mongolia being much more closely integrated with China. Although administrative distinction between Inner and Outer Mongolia was formally introduced by the Manchu-Qing dynasty, its origin was much older and can be traced back to the period of Dayan Khan in the fifteenth century.

As regards the Outer Mongols and the Western Mongols, tribal war between them continued until 1688 AD when the Western Mongols under the leadership of Galdan Boshigt (1651 AD-1696 AD) invaded Outer Mongolia. In order to fight back the Western Mongols, the Khalkha nobles of Outer Mongolia requested for military aid from the Manchu rulers of China,[24] who quickly responded as the prevailing situation was conducive to their expansionist designs. Having succeeded in subjugating the Western Mongols or *Oleuths*, Manchu Emperor K'ang-hsi called a convention of the Khalkhas at Dolon-nor in Inner Mongolia in 1691 AD,[25] where the Khalkha nobles recognized the Manchu Emperor as their great Khan. The struggle between the Manchus and the Western Mongols, however, continued, and it was not until 1750s that the Manchus finally dealt a crushing blow to the Western Mongols. Whereas the main body of the

Western Mongols still remained in the northern part of what is today Xinjiang Uighur Autonomous Region, a portion of their territory was annexed to the north western part of Outer Mongolia where they had been at war among themselves. As a result, one group split up to migrate to the lower Volga in Russia, where they came to be known as Kalmyks.[26] After conquering Western Mongolia, the Manchus ruled the two Mongolias-Inner and Outer till 1911, though Outer Mongolia was administratively ruled more loosely and indirectly while compared to Inner Mongolia.

Qing Policy towards Inner Mongolia

The close integration of Inner Mongolia into Manchu-Qing rule was influenced by geographical setting of the region which proved to be a vital link for spreading Manchu control over other parts of Mongol inhabited territories. Obviously, the use of Inner Mongol tribes as allies constituted an "essential factor" in the rise of the Manchus. The first documented evidence dealing with relations between the Manchu Emperor and the Inner Mongol tribes has been found to be dated 1636, which marked the acknowledgement of Manchu emperor's suzerainty, though it was stipulated that "should the dynasty [Qing] fall, all the laws previously existing should come into force again."[27] But Inner Mongolia never returned to its previous status, as it became more of a "province" than a mere territory of Manchu-China.[28] It appears that what was begun as subjugation of the Mongols of Inner Mongolia following their defeat by the Manchus culminated in their enrolment as vassals and yet simultaneously as allies in the Mongol banners. The Ming Chinese devices were further strengthened to keep the Mongols in check, mainly by "assigning the [various Mongol] tribes to fixed geographic areas, confirming new chiefs in their succession, conferring titles and honours, supervising inter-tribal councils and postal communications, permitting regulated trade at fixed markets, and bestowing the customary gifts on regular tribute missions."[29]

Whatever policy with regard to the Mongols was followed, it was essentially targeted to prevent the accumulation of power by any single Mongol leader, and herein lay the key to Manchu success in keeping Inner and Outer Mongolia separate ever since the two areas came under Qing rule. However, as Rupen argues, although the seventeenth century internal strife among the Mongols benefited the Manchus in gaining slow but steady control of Mongol areas, it was revealed that the identical policies proclaimed particularly for both the Inner and Outer Mongolia often differed in practical results. It was basically due to the fact that the Qing rulers enforced their will more effectively in contiguous Inner Mongolia than in distant Outer Mongolia.[30] For all practical purposes Inner Mongolia was treated more or less like the "interior" of China. For the smooth functioning of administration in Inner Mongolia, the whole region was divided into six leagues, embracing 24 tribes, which in turn consisted of 49 banners altogether.[31] Sometimes Inner Mongolia was also referred to as "the country of Forty-nine Banners,"[32] thus signifying the importance of institution of the banner system.

Unlike Outer Mongolia where a league was made up of at most two tribes, in Inner Mongolia the Qing policy to break up their tribal organisation and tradition worked so forcefully that several tribes, sometimes as many as eight, were brought together to form a league.[33] As already mentioned there were six leagues known as Jirim, Josotu, Juu Uda, Shili-yin Gool, Ulaanchab and Yekhe Juu which were composed of 24 different tribes to be organized into 49 banners in Inner Mongolia.[34] Besides, there were also a number of other Inner Mongolian groups who remained outside the system of league administrations and were not subjected to be ruled directly by their hereditary princes, such as the eight banners of Chahar, divided into right and left wings with four banners each, as well as those of the Tumet and Barga Mongols.[35] Typically in the league system, the banner was the local unit, and hence not only the leagues but also the banners were considered to be the real administrative units. Theoretically, the local administration enjoyed self-autonomy i.e., the Mongol elements were continued to be ruled by the hereditary Mongol chieftains, yet in practice the Manchu administrative organs exerted vigorous influence over the Mongols.[36] In this respect, the head of the banner called

Jassak (Administrator), who held the position with the approval of the Manchu emperor, resembled the character more of a vassal lord than of an official. Moreover, he was assisted by a number of staff to carry out administrative work.

The status of Inner Mongolia under the Qing administration remained as a subject of close supervision or rather governance of the imperial court in Peking. But the understanding of "closeness" on the part of the Inner Mongols basically worked in two ways: while on the one hand it helped the Manchus to maintain the Inner Mongols as their allies, on the other it strengthened the Qing policy of keeping the Mongols of the two regions divided. As Lattimore points out, "the policy in question had been based on the sound theory that the Manchus could hold China in peace if the Mongols were unable to unite".[37] This unity was prevented by, apart from others, granting the Inner Mongol tribal chiefs a privileged position, particularly subsidizing them with award of honoured titles and local power, something that could help the Qing rulers to win their loyalty. Another method that proved to be most effective in ensuring the Mongol loyalty was the matrimonial alliances between the Mongols and the Manchus. Initially, discouraging Han Chinese to intermingle with the Mongols was part of the overall Qing frontier policy of playing one race against another in order to have their supremacy over all of them. However, it was in the beginning of the twentieth century when the Manchus identified their interests more closely with the Han Chinese interests that the Qing imperial rulers began to realize the folly of their frontier policy. Consequently, a major policy shift took place that encouraged the Han Chinese immigration to settle in the frontier regions including both Outer and Inner Mongolia.

This policy of encouraging Han migration was also aimed at counteracting Russian settlement in eastern Inner Mongolia, which at that time was intensified in search of economic prosperity. Commenting on the folly of Qing frontier policy, Pao Chao Hsieh says, "Had these suicidal territorial policies [discouraging Han migration to frontier areas] been changed earlier, China's frontier troubles would have been reduced and her frontier development [would have been] much more advanced.[38] By the time the Qing dynasty fell, it was too late to get rid of all the social prejudices as long separation had already created enough "misunderstanding" and "distrust" between the Han Chinese and the Mongols. China, thus, had to pay the price for it because at least Outer Mongolia conditioned by the colonial legacy of the Qing dynasty finally became independent. On the other hand, situation in Inner Mongolia was very different on both the political as well as demographic levels. Politically, Inner Mongolia's close association or rather incorporation into the Qing Empire proved to be a permanent arrangement as it outlasted the demise of the last dynastic rule in China and exists even today as an autonomous region; demographically, the Mongol population had been swamped by the Han Chinese settlers.[39]

One of the main reasons for an extensive Han Chinese settlement in Inner Mongolia was to increase population density in the northern frontier areas so as to defend the country against potential Russian invasion.[40] The activities of these Chinese settlers in Inner Mongolia from the economic point of view were limited not only to cultivate grasslands for agricultural production but also to raise revenues through their commercial activities in order to support the imperial government's Mongolian administrative apparatus. Han Chinese economic penetration, thus, served the dynasty's interests, which resulted in binding the Mongols "more tightly to the rest of the empire."[41]

Interestingly, the glory of Chinese culture, which had taken a back seat for quite some time, now suddenly came into the forefront and the Qing rulers began to believe that "the Chinese civilisation must be extended to the non-Han nationalities, not only for the benefit of China itself, but for the regeneration of the 'benighted' frontier peoples."[42] And to make it a reality, every possible obstacle was dealt with firmly. Realising that this might lead to assimilation and ultimately to Sinicization, the Mongols out of their resentment took to uprisings. These uprisings were essentially local in character far from being well-organised "national revolts", though later on in 1911 Outer Mongolia witnessed a national liberation movement. But Inner Mongolia, where uprisings against Qing rule and Chinese merchants took place relatively earlier than in Outer Mongolia, never found such an opportunity to become independent. Some primary sources released in the 1970s point to the occurrence of insurrections definitely in Inner Mongolia as far back as in 1861 and further in 1864, 1870, 1890, 1899 and 1901.[43] Thus, it confirms the suggestion by numerous scholars that in most of the key developments of nineteenth and early twentieth century Mongol history, it was Inner Mongolia, which showed the way and Outer Mongolia simply followed.

In spite of various difficulties surrounding the Mongols, seeds of nationalism were already sown particularly in Inner Mongolia, where resentment further grew against the underhand practices of the Chinese merchants and attempts by the Qing rulers to implement reforms as part of their policy shift. Moves towards implementing reforms, as Baron Korff observes, were considered by the Mongols "to be interferences with their local self-government."[44] This was the situation of the Mongols at the turn of the twentieth century. Finally, in 1906, following the Russo-Japanese War (1904-05) the Qing government announced the application of "New Administration" (*Hsin Cheng*) policy to Inner Mongolia. As such, several plans were devised on the basis of investigations carried out by the Qing officials. One such investigation was conducted by Prince Shu who recommended the plan for "extensive Chinese colonisation of Inner Mongolia with the aim of absorbing the Mongols into the Chinese nation."[45] The recommendation, however, was described as being a developmental plan for the whole region.

Yet, the Chinese influence on the Mongols of Inner Mongolia, or in this case impact of Sinicization process was not always negative. It is evident from the fact that a few Mongol nobles who were educated in Chinese ways put their demands before the Qing court for socio-economic changes in Inner Mongolia. For example, in 1908, Gungsangnorbu (1871-1931), the Prince of Kharachin tribe, gave a petition to the Qing court, which contained eight demands:[46] (a) to establish banks as soon as possible; (b) to hasten the construction of railroads; (c) to develop mineral resources; (d) to develop farming, industry and commercial enterprises; (e) to take special care of diplomatic matters; (f) to popularise and elevate education; (g) to modernise military forces; and (h) to establish a police administration. The very next year in 1909, Ghonchughsereng, another Prince who belonged to the Khorchin tribe, petitioned the court on following four items:[47] (a) to control religion to stop superstition; (b) to develop education to increase the knowledge of the people; (c) to train Mongolian troops to fortify border defence; and d) to select land for cultivation to protect the livelihood of the people. But all these demands failed to receive desired response. It means, although Sinicization somehow provided an opportunity to the Mongol nobles to think constructively, the Manchus even to the end of their rule were unwilling to encourage them in their constructive efforts.

What is worth to be noted here is that after the Qing policy shift the key issue before the imperial government was to reorganise banner lands into Chinese administrative units not only in the Mongol inhabited areas including Manchuria but also into other Qing domains in Inner Asia. But the situation was not favourable to the imperial rule as anti-Manchu and anti-Chinese sentiments were expressed in vary many ways. Besides, it was also the time when "the nationalist currents that had swept over Europe in the nineteenth century now began to reach Inner Asia."[48] Consequently, the Mongols of Inner and Outer Mongolia as well as the Uighurs and Kazakhs of Xinjiang started dreaming of establishing their "own national states". However, except Outer Mongolia none of the Chinese domains in Inner Asia were able to sever their ties completely with China even after the fall of the Qing rule in 1911. The fate of Inner Mongolia too fell victim to circumstances of the day and despite strong urge for "nationalism" or in other words "Pan-Mongolism", nothing substantial similar to what Outer Mongolia achieved in terms of independence from the Qing rule, could be realised.

Establishment of Inner Mongolia Autonomous Region

Post-Qing period saw the emergence of a new phenomenon in Inner Mongolia, particularly in the 1920s partly under the impact of the Outer Mongolian revolutionary developments. This was the emergence of what Lattimore calls "Young Mongols" as a more and more coherent party, which actually was the result of "the failure of princes on one side to organise a more hopeful policy than intermittent, negative resistance, and the failure of Outer Mongolia on the other side to organise a workable union of all Mongols."[49] In fact, it was under the influence of the teachings of Sun Yat-sen, the founder of the Chinese Kuomintang, the Young Mongol party also referred to as "Young Mongol Movement" or "National Revival Club" came into existence in 1922 and was later in 1925 reorganised as the Inner Mongolian People's Party, sometimes also referred to as the Inner Mongolian Kuomintang. The first Congress of the Inner Mongolian People's Party was held in Kalgan in October 1925. In its declaration the Congress, which was also attended by the MPRP representatives (Outer Mongolia) and representatives of the Chinese Kuomintang, came out with certain demands,[50] including a call to the whole Inner Mongolian population, such as labouring class, the middle and lower lamas, as well as intelligentsia to join the party, and under its guidance "wage a struggle for the liberation of the Mongol people."[51]

From the ideological and strategic point of view, the most important aspect of the declaration in the documents from the First Congress of the Inner Mongolian People's Party was "the placing of Inner Mongolian liberation entirely within the context of the Republic of China."[52] After the "war of unification" was won by the Chinese Kuomintang and the Nationalist government of Chiang Kai-shek was established, "the Young Mongols hoped to be allowed to reform and reorganise Inner Mongolia on Kuomintang lines, on a basis of federation with the Chinese Kuomintang but with a recognised regional standing."[53] However, nothing substantial could be achieved as having emerged victorious the highly centralised organisation of the Kuomintang ruled out the possibility of giving a green signal to such an idea of a semi-independent Inner Mongolian Kuomintang. Therefore, it was dissolved in its original form and the central authority began to appoint representatives for the Mongol regions from among those who were not necessarily the Mongols.[54] As Lattimore observes, "The Mongol policy of the [Chinese] Kuomintang became essentially the old Chinese policy of exterminating the Mongols, or forcing them to turn into Chinese, as far as possible."[55]

That the main intention of the central government was to assimilate the Mongols with the Chinese, became increasingly clear when four new provinces were carved out of Inner Mongolia in 1928. These provinces came to be known as Jehol (Rehe), Chahar, Suiyuan and Ningxia.[56] However, creation of new provinces appears to have broken "the Inner Mongolian territory into isolated parts and separated the Mongolian land from any unified Inner Mongolian administration."[57] The next step was to step up efforts for the Sinicization of the Mongols, and for this purpose "a certain amount of money was spent on schools at the edges of Mongol and Tibetan territory to teach the Chinese language and the principles of the Kuomintang, but no money was spent to educate them in their own languages."[58] Such a situation led to the emergence of more aggressive Inner Mongolian nationalist movement, which also gave way to princely nationalism because they feared the loss of princely titles and privileges following the establishment of new provinces and counties. The symbol of this movement was Prince Demchukdonggrub of West Sunid banner in Shili-yin Gool (also spelled as Silingol) League, who is popularly known as Te Wang or Prince Te. In fact, it was in 1929 that Prince Te came forward with firm determination and decided not only to fight for Inner Mongolian autonomy but also to abolish Chinese provinces and counties. It was also the time which coincided with the well targeted Japanese advance in Manchuria and the inability of the Chinese government to check it.

It all began in 1931 with the Japanese occupation of Manchuria and consequently the establishment of the new state of "Manchukuo", which completely altered the Chinese frontier situation. Meanwhile, Inner Mongolian nationalist movement or in more specific term "autonomy" movement under the leadership of Prince Te spread across all over Inner Mongolia, from Manchuria to the Ordos. On the other hand, in order to thwart Japanese pressure the Chinese Nationalist government considered it necessary to first of all try everything possible to keep the Inner Mongols well within China and, therefore, in

October 1931, they passed a law, which provided some concessions to the Mongols. The law stipulated that not only the league and banner system would be retained, equivalent in status to provinces and counties, but princely titles and privileges would also continue to remain as ever.[59] However, the concessions given to the Inner Mongols did not bring the desired results for the Chinese as the Kuomintang government outrightly rejected the former's main demand of "regional autonomy". Throughout the 1930s, Japanese advance overwhelmed almost all of Inner Mongolia, though to a large extent it was seen as a move favourable to the Mongols. What was considered as the most significant development, which took place in 1932 was the creation of predominantly Mongol inhabited Hsingan province of Manchukuo in the northwestern Manchuria. Afterwards the Japanese moved into Jehol and in 1934 they succeeded in taking over the control of this area.

Furthermore, the Japanese occupation of large parts of Inner Mongolia in 1937-38 led to the creation of another separate Mongolian area that came to be known as "Mengjiang" with its capital at Kalgan and Prince Te as the head of its government. Though the creation of two distinct areas i.e., Hsingan and Mengjiang, was generally considered to be the Japanese scheme of supporting the Inner Mongols against the Chinese, in practice it was revealed that complete freedom to the Mongols was no where in sight, not even the union of the two areas was allowed at any point of time under the Japanese occupation. Surely, while the Inner Mongols on the one hand found themselves disappointed for being unsuccessful in their desire for "real autonomy and freedom", on the other hand they became disillusioned also with the Japanese policy as in the words of Rupen:[60] "Japan seems to have thrown away her initial advantage of Mongolian support by blatant propaganda and a general attitude of racial superiority, a parallel to German conduct in Russia in World War II." Besides, Japan's involvement in the military conquest of China from 1937 onwards contributed much to divert its attention from Inner Mongolia, which never revived especially after the Japanese defeat in the World War II.

Nevertheless, it was not the Kuomintang government of Chiang Kai-shek but the Chinese communists who succeeded in filling the vacuum created by the departure of the Japanese. The significance of this success lies into the fact that the Chinese Communist Party (CCP) had, at that time, the most trusted Sinicized Tumet Mongol called Ulanfu (also spelled Ulanhu) who ultimately led Inner Mongolia into "the Chinese jurisdiction in 1947."[61] The end of the World War II in 1945 witnessed new developments in Inner Mongolia such as the establishment of the Association of the Inner Mongolian Autonomous Movement, which soon began its work in Silingol and Chahar regions.[62] Meanwhile, in March 1946 the Inner Mongolian People's Party was dissolved only to merge with the Chinese Communist Party for failure to submit itself to the later.[63] Next month a conference popularly known as "April 3 Conference" was held under the leadership of Ulanfu which decided to unite eastern and western Inner Mongolia, thus clearing the way for the incorporation of Inner Mongolia into China. But it took almost one year to declare the founding of the Inner Mongolian Autonomous Region (IMAR) of China. Prince Te had already lost ground for champion the cause of Inner Mongols, while on the other side Ulanfu under the guidance of the Chinese Communist Party made considerable impact to rally the people behind him. Finally, on 1 May 1947, the Inner Mongolian Autonomous Region was established with Ulanfu as the head of the government of the IMAR.[64]

As such, in the contemporary history of China Inner Mongolia has the distinction of becoming the first region to have been granted autonomy, though at the cost of Pan-Mongolist movement which never succeeded. Considering the external factor it appears that in 1945-46 the future of Inner Mongolia was somehow uncertain but once the Soviet Union, the Mongolian People's Republic and China accepted in principle the separation of Inner and Outer Mongolia, nothing could deter the Chinese communists from consolidating Inner Mongolia as an Autonomous Region with limited powers of self-government. With Barga (eastern Inner Mongolia) too was included into IMAR in January 1948, the whole region was turned into a major strategic base for the Chinese communists to defeat Chiang Kai-shek's Kuomintang government. Since 1949 when People's Republic of China was established under the aegis of the Chinese Communist Party, several significant changes in administrative policies and planning took place in Inner Mongolia, including the reorganisation of boundary and shifting of its capital. While Ulaanhot (Ulan Hoto) served as the capital from 1947 to 1950, Zhangjiakow (Kalgan which is now in Hebei province) served from 1950 to 1952, until Guisui, renamed Höhhot (Koke Khota) in 1954, became the capital of the IMAR. Höhhot, meaning "Green City" in Mongolian, is now known as "The Dairy Capital" in China as it is home to the country's two leading dairy producers – Mengniu Milk Industry Group and Yili Industrial Group.

INNER MONGOLIA'S ROLE IN SINO-MONGOLIAN TIES

Due to its (i) geopolitical importance of being in the close proximity to Mongolia, i.e., being the Chinese border region adjoining Mongolia, and (ii) similar ethno-cultural background as that of Mongolia, Inner Mongolia Autonomous Region (herein after referred to either as Inner Mongolia or IMAR) has been playing a significant role in the Sino-Mongolian ties.

Geopolitical Importance

Inner Mongolia, a deep hinterland region, has a geopolitical importance due to its strategic location along China's northern boundary, where it is bordered by Heilongjiang, Jilin and Liaoning provinces in the east, Hebei, Shanxi and Shaanxi provinces and the Ningxia Hui Autonomous Region in the south and south west, Gansu province in the west, and Mongolia as well as Russia in the north and north east respectively. It is, therefore, a landlocked province with the distinction of being the first national minority Autonomous Region of China; the other four include the Guanxi Zhuang, the Xinjiang Uighur, the Ningxia Hui and the Tibet Autonomous Regions. With a total land area of 1,183,000 sq. kms., accounting for 12.3 per cent of China's entire territory, Inner Mongolia is the third largest among the provinces and autonomous regions of China, exceeded only by the Xinjiang Uighur and the Tibet Autonomous Regions.

Inner Mongolia's importance also lies into fact that it has comparative advantages over other regions due to its being a considerable natural resource base, with the potential to serve as the basis for China's future economic development. A study conducted by the Asian Development Bank (ADB) has discovered that Inner Mongolia has deposits of 134 types of mineral resources.[65] Six of these mineral resources, including rare earth elements and columbium, rank number one among China's provinces; 11 resources, including coal and chromium, rank second among provinces; and 63 rank in the top 10. According to the findings of the ADB study, Inner Mongolia is rich in energy resources as well, which is evident from the fact that proven coal reserves are estimated as 223 billion tons, while prospective coal reserves stand at 1200 billion tons. Similarly, the proven and estimated oil reserves constitute 700 million tons and 4 billion tons respectively. Whereas the proven gas reserves are 1 trillion cubic meters, the potential reserves are 4.2 trillion cubic meters. It is to be noted here that Shan'xi-Gansu-Ningxia Oil and Gas Field, a recognized world-class oil-gas field, is located mostly in Inner Mongolia's Erdos Basin.

Having natural resources in abundance and unique strategic geographic advantage Inner Mongolia has the potential for connecting the East with the West. It is more so because it shares a 4,221 kms. long borderline with Russia and Mongolia, thus serving as an important transportation channel between China, Russia and Mongolia. Besides, as an intersection point for the Trans-Asia rail, the railway linking Inner Mongolia's capital Höhhot to Frankfurt has been playing an important role for the bilateral trade between China, Mongolia, Russia and the European countries. Furthermore, Inner Mongolia occupies 3,193 kms, i.e., 70 per cent of the borderland area of the 4,677 kms. long Sino-Mongolian border. Also the Gobi Desert, which is the largest desert in Asia and the fourth largest desert in the world, stretches across the IMAR and crosses over the border with Mongolia. Moreover, with its 15 banners (*hoshuns*) sharing common borders with Mongolia and having five trading ports of first and second-class categories, Inner Mongolia acts as a sort of bridge between China and Mongolia.

The other factor which signifies the role of Inner Mongolia in Sino-Mongolian relations owes much to the ethno-cultural and linguistic background of the region. Although the Mongols in Inner Mongolia and Mongolia have two different nationalities, ethnically they belong to one group as discussed earlier and share same language (at least spoken), culture and the lifestyle.[66] In the psyche of Mongols of Inner Mongolia, there is a strong feeling for Mongolia's position at the international level. As a first Indian researcher to visit Inner Mongolia University (IMU) in Höhhot on 8 June 2006, this author was informed during his interaction with academics at IMU's Research Centre for Mongolian Studies that Inner Mongolia would like to see a strong and economically self-sufficient Mongolia so that it could raise its international status because it also influences the position of ethnic Mongols within China. Besides, the Mongols of Inner Mongolia have learnt a lot from Mongolia, especially how to keep a separate identity alive in a "sinicized" world. All these factors have contributed much to the development of the Sino-Mongolian border trade as the central government in China has been exploiting all possible resources of Inner Mongolia, both the natural as well as Mongolian speaking manpower, in order to keep its foothold in Mongolia.

Now a word for demography of Inner Mongolia which gives an impression that having a total population of 24.05 million people,[67] Inner Mongolia has greater number of people than the independent State of Mongolia which has just a little over 2.6 million population (2.4 million as per 2000 population and housing census of Mongolia). Even the population of ethnic Mongols alone in Inner Mongolia today stands at 4.2 million which is larger than the total population of Mongols in Mongolia. In all 49 ethnic groups live in Inner Mongolia including the Mongol, Han Chinese, Manchu, Hui, Daur, Ewenks, Oroqen, and Korean. The population of Inner Mongolia also include many diverse Mongolian-speaking groups, such as the Buryats and the Oirats, all of whom are officially considered as Mongol. Besides, there are several thousand of Mongols who live in other regions of China such as Xinjiang, Qinghai, Heilongjiang, Jilin, Gansu, Liaoning and Beijing. As per the 2000 population Census of the People's Republic of China, **Table 1** shows the population of different ethnic groups and their percentage share in the total population of Inner Mongolia, which excludes members of the People's Liberation Army in active service, though others and total in the table include the same.

Table 1: Ethnic Composition of Population in Inner Mongolia (2000 Census)

Ethnic Group	Population	
	Number	Percentage
Han Chinese	18,465,586	79.17
Mongol	3,995,349	17.13
Manchu	499,911	2.14
Hui	209,850	0.900
Daur	77,188	0.331
Evenks	26,201	0.112
Koreans	21,859	0.094
Russians	5,020	0.022
Others	459,036	-
Total	23,760,000	-

Source: Tabulation on the 2000 Population Census of the People's Republic of China, compiled by Population Census Office under the State Council & Department of Population, Social, Science and Technology Statistics, National Bureau of Statistics of China (Hong Kong: China Statistics Press, 2001).

Trade and Economic Relations

Having a least developed economy in comparison with China's other regions, Inner Mongolia until recently has been a remote area of China. But once the "Western Development Programme" was implemented along with development of China's border regions, Inner Mongolia figured prominently in the Beijing's domestic policy. In addition, Inner Mongolia also came in to lime light after a final agreement on the exact demarcation of Sino-Mongolian border took place during Mongolian President Nambaryn Enkhbayar's visit to China in

November 2005. This provided opportunities for the two countries to conclude a series of border-related agreements, including the cross border trade. It is significant to note here that since the first Sino-Mongolian border trade agreement was signed in November 1985 followed by the signing of another agreement in 1990 on border areas emigration control points and their administrative system, there has been dramatic growth in the Sino-Mongolian border trade. Among the ten pairs of border posts, which have already been opened, Inner Mongolian city of Erenhot or Erlian/Erlianhot (as called by the Chinese) and Zamyn Uud of Mongolia now remain open throughout the year, the rest nine pairs being seasonal. Erenhot city has not only become a main point of goods clearance, processing and manufacturing, trading and logistics but also a platform for exchange of communications between Chinese and foreign enterprises including Mongolian ones.

Currently, border trade is being carried out between China's Inner Mongolia, Xinjiang-Uighur and Ningxia Hui Autonomous Regions, Hebei and Jilin provinces and Mongolia's related regions and departments. However, Inner Mongolia and Xinjiang have comparatively larger share in the border trade with Mongolia due to the advantage of their being the direct border regions of China. Since China became the largest trading partner of Mongolia in 2000, there has been tremendous growth in the bilateral trade and economic cooperation, particularly with Inner Mongolia which continues to be the largest trading partner of Mongolia among the Chinese provinces and regions. By and large, Inner Mongolia has been conducting trade, economic and technological cooperation with nearly 160 countries and regions in the world. In terms of total value of Inner Mongolia's trade (imports and exports) with the world, the contribution of Russia and Mongolia is of vital importance. This is largely due to geographical factor as Inner Mongolia, Russia, and Mongolia share the borderline significantly. According to a market research conducted by China based Starmass International, the total imports and exports of Inner Mongolia has grown from US$ 1,070 million in 1997 to over US$ 7,740 million in 2007, representing a 7.2 times growth over a period of ten year.[68]

Further analysis shows that Inner Mongolia's value of imports has risen from US$ 420 million in 1997 to over US$ 4,790 million in 2007, reflecting an 11.5 times increase over the same period. Similarly, Inner Mongolia's total exports too has shown an upward trend from being US$ 660 million in 1997 to crossing the figure of US$ 2, 940 million in 2007, thus registering a 4.5 times growth over the years.

Graph 1 and **Table 2** present Inner Mongolia's world trade and trade with Mongolia during the period between 2000 and 2007 in US Million Dollar value. It can be observed that Inner Mongolia's exports amounted to US $ 1021.85 million in 2000 which significantly increased in succeeding years and became tripled in 2007 to register a figure of US $ 2947.41 million, while imports increased to four-times from US $ 1014.11 million in 2000 to US $ 4797.19 million in 2007. It indicates that Inner Mongolia has been facing a trade deficit with world as its world imports are increasing at faster pace as compared to its exports. Even the trade deficit is significantly increasing year by year to reach at the highest ever level of US $ 1849.78 million in 2007 as compared to merely US $ 7.74 million in 2000.

Graph 1: Inner Mongolia's World Trade (US $ Million)

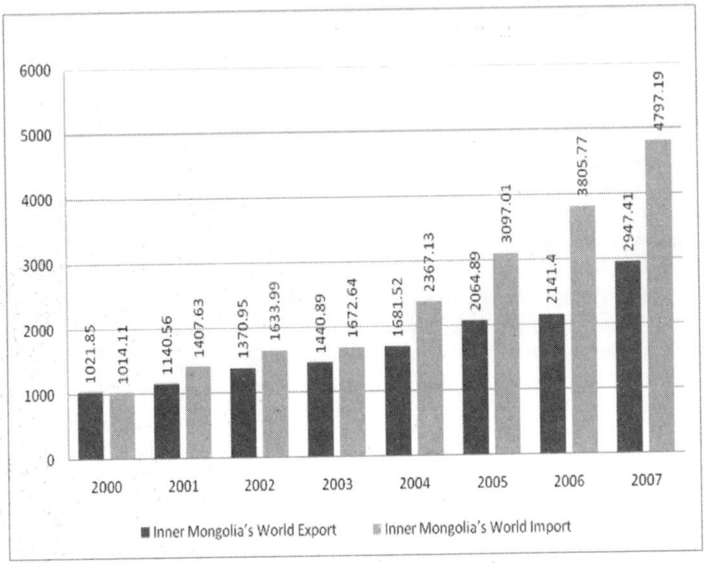

Looking at the figures for Inner Mongolia's trade with Mongolia over the same period, it is visible that Inner Mongolia's exports to Mongolia, which was merely US $ 84.87 million in 2000, increased significantly to reach the level of US $ 184.21 million in 2007, while imports from Mongolia increased from US $ 172.49 million in 2003 to US $ 272.79 in 2005. It can also be observed from **Table 2** and **Graph 2** that although Inner Mongolia's trade with Mongolia is increasing in value terms, its share in Inner Mongolia's world trade is quite fluctuating and decreasing year by year.

Table 2: Inner Mongolia's World Trade and Trade with Mongolia (2000 to 2007)

Year	Trade with World (US $ mln.)		Trade with Mongolia (US $ mln.)		Share of Inner Mongolia's Trade with Mongolia as % of World Trade	
	Exports	Imports	Exports	Imports	Exports	Imports
	1	2	3	4	(5 = 3/1)	(6 = 4/2)
2000	1021.85	1014.11	84.87	n/a	8.31	n/a
2001	1140.56	1407.63	134.09	n/a	11.76	n/a
2002	1370.95	1633.99	148.53	n/a	10.83	n/a
2003	1440.89	1672.64	50.16	172.49	3.48	10.31
2004	1681.52	2367.13	84.64	222.55	5.03	9.40
2005	2064.89	3097.01	93.93	272.79	4.55	8.81
2006	2141.4	3805.77	118.77	n/a	5.55	n/a
2007	2947.41	4797.19	184.21	n/a	6.25	n/a

Note : n/a denotes Not Available.

Sources: Compiled by author on the basis of data collected from *Nei Meng Gu Tong Ji Nian Jian* [Inner Mongolia Statistical Yearbook], 2001 to 2008. Inner Mongolia Autonomous Region Bureau of Statistics, China Statistical Press. Figures for Inner Mongolia's imports from Mongolia during 2003-2005 are taken from Asian Development Bank (2006), *Inner Mongolia Autonomous Region: Trade Facilitation and Logistics Development Strategy*, TA-6058 (REG), Report prepared by Robert L. Wallack, p.8.

Graph 2: Inner Mongolia's Trade with Mongolia (US $ Mn)

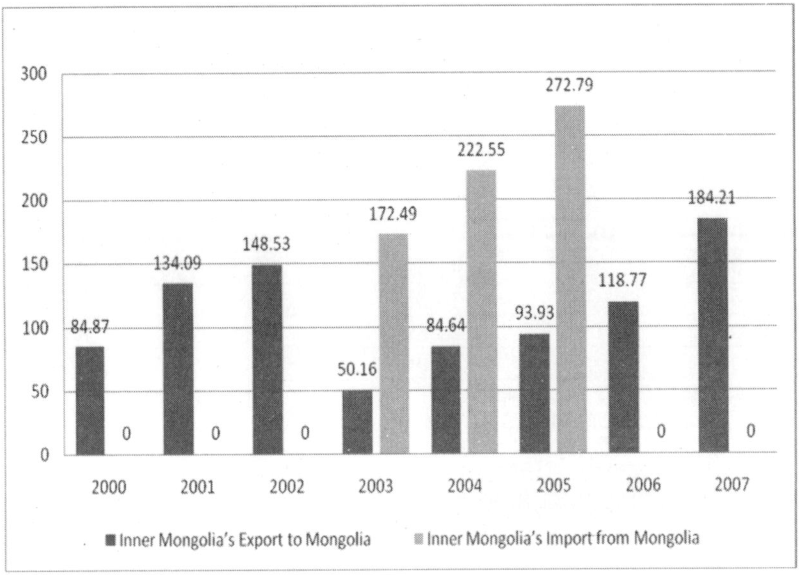

Whereas Inner Mongolia's major export destinations include Japan, the USA, South Korea, Italy and Mongolia, the main export goods include base metals, textile materials, chemicals, electronic products, vegetables, fruit and cereals. Similarly, Inner Mongolia's major import sources consist of Russia, Mongolia, Australia, Germany and the USA, while major import goods include minerals, wood and wooden products, charcoal, cork and related products, straws, plaited products, baskets and wickerwork, chemical raw material and electronics. **Table 3** presents the growth rate over previous period of Inner Mongolia's trade with world and Mongolia from 2000 to 2007. It is quite evident from this table that in 2007 the growth in Inner Mongolia's exports to world is 37.64 per cent which is higher as compared to imports from world, i.e., 26.05 per cent. Obviously, it is a good sign of recovery of trade deficit. It can also be observed from this table that there is a fluctuating trend in the growth rate of Inner Mongolia's exports to and imports from Mongolia during the period from 2000 to 2007.

Table 3: Growth Rate (%) over Previous Period of Inner Mongolia's Trade with World and Mongolia

	Exports to World	Imports from World	Exports to Mongolia	Imports from Mongolia
2000	---	---	---	---
2001	11.62	38.80	57.99	n/a
2002	20.20	16.08	10.77	n/a
2003	5.10	2.37	-66.23	---
2004	16.70	41.52	68.74	29.02
2005	22.80	30.83	10.98	22.57
2006	3.71	22.89	26.45	n/a
2007	37.64	26.05	55.10	n/a

Note : n/a denotes Not Available.
Source: Estimation is based on Table 2.

As regards foreign direct investment (FDI) in Inner Mongolia, the total investments, which mainly came from Hong Kong, Taiwan, Japan, the USA and Australia, amounted to US$ 1.7 billion in 2006, thus revealing a year-on-year surge of 47 per cent. Most of the FDI was channeled into manufacturing (US$ 949.3 million), energy (US$ 499.6 million), real estate (US$ 100.8 million) and resident services as well as other services (US$ 37.4 million). Since Inner Mongolia is rich in resources, especially cashmere, coal, rare-earth and natural gas, there is a scope of increasing cooperation particularly in these areas with the outside world including Mongolia. In the past, the exploitation and utilisation of resources were rather inefficient, which resulted in the so called "poor returns from rich resources".[69] Despite the fact that Inner Mongolia has well-developed agriculture and livestock husbandry, which makes it an important production base for grains, oil, sugar and livestock in China, it is now the industrial structure mainly consisting of energy and raw materials industries which is playing major role in the economic development of the region. In fact, it was during the period of Tenth Five-Year Plan (2001-05) that Inner Mongolia laid emphasis on developing six unique and competitive industries, namely energy, chemicals, metallurgy, equipment manufacturing, processing of farm produce as well as hi-tech products. As a result, competitive capacity of these industries on the market started showing positive outcome, and well-known enterprises such as Erdos, Yili and Mengniu and their products have now become brand names of Inner Mongolia.[70]

Past few years have witnessed Inner Mongolia and Mongolia expressing their commitment to boost cooperation in various fields. Evidently, both sides made such remarks at the 8th Conference on the Economic Cooperation Standing Working Group held in Ulaanbaatar on 15 November 2007.[71] They spoke highly of the development of cooperation in the fields of economy, culture, health and science in recent years. While outlining the aim of the conference, Yu Dehui, Vice Chairman of People's Government of China's Inner Mongolia Autonomous Region, stressed on strengthening Inner Mongolia-Mongolia cooperation on mining, ports and transportation besides resolving some problems that occurred in these fields. B. Nyamsuren, Secretary of the Mongolian Industry and Trade Ministry, expressed hope that more Chinese high-tech enterprises would invest in Mongolia. Recently, due to the increased demand from Mongolia, the steel exports of Inner Mongolia through the Erenhot port registered a sharp growth in March 2009. The Erenhot port recorded exports of 75.2 tonnes of steel on March 18 itself, with a single day steel export tax amounting to US$1.7 thousand, more than 3.9 times of the figure for the first two months.[72]

However, there is a serious problem of desertification along both sides of Inner Mongolia-Mongolia borders, which in recent years raised concerns in Sino-Mongolian relations. China has suffered from nine sand storms in 2004, which caused great economic losses and left adverse impact on people's lives. Several sand storms originate in Mongolia too, which seriously affect Inner Mongolia region. Keeping the severity of the problem in mind, China had already planned to cooperate with Mongolia in the transformation of desert. This was suggested by some 100 Chinese experts on 5 April 2004, at an annual regional sand control meeting.[73] They unanimously favored to conduct a joint research on sand storm control efforts along the Sino-Mongolian border with the Mongolian counterparts.

Integration of Infrastructure Network

The increasing role being played by Inner Mongolia in Sino-Mongolian ties becomes evident from the fact that the Municipal Government of Erenhot and Mineral Resources Association of Mongolia jointly held "2005 Friendly Neighbour and Cooperation: China-Mongolia Enterprise Investment Negotiation Conference" in Erenhot on 15-16 November 2005. This Conference provided an excellent opportunity for both Chinese and Mongolian enterprises to explore the mineral resources in Mongolia and contribute positively to local economy on the one hand and Chinese economy on the other. As a point of goods clearance, processing and manufacturing, trading and logistics the Erenhot city offers a mutually beneficial platform for exchange and communication between the Chinese and foreign enterprises, particularly those operating in China's neighbouring countries on the northern side of the border.

In this regard a report prepared for the Asian Development Bank's project entitled *Inner Mongolia Autonomous Region: Trade Facilitation and Logistics Development Strategy* reveals that the development of Inner Mongolia's logistics industry has become a strategic agenda which needs to be implemented in order to fully develop the economy of the region, particularly in mining, agriculture and animal product sectors.[74] It further points to the integration of the logistics industry with plenteous human and natural resources of not only Inner Mongolia but also Mongolia which could go a long way in benefitting the long term bilateral and international economic growth. It is more so because there are commonalities and complementarities in the grassland economies and cultures and in mining which provide ample scope for cooperation, collaboration and interdependence in cross-border trade. The study made several recommendations for action to be taken by both Inner Mongolia and Mongolia with the support of international organizations like Asian Development Bank (ADB), United Nations (UN) and World Customs Organization (WCO) for the development of IMAR's logistics industry. As regards legal framework and policy related actions, the study underlines that given the fact that the People's Republic of China issued suggestions to promote the development of a modern national logistics industry in August 2004, "it is important that IMAR and Mongolia find a way to integrate infrastructure resources among the different departments at the local government levels and not just from the central governments so that intergovernmental agreements are implemented and transport disagreements are resolved at the borders, expeditiously."

Stressing that the existing key dry ports of Erenhot and Ganqimaodao and the inland depots of Baotou, Linhe and Jining need to expand in order to increase the value add activities required by logistics providers to serve customers, the report notices that "a higher value add to weight ratio of products reduces the high cost of transport to the total value of a product and thereby lessens the impact of IMAR and Mongolia's distance to markets." Besides, it also points out that "Information and Communication Technologies (ICT) software and networks can bridge IMAR and Mongolia to international markets, improve transport efficiency by instituting performance measurements and provide automation of trade and Customs documentation." As such, the report outlines that "the IMAR e-Port platform is a starting point to build ICT applications and an excellent means to train the logistics industry community." In such a scenario, the key recommendations, among others, for action on the part of Inner Mongolia and Mongolia made in the study include the following:

(i) IMAR and Mongolia should meet regularly to review and amend the road transport agreements to eliminate disputes on the crossing of trucks over each countries' border and not just at the central government, but also at the local government levels;

(ii) IMAR and Mongolia should devise a plan to form joint venture trucking firms to share transport and logistics resources for the common goal of raw materials' transportation;

(iii) IMAR and Mongolia should form a bilateral committee to review the TIR system for cooperation and training purposes;

(iv) IMAR should strengthen the *IMAR-Mongolia Network* that began with the respective Chambers of Commerce and information technology departments. The networks should be developed to provide connections at Erenhot and Baotou with the other dry ports and to the inland depots in a defined time frame. Besides, Inner Mongolia should work to overcome the incompatibility of the IMAR-Mongolia (GAMAS) Customs' systems;

(v) IMAR should explore the upgrading of e-Port to a "One Window" system by using the United Nations' model as technical advice or the Automated System of Customs Declarations (ASYCUDA);

(vi) IMAR should provide an open forum for the Customs' initiatives of the *China-Mongolia Customs Cooperation Expert Group* with other interested groups in attendance such as the Port office and Information Promotion office.;

(vii) IMAR should consider a dry port (Erenhot) to have a common facility to ensure inspection and approval of animal products from Mongolia; and

(viii) IMAR should initiate and facilitate meetings by local governments of Mongolia and China of dry ports to discuss banking issues related to improving systems to process border transactions and to coordinate policies from the central governments. The goal is to have IMAR-Mongolia systems on equal levels of development for all financial services.

Similarly, the recommendations also outline the supporting role to be played by international organizations, which are as follows:

(i) ADB should assist in articulating and documenting the problems faced by local transport providers and serve as a mediator to resolve the disputes between the local governments, besides making possible suggestions for amending the road transport agreements;

(ii) ADB should provide information on best practices for bilateral joint venture transport and logistics firms, besides facilitating meetings and set agendas to bring concrete results in the short term;

(iii) ADB should assist in organizing the meeting between the responsible departments of IMAR and Mongolia for establishing a committee to review the Transport Internationaux Routiers (TIR) system issues on a regular basis and seek assistance from the China Road and Transport Association and the National Road Transport Association of Mongolia;

(iv) ADB should assist in organizing meetings and agendas with IMAR, Mongolia and key industry players to map out short, medium and long term rail and road transport needs;

(v) ADB, UN and WCO should assist IMAR and Mongolia in developing a plan and implementing a common platform based on the United Nations' Automated System of Customs Declaration (ASYCUDA), "One Window" and/or World Customs Organization standards;

(vi) ADB, UN and WCO should ensure input from WCO and ADB customs experts so that the *China-Mongolia Expert Group* brings meaningful change; and

(vii) ADB, UN and WCO should offer assistance to local governments and local branches of banks in IMAR and Mongolia on issues of letters of credit and foreign exchange forward contracts as well as other financial instruments and systems needed to conduct border trade in a secure and efficient manner.

Such a study seems to have started striking the right chord as recently there have been concerns from both China and Mongolia to take initiatives towards integration of infrastructure network involving Inner Mongolia. Earlier on 15 February 2005, the World Bank too had shown interest in such initiatives when it approved a US$100 million loan to China to help finance the Inner Mongolia Transport and Trade Corridor Project. The project aimed at promoting and sustaining the development of

China's cross-border trade between China on one hand and Russia and Mongolia on the other by way of improving transport infrastructure and logistics. These improvements, in turn, would lower transport costs, increase income from external trade, and raise incomes in Inner Mongolia.[75] Again the role of Inner Mongolia's border town of Erenhot becomes important whenever any initiative is taken to promote Sino-Mongolian relations. Recognising the importance of this town, Mongolia opened a consulate in Erenhot on 7 April 2007.[76] After the opening ceremony, Chinese and Mongolian officials exchanged views and conducted in-depth discussions on a wide range of issues, including cooperation in tourism and transportation. It is to be noted that earlier in 1996, the Consulate-General of Mongolia in Höhhot opened an office in Erenhot and that upgrading the office into a consulate only confirms growing ties between the two sides.

There are quite a few evidences of connecting China with Mongolia through Inner Mongolia by road, railways and air. For example, on 17 August 2005, over 700 km-long Beijing-Erenhot-Zamyn-Uud transnational self-driving trip route was opened, which was followed by the construction of a China-Mongolia bridge known as "Ebudege-Bayan Wesh Bridge". On 3 November 2005, the bridge was formally opened for traffic at Ebudege Port in Xinba'erhu Left Banner of Inner Mongolia's Hulunbuir city.[77] It is to be noted that Xinba'erhu Left Banner has 207 kms. long frontier with Mongolia. Though Ebudege port, which faces Bayan Wesh port across Harlahar river, became a first-class seasonal port of China in 1995, its significance increased in 2004 when the export-import cargo volume of the port surpassed 3000 tons mark, thus creating a new high in its history. The same year in June 2004, the construction work of "Ebudege-Bayan Wesh Bridge" was launched in order to give boost to further expansion of Sino-Mongolian trade and energy cooperation. The opening of the bridge has enabled Ebudege port to get rid of the restriction of season and make round the year pass possible.

As regards railway, in November 2007, China started construction of a railway line dubbed as "energy line", which is to run across northeast China and eastern Mongolia and eventually lead to Russia.[78] In comparison to road transport, the completion of this railway would boost transportation of not only coal in terms of its output but also the growing number of trade items between Inner Mongolia and Mongolia. Given the fact that of late, almost 20 billion tons of coal has been discovered in three basins of Inner Mongolia's Xi Ujimqin Banner where Bayan Ul is located, it is likely that a large amount of coal can also be transported to Liaoning province in order to help revive northeast China's old industrial base. This railway project is undergoing three phases of construction: The first phase involves a 487 kms. long Xinqiu-Bayan Ul section, the longest of the three sections, which connects Xinqiu in Fuxin city of northeast China's Liaoning province to Bayan Ul in northern Inner Mongolia. At a cost of nearly US dollars 790 million, the first-phase construction is expected to be completed in 2010. The second phase of construction would lead the 230 kms long railway northward from Bayan Ul to Zhuengadabuqi port, on the border of Mongolia, while the third phase would stretch further northward to Mongolia's Choibalsan city, where it would join the railway to Borzya in Russia's Chita region. After completion, the railway would be connected to the line leading to Jinzhou port in Liaoning, thus providing inland Mongolia a convenient sea access and cutting almost 1,000 kms. from the present route by way of Inner Mongolia's Erenhot port and the northern Tianjin port.

As Lu Chao of Institute for Borderland History and Geography Studies at Liaoning Academy of Social Sciences explains, "The railway, connecting Mongolia's inland port with China's sea port, will contribute to fluid transportation of China's merchandise and agricultural products to Mongolia. It will also provide Mongolia more convenient shipment of its abundant coal and other resources by sea."[79] Similarly, air connection between China and Mongolia through Inner Mongolia has also been gaining momentum. Recently, on 5 August 2009, the first flight from the Mongolian capital Ulaanbaatar to Hailar in Inner Mongolia region took off, marking the opening of the third air route between Mongolia and

China and second air route between Mongolia and Inner Mongolia after Ulaanbaatar-Beijing and Ulaanbaatar-Höhhot air routes. While Yu Hongyao, the Chinese Ambassador to Mongolia stressed that "this air route would promote the exchanges and cooperation between the two countries and enrich bilateral relations," G. Davaa, Director of the Civil Aviation Authority of Mongolia, expressed hope that this air route would prove to be "a new bridge" linking China and Mongolia.[80]

Cultural and Educational Cooperation

Sharing similar ethno-cultural legacy the Mongols of Inner Mongolia like Mongolia celebrate one of the most exciting and colorful festivals- the annual *Nadaam* Festival (*eriin gurvan nadaam*), usually held in July every year. It has been held for centuries to exhibit the courage and strength of the nomadic Mongols. The main attraction of the festivities are the fierce horse racing, archery and wrestling competitions, the traditional sports of the Mongolian warriors. In Mongolian, the word *Nadaam* means "amusement and entertainment" which can be traced back to the year 1225 AD, when Chinggis Khan led an expedition to the west and conquered Khwarezm. In order to celebrate the victory the Mongols organized the magnificent *Nadaam* Fair and used this exciting gathering as a big occasion to compete in the horseracing, wrestling and archery, which were regarded as the three basic skills of men.[81] Recently, Mongolia's ethnic culture, including *Nadaam* festival became the highlights of the 11th Asian Arts Festival, which was jointly sponsored by China's Ministry of Culture and the People's Government of Inner Mongolia Autonomous Region, and was held from 18 to 26 August 2009 in the city of Ordos in Inner Mongolia.[82] The Festival saw the participation of 17 Asian countries, who signed an initiative on cultural cooperation by which they committed to carry out a "wide-ranging and substantial cooperation" on cultural development and human resources. The idea was to contribute to restoring the confidence of the society and promoting the economic revival via cultural exchanges and dialogue between different civilizations. Indeed, holding such festivals greatly help bring the people of different civilizations including China and Mongolia more close to further strengthen their relations in other areas.

It was from the beginning of the 1990s that Sino-Mongolian cultural relations witnessed a thaw when in 1991 alone cultural groups of the two sides visited each other's countries 20 times. With the visit of Mongolian Buddhists to Inner Mongolia exchanges in other fields such as art, radio, literature, TV, films and academics became more frequent in succeeding years. Encouraging signs further emerged when in 1999 during his visit to Inner Mongolia, Mongolian President Bagabandi remarked that he "was impressed with China's efforts to protect the culture and education of the Mongolian minority," a sharp difference in earlier version of Mongolian statements alleging ruthless Chinese rule in Inner Mongolia.[83]

Since Höhhot and Ulaanbaatar enjoy a sister city relationship, in 2001 they celebrated tenth anniversary of their becoming friendly cities. In Ulaanbaatar, several activities including the film shows, art performances as well as conferences on Sino-Mongolian economic and trade cooperation, particularly on cross-border trade involving Inner Mongolia took place. As the year 2009 marked the 60th Anniversary of diplomatic relations between Mongolia and China, Inner Mongolian Cultural Day was held on June 25-27 in Ulaanbaatar which was jointly organized by the Mongolian Ministry of Education, Culture and Science as well as Chinese Embassy in Mongolia. On this occasion, the artists from Inner Mongolia visited Ulaanbaatar and performed the concert *Nairamdliin Magtaal* (Tribute to Friendship). The concert began with an unaccompanied choral singing *Naiman Shargin Magtaal* (Tribute to Eight Yellow Horse) sung by Young Choral Band of Inner Mongolian National Song and Dance Ensemble.[84] Further, a delegation from Höhhot visited Mongolia to celebrate Ulaanbaatar's 370th anniversary which was held on 29 October 2009. On this occasion, both sides expressed hope that they would strengthen friendship and collaboration in the future as well.

Earlier in 2005, *Xinhua News Agency* reported that China and Mongolia announced to jointly work for protecting the ethnic Mongolian traditional folk song *Urtiin Duu* sung by the people in both countries after UNESCO approved it for designation as "oral and intangible heritage" song.[85] The heritage designation requires China and Mongolia to train musicians, build a database of people who can sing the songs, popularize the songs and set up a platform for the two countries to exchange song-related information. Besides, the two countries are also expected to work for the revival of traditional ceremonies where the song, which made entry into UNESCO's 2005 list of 43 "masterpieces", can be played. Described as a "lyrical chant" that praises natural scenery and love for family and friends, the song *Urtiin Duu* goes back to 2000 years as songs for rituals such as births and weddings.

In recent years, educational cooperation between Inner Mongolia and Mongolia has also grown and several agreements to exchange students between Inner Mongolia University and National University of Mongolia, especially in Mongolian Studies and Nomadic Civilization Studies, have been signed. Number of students from Mongolia in Inner Mongolia has been increasing tremendously.[86] This author was informed during his visit to Inner Mongolia University that since 2000 Inner Mongolia University, Inner Mongolia Normal University and Inner Mongolia Academy of Social Sciences have been participating in research activities on the Central Asian Nomadic Civilization jointly undertaken by China, Mongolia and Russia. Besides, Inner Mongolia University for the Nationalities has established friendly cooperative relationships with National University of Mongolia as well as Mongolian University of Health Science and Technology. Already in the year 2000, a hospital located in Inner Mongolia reached an agreement with a medical center in Ulaanbaatar to cooperate on prevention and control of tuberculosis.[87] The agreement stipulated that the hospital in Inner Mongolia will help Mongolia train professionals and set up a tuberculosis control center at the grassroots level. In return, Inner Mongolia will receive interns from Mongolia to participate in the research on the treatment of lung disease. Both sides will also cooperate on conducting research on problems related to heart and respiratory system. As part of educational cooperation Inner Mongolia also presented 350 books of eight categories to the National Central Library of Mongolia on the occasion of Inner Mongolia cultural days held in January 2008 in Ulaanbaatar.[88] The books included modern classic stories, essays and poems of Inner Mongolia, apart from collection of stories written by Ayanga and a novel by Lyau Kuai, translated from the Mongolian classic alphabet into Cyrillic.

CONCLUSION

Though Inner Mongolia presents a "paradox" for understanding contemporary ethnic politics in China,[89] it also demonstrates as to how an ethnic minority region could play a significant role in cementing the ties between the two countries- one to which it belongs in terms of territory and nationality and the other to which it identifies its ethno-cultural identity. Basically, it is the result of the post-Soviet normalization of Sino-Russian relations which made China's northern boundary less vulnerable. It is more so because China's military burden to a great extent has been relieved due to the disappearance of Mongolia as a springboard for Soviet offensive against China proper. This, in turn, "resulted in diverting Chinese resources from military spending to promoting economic development," which also witnessed changes in China's thinking of its international relations, particularly in the Asia-Pacific. Moreover, China's realization to maintain cordial relations with neighbouring countries became the central point of its periphery policy. As such a new equation emerged in the Sino-Mongolian relations in which Inner Mongolia's role to a considerable extent holds importance. For China still considers Mongolia as a country of "crucial geopolitical interest" despite the fact that the ongoing Sino-Russian relations have substantially lessened Mongolia's buffer role in the security policy of its two neighbours. And that is where China's Inner Mongolia provides Beijing with a ready supply of Mongolian-speaking market personnel to help maintain the stability in the Sino-Mongolian ties.

Notwithstanding the warm cooperation between China and

Mongolia in general and Inner Mongolia and Mongolia in particular in the trade, economic including infrastructure network, cultural, scientific and educational fields, the key question that today several young Inner Mongolian scholars have been confronting remains to be the issue of "Mongolian identity."[90] This also brings into focus the issue of "Pan-Mongolism" or Mongolian nationalism which is still considered to be a bone of contention between China and Mongolia. Year by year China is increasing its economic leverage in Mongolia in order to ensure the non-involvement of Mongolia in any kind of ethnic resurgence of Inner Mongols for the Pan-Mongolist cause. On its part, Mongolia too seems to be no more interested in supporting such a cause which could adversely affect its relations with China, especially at a time when the priority lies in country's security on all fronts-political, economic and military. What is praiseworthy at the moment is that geographical proximity and economic complementarities as well as ethno-cultural linkages make both Inner Mongolia and Mongolia natural partners for strengthening Sino-Mongolian ties. Even Mongolia's Foreign Minister S. Oyun, during her visit to China on 24-26 March 2008, recognized that "Inner Mongolian Autonomous Region has served as a bridge between the two countries [China and Mongolia] in their bilateral exchanges and made contributions to the development of cross-border economic and trade cooperation."[91]

However, there are still some serious problems which need to be sorted out. Mismanagement at the border posts gives way to illegal acts, such as tax evasion and smuggling that appear to be affecting the reputation and mutual confidence of both sides and hence the foreign trade. Even Mongolia accuses the Chinese customs authorities of levying unfairly high taxes and other duties on Mongolian traders and their vehicles. This factor points to the one-sided nature of border trade that favours Chinese traders. Besides, there is a lack of awareness among the businessmen of Inner Mongolia about the investment law as well as how to compete with other investors in Mongolia. Hence, government should pay more attention towards not only educating them but also creating viable environment to do business in new areas as well. According to the ADB (2004) study, given its large reserves of coal and successful transformation of coal to oil production, Inner Mongolia has already demonstrated its potential to develop "coal to oil" projects, apart from showing potential to develop wind and solar energy. If developed in a strategic manner, the energy sector would prove to be a major driving force behind economic development of China in general and the IMAR in particular. This may also give an impetus to Sino-Mongolian energy cooperation on the long term basis, which in the foreseeable future remains to be seen.

REFERENCES

1. Morris Rossabi, *Modern Mongolia: From Khans to Commissars to Capitalists* (Berkeley: University of California Press, 2005), p.225.
2. China's Western Development Programme covers ten western provinces plus two other provinces of Inner Mongolia and Guangxi which have large ethnic populations. For more on China's western initiative, see Hongyi Harry Lai, "China's Western Development Program: Its Rationale, Implementation, and Prospects", *Modern China*, vol. 28, no. 4, October 2002, pp. 432-466.
3. Cited in Xu Bingxun and Wang Songtao, *Inner Mongolia* (Höhhot: Inner Mongolia University Press, 2001), p.19.
4. For different names of Mongols and their predecessors at different times, see Chang Yin-T'ang, *The Economic Development and Prospects of Inner Mongolia* (Shanghai: The Commercial Press, 1933), pp.56-57.
5. *Ibid,* p.57.
6. For more on the Rise of Mongols and their conquests see Sharad K. Soni, *Mongolia-Russia Relations: Kiakhta to Vladivostok* (Delhi: Shipra and MAKAIAS, 2002), pp.13-16.
7. John K. Fairbank, Edwin O. Reischauer and Albert M. Craig, *East Asia: Tradition and Transformation* (Delhi: World View Publications,1998), revd. edn, p.164.
8. For more on early contacts between Mongolia and China, see Sharad K. Soni, *Mongolia-China Relations: Modern and Contemporary Times* (New Delhi: Pentagons, 2006), pp.1-18.
9. Fairbank and others (1998), p.200.
10. *Ibid.*
11. Morris Rossabi, "The Ming and Inner Asia", in Denis Twitchett, Frederick W. Mote and John K. Fairbank (eds.), *The Cambridge History of China,* vol. 8, Part-II, 1998, pp.225-6.

12. Peter S.H. Tang, *Russian and Soviet Policy in Manchuria and Outer Mongolia,* 1911-1931 (Durham, N.C.: Duke University Press, 1959), p.276.
13. Tsedendambyn Batbayar and Sharad K Soni, *Modern Mongolia: A Concise History* (New Delhi: Pentagon Press, 2007), p.8.
14. O. Edmund Clubb, *China and Russia: The Great Game* (New York and London: Columbia University Press, 1971), pp.6-7.
15. Cited in Morris Rossabi, *China and Inner Asia: From 1368 to the Present Day* (London: Thames and Hudson, 1975), p.45.
16. *Ibid.*
17. David Sneath, *Changing Inner Mongolia: Pastoral Mongolian Society and the Chinese State* (New York: Oxford University Press, 2000), p.7.
18. See Morris Rossabi, "Altan Khan," in Ainslie Embree, ed., *Encyclopedia of Asian History,* (New York, 1987), vol. I, p.50.
19. Rossabi (1998), p.237.
20. B. Shirendyb and others, eds., *History of the Mongolian People's Republic* (Moscow: Nauka Publishing House, 1973), p.171.
21. See Baabar [Bar-Erdene Batbayar] (1999), *Twentieth Century Mongolia*, C. Kaplonsi, ed., D. Sühjargalmaa, S. Burenbayar, H. Hulun and N. Tuya, trans.(Cambridge: The White Horse Press, 1999), p.61.
22. Clubb (1971), pp.19-20.
23. See Urgunge Onon and Derrick Pritchatt, *Asia's First Modern Revolution: Mongolia Proclaims its Independence in 1911* (Leiden: E.J. Brill, 1989), p.2.
24. *Ibid*, pp.2-3.
25. Tang (1959), p.279.
26. Owen Lattimore, *Nationalism and Revolution in Mongolia*, (Leiden: E.J. Brill, 1955), p.7.
27. See G.M. Friters, *Outer Mongolia and its International Position* (Baltimore: The Johns Hopkins Press, 1949), p.151.
28. Ken Shen Weigh, *Russo-Chinese Diplomacy: 1689-1924*(Banger, Maine: University Prints and Reprints, 1928), p.147.
29. Fairbank and others (1998), p.218.
30. Robert A. Rupen, *Mongols of the Twentieth Century* (Bloomington: Indiana University, 1964), pp.70-71.
31. A league was called *mêng* in Chinese and *chulgan* in Mongolian; a tribe – *pu* in Chinese and *aimak* in Mongolian; a banner or military unit – *chi* in Chinese and *heshun* in Mongolian. See Chang Yin-T'ang (1933), p.6.
32. Great Britain, Foreign Office, *Mongolia*, Handbooks Prepared under the Direction of the Historical Section of the Foreign Office – No. 68, (London: H.M. Stationery Office, 1920), p.16.
33. *Ibid*, p.326.
34. The spellings of League names follow the same pattern as given in Christopher P. Atwood, *Young Mongols and Vigilantes in Inner*

Mongolia's Interregnum Decades, 1911-1931, (Leiden, Boston, Köln: E.J. Brill, 2002), vol. I, p.60.

35. Sneath (2000), p.9.
36. Chang Yin-T'ang (1933), p.6.
37. Owen Lattimore, "The Historical Setting of Inner Mongolian Nationalism", in *Studies in Frontier History: Collected Papers, 1928-195,* (Paris: Mouton & Co., 1962), pp.442.
38. Pao Chao-Hsieh, *The Government of China: 1644-1911* (Baltimore: The John Hopkins Press, 1925), p.341.
39. See Svat Soucek, *A History of Inner Asia* (Cambridge: Cambridge University Press, 2000), p.171.
40. Rong Ma,"Changes in Local Administration and their Impact on Community Life in Grasslands of Inner Mongolia, China", *China Report*, vol.39, no.4, 2003, p.460.
41. Joseph Fletcher, "The Heyday of the Ch'ing order in Mongolia, Sinkiang and Tibet," in John K. Fairbank, ed., *The Cambridge History of China: Volume 10: Late Ch'ing, 1800-1911,* Part I ,(Cambridge: Cambridge University Press, 1976), p.353.
42. Thomas E. Ewing, "Ch'ing Policies in Outer Mongolia, 1900-1911", *Modern Asian Studies*, vol.14, no.1, 1980, p.152.
43. See Rossabi (1975), p.212.
44. Baron S.A. Korff , "Russia in the Far East", *American Journal of International Law*, vol.17, 1923, p.277.
45. Cited in Chang Yin-Tang (1933), p.70.
46. Sechin Jagchid, *Essays in Mongolian Studies* (Provo, Utah: David M. Kennedy Centre for International Studies, 1988), p.202.
47. *Ibid.*
48. The credit for introducing the idea of nationalism into the Chinese domains in Inner Asia goes largely to the Russians and the British, see Rossabi (1975), pp.218-19.
49. Owen Lattimore, *The Mongols of Manchuria* (New York: The John Day Company, 1934), p.128.
50. For details of the demands, see Xenia Joukoff Eudin and Robert C. North, *Soviet Russia and the East, 1920-1927: A Documentary Survey* (Stanford, California: Stanford University Press, 1957), pp.259-60.
51. *Ibid*, p.260.
52. Atwood (2002), pp.466-7.
53. Lattimore (1934), p.130.
54. *Ibid.*
55. *Ibid*, p.131.
56. To know more about capitals, areas and dates of assimilation of these provinces into China, see Chang Yin-T'ang (1933), p.74.
57. G. Tsengelt, "The Nationality Question in Inner Mongolia and the Ethnic opposition," at http://www.radicalparty.org/humanrights/mon_doc2.htm

58. Owen Lattimore (1955), p.27.
59. Uradyn E. Bulag, *From Empire to Nation and Back: Tibeto-Mongolian Buddhism, Nationalism and the Challenge to Chinese Sovereignty* at http://www.intlstudies.ucsd.edu/iicas-research_paper/Empire to Nation11/Bulag.pdf
60. Robert A. Rupen, "Mongolian Nationalism, Part I," *Journal of Royal Central Asian Society*, vol.45, 1959, p.164. Also see James Burke, "China's Losing Game in Mongolia", *Far Eastern Survey*, vol.17, no. 13, 7 July 1948; G.D.R. Phillips, *Russia, Japan and Mongolia* (London, 1942).
61. For more on Ulanfu's (1906-1988) contribution to Inner Mongolia in particular and China in general, see Uradyn Erden Bulag, "The Cult of Ulanhu in Inner Mongolia: History, Memory and the Making of National Heroes", *Central Asian Survey*, vol.17, no.1, 1998, pp.11-33.
62. Zhao Zhenbei, "A New Appraisal of Democratic Reform in the Pastoral Zone of Inner Mongolia in the 1940s", *Central Asian Survey*, vol.17, no.1, 1998, p.109.
63. Rupen (1964), pp.259-60.
64. Zhang Zeyi, "Inner Mongolia: China's First Autonomous Region 40 Years Old", *Beijing Review*, vol.30, no.18, 4 May 1987, p.16.
65. Asian Development Bank (2004), *Technical Assistance to the People's Republic of China for Energy Development Strategy for the Inner Mongolia Autonomous Region*, TAR: PRC 38511, Report prepared by Longyun Peng.
66. Tumenceceg, "Mongol-xiatadin ediin zasag, xydaldaanii xapilcaand OMOZU-in guicantgaj bui uureg" [Inner Mongolia Autonomous Region's Role in Mongolia-China Trade and Economic Relations], *International Studies* (Ulaanbaatar), February 2002, p.98.
67. This figure has been taken as of 31 December 2007 as recorded in *China Statistical Yearbook 2008*. However, according to the 2000 National Population Census of China, the total population of Inner Mongolia stands at 23.76 million with almost 4 million Mongols, see "Inner Mongolia" at http://en.wikipedia.org/wiki/Inner_Mongolia.
68. Starmass International, "Inner Mongolia Imports and Exports", at http://www.starmass.com/china_review/provincial_overview/inner_mongolia_imports_exports.htm
69. People's Daily Online, "Inner Mongolia's Economy Maintains a Rapid Growth Momentum", 5 February 2006 at http://english.people.com.cn/200602/05/eng20060205_240396.html
70. *Ibid.*
71. People's Daily Online, "Chinese Inner Mongolia to enhance cooperation with Mongolia", 15 November 2007 at http://english.people.com.cn/90001/90776/6303523.html
72. China Real News, "Steel exports through Inner Mongolia's Erenhot port rebound in March", 31 March 2009 at

http://chinarealnews.typepad.com/chinarealnews/2009/03/steel-exports-through-inner-mongolias-erenhot-port-rebound-in-march.html

73. Xinhua News Agency, "China Seeks Cooperation with Mongolia in Sand Control", 6 April 2004 at http://china.org.cn/english/international/92233.htm
74. Asian Development Bank (2006), *Inner Mongolia Autonomous Region: Trade Facilitation and Logistics Development Strategy*, TA-6058 (REG) Report prepared by Robert L. Wallack, and Executive Summary presented at a Workshop held in Tashkent, Uzbekistan on 2-4 September 2008.
75. China Development Gateway, "World Bank Helps Inner Mongolia Facilitate Cross-border Trade through Improved Transport Infrastructure," at http://www.chinagate.cn/english/34425.htm
76. CRI English.com, "Mongolia opens Consulate in Erenhot," 7 April 2007 at http://english.cri.cn/2946/2007/04/07/272@213647.htm
77. "Open ceremony of 'No.1 China-Mongolia Bridge' held in Xinba'erhu Left Banner", at http://www.nmgnews.com.cn/eng/article/20051107/24929_1.html
78. Xinhua, "China Exclusive: Construction Starts on Railroad Linking China, Mongolia, Russia", 10 November 2007, at http://www.smhric.org/SMW_43.htm
79. Quoted in *ibid*.
80. China View, "China, Mongolia open new air route", 5 August 2009 at http://news.xinhuanet.com/english/2009-08/05/content_11829639.htm
81. Xinhua, "Inner Mongolia Naadam Festival", 2 August 2009 at http://www.chinaethnicgroups.com/2009-08/02/content_8561143.htm
82. "Asia Arts Festival highlights Mongolia's Ethnic Culture", *China Daily*, 20 August 2009.
83. The Economist Intelligence Unit, *China and Mongolia*, First quarter. 1999, p.47.
84. M. Bayarmaa,"Inner Mongolian Artist Performed in Ulaanbaatar", 30 June 2009 at http://ubpost.mongolnews.mn/index.php?option=com_content&task=view&id=3146&Itemid=45
85. Asian Economic News, "China, Mongolia to protect endangered ethnic song", 5 Dec 2005 at http://findarticles.com/p/articles/mi_m0WDP/is_2005_Dec_5/ai_n15899944/?tag=content;col1
86. Tumenceceg (2002), p.100.
87. People's Daily, "Inner Mongolia, Ulan Bator to Jointly Fight TB", 21 October 2000 at http://english.peopledaily.com.cn/english/200010/21/eng20001021_53222.html
88. See *The Mongol Messenger*, 9 April 2008 at http://www. mongolmessenger.mn/issue/080104.php

89. Uradyn E. Bulag, "Inner Mongolia: The Dialectics of Colonization and Ethnicity Building", in Morris Rossabi, ed., *Governing China's Multiethnic Frontiers* (Seattle and London: University of Washington Press, 2004), p.84.
90. See Alicia Campi, "Mongolian Identity Issues and the Image of Chinggis Khan", *Bimonthly Journal of Mongolian and Tibetan Current Situation*, vol.16, no.3, 2007, p.23.
91. Ch. Sumiyabazar, "Ties with China Developing Smoothly: FM Oyun", *The UB Post*, 3 April 2008.

Dr. Sharad K. Soni meeting with Mongolian President N. Enkhbayar on 30 June 2006 at President Office in Government House, Ulaanbaatar, Mongolia

Dr. Soni at Research Centre for Mongolian Studies, Inner Mongolia University (IMU), Höhhot

Dr. Soni with Prof. J. Chimeddorji, Dean of Research Centre for Mongolian Studies and Dr. Nasanbayar, Director, Anthropology Department, IMU, Höhhot

Sculpture of Mongolian music instrument Morin Khuur inside IMU Campus, Höhhot

Dr. Soni at the traditional dwelling of Mongolian Nomads (ger), Inner Mongolia

Dr. Soni at Inner Mongolia Museum, Höhhot that exhibits Revolutionary Struggle in Inner Mongolia (1925-1949)

CHAPTER 22

TRANSFORMATION OF TRADITIONAL CULTURE IN INNER MONGOLIA

Baohua

Can the nomadic society be nomadic in the modern era? What has been happening to Inner Mongols during the last few decades due to the influence of modern technology? Globalization and industrialization have now become the most significant feature of modern society having great impact on traditional culture and society, especially to those societies which had been seen as barbarous, undeveloped and primitive, of course, including nomadism. For quite a long time, people influenced by cultural hegemony and the European center principle believed that animal husbandry and nomadism is less developed than agriculture and industry, So people were proud of developing industry. While going through the newspapers and magazines of Inner Mongolia published in the initial stage of establishment of People's Republic of China, one would find so many pictures of factories and chimneys which were seen as the symbol of new development. People were considering that agriculture and industry are the true and only way of development. But after half a century's so-called-development, our environment has been damaged badly, traditional religion has diminished and herdsmen became poor, and so neither the government nor the people have realised the benefit of fully industrialization. Thus in the twenty first century, China appears to be increasingly nature-oriented, and people now have started paying attention to nomadism and traditional culture, re-thinking about the consequences of industrialisation and globalization mostly because of the Black-Sandstorm. But this is just the beginning, if we want to solve and overcome the great changes and their consequences, one has to know the reasons and process of the transformation. Using concrete examples in Alaxia Aimak, one is concerned with the reasons and impact of transformation of traditional culture in modern Inner Mongolia. This paper is an attempt to critically analyze the significant changes occurring in modern society from the perspective of the everyday life of rural communities in Inner Mongolia.

When I was four or five years old, I first remembered things (late 1980s) that my parents have all five kinds of livestock, and our family moves to long distance for the sake of letting animals to eat more and nutritional grass just like our ancestors did for centuries. But in the year 1994, when I entered fifth grade, primary school, arose the sandstorm first time. Since then it has been occurring every year and several times a year. The weather is getting worse and worse. It rains rarely, so there is heavy drought all the year round and almost everywhere. Grassland grows so little vegetation that livestock have little to eat. So our family has camel, sheep and goats, three kinds of animals only now. I have witnessed these changes, that is, transformation of traditional culture which is an ongoing process. When interviewing local residents, we found that in older people's memory, their life, production and environment was almost totally different from now. So we can see the process of changing traditional culture through interviewing, observing and going through the government documents, which are the methodologies of my study.

Mongols used to live a nomadic life, move within four pastures logically according to the weather, topographic features, vegetation and water supply, so that the vegetation of all pastures could grow well and stay away from disaster and drought easily. However, Inner Mongols now have chosen to settle down developing sedentary husbandry, so that most families have only one pasture. In traditional nomadic life, there are five kinds of animals: horse, cattle, camel, sheep and goat, which are called *tavan hoshuu mal* in Mongolian, some of which are mainly used for transport, some produce wool and milk, while some mainly produce meat and skin. All the five kinds of animals played their own special role in nomadic life. But now in Inner Mongolia, few families have all these five kinds of livestock. Generally the families have only two or three kinds of animals. In such case the life and husbandry economy of the people has changed. Many herdsmen are now buying milk from city market. It sounds ridiculous: herdsmen, who herd livestock and produce milk, couldn't have milk and bought the same from city. But this is the fact in case of many places of Inner Mongolia. Herdsmen who used to herd livestock have their livestock and get meat and milk, and earn some money from selling sheepskin. Unfortunately, due to the great changes in environment and desertification, little vegetation grows on the grassland forcing the herdsmen to buy so much hay and forage to feed their animals which cost almost all of their income. So herdsmen are feeding their livestock now and getting poorer. Then what are the reasons for such great and quick changes? Let's look at the reasons.

Firstly, enormous increase in population poses the potential danger. In the years 1958-1960, there was a heavy draught disaster in Gansu province, which is located adjacent to Alaxia Aimak, Inner Mongolia that caused the immigration of a large people to Alaxia. Both Mongols and Han Chinese who witnessed development, state that the environmental condition and the social life was totally different from which is today in Inner Mongolia. One the one side (Gansu) there was disaster and difficulties, on the other side (Alaxia) there was good life. The disaster encouraged refugees to move out of Gansu province, and the better condition in Alaxia attracted them into Inner Mongolia. Whereas these immigrants were looking for a way out, the nomadic society required more work-force. Thus, the immigrants were pushed out of Gansu and pulled into Alaxia (west to east). This is the "Push" and "Pull" theory of sociology. Besides, many Mongols from western part of Alaxia settled in the eastern part, due to nation building and construction of military bases, etc. As such the population of Alaxia increased hugely due to migrantion from both within and outside of western Alaxia. But the pastoral area was decreased in the eastern part of Alaxia.

This made the herding space much smaller than it used to be for an average family. People had no other option but to settle down and raise animals just in one place instead of following the nomadic life moving around all the year round based on its water supply and vegetation. Since the livestock eats the limited vegetation of only one pastoral area everyday, plants could grow very little. And recently, contract responsibility system has been carried out under which local government contracts for certain piece of grassland to every family for its age and care. Most families have encircled their "own" pastoral area with wire nettings, and donot want to share the steppe with others any more. In addition, with the arrival of modern technology, many highways and railroads have been constructed, thereby dividing the natural herding place into so many smaller pieces that are not suitable for big animals like cattle, horses and camels, which are accustomed to go a far to find food. Thus such division of grassland adversely influenced the traditions of nomadic economy. This is the second reason for changes in nomadic life: smaller and only one pastoral area makes it hard to grow all five kinds of animals.

Railroad dividing the natural pastoral area

Cars always disturb animals

Due to bigger population and less grassland, Alaxias had no option but to settle down on only one pastoral area and develop sedentary husbandry. Many people believe that sedentary life is more comfortable than nomadic and moveable one, but it has counteracted upon traditional nomadism and natural conservation. Once people settle down, their demands grow and they need to construct their houses, get furniture and so on and do not feel satisfied with Mongol *Ger* and whatever things they had in the nomadic life. To fulfill all these needs, people began to cut down trees and bushes in the local area damaging the environment. Modern society, including sedentary life is characterized by its high technology and high consumerism.

Herdsmen have settled down, living sedentary life

Traditional minded Mongols believe that every trees and plants have life and if we cut down or hurt them, we would be punished by gods. But due to globalization, people's beliefs and traditional religion have been vanishing. People are destroying nature without any fear for the sake of earning more money, and this has badly damaged the natural environment.

At the beginning of the twenty first century, global environmental issues are much closer to daily life. Only a few decades ago, environmental issues were typically framed within a stereotypical dichotomy of perpetrators and victims; namely, between those producing gases or excessive noise or toxic waste, and those who suffer from such pollution. Today, however, it has been seen from perspectives that go far beyond this perpetrator-victim dichotomy and beyond the boundaries of the regions and countries in which such dichotomous relationships must be located. Black-sandstorm in China has drawn global attention and source of the sand-storm is seen as Ejene, Alashan.

Increasing population, sedentary husbandry, high consumption, unsuitable exploration of agriculture and industry has contributed to desertification and environmental degradation.

Grassland today in Alaxia

Little vegetation on grasslands

As nomadism is a kind of economy which relies upon natural environment, herdsmen's life has become poor during the recent years. Herdsmen, who used to herd animals, are now feeding animals due to poor vegetation on grassland. Since herdsmen spend almost all their income from selling wool and sheepskin to buy hay to feed their livestock, they are becoming poorer. Many people believe that the decrease in the number of big animals like cattle and horse is due to poor environmental situation. As there is no vegetation for animals to eat, they cannot survive any more. However, in my opinion, it is the imbalance within the five-kinds of animals, which accelerated the changes in environment.

With the advent of power-driven machinery, traditional communication system has given way to machine-based transport. People prefer to use cars and motorcycles, and they are satisfied with herding sheep and goat with their supply of meat and milk. So camel, oxen and horses are seen as useless animals in the sedentary modern society. People prefer to herd so-called financially useful animals rather than practically helpful animal in modern society.

Herdsman riding motorcycle

Herdsmen decorate motorcycle with horse saddle

But the modern means of communication need finances. They raise money by increasing useful and financially beneficial animals unceasingly, which causes overload on grassland which in turn leads to environmental degradation.

To conclude, traditional nomadism and herding economy sustain the growth of production, which also sustains natural recourses. It makes use of grassland and conserves it by moving around and not by consuming it. However, in the industrial society, people won't stop exploring and consuming until they have finished or explored all the mineral resources. But sedentary herding in Inner Mongolia today is similar to industry that is settling down in a place and not storing and conserving the natural resources. So shift from the traditional nomadism has caused environmental changes in Inner Mongolia.

REFERENCES

1. *Alashan Youqi Zhi* (*Annals of Alaxia Western Banner*), Neimenggu Jiaoyu Chubanshe (Educational Press of Inner Mongolia), 2000.
2. Robert L. Bee, *Pattern and Processes: An introduction to Anthropological Strategies for the Study of Socio-cultural Changes*, New York: Free Press, 1974.
3. *Ejina Qi Zhi* (*Annals of Ezene Banner*), Zhifang Chubanshe (Zhi Fang Press), 1998.
4. KuiLi Liu, BinZhong Gao edited, *Alashan Shengtai Huanjing de Ehua yu Shehui Wenhua de Bianqian* (*Environmental changes and cultural transformation of Alaxia*), Xueyuan Chubanshe (Xue Yuan Press), 2007.
5. G.J. Lewis, *Human Migrants*, London: Groom Helm Ltd, 1982.
6. Xinjiletu, ed., *Zhongguo Huanjing Zhengce Baogao – Shengtai Yimin* (*Report of China's Policy on Environment – Ecological Migrants*), Neimenggu Daxue Chubanshe (Inner Mongolia University Press), 2005.

CHAPTER 23

BURYATIA AND THE IDEA OF UNITED MONGOLIAN STATE

M.N. Baldano

The idea of uniting the Mongolian peoples for creating the ethnically homogeneous state emerged among the Buryat intellectuals who had received European education, in late 19th and early 20th centuries. It became one of the components of national ideology which was named Pan-Mongolism. Geographical proximity, common cultural roots, traditions of statehood, preservation of spiritual ties with the related Mongolian world formed the basis of this Pan-Mongolism.

The idea of uniting Mongolian peoples came up within the limits of political discourse and was mainly due to the crises in China and Russia, which incorporated Mongolian speaking population. Concerned over the strengthening of China and Japan in Mongolia, the Buryat national democrats thought that bringing Mongolia in Russian sphere of influence would provide conditions for uniting the Buryat and Mongolian peoples and developing their cultures by combining both the eastern and western cultures.

The essence of the political doctrine of Pan-Mongolism was stated by Ts. Zhamtsarano, which was to unite Mongolia with Inner Mongolia, Buryatia, Kalmykia, Mongols of Xinjiang and Tuva. It would give an opportunity to restore historical region of Mongol settlements and to transform new country into really independent sovereign state.[1] He saw in the state a way to national consolidation and integration.

This approach to the integration of peoples in Central Asia into one cultural space by gradually erasing the distinctions between separate regional groups and achieving ethnic unification and solidarity of the population of Mongolia reflected the European paradigm of nation. Ts. Zhamtsarano's "Manifesto" underlined that it's necessary "to be released from the power of aggressive state... and create in future huge state uniting all Mongolian tribes" on a federal basis. Defining its foreign policy, Ts. Zhamtsarano put forward the idea that the country should be neutral like Switzerland.

The Russian-Chinese Declaration of 1913 on the Mongolian question and Kyakhta tripartite agreement of 1915 defined the international legal status of the Mongolian state, having reduced it to the level of Outer Mongolia's autonomy. It was recognized and signed by official representatives of Bogdo Gegen. Probably, these events influenced the Buryat people in search for new forms of state system for Mongolian speaking peoples, especially during the Burnatskom's and Burnarduma's activities. Thus the idea of obtaining autonomy for Buryatia as a part of the Great Mongolian state independent of the influence of Japan, China and Russia emerged. Ts. Zhamtsarano, E. D. Rinchino, B. Baradin and others adhered to this idea. E. D. Rinchino wrote in his letter to D. Sampilon: "The old Natskom considered that Manchuria and East Mongolia will entirely stay in the sphere of Japan. Southern, northern and western Mongolia including the Buryats will form the independent neutral buffer state. And Buryats should move to Halh or to the borders of Transbaikalia with exchange of their lands."[2]

The attempts of practical realization of the idea of political unity of the Mongolian peoples were made in 1919. The Conference held in Chita (frontier station of Daurya) on February 25, 1919, accepted the decision about formation of the independent federal "Great Mongolian State" including four *Aimags* – Outer Mongolia, Inner Mongolia, Barga and the lands of Transbaikalian Buryats. The Mongolian prince Neyse Gegen became the head of the new state. However, as shown by the subsequent events, the idea of political consolidation of the Mongolian peoples appeared insolvent: first, it hadn't mass support; secondly, neither party, nor the cultural elite of Mongolia, Buryatia and Tuva were really interested in unity. The delegation from Outer Mongolia didn't participate in the Conference.

Despite internal disorders, Russia and China continued to defend their own interests in Central Asia. Kolchak's government and Republican China, using the inconsistency in the actions of Congress participants and Urga sabotage, successfully counteracted the realization of Daurya's Congress plans. Prince Neyse Gegen was captured and shot dead by Chinese troops.

In 1924 the first Great *Khuruldan* in Outer Mongolia adopted the Constitution proclaiming the Mongolian People's Republic (MPR). It was declared that one of the goals of MPR's foreign policy was "uniting of Mongolian tribes into common free state capable to protect religion and people's interests."[3] Mongolia started to realize the "nation-state" principle.

One year before in 1923, Buryat-Mongolian Autonomous Soviet Socialist Republic (BMASSR) was created in Soviet Russia. The Bolsheviks being under strong influence of the theory of "world revolution" were guided by class interests. In the report to the Central Committee of the Communist Party on December 8, 1922, the Buryat-Mongolian party's committee marked: "Establishing of the Buryat-Mongolian Autonomous Republic, being the demonstration of the Soviet principles of solving national-colonial question and politically impressing to all Mongolian and Tibetan world, is the big plus for strengthening the Soviet foreign policy in the Far East and in Central Asia."[4]

In spite of the establishment of BMASSR's, the idea of uniting the Mongolian peoples continued for some time to have a place in theoretical directions of new leaders of the autonomy moves. However, the process of nation-building in Buryatia (like in Mongolia) was developing in another direction. It cardinally differed from the project of Pan-Mongolists, aspiring to create the Buryat statehood in the form of cultural-national autonomy (the Bryunn compromise variant) with the subsequent allocation of compact territory for settling the Buryats, or in the form of the state unifying the Mongolian historical and cultural community.

The Soviet model of nation-building didn't exclude the potential possibilities of unity dictated by reasons than other Pan-Mongolism. The question of uniting all Mongols with Outer Mongolia was raised by Choybalsan and Yu. Tsedenbal with the Soviet Union.[5] During the 1920s, Pan-Mongolian factor played important role in the revolutionary movement in Central Asia. At that time the Comintern sought to use it for its purposes, as Mongolia was considered to be a corridor to China. Comintern supported the Pan-Mongolian moods. In the spring of 1925, the member of Executive Committee of the Comintern, Sen Katayama visited Ulan Bator, on his way from China to Moscow. In his speech at the session of Central Committee of the MPRP, Katayama underlined: "Gomindan will have nothing against the independent existence of Outer Mongolia. The idea of reunion of all Mongolian tribes into one independent federal republic with the nearest course on Sovietization and with the remote prospect of joining the USSR... It is beautiful idea... Let Outer Mongolia go to the relatives in Inner Mongolia and Barga, Xinjiang and will organize all of them against world imperialism."[6]

The sharp ideological and political struggle between the "old" and the "new" intelligentsia started in Buryatia. Those who for a long time were developing ways of state system in Buryatia were accused of "bourgeois nationalism" and were severely criticized. Then came to the period when the representatives of "old" Buryat intelligentsia gathered on the Mongolian territory and played important role in the social and political life of the Mongolian state.

After defeating the group of national democrats in the Mongolian People's Republic in 1928, Pan-Mongolian factor ceased to be of any value for the USSR in the geopolitical game. On the other hand, it became even dangerous, mainly due to increased political activity of Japan in the Far East, as Japan was interested in the spread of Mongolian national movement. In the 1930s, the situation abruptly changed in Buryat-Mongolia. Members of Anti-Soviet insurgent Pan-Mongolian organization on the both sides of border were repressed. As a result of repressions, thousands of the Soviet and Mongolian citizens suffered. The terms "Pan-Mongolism", "bourgeois nationalism", "Pan-Mongolist" and "Pan-Mongolian" became dangerous political labels.

On September 26, 1937, the Central Executive Committee of the USSR approved the decision "About dividing East-Siberia into Irkutsk and Chita areas", without any consultation with the Buryat-Mongolian republic authorities. This decision ran contrary to the accepted Constitution of BMASSR, particularly with the 15th article regarding its territorial integrity. The Soviets feared that the Buryat population, the largest ethnic formation in this region, might collaborate with Japan in the event of war with USSR, and hence such preventive measures were taken. One of them was administrative division of Buryat-Mongolian territory, which would essentially strengthen the region's safety and weaken the Republic as a national formation.

Creation of the Buryat-Mongolian national areas formally provided national-administrative autonomy to the Buryat population in their concentration outside the BMASSR area, but at the same time it had negative consequences for the Buryat people. Professor Sh. Chimitdorzhiev, one of the ideologues of the Buryat national movement in 1990s underlined, that "as the result of this anti-constitutional act the unity of the Buryat-Mongolian people was undermined and difficulties in its consolidation were caused. Thus started deformation of culture, national traditions, customs and ceremonies, language."[7] The 1937 decision has remained one of the actual problems of the Buryat people, "which reflected in the people's consciousness, accumulating other acute problems of the Buryat culture and language, strengthens its frustration, on the one hand, and on the another – promotes radicalization of Buryat nationalism."[8]

At the end of 1950s, the idea of unity and the idea of trans-border community lost its relevance, as the new historical community – Soviet people – was created on this side of the border, and the Buryat-Mongols were part of it. However, the Mongolian researchers Sh. Luvsandorj and A. Enhbat note, the unifying idea still remained a cherished dream of the Mongolian scientists and intellectuals, such as S. Danzan, C. Dandaa, N.

Amar, T. Dambadorj, N. Jadamba, D. Dogsom, B. Rinchen, Gombojav and others.[9]

In 1958, a Decree of Presidium of the Supreme Soviet of the USSR, renamed the areas and the word "Mongols" disappeared from the people's name. Legitimacy and necessity of renaming the republic was still discussed by a part of intelligentsia and public organizations of ethnic orientation. Changing the names of Republic and areas, according to some Buryat researchers, was dictated by ideological and to some extent by foreign policy considerations. Professor G. Sanzhiev supposed that "N. Khrushchev insisted on renaming of the Republic as the preservation of its former name could be used by Chinese leadership in course of complicated relations between the USSR and the People's Republic of China (PRC) as a ground to make claims for ethnic territories of Mongols."[10]

With the crash of socialism and disintegration of the USSR, the Soviet model of nation-building became history. At the end of 1980s and the beginning of 1990s the tendency of regeneration of "cultural Pan-Mongolism" emerged once again. In Buryatia and in Mongolia, its ideas were revived in the course of discussions among the intelligentsia. These debates were devoted to the problems of trans-border integration of the Mongolian historical and cultural community. Sometimes this integration was perceived as the state unification.

The slogans of national revival of the Buryat people were firstly put forward in November 1988 by supporters of the People's Front of Assistance to Perestroika (PFAP), which was part of the ecological movement. Radical wing of PFAP asked for raising the status of the Buryat ASSR to the level of Union Republic, and also to return the territories, torn away in 1937. The theme of division of Buryat people was echoed in political circles and affirmed in ideological discourse. Appearing of PFAP was connected, first of all, with the dismantling of the Soviet system. On the one hand, it showed the rise of civil activity, and on the another, the attempt of new political opposition to mobilize civil activity for supporting its own policy. Though the questions of nationality and identification gained importance, they remained out of the programme of PFAP.

In the early 1990s, different public organizations and political movements, like the society *Geser*, later transformed to the *Buryat-Mongolian People's Party* (BMPP) (1990), and social movement of national orientation *Negedel* (Unity) (1992) appeared. BMPP and *Negedel* perceived themselves as political movements in tradition of modern patriotism, having special value in the course of nation-building. *Negedel* supported the separation of Buryatia (with Buryat areas) from Russia, consolidation of the Mongolian-speaking peoples and creation of Central Asian federation including Tuva, Kalmykia and two Mongol areas of the People's Republic of China.

New changes in public life and replacement of the republican leadership gave fresh impetus for discussion of the problems of Buryatia. In this connection the issue of territorial division of BMASSR in 1937 was revived and became the basis for demanding restoration of Buryatia to the old borders of 1937 and return of the republic's old name to Buryat-Mongolia. It was the sensitive issue, actively and emotionally discussed by the population of Republic and Buryat areas.

National history was actively used in the mobilization of opposition movement, based on national identification. The question of national identity took a special place in the Buryat political discourse. "The Buryats-Mongols: who are we?" – this question rested on the definition of priority criterion among existing markers of ethnic identification. The appeal to revive the Buryat-Mongolian people "through the spiritual and territorial reuniting of Buryatia with Ust-Ordynsky and Aginsky Buryat autonomous areas and returning the historical name – Buryat-Mongols was part of the Charter of BMPP.

In August 1990, a group of veterans sent a letter addressed to the Chairman of the Council of Nationalities of the Supreme Soviet of the USSR, R.N. Nishanov. They sought the cancellation of anti-constitutional act of 1937 and restoration of the Buryat Republic to its former borders. "Formal reason to divide the people, as it was pointed out, was territorial sparseness, actually judging by the time of this lawless act, the initiators and organizers of dividing the small people wished to liquidate an economic and territorial basis of Pan-Mongolism."[11]

The letter received wide resonance not only in the republic, but also in the Buryat areas.

On February 22, 1991, the first All-Buryat Congress devoted to the problems of consolidation and spiritual revival of nation was opened in Ulan-Ude. Leitmotif of all reports was "Buryat people and Buryat culture are in crisis, and the urgent measures of revival are required". The Congress unanimously condemned the anti-constitutional act of dividing the Republic in 1937. But the participants were divided in their opinion on the question of reuniting of Buryat territories. The problems of national policy, history, Buryat culture and language received wide discussion, and concrete decisions were made. The establishment of All-Buryat Association for Cultural Development (ABACD) became a practical step in the field of spiritual consolidation of the Buryat people and revival of Buryat culture.

Second All-Buryat Congress which became the indicator of ethno-political processes in the Republic and Buryat areas was held in March 1996. Attempt by radical section of the intelligentsia to transform ABACD into political organization at the Congress did not succeed. However, few months later, the Congress of the Buryat People (CBP) was created in July 1996 with a goal to expand influence on various spheres of social and political life of republic and areas. The Congress paid special attention to the problem of division of BMSSR in 1937, restoring the Republic in former borders and returning the old name – Buryat-Mongolia. However, due to legal complications, the problem of reunification began to lose its appeal, especially in the public opinion of the Buryat population in the national areas.

The CBP and ABACD supported close cooperation between Buryatia and Mongolia in the field of culture. So, at the third All-Buryat Congress which has held in Ulan-Ude on February 16, 2002, the necessity of strengthening international ties, first of all, with related Mongolian-speaking peoples and diasporas was especially underlined. The beginning of 1990s was marked by gradual transition from a problematic cultural revival processes into the sphere of political discourse, and the end of 1990s was characterized by the reverse course.

Speaking about 1990s, one of the leaders of *Negedel*

movement V.A. Khamutaev in his interview to the author of this article underlined that "despite the certain degree of attraction of nationalist slogans and ethnic aims, the main peculiarity of the Buryat national movement at that time was that its representatives struggled for creation of the political community of new type".

In general, the idea of unity of the Buryats and Mongols both in the beginning and in the end of the twentieth century in Buryat national movement emerged not only in socio-cultural practice, but also in the attempts to construct All-Mongolian ethno-political system. Leaders of the Buryat revival movement were inclined to the need to expand people's political rights (up to full separation from Russia and creation of independent All-Mongolian national state). But the idea of unity did not find mass support neither in Buryatia, nor in Tuva or Kalmykia. Strengthening statehood in Russia, growing China's power, and absence of real interest of political and intellectual elite of Mongolia (seeing their future within the limits of existing statehood) were the ground realities due to which the unifying project proved to be illusive. However, the idea of political unity of the Mongolian community did not disappear, it continued to exist with full understanding that practical unification is impossible. Probably, it began to gain another functional meaning. It is also possible to suppose that the dream of unification became the instrument of nation-building.

References

1. Sh. Chimitdorzhiev, "Panmongolian Movement: It is all-Mongolian National Movement", *Mongolian Studies*, Issue.III, Ulan-Ude, 2000, pp.15-16.
2. E.D. Rinchino, *Documents, Articles, Letters*, Ulan-Ude, 1994, p.143.
3. S. Luzyanin, *Russia-Mongolia-China*, Moscow, 1997, p. 207.
4. N. Shulunov, *Formation of the Soviet National Statehood in Buryatia (1919-1923)*, Ulan-Ude, 1972, p. 396
5. L. Shinkarev, *Tsedenbal and Filatova: Love, Power, Tragedy*, Irkutsk, 2004, p. 79.
6. *Ibid*, p. 219.
7. Sh.Chimitdorzhiev, *Buryat-Mongols: History and Presence*, Ulan-Ude, 2001, p.38.

8. A. Elaev, *The Buryat People: Formation, Development, Self-identification*. Moscow, 2000, p. 287.
9. Sh. Luvsandorj and A. Enhbat, "National-Socialist Thought of Tsevena Zhamsaranova", *Mongolia-Buryatia-Tuva-Irkutsk Region: Development, Interaction and Challenges in and out of the Baikal Region*, Materials of the International Seminar, Ulan Bator, 2002, p.73.
10. *Pravda Buryatii*, 3 October 1991.
11. *Pravda Buryatii*, 24 August 1990.

CHAPTER 24

TRADITION AND CULTURE IN BURYATIA

K. Warikoo

Covering an area of 3,51,000 sq.kms. and situated in the southern part of East Siberia to the southeast of Baikal Lake, the Republic of Buryatia has its borders touching Mongolia in the south, the Republic of Tuva in the southwest, the Irkutsk oblast in the northwest and the Chita oblast in the east. The major part (about 60 per cent of coastline) of the 636-kms long Baikal Lake, the deepest freshwater lake in the world, falls within the territory of Buryatia. Buryats, Evenks and Soyots constitute the main indigenous nationalities, besides Russians, Ukrainians and others. By 2002, the population crossed one million, with Russians and Buryats constituting over 68 and 28 per cent respectively. Buryats, who are the largest ethnic group of indigenous people of Siberia, inhabit huge areas to the northeast from Lake Baikal. According to the 1989 Census, the population of Buryats in the former USSR was 4,21,600 (2,49,500 in Buratia Republic, 77,300 in Irkutsk Oblast, 66,100 in Chita Oblast and over 5000 in Moscow City.[1] Buryat Mongols also live in significant numbers in Dornod, Hentii, Selenge Tuv, Bulgan and Huvsgul *Aimags* of Mongolia, most of which border on Buryatia Republic and Chita region of Russia. Similarly in Inner Mongolia, the Hulun Buir region bordering Dornod *Aimag* also has a Buryat group called Shinheeni Buryats.

Zabaikalye – the richest part of Siberia – has been an integral part of the historical and cultural processes in Central Asia since ancient times. Until the establishment of the Mongol Empire, different forms of nomadic states had subsequently appeared and vanished over the centuries. It was in the 17th century that major part of Buryat territory was incorporated in the Russian empire. The Russian colonisation of this region resulted in the separation of a vast territory on both sides of the Baikal from the Mongolian world and the socio-political system of Mongols. Thus the dominant ethnic group in this area, who were Mongolian speaking tribes, clans and sub-groups, got isolated from the original ethnic Mongolians. After joining Russia, the new ethno-national identity of Buryats shaped up in the evolving historico-political situation. With the growing inter-ethnic social and cultural relationship including mixed marriages, a new class of assimilated Russian-Buryat families came into being. Interestingly, many Buryats played a positive role in the development of culture and self-identity of Buryats. For instance, Dorji Banzarov (1822-1855), Galson Gomboev (1822-1863), Zamtsarano (1880-1940), Bogdanov (1878-1919), Rinchino (1885-1937), Dorjiev (1853-1938), Ochirov (1875-1914), Baradin (1878-1937), Taysbikov (1873-1930) and Solbone Tuya (1892-1937) were the prominent Buryat intellectuals, who highlighted national Buryat culture, history and identity and also wrote and published in Russian journals and publications.[2] Buryat litterateurs adopted modern Russianised approach to traditional Mongolian themes. Zamtsarano's publications revolved around the themes of Buryat culture, folklore, epic poetry, shamanism, Buryat and Mongolian history, indigenous law etc. Buryat intelligentsia also translated works of Russian and Western literature into Mongolian. Bogdanov wrote important historical studies and also translated some German literary works into Mongolian. Agvan Dorjiev worked on language reform. Ochirov worked on a Russian-Mongolian newspaper for sometime and translated Russian laws and literary works into Mongolian. Baradin devoted himself to Buddhist and Tibetan studies. Both Baradin and Tsybikov wrote extensively about the Mongolian language. These Buryat intellectuals who were educated and trained in Russian institutions, led the Buryat movement for cultural revival.

In 1666 AD, Russian Cossacks built a wooden fortress on the bank of the Uda River, which turned into a large city

Verkhneudinsk and later became the capital city of Buryatia under the new name of Ulan-Ude. The capital city of Ul'an-Ude is the administrative, political, economic, and cultural centre of the Republic of Buryatia. It is one of the oldest and large cities of Siberia. Ulan-Ude city is small, compact and well organised. The Trans-Siberian railway which has been played key role in the economy of the region, passes through Ulan-Ude. The city is located on the tea road from China via Kiakhta port to Russia. On the main Arbat Street, we see a symbol of Ulan-Ude city – the *Swayambo* placed above two dragons, which reminds of close Indian cultural influence. On a visit to the Rimpoche Baksha Temple in Ulan-Ude city, this author met a Buddhist Lama from Ladakh (India), who was spending over three months in this monastery. On the outskirts of Ulan-Ude city, there is a traditional Buryat restaurant – *Yurt*. I spent an evening in the *Yurt* enjoying the ethnic Buryat cuisine and national music and dance. We made circular dance around *Ogun* (fire place), which is placed in the centre of the restaurant. That *Ogun*, the Sanskrit term for fire is still in vogue here, only testifies to the continuing Indian connection with Buryatia.

Selenga, which is the largest river having a length of over 1,200 kms and flowing through Russia, Mongolia and Buryatia, falls in the Baikal Lake. Selenga river has strong flow of water and depth. It is like the Ganges of India and is an integral part of Buryat culture. So many national Buryat songs have been written about the Selenga. Well known Buryat artist Anna Subonova has composed several songs eulogising the grandeur and essence of Selenga for Buryatia. Selenga river flows along the road to Baikal lake and the clouds of vapour over the course of the Selenga river present an extraordinary sight.

Though the Tsarist government had its own system of administration in Zabaikalye, local administration remained in the hands of Buryat nobles. Traditional caravan routes connecting Russia to the Far East as well as the construction of the Trans-Siberian railway that crossed the territory of Zabaikalye contributed to the economic development of the region during the 18th and 19th centuries. The settlement of Russian peasants, missionary work of Orthodox Christians, the presence of local Cossacks and widespread usage of Russian language, led to the Russification of this area. With the introduction of Russian language, culture and education, a new powerful class of Buryat intellectuals came into existence and they wielded considerable influence in Russian politics particularly in its dealings with Mongolia and Tibet. Buddhist lamas from Buryatia had access to the rulers of Russia from the time of Empress Elizabeth (1741-1762). They became influential at the Tsarist Russian courts of Alexender III and Nicholas II, through the efforts of the Peter Alexandrovich Badmaev (1851-1919), a Buryat physician and practitioner of Tibetan medicine at the Court.[3] Badmaev, who served in the Asiatic Department of the Russian Ministry of Foreign Affairs from 1875-1893, advocated active Russian expension into Mongolia and Tibet, in his memorial submitted to Alexander III in 1893.[4] Well known Buryat Lama Agvan Dordji (Dordjiev) had gained substantial influence with the Dalai Lama in early 20th century. When he was received by Nicholas II in Otober 1900 and in July 1901, Dordji proposed to the Tsar that "Russia should proclaim herself the champion of Asia and the defender of Buddhism."[5] In early 20th Century, some leading Buryat intellectuals like Bazar Baraadin, Elbegdorj Rinchino and Zhamtsarano promoted the idea of pan-Mongolism. Baraadin even developed the script for the Mongolian language using Roman letters. Baraadin script was used in Buryatia, Outer Monglia and Inner Mongolia for about thirty years, alongside the old Mongolian script.

In 1741, the Empress Elizabeth Petrovna issued an imperial decree "recognising Buddhism in Buryatia and 11 *datsans* which existed at that time were confirmed with 150 lamas in them".[6] In 1764, Russian government appointed the Buryat lama Dambadarja Zayayev as the Chief Bandida Hambo Lama of all Buddhists living to the south of Lake Baikal. He became the supreme official head of the Buddhist order in Buryatia as the first Bandida Hambo Lama (1766-77).[7] And this tradition has continued till modern times. In 1811 the foremost Aginsky monastery with separate departments of philosophy, tantras and medicine, was set up. Its degrees were recognised. In 1853 Russia issued a decree on "the Status of the Lamaist Clergy in

Eastern Siberia" which regulated the administrative and economic status of datsans and lamas until the 1917 Revolution.[8] By 1917, there were 47 Buddhist monasteries (*datsans*) in Buryatia, each being a spiritual and cultural centre.

The October Revolution of 1917 led to further integration of Zabaikalye with Soviet Russia. The Buryat-Mongol Autonomous Soviet Socialist Republic was established in the year 1923. All Soviet and administrative personnel in Buryat Republic were initially recruited from lamas, ex-lamas and students of lamaist monestries. These lamaist modernists projected Buddhism as atheistic and Buddha as a predecessor of Lenin. The leading Buryat historian Zhamtsarano stressed that "Gautam Buddha had given the world an accomplished system of Communism".[9] But despite the efforts of Buryat lama ideologues and Communists to adapt to the Soviet system, Lamaism was crushed in Stalin's period. Prominent Buryats like Rinchino, Baraadin, Zhamtsarano, Agvan Dordji and others were liquidated during Stalin's purges.[10] In the year 1936 the official name of Buryatia became Buryat Autonomous Soviet Socialist Republic, after dropping the term 'Mongol'. It was in 1937 that the Republic was split into three parts separating Buryat autonomous areas of Ust-Orda and Aginsky from Buryatia and merging them in the Irkutsk (Ust-Orda Buryat Autonomous Okrug) and Chita (Aginsky Buryat Autonomous Okrug) regions respectively, thereby diluting the consolidation of Buryats into one political-administrative unit. Mongolian script was also changed to Russian Cyrillic script. Many Buryat monasteries were closed and destroyed during this period of Stalin's repression. It was an anathema to speak about Buryat traditional heroes such as Geser and Chinggis Khan. At the same time a local dialect *Khori Buryat* was promoted as the literary language. All these steps were taken by the Soviet authorities to curb the idea of pan-Mongolism affecting the Mongol territories of the former USSR in Buryatia and adjoining areas in Iskutsk and Chita oblasts. Following the death of Stalin and the growing cold war between USSR and China, things began to change but slowly. A new generation of Buryat intellectuals who had grown up in the 1950s, now started writing in Russian and Mongolian languages about Mongolia and Mongols. Several Buryat poets such as Dondok, Dashi Dambaev, Lopsan Taphkaev and Bayar Dugarov played key role in the reawakening of Buryat Mongol consciousness. One Buddhist monastery became the centre of Buddhist preaching and practice and several Buryat Lamas even represented the USSR at international peace conferences.

Gorbachev's policy of *glasnost* and *perestroika* facilitated the revival of Buryat culture and traditions. In 1989 Bayar Dugarov led a successful campaign for the celebration of the ancient Buryat holiday Sagaalgan (New Year). First such festival was celebrated on 14 February 1991, when national food was served, national Buryat songs were sung and the round dance *yokhor* was performed.[11] In 1990 Dugarov and other Buryat cultural personalities initiated the five year celebrations of *Geser*, thus reviving the local heritage. The process of promoting Mongolian culture and traditions in Buryatia received further fillip after the fall of the Communist government in Mongolia in 1990. And with the weakening of Soviet authority, the state sovereignty of Buryat Soviet Socialist Republic was proclaimed on 8 October 1990. On 27 March 1991, the Republic was named as the Republic of Buryatia of the Russian Federation. Now Buryatia established closer ties with Mongolia which opened its consulate in Ulan-Ude in 1992. All-Buryat Cultural Association was formed with the objective of promoting Mongolian language, culture and contacts between Buryat Mongol areas. Buryatia also witnessed the revival of Shamanism and Buddhism. Teaching of Mongolian in schools and writing of poetry, literature and history of Buryatia both in Mongolian and Russian languages was started. A new Constitution was adopted in Buryatia in 1994 and the first elections elected Leonid Potapov, a Russian former communist as the President of Buryatia.

Despite having a long chequered history, Buryats have always demonstrated benevolence and respect to their neighbours, who arrived in the Baikal region at different periods of time. Notwithstanding their Russian education and training, Buryat intellectuals played key role in retaining the Buryat traditions and culture while modernising themselves. In this process of syncretisation, as a result of application of Russian science, technology, language, literature and culture in the traditional nomadic society of Buryatia, the indigenous Buryats retained their local tradition and ethos adjusting themselves to the new wave of dominant Russian and later Soviet cultural and political influence. Even though the use of Russian language became widespread amongst the Buryats, they retained the indigenous Mongolian characteristics, nomadic lifestyle, Buddhist and Shamanist religion and traditions, Tibetan language, Buryat history and folklore. Today, cultural, religious and social traditions of different peoples in Buryatia are closely interwoven forming a unique pattern of peaceful coexistence. Buryats have maintained their Shamanist and mythical traditions and practices. The heroic epic *Geser*, whose 100th anniversary was celebrated in 1995, glorifies the idea of equality and collectivism of the people. Buddhism and Buddhist tradition which was brought to Buryatia from India, Tibet and Mongolia, forms the main base of its culture. The Buddhist philosophy, Tibetan system of medicine, astrology, language and printing of literature have not only survived but even developed in Buryatia. The Russian element in Buryatia's culture is represented by Russian literature, opera and ballet, drama, cinema, musical performances, circus, cultural centres and clubs.

Harsh climatic conditions, nomadic lifestyle, dependence on natural resources – forests, mountains, lakes etc., sparsely populated settlements situated at a distance from each other and other environmental factors played their role in the development of various rituals, traditions and culture of the Buryats. Thus we see the Buryats revering the elements of nature – earth, sun, moon, fire and water. Similarly collectivism, mutual help and hospitality are accorded importance in their day to day life. For instance, it is "considered sinful to defile fire and water. Also one must not break trees, instead one should give them gifts by hanging coloured pieces of cloth on its branches." The practice of tying coloured pieces of cloth on the branches of trees is quite prevalent in Buryatia as in most parts of India. On both sides of the highway from Ulan-Ude to Lake Baikal, the birch and pine trees are in abundance. Golden yellow leaves of birch trees provide a beautiful sight in autumn. On the way to Lake Baikal, we stopped at a place and bowed before the birch trees offering tea, bread, coins etc. Further moving towards Lake Baikal, we reached a point where we paid obeisance to *Usan Lopsan* – the god of Baikal, offering coins to its wooden statue. We made three rounds from the left clockwise around the statue like the one we have in Hindu tradition. Buryats attach great importance to colours, certain numerals etc. White (*saagan*) is considered to be the colour of sanctity and well-being. Black symbolises danger, grief or death. Red is revered as it is related to fire, light and warmth and it is believed to bring power, joy and well-being. So we find *Ulaan* (red) in the words Ulaan-Baatar, Ulaan-Ude, Ulaan-Hongor etc. Yellow is associated with the Sun and gold and is given prominence in the palette of colours in Buddhism. Blue denotes the eternal sky and water. Green symbolises the earth, vegetation and growth.

Today there are eighteen Buddhist *datsans* (monasteries), twelve Buddhist communities, seventeen Orthodox temples and parish churches, seven ancient Russian Orthodox communities, and over twenty religious denominations and movements of various kinds in Buryatia. A temple complex called Jarun Khashor, which unites different Buddhist sects was opened in Kizhinga. The past several years have witnessed the revival of old traditions in Buryatia. Old *datsans* are being restored and new temples and Christian churches are being constructed. Today cultural traditions of the people in Zabaikalye are preserved in all its aspects, be it national cuisine or theatre. In July 1991, a jubilee was celebrated in Buryatia to mark 250 years of the official recognition of Buddhism in Russia and 14th Dalai Lama was invited to Buryatia on this occasion, which turned the event extraordinary and historic. People in Buryatia and Chita Oblast braved heavy rains and stood waiting to see the Dalai Lama. Buddhists of Mongolia and the Russian Federation, particularly the Republics of Buryatia, Kalmykia and Tuva, look towards the Dalai Lama as their spiritual leader. In early November 2007, about 4000 Buddhist from Mongolia and the Russian Federation visited India and organised a week-long cultural festival in Dharmshala, the seat of the Dalai Lama and

Tibetan Government-in-Exile. They held an exhibition showcasing Buddhist culture and traditions in the Russian Republics, besides having concerts and performances by visiting cultural group. This was a major organised effort by the Buddhists of Buryatia, Kalmykia and Tuva to revive their ancient historical and spiritual ties with homeland of Buddha.

In 1990-91 several monasteries were renovated and new ones constructed at Tsugol, Gusinoozersk, Kyrensk, Atzgat, Egituevsk, Murochinsk, Gegetui, Anninsk, Sanaginsk and Ust-Ordynsk.[12] A School for higher Buddhist studies was opened in 1991 at Ivolginsk *Datsan*, with a few students having enrolled there. The year 1991 also witnessed the establishment of several social, cultural and political organisations such as All-Buryat Association for Cultural Development, Lay Buddhist Association, Buryat-Mongolian People's Party etc. All these organisations aimed at the consolidation of Buryats into one territorial unit, revival of the national Buryat culture and promotion of close cultural cooperation between Buryats and Mongols. Now steps for teaching Buryat/Mongolian language, publication of books, celebration of national festivals and organization of lectures on Buryat history and culture were initiated.

Inhabitants of the Republic have strong ties with Buryat ethnic groups in other cities and countries. Buryat Culture Societies are registered in Moscow, St. Petersburg, Kiev and Irkutsk. Over 300 public organizations and associations are registered in Buryatia. Today, the Republic is the centre of Buddhism in Russia, Ivolginsky *datsan* (monastery), being located in Buryatia. The Republic has been rightfully considered as one of the popular cultural centres of East Siberia. The glorious traditions and cultural activities of the Republic are preserved and promoted through the existence and functioning of theatres, writers, ballets and dances.

The combination of the influences of Buddhism, Shamanism of indigenous peoples, and *Staroobryadchestvo* (Old Russian Orthodox Christianity) has enriched the spiritual sphere of the society in Buryatia. The most ancient traditional religion of Buryats and Evenks has been Shamanism since ancient times.

Both the Indo-Buddhist, Mongolian and Russian-European cultures and Shamanism, Buddhism and Christianity have played their role in the formation and development of Buryat culture through history. Due to its unique geographical location (being situated on the borders of Russia, Mongolia and China) and historico-cultural development, Buryatia and Buryats present a unique synthesis of both culture of the East through Buddhism and Mongolian language and culture and that of the West through the medium of Russian language and culture. However, during the past two decades, there has been resurgence of indigenous traditions and practices among the Buryats. The three main value system of the Buryats – Buddhism, Shamanism and epic-heroism (*Geser*) have become important for the preservation and promotion of Buryat ethno-cultural identity. Reopening of Buddhist monasteries, forging of close contacts with Mongolia and the Dalai Lama, renewal of shamanist practices and claims, and the promotion of heroic figure of *Geser* signify the assertion of their distinct and indigenous identity by the Buryats.

REFERENCES

1. Cited in N.L. Zhukovskaya, "Buddhism and Problems of National and Cultural Resurrection of the Buryat Nation." *Central Asian Survey,* Vol. II(2), 1992. p. 27.
2. For further details see, Robert A. Rupen, *Mongols of the Twentieth Century, Part I*, Bloomington: Indiana University, 1964, pp. 42-46
3. Emanuel Sarkisyanz, "Communism and Larmaist Utopianism in Central Asia". *The Review of Politics* Vol. 20 (4), October 1958. p. 627
4. Ibid.
5. Ibid p. 628.
6. Ibid p. 29.
7. Lokesh Chandra, "Life of Damba Darja Jaya Yin". *In Cultural Horizons of India*. Vol. 7, New Delhi, 1998. pp. 265-66.
8. Zhukoskya (1992).
9. Ibid p. 632.
10. Ibid.
11. Zhukovskaya (1992), p. 31.
12. Lokesh Chandra (1998).

Prof. K. Warikoo standing in front of Swayambo placed above two dragons (symbol of Ulan-Ude city) at Arbat Street, Ulan-Ude.

Prof. Warikoo (third from the left) standing in front of Usan Lopson (the God of Baikal Lake)

Notice Board describing Usan Lopson near the Baikal Lake

Prof. Warikoo standing third from left making offerings at Baikal Lake

Statue of Gesar seated on horse, Ulan-Ude

Offerings made at birch trees

CHAPTER 25

BUDDHIST CHURCH IN SOCIO-CULTURAL SPACE OF RUSSIA

V.M. Mitypov

Perestroika and the subsequent events of 1990s brought cardinal changes in the situation of all religious confessions and in relations between state and church. The Republic of Buryatia, as well as the Russian Federation, in that period suffered from deep crisis which had affected all spheres of public life, including state-political and spiritual. Absence of general concept of future development of the country and strategy of its reform, and also refusal to abandon former system of values led to the formation of certain vacuum in people's minds. In these circumstances, religion began to play more important role in social life.

The period beginning with late 1980s up to 1990s witnessed, in essence, the renaissance of religious life in the former USSR including Russia. Revival of Buddhism can be seen since 1988, when a few Buddhist communities were registered. The process of Buddhist revival was marked by splash of interest and growth of religiousness among population, restoration of old and building new Buddhist temples in Buryatia, Aginsky and Ust-Ordynsky Buryat national areas, Kalmykia and Tuva.

In 1990, a new state law "About Liberty of Conscience and Religious Organizations"[1] was adopted. It became a quite strong legal base for the democratization of state-church relations and providing guarantees for the liberty of conscience. The democratic principle of equality concerning all confessions is enshrined in this law. The church and religious organizations received an opportunity to propagate religion and participate in the political life of the country. The restrictive acts concerning church and clergy were annulled. With the disintegration of the former USSR all-union governmental structures, including the Council on Religious Affairs under the Council of Ministers of the USSR, were abolished. New Interreligious Council of Russia with representatives of all traditional confessions of the Russian Federation has now been organized. The head of the Buddhist church, Pandido Khambo Lama joined the Council. This analytical consultative and coordinating centre was created for rendering assistance to the state and church structures to facilitate optimum interaction between them.

At that time, political activity of the Buddhist clergy increased: its representatives took direct part in the public policy and activity of state bodies. In 1989, lama E. Tsybikzhapov became a Deputy of the Supreme Soviet of RSFSR, lama D. Marhaev became a member of the Constitutional Assembly of the Russian Federation, in 1994 lamas F. Samaev and M. Choibonov became Deputies of the Peoples Khural of the Republic of Buryatia.

According to the Buryat historian A. Elaev, "political activity of Buddhist priests did not evoke condemnation, but at the same time it was viewed by public rather differently. But during the period of revival of Buddhism in Buryatia, which became a part of culture, national psychology, a way of life of the Buryat people, such non-standard forms of activity of some lamas were regarded by public as manifestation of activity of the Buddhist church and growth of its popularity which, finally, propagate the moral-religious values of people."[2]

Process of Buddhist revival had contradictory character. It is possible to agree with well-known scientist K. Gerasimova, who wrote that "conditions have cardinally changed – enlightened century with official bourgeois orientation has come, but it's not clear, which Buddhism will revive – Indian or Tibetan, or any mix of them. Quality of clergy's education has changed, and believers are not the same, they have lost knowledge of ethnic customs and traditions and do not know any more the purity of classic religious canons of Buddhism or lamaist sense."[3]

In 1990s, during the celebration of *Sagaalgan* in some

Buddhist communities *mantras* were translated into the Buryat language and were distributed among believers. However, today the majority of lamas are drawn from *datsans* not by the content of divine, but by some ritual moments. They come to take home the sanctified water-*arshan*, aromas-*sanzai*, to order church service for good health, successful reincarnation, good study, military service, etc. Earlier, people would come to Ivolginsky *datsan* for worshiping to imperishable body of Khambo Lama Itygelov. Believers pay more attention to ceremonial part – to receive blessing (*adis*), to make *goroo*, to twist *hurde* – a sacred drum, etc. Thus many of them start to perceive faith as ritual. Position of some lamas connected with such religious "materialism" and sometimes they can be too sharp to parishioners, turning the visit to *datsan* into the system of certain prohibitions.

One of the basic characteristics of church community in 1990s was prevalence of neophytes – people who started to believe only for the last few years. As a sample of behavior which was inherent in the generation of their mothers and grandmothers they choose imitation of that life style. One may state that not only behavior of common believers, but also, as a whole, imitation has become one of the main features of religious consciousness today.

According to the sociological investigations, religion takes only the fifth position in consciousness of people equally with others: 32.4 per cent of respondents consider themselves to be followers of Buddhism, 5.3 per cent are followers of Shamanism, 38.8 per cent just believe in God. Certain religious attitudes are shown among respondents, some of them who have Christian ancestors now aspire to be Buddhist, some stress their aspiration to comprehend philosophical depths of Buddhism, which in their opinion, can help to come to real sincere faith.[4]

In the early 1990s, changes in the social order in the country and refusal to follow the former value system objectively promoted the spontaneous growth of people's interest in religion. Certainly, this opened wide opportunities to churches for strengthening their influence on masses. However, the churches being not ready for such events, these could not use this situation to improve their position in society. Liberalization of inter-confessional relations, opening discussion on the problems of real situation in the Central Religious Board of the Buddhists (CRBB) aggravated the internal problems of the Buddhist church.

Till 1990s, the CRBB kept a traditional hierarchical principle of management and mutual relations. But in 1992, after the death of Pandido Khambo Lama M. Tsybikov, during the short period (since 1992 till 1995) three heads of the CRBB – representatives of young generation – were replaced. The CRBB as a structure has not adapted to innovations, and after introduction of the democratic standards and procedures it began to lose control with separate independent structures quickly beginning to follow numerous schools and currents, existing in Buddhism, in order to strengthen their autonomy.[5] The clergy believed that one of the reasons for these problems was absence of organizational unity and stability in the Buddhist confession. Without real autonomy from the state, the Buddhist church appeared to be dependent and came under the strong influence of state's political institutions. The demise of totalitarian system and long-term pressure upon the church led to the crisis in religious sphere.

In April 1995, new council of the CRBB and its chairman Damba Ayusheev, current Pandido Khambo Lama, were elected. According to the decision of *Sugundy* held on March 22, 1996 the Central Religious Board of the Buddhists was renamed as the Buddhist Traditional Sangha of Russia. 20 *datsans* and Buddhist communities joined to this structure. Transition to positions of renovation of Buddhism was one of the important decisions which should be understood not only as radical recombination of the church organization but also as new approach to the changing world, as an attempt to meet the challenges of time.

According to a Decree of the President of Buryatia, "The Concept of State–Church Relations in the Republic of Buryatia" in 1996 was confirmed. It "was supposed to reflect condition, maintenance and character of relations between state and church, to define prospects of development of state-church relations in republic, to give reference points to state and local authorities, public associations in their practical activities."[6] It was almost revolutionary step of the state which had to reckon with the growing authority of confessions. The Concept stated that "the Buddhist church in the republic is presented in the form of widely branched out hierarchical system with the staff of clergy, educational institutions and management – the CRBB of the Russian Federation. Presence of the CRBB in the republic is of great importance not only for Buryatia and Russia, where the number of followers of Buddhism is about one million, but also for external relations of the country in Asia-Pacific region. The Concept, while acknowledging the role of state in the religious matters of society and solution of the problems,[7] coordination of activity of the state structures put forth its priorities as in the sphere of state-church relations and the creation of special body at the republican level and also in the countryside.

In December 1997 the new "Law on Religious Activity on the Territory of the Buryat Republic" No. 610-1 was adopted.[8] According to this law on religious confessions, including the Buddhists, had the right to treat people using traditional medicine, to conduct economic activities, to carry out religious practices and ceremonies. Besides, social insurance of priests and citizens working in the religious organizations, was guaranteed.

As a follow-up to "Concept of State–Church Relations", an Expert-Consultative Council on the Religious Affairs under the Government of the Buryat Republic, has been created for normalising of religious situation and resolving the problems of interaction between state and religious associations.

However, in spite of improvements in legal framework and its implementation, the situation in the Buddhist church remained strained. In spring 1998 it was aggravated by the events connected with exhibiting *The Atlas of the Tibetan Medicine* in USA and counteraction of the Buddhist Sangha leaders, who declared their rights to this rare artifact.

A. Elaev noticed that the time of "sending the *Atlas* coincided with presidential and parliamentary elections of 1998 and has been used for political aims, which negatively reflected on the authority of the Buddhist church leaders."[9] According to the famous researcher B. Bazarov, "this conflict, having political overtone, pursued the obvious aim to compromise the state power during election campaign. The 1980s-1990s is the period of cultural and religious renaissance. The state support to the process of the church revival as well as carrying on dialogue with *datsans* actually recognized that persecution of Buddhism in the recent past was not justified. With the fast increase in the number of priests at a time when old monks, the bright and unordinary people, have gone, mass rejuvenation of clergy led to inevitable consequences. Nowadays the Buddhist confession is faced with the problem of personnel, plunging it in to deep crisis. Internal dissociation of Buddhist communities has the potential of transforming the spiritual estate in to some caste "in itself and for itself". They are more concerned with material things – maintenance and building – than the questions of faith. Khambo Lama D. Ayusheev obviously knew that the CRBB is "not the proprietor of the *Atlas*, that he is fighting not for a cult subject, not for sacred object, and, nevertheless, he led priests to attack."[10]

An attempt to prevent the *Atlas's* removal ended with beating of the Buddhist monks by special military detachment and the beginning of a big scandal directly connected with forthcoming election campaign. The "Atlas conflict" was used by all concerned persons for their interests. With the society being not ready to accept divergent views, tolerance for heterodoxy and peaceful resolution of problems on the basis of compromise and mutual respect, only led to monopolistic and regimented view of the problem by different sides, with negative consequences. The agreement on export of the Buddhist artefacts would be coordinated with the Buddhist Traditional Sangha of Russia, but it was concluded with the Ministry of Culture of the Russian Federation.

On April 27, 1998, next *sugundy* took place, with 127 delegates from Buryatia, Tuva, Altai and Kalmykia participating in its work. A new Charter of the Buddhist Traditional Sangha of Russia was accepted by the majority of votes. According to this Charter, the Buddhist Traditional Sangha of Russia is successor of the CRBB uniting the Buddhist organizations of the Russian Federation professing the traditional Mahayana Buddhism in

Russia. The Sangha of Russia carries out the activity according to the Constitution of the Russian Federation, the current legislation and this Charter. The purpose and aims of the CRBB are: "confession, distribution, studying, careful preservation and propagation of spiritual heritage and precepts of the Buddha, culture and traditions of the Buddhist doctrine, its philosophical, moral and ethical bases, educating people in the spirit of compassion and love to all living beings". Essential changes have been brought to the structure and activity of the *Sangha*. According to the Charter, "decisions are accepted jointly at the congress of representatives of the Buddhist clergy and believers with preliminary discussion of questions on local *khurals*, regular sessions of priests and heads of religious organizations. The Charter reflects new forms of the Buddhist church activity: release of the Buddhist literature, TV and radio programs, periodical publications, organization of pilgrimages, establishment of institutions of the Buddhist religious education, charitable funds, publishing, polygraphic and other economic societies.

The Buddhist Traditional Sangha of Russia was registered on June 9, 1999 by the Ministry of Justice of the Russian Federation. Other than ethnic Buryatia's *datsans*, the association *Ak-Burhan* (the Republic of Altai), St. Petersburg *datsan Gunzenchoinei*, the *Centre of Tszonhava* (Moscow), *Maitreya* (Novosibirsk), *Green Tara* (Ulan-Ude), *Vadzhra* (Irkutsk), *Zambala* (Abakan), *Namsal* (the Republic of Sakha) being part of the structure of the CRBB. The republican newspaper mentioned: "Such a decision put an end to the ambiguous situation in connection with the re-registration of the largest Buddhist association of Russia."[11]

The current federal law "About Liberty of Conscience and Religious Organizations" (26.09.1997), in essence, proclaimed the policy allowing administrative-legal relations, and formation of religious associations. Unlike the previous laws the activity of so called "atheistic public organizations" was not regulated. Along with the basic federal law "About Public Organizations" (19.05.1995), the new legislation defined the status of the optional and imperative modes of registration depending on intentions of the persons who have created a religious group, thereby giving the right to choose the form of further existence.

As stated earlier, the Council on the Religious Affairs under the Council of Ministers of the USSR was dissolved in 1991, and all contacts (first of all, registration) with existing and new religious organizations and in regions were transferred to the departments of justice. Those clergymen who in the past demanded to abolish the Council on the Religious Affairs restricting free activity of religious confessions, now began to speak about their incorrect statements. This came out during my personal conversations with the Buddhist priests. It's quite clear that instead of one body, responsible for all questions of coordination between state and church, now appeared several bodies: the Justice Department registering religious organizations; Committee of the National Policy, Communications with Public and Religious associations of the Administration of the President and the Government of the Republic of Buryatia; similar committee of the National *Khural*; the Advisory Council making recommendations to different organizations (religious or not), and, at last, Inspection on Protection of Monuments of History and Culture. This situation creates problems in making decisions on the problems of religious associations.

Concerning the questions about inter-confessional relations, in the Concept of state-church relations in the Republic of Buryatia underlined: "Now relations between followers of two basic faiths: Orthodox Russian church and Buddhism, in general are good. Inter-religious tolerance, typical of Buryatia, has a basis, as each of these religions has been spread in a certain national-ethnic surroundings: "Orthodoxy among the Russians, Buddhism among the Buryats. The followers consider their religion as their national-cultural heritage. They do not try to make other people as a subject of their religious mission as they are not afraid of religious expansion from their side."[12]

According to a well-known researcher T. Skrynnikova, "character of the Buddhist institutions on the territory of Buryatia (the Buddhist church, public organizations) implicitly contains an idea of forming a community, not on ethnic, but on a civil basis. The Buryats are not only members of the public

Buddhist organizations, members of the *Sangha*, teachers of the Buddhist institute *Dashi Choinkhorlin* formed in 1991, as well as the authors of the journal *Legshed.*[13]

In general, the current situation has shown the actual need for inter-church renovation, particularly with regard to the training of young lamas studying at the Buddhist institute *Dashi Choinkhorlin*, Aginsky Buddhist Academy, Buddhist monasteries of India and Mongolia. Speaking about the students, Khambo Lama D. Ayusheev underlined that: "They are the future of the Buryat Buddhism. We, present lamas, carry out an intermediate link role, and everything should be recreated by them in future". In the past few years, the Buddhist church was replenished with the lamas who have got education in Buddhist monasteries of India – Goman, Namgyal, etc.

The general strategy of developing the *Sangha* of Russia is based on the federal policy of decreasing the influence of Tibetan clergy, providing conditions for training of students in India. The Buddhist church has been legally separated from the state. Whereas it can not intervene in the internal affairs, there are wide opportunities for preaching and social activity in the world. There is no discrimination against priests and believers, and confiscated religious buildings and their artifacts have been returned. Besides, there are opportunities for constructing new temples.

Rapprochement between the church and state has taken place in many spheres, including the issues of citizen's education and moral revival. After the disintegration of the former USSR, problems of building a lawful state, democratization of society, maintenance of human rights, and humanization of interpersonal relations have been the focus of public attention. Cultural workers, scientists, publicists, priests and lawyers express different points of view, sometimes quite opposite, about the development of mutual relations of the church, religious organizations and the state, about the place of liberty of conscience in the system of human values, democratic rights and freedom. Though the church and religious organizations are separated from the state, these as well as the believers can not be kept separate from the social life. Each person inspite of his attitude to religion and atheism has the right to follow his belief. Religion, free-thinking and atheism are integral parts of world culture.

REFERENCES

1. *Registers of the Congress of the USSR People's Deputies and the Supreme Soviet of the USSR*, no.16, 1990.
2. A. Elaev, *The Buryat People: Formation, Development, Self-identification*, M., 2000, p. 293.
3. K. Gerasimova, "About Buryat 'bourgeois intelligentsia' of the beginning of XX century", *National Intelligentsia, Clergy and Problems of Social, National Revival of the Republic of Buryatia*, Ulan-Ude, 1995, p.26.
4. A. Biltrikova, "National Intelligentsia in the Processes of Consolidation of the Buryat People", *Modern Status of the Buryat People and Prospects for its Development*, Ulan-Ude, 1996, pp. 74-75.
5. Elaev, (2000), p. 294.
6. "The Concept of State--Church Relations in the Republic of Buryatia", *The Baikal Region: Legal Aspect of Ethno-Political Situation (1992-2001)*, M.-Irkutsk: Natalis, 2002, p. 123.
7. *Ibid*, p.124.
8. *Ibid*, pp. 131-135.
9. Elaev (2000), p. 295.
10. *Pravda Buryatii*, 12 June 1998.
11. *Pravda Buryatii*, 22 June 1999.
12. "The Concept of State–Church Relations in the Republic of Buryatia" (2002), p. 125.
13. T. Skrynnikova, "Traditional Culture and Buddhism in Self-Identification of the Buryats", *Religion and Identity in Russia*, M.: Vostochnaya literatura, 2003, p. 152].

CHAPTER 26

TUVA-RUSSIA RELATIONS IN HISTORICAL PERSPECTIVE

Sharad K. Soni

Formerly known as Tannu Tuva, the Republic of Tuva (Tyva) is located in the central part of the Asian continent surrounded by Eastern Siberia on the north, Mongolia on the south and east, Irkutsk Region on the northeast, the Buryat Republic on the east, and the Altai Republic on the west. It covers a geographical area of 170,500 sq. kilometers, which is separated from Mongolia by the Tannu Ola range and from Russia by the Sayan range of mountains. Sometimes also referred to as Uryankhai (distant forest people), Tuva is now the smallest and most remote republic of the Russian Federation, having a population of just a little more than 300,000 with 90,000 people alone are staying in the capital Kyzyl earlier known as Belotsarsk. However, its importance lies in to its strategic location rather than population which is evident from the fact that at least from the eighteenth century onwards Tuva emerged as a geo-political entity due to its being in the zone of Sino-Russian rivalry. Besides, the "Great Silk Road" passed over the land of Tuva that also contributed much to attract Russian interest in this area, thus finally leading the former to come under Moscow's domain in 1944.[1]

What impression one could get from Tuva's incorporation into erstwhile USSR is that it reflects the whole history of Sino-Russian/Soviet rivalry for dominating the Mongolian borderlands. And this rivalry always prevented attempts of unification of Tuva with Mongolia on the basis of their ethnic and cultural links, and Russia succeeded in outweighing Chinese claims over Tuva.[2] The Chinese claim was inspired by the assumption that so long as Mongolia remained under formal Chinese rule during Qing dynasty, Tuva being a part of one of the provinces of Mongolia. But in reality nothing could deter Tuva, not even the Buddhist religious factor from its becoming a part of Russia.

HISTORICAL BACKGROUND

Recorded history suggests that the Tuvans of Turkic Uryankhai-Tuva – developed from ancient indigenous tribes and some groups such as Tugiu-Turks, Uyghurs and Kyrghyzs besides absorbing some Mongolian tribes who came to be Turkicised.[3] This Turkic influence on native Tuvans in addition to the geographical and religious considerations, became the basis of claims made by Russian scholars that the Tuvans are different from Mongols in their origin, culture and language, i.e., they are Siberian and Turkic-oriented, hence somehow closer to Russia than to Mongolia.[4] Western scholars, Rupen also agrees with this point of view, when he says, "There clearly exists some genuine basis for distinguishing Tuvans and Mongols."[5] But at the same time he argues that "the former [Tuvans] do display far greater Turkic influence, yet it is also true that Western Mongols, the Oirats, differ from the predominant Khalkha Mongols in many of the same characteristics that differentiate Tuvans from Khalkhas." According to him, "some Tuvans are 'very Mongols,' while other are 'very Turkic,' so they could be described as constituting an ethnic and cultural bridge between Central Asian Turkic and Central Asian Mongol group."

The Tuvan territory remained under Mongol control from thirteenth to the first quarter of eighteenth centuries. It was an industrial and raw material base for the Mongol army under Chinggis Khan and his successors, which carried out campaigns to the west. Though Chinese sovereignty over Tuva was recognized by Russia in 1728 Kiakhta Treaty,[6] the area had formally come under the Manchu-Chinese Qing rule in 1757 and a year later it was administratively attached to Outer Mongolia (now known as simply Mongolia) under Sain Noyan Khan *aimak* (province).[7] Since then, throughout the eighteenth, nineteenth and early twentieth centuries, the area remained a Qing dependency not only politically but to some extent economically as well.[8] It was only in 1911 when a liberation movement provided Mongolia an opportunity to declare its independence from the Qing rule, Tuva too found itself outside the Manchu sphere. However, it may be noted here that although Tuva was under Qing control for almost 150 years, the latter "never exercised close control there."[9] Instead, it were the Russian settlers who entered the territory during the middle of the nineteenth century, most of them for trade purposes, who ultimately played significant role in deciding Tuva's future. The issue of their protection from Chinese traders often invited concerns of the Russian Government, which took a political form.

Increasing Russian settlement in Tuva region particularly since 1910 owes much to the foresightedness of Tsar Nicholas II who, in 1908, had acknowledged Tuva as an area, which "may become very useful for Russia in the future."[10] Tuva's geo-political importance, thus, was one of the key reasons for encouraging Russian settlement in the area and as time went on, more and more Russians including merchants and farmers crossed the border. Consequently, the number of Russian settlers increased considerably so much so that the figure rose from 2,100 in 1910 to 8,200 in 1916, which further grew constantly to reach the figure of almost 12,000 in 1944.[11] Moreover, nonexistence of any permanent Chinese settlement in Tuva also smoothen the progress of Russian settlement as Rupen notes down that "the Manchu administrative system operated indirectly through Tuvan and Mongol agents, whereas Russian control was more direct and straightforward."[12] This apparently helped prevent Chinese ambitions in that area.

Since Tuva was known to be rich in natural resources especially minerals, the activities of mineral explorers also gave way to the Russian penetration in this area. The motivation for Russian penetration was that Tuva was "an extremely valuable colonisable territory with fertile soil, good pastures and rich mineral deposits, above all gold."[13] Many Russian merchants, who came to Tuva in search for gold, returned with such considerable amounts of gold that "Russian government agencies began to be interested in the natural resources of the region."[14] In fact, Russians were the first to do business in Tuva.[15] Since 1867 when the first Russian merchants came and established three trading stations in Tuva, there had been sharp increase in their business as well as their penetration. By 1890s, almost the whole Tuvan territory seemed to have been covered with Russian trading stations.[16] These commercial activities further continued in the Soviet period as well mainly due to the fact that Tuva's richness in natural resources had shaped the area largely as "economic necessity to the Russian centre."[17]

The beginning of twentieth century witnessed new developments on the political front due to the circumstances of the day. Encouraged by the permanent Russian settlement Tsarist Russia became interested in adding Tuva to its territory. The first attempt in this direction was made in November 1911 after the Mongols of Outer Mongolia proclaimed their autonomy following the success of their liberation movement against the Manchu-Qing rule.[18] But the Tsarist government decided to follow the policy of what Morgen Mongush describes as "peaceful penetration".[19] After the Autonomous government of Outer Mongolia was established in Urga, Jebtsun Damba Khutukhtu, the Urga living Buddha whose area of control bordered Tuva, tried to encourage Tuvans for joining the new state. Moreover, since the Mongols considered Tuva as legitimately falling within their own territory, they wanted the area to be incorporated in Autonomous Mongolia. At that point in time, most of the native Tuvans too, desired for the same, which is evidenced by the fact that in 1912, even a Tuvan *amby-noyon* (feudal lord) Gombodorji applied to the Urga government for inclusion of Tuva in latter's territory.[20] Despite the fact that his application was accepted without any delay and soon he was made Urga's official representative,[21] he, on the other hand, came under the influence of Russian forward policy in Tuva. The Russian policy with regard to Tuva can be understood by a statement of the Imperial Council of Ministers issued in 1913.

The statement stressed that the Russian recognition of the autonomy of Mongolia as per the Treaty of October 21, 1912 [old style] and the departure of Chinese officials not only from Mongolia but also from Uryanghai [Tuva], placed the issue of Russian government's relation with the latter in a new direction.[22] It further said:

> The proclamation of the Republic in China and Mongolian independence, and the departure of the Chinese officials who had been responsible for Uryanghai from Ulyasutai has as a consequence put an end to the departure of Uryanghai on China; also Khalkha [Outer Mongolia], now first entered into political life, can not claim this land. Therefore, His Majesty suggests to Minister Sazonov that Russian policy concerning Uryanghai should take the direction of fixing this land in Russian interests.[23]

And in fact, as recorded in the third edition of the *Great Soviet Encyclopedia*, "in 1912-13 many big landowners and officials repeatedly appealed to the Russian Tsar to incorporate Tuva in to the Russian empire."[24] Gombodorji, however, made a request to the Russian government in St. Petersberg through a letter dated October 26, 1913 for the establishment of a Russian protectorate, an idea which was originally advocated by Sazonov. After prolonged discussion, the idea was accepted by the Russian cabinet and on April 5,1914, a Russian protectorate over Tuva was announced. But Sazonov was calculated so much so that he declared that in exchange of getting Russian protection "the Uryanghais [Tuvans] must first of all give up the right of external relations and must pledge themselves to form connections with their neighbours only through the official stationed in the territory by the Governor-General of Irkutsk."[25] A few months later in July 1914, an instruction was communicated to Gombodorji by a Russian border Commissioner, Zererin saying, "Your duty is to maintain no relations of any kind with foreign states, including Mongolia...."[26] Gombodorji immediately agreed to abide by the instruction. Tuva, henceforth, remained under Russian protection until 1917 when the Russian Revolution overthrew Tsarism. However, during this period, neither Chinese nor Mongolians stayed away of the Tuvan affair. They repeatedly argued that Tuva was an integral part of Outer Mongolia but nothing substantial they could achieve due to the success of diplomatic maneuvering on the part of Tsarist Russia.

At that time Russian policy towards Outer Mongolia and Tuva differed in its nature. According to Dallin, "the old Russian governments strove to achieve 'independence' and 'autonomy' for Mongolia, whereas Tuva was to be subjected to direct control by Russia."[27] Nevertheless, the Revolution of 1917 in Russia changed the scene and the course of events in both Tuva and Mongolia from 1918 onwards was similar, as their territories became a battleground due to the civil war between Red and White Russians. It was only in 1921 when White Russian troops, who had overrun Mongolia and Tuva, suffered a heavy defeat at the hand of the Red Army that the Soviet period in Tuva's history began. The first step taken by the Soviet government was to abolish Russian protectorate "forever" and proclaim Tuva's independence.[28] In fact, it was at the first Congress of the Representatives of the Tuvan *Khosuns*, which took place from August 13 to 16, 1921, that the declaration of Tuva's independence and sovereignty as well as the first draft Constitution were adopted.[29] Subsequently, a Tuvan government was formed and on September 9, 1921, the RSFSR declared that "it did not consider Tuva to be Russian."[30] Tuva, thus, was recognized by Soviet Russia in the same year and just a little over one and half months after Mongolia became a People's Republic.

INCORPORATION OF TUVA INTO USSR

On October 29,1921, a Tuvan People's Revolutionary Party (TPRP) was formed following the establishment of the Tuvan People's Republic (TPR). The TPRP issued its first manifesto to the people of Tuva on December 20, 1921.[31] Significantly, the party soon became pro-Soviet in the same manner as was the case with the Mongolian People's Revolutionary Party (MPRP) that ruled Mongolia. Three successive Tuvan Constitutions were also drafted in 1922, 1924 and 1926. But it was the third Constitution which was adopted on the Soviet model and was finally confirmed by the Fourth Great *Khural* on November 24, 1926.[32]

Although Tuva proclaimed its independence, it maintained its aspiration to unite with Mongolia. There existed a tendency to participate in the Pan-Mongolist movement. Tuva constituted one of the territories to be included in the unified state. In fact, Pan-Mongolism represented the desire of indigenous Mongols to have a united state based on the model of the Empire of Chinggis Khan. This concept was so deep rooted that it called for reunification of all the Mongols wherever they were as well as all the Mongolian areas into a single "Greater Mongolian state." The idea of creating such a state that would essentially be a Pan-Mongolian in nature, primarily focussed on including territories comprising of not only Outer and Inner Mongolia as well as Buryat and Tuva regions of Siberia but also the territories of Tibetans, the Kyrgyzs and Kalmyks; thereby stretching the whole area from the Caspian Sea to Lake Baikal. However, Pan-Mongolism could not grow into a movement for a single unified state against the desire of the native Mongols whose region was now segregated in different areas by different powers.

The key factor behind this denial was the geopolitical importance of Mongolian areas, which attracted various powers mainly Russia, China and Japan for establishing their hegemony over there. In doing so these powers exploited the concept of Pan-Mongolism in various situations for their own benefit and the Mongols were left with nothing but a dead desire of having a Pan-Mongolian state. Tuvans were also discouraged and forced to remain separate from Mongolia despite their continuous urge for unity. In early 1920s, Donduk, the Tuvan Prime Minister explained: "The Tuvinian people is small, poor and backward in the cultural aspect. That is why it must be united with Mongolia."[33] Even in 1924, the Tuvan people went to the extreme by declaring their "affiliation" with Outer Mongolia.[34] But they received a setback when Soviet troops were sent to suppress the revolt successfully.

Nevertheless, the events that followed were of vital importance in the history of Tuva-Mongolia linkages. The issue of Tuva's union with Mongolia was again placed on the agenda at a Tuvan Great *Khural* session in 1924. But soon after in July 1924, three-sided talks among Mongolia, Russia and Tuva in

Kyzyl ended with "the *de facto* recognition of the country".[35] Yet, in August 1924, the matter of Mongolia-Tuva unity was placed at the Third Congress of the MPRP. During its deliberations it became clear that the Mongol side wanted to include Tuvan territory into the Mongolian People's Republic. Almost all the Mongols were unanimous on the question of Tuva despite objection made by Soviet representative A.N. Vasiliev at the Congress. He made it clear that the Russians would not allow Mongols to regain Tuva. In the end, the Congress adopted a resolution seeking for a mixed Russian-Mongolian Commission to settle the question of Tuva. Moscow agreed to send the mixed Commission and finally Mongolia's aspirations were met on only one point. A very small sector of the Tuvan territory called, Darkhat was given to Outer Mongolia.[36] This was how Mongols and Tuvans were prevented from uniting themselves. But Mongolian side did not stop to lay claim over Tuva. For instance, a Mongol leader, Amor is said to have told the MPR's First Great *Khural* held in November 1924 that "Uryankhai [Tuva] was part of Mongolia."[37] At the Fourth MPRP Congress held during September-October 1925, the Comintern representative, Amagaev was of the opinion that "... up to this time the so-called 'Uryankhai question' has not been resolved. Perhaps Mongolia will require the union of the Uryankhai people with it."[38]

However, nothing substantial could be achieved and in July 1926, Soviet diplomatic initiatives resulted into the signing of a treaty of friendship between the Tuva People's Republic and the Mongolian People's Republic. By this agreement Tuva was recognised as a fully equal and independent sovereign state, entirely separate from the Mongolian People's Republic. One month later, another treaty of friendship was signed between Tuva and the Soviet Union which was modelled on the Soviet-Mongolian agreement of November 5,1921.[39] The agreement among other things included "reciprocal recognition of independence and exchange of representatives." Thereafter Soviet influence over Tuva remained undisturbed and what followed next was the beginning of a period of "Sovietization" of Tuvan politics, economy and culture. The Sovietization drive in Tuva lasted from 1929 to 1933,[40] which not only kept Tuva separate from Mongolia but also isolated it from the outside political influences. Every Tuvan leader who tried to advocate Tuva-Mongolia unity was declared to be "pro-Chinese" and a "traitor". Peter Tang attributes Moscow's success in Tuva in the following way:[41] Firstly, China was used to keep foreign powers out of Outer Mongolia as a whole. Secondly, Outer Mongolian "independence" was used to oust China and lastly, Tuvan "independence" was used to prevent Pan-Mongolist moves for unity.

Significantly, Soviet policy in Tuva met with a positive response from the Tuvan leader Solchak Toka who became the General Secretary of the Central Committee of the TPRP in 1932. In fact, the government of Tuva headed by Toka sought to integrate Tuva into the Soviet Union thrice, first in 1939, second in 1941 and the last in 1943.[42] But due to Soviet engagement in the Second World War, their petitions received a delayed response. On August 17, 1944, a special session of the Little *Khural* of the TPR met and signed a petition addressed to the Moscow government requesting for the incorporation of Tuva into the USSR. The request was approved on October 11, 1944 by the Presidium of the Supreme Soviet of the USSR and two days later Tuva was officially declared to have become an autonomous *oblast* of the Russian Socialist Federated Soviet Republic (RSFSR).[43] This was announced on November 1,1944 at the Eighth Extraordinary session of the Little *Khural* in the Tuvan capital Kyzyl.[44] Later on by a decree issued on October 9, 1961 at the Presidium of the Supreme Soviet of RSFSR, Tuva's status of autonomous *oblast* had been transferred to autonomous republic known as Tuva ASSR.

POST-SOVIET TUVA AND RUSSIA

Since December 1991, Siberian regions have been assuming an increasingly prominent role in Russia's foreign, economic and security policy towards Eurasia. Geographically, politically and culturally Tuva has come a long way in getting recognition of being a significant peripheral area of Moscow. While its geographical importance remained intact due to strategic reasons, politically it has witnessed new developments at the domestic front. Earlier, Tuva's incorporation into former USSR strengthened Moscow's hand in the Siberian region, which touches the border with Mongolia thus keeping aside other powers particularly China from exerting any influence in the region. It was more so because Tuva had traditionally been regarded as part of Outer Mongolia and hence the Chinese made their claims. For Mongolia, both the downfall of Buryats as well as Tuva's incorporation into the USSR proved to be a major set back in its aspirations of a Pan-Mongolian state which never came into being. However, the Buddhist factor in Tuva-Mongolia relations in particular and Russia-Mongolia relations in general may prove to be politically advantageous. This factor can play a bigger role in ensuring the security of Siberia from any potential threat from the outside world. Besides, Buddhism provides an excellent opportunity for the Siberian people to remain connected with the people of other Buddhist nations in Asia.

After the collapse of the former Soviet Union, Tuva retained its autonomy in 1993 as a Republic within the Russian Federation. The same year witnessed the adoption of a new Tuvan constitution, the first post-*perestroika* constitution, which was written under Yeltsin's slogan "Take as much sovereignty as you can swallow!"[45] The 1993 constitution created a parliament that became responsible for foreign policy as well. The latest constitution, the ninth in its history since the first one came in to existence in 1921, was adopted at an All-Republican Referendum on May 6, 2001. This document has become the guiding principles for Tuva's domestic and external affairs. In August 2007, Tuva was much in news as it was chosen out of 88 Russian regions by the Russian President Vladimir Putin to host Monaco Prince Albert II for a 3-day holiday.[46] Tuva's geopolitical importance as well as its cultural heritage and natural beauty must have attracted Putin to spend holidays with his guest there. As regards, Tuva's linkages with Mongolia, the Tuvans are a Turkic speaking people with Mongol influences. They are mainly adherents of Tibetan Buddhism, along with native Shamanism. This factor has been playing an important role in strengthening the Tuva-Mongolia linkages. The other factor which contributes to the growth of people to people contacts between Tuva and Mongolia is Tuvan ethnic minority itself, which outside Tuva, is concentrated mainly in northwestern Mongolia.

Whatever may have been the state of Buddhism in Tuva during the Soviet period, it is now gaining ground to even play a significant role in Tuva-Russia relations to be exemplified as another dimension of the center-periphery relations. It is more so because in the post-Soviet period, Tuva has been trying to relink itself with the Buddhist world in Asia following the revival of Buddhism in Siberia, which can be termed as Russia's new cultural diplomacy to enhance its stakes in Asia. Besides, given the fact that Tuva continues to be economically dependent on Moscow, overall development of Tuva depends on what resources and concessions the Tuvan leadership can extract from Moscow. It now appears that Tuva's course, like that of other Siberian parts of the Russian Federation, would be influenced largely by developments in Moscow.

REFERENCES

1. For a detail account of Soviet take over of Tuva, see Sharad K. Soni, *Mongolia-Russia Relations: Kiakhta to Vladivostok*, Delhi: Shipra Publications, 2002, pp.73-80.
2. Robert A. Rupen, "The Absorption of Tuva," In *The Anatomy of Communist Takeovers*, edited by T.T. Hammond, New Haven: Yale University Press, 1975, p.145.
3. *Great Soviet Encyclopedia*, vol.26, 1977, p.523.
4. For more details, see Rupen (1975), pp.153-157.
5. *Ibid.*, p.154.
6. Peter S. H. Tang, "Sino-Soviet Territorial Disputes: Past and Present," *Russian Review* 28, no.4 (1969), p.406.
7. Robert A. Rupen, *Mongols of the Twentieth Century*, Bloomington: Indiana University Press, 1964, p.74.
8. *Ibid.*
9. Robert A. Rupen, "Mongolian Nationalism: Part I," *Journal of Royal Central Asian Society* .vol. 45, 1959, p.163.
10. *Ibid.*
11. Rupen (1975), p.150.

12. *Ibid.*, p.159.
13. Toomas Alatalu, "Tuva – A State Reawakens", *Soviet Studies*, vol. 44, no.5, 1992, p.882.
14. David J. Dallin, *The Rise of Russia in Asia*, London: The World Affairs Book Club, 1950, p.138.
15. *Ibid.*, p.137.
16. Peter S. H. Tang, *Russian and Soviet Policy in Manchuria and Outer Mongolia, 1911-1931*, Durham NC: Duke University Press, 1959, pp.403-404.
17. Albert L. Weeks, *The Other Side of Co-existence: An Analysis of Russian Foreign Policy*, New York: Pitman Publishing Co., 1970, p.43.
18. See Morgen Mongush, "The Annexation of Tannu Tuva and the Formation of Tuva ASSR," *Central Asian Survey*, vol.12, no.1, 1993, p.81.
19. *Ibid.*
20. Rupen (1964), p.75.
21. *Ibid.*
22. See Rupen (1975), pp.159-160.
23. Cited in *Ibid.*
24. *Bol'shaya Sovetskaya Entsiklopediya* (Great Soviet Encyclopedia), 3rd ed., vol.29, Moscow, 1977, p.284, cited in Alatalu, p.882.
25. Cited in Tang (1959), p.410.
26. *Ibid.*
27. Dallin (1950), pp.84-85.
28. *Ibid.*, p.85.
29. Cited in Mongush (1993), p.82. In fact, it was on August 14, 1921 that the Tannu Tuva People's Republic was proclaimed. Later on, in 1926 the word Tannu, meaning *taiga*, was dropped to remain just as Tuva People's Republic, see Alatalu (1992), p.883.
30. Cited in Rupen (1964), p.189.
31. Xenia J. Eudin and Robert C. North, *Soviet Russia and the Far East*, Stanford: Stanford University Press, 1957, p.259.
32. *Ibid.*, p.258.
33. Rupen (1975).
34. G. M. Friters, *Outer Mongolia and Its International Position*, Baltimore: The John Hopkins Press, 1949, p.130.
35. Alatalu (1992), p.884.
36. Friters (1949), p.131.
37. Cited in Rupen (1964), p.189.
38. *Ibid.*
39. See Robert M. Slussar and Jan F. Triska, *A Calendar of Soviet Treaties, 1917-1957,* Stanford: Stanford University Press, 1959, p.57.
40. William B. Ballis, "Soviet Russia's Asiatic Frontier Technique: Tannu Tuva," *Pacific Affairs*, vol.14, March 1941, pp.91-96.

41. Tang (1959), p.419.
42. Mongush (1993), p.83.
43. *Ibid.*
44. *Ibid.*
45. "Tuva celebrates Constitution Day," 6 May 2007, at http://en.tuvaonline.ru/2007/05/06/constitution-day.html
46. "Putin Chose Tuva as a Holiday Place for his Honourable Guest", 16 August 2007, at http://en.tuvaonline.ru/2007/08/16/1946_putin-in-tuva.html

CHAPTER 27

MONGOLIA AND KALMYKIA: PAST AND PRESENT

Yelena B. Pokaninova

The relations of Russia with countries of the Orient count several hundred years. The Kalmyks became a part of Russia at the beginning of the seventeenth century and made great contribution to formation and development of relations between Russia and Mongolia. In the nineteenth century the first Department of the Mongolian language was opened in Kazan and later in Petersburg. Today knowledge of the language, history and culture of the Mongolian people is a key to fruitful cooperation.

The Kalmyk people evince special interest in their culture and history. They consider themselves as a part of the Mongolian world both in respect of language, and in respect of its history and culture. Much of the original ethnic and cultural colouring of Elista comes from a unique Eurasian culture of the Kalmyk people, the only Asian Buddhists living on the territory of Europe. The Kalmyk ancestors, Western Mongols (*Oirats*), used to live in Central Asia (*Djungaria*) roaming as far as Altai, Tarbagatai, Western Sayans and southern Siberia. Their cultural roots go back to ancient times of pan-Mongol history.

The Kalmyks as a nation descend from the *Oirats* – Western Mongol tribal union. Kalmyk language belongs to the Mongol language group. Written language used to be based on Mongol alphabet, at present it is based on Russian one. In early XVII century all the *Oirats* moved to Lower Volga region and Caspian steppes having sworn allegiance to the Russian king. This event occurred in 1609. Soon there will be the celebration of 400th

anniversary of voluntary merging of the Kalmyks into the Russian state.

The period from the 16th to the 14th centuries BC was the time of Andronovskaya culture characterized by a transition from sedentary lifestyle to nomadic cattle breeding and exploitation of copper, tin, silver and gold. In the period from the 13th to the 10th centuries BC Bronze age reached its peak marked by the development of metalworking and famous Karasukski style in art to be replaced by a more advanced Togarskaya culture in the 7th century BC. A nomadic civilization, or “a culture best suited for the lifestyle of nomads”, was emerging. A number of tribes of Central Asia joined to form the state of Hunnu at the close of the first millennium BC. The northeastern and northern tribes founded the state of Syanby in the early first millennium AD. According to N.Y. Bichurin, the language of ancient Mongols had an advanced written form as early as the epoch of Hunnu-Syanby (3rd century BC–5th century AD).

In the period from the 8lh to 9th centuries AD, the Mongol-speaking Kidani were involved in farming and handicrafts, increased the total number of their cattle and built new settlements and towns. At their highest period (10th–12th centuries) they founded the empire of Lyao, practiced Buddhism, had their own Literature and two writing systems: a major script after Chinese writing model and a minor one based on Uighur alphabet.

In the mid-12th century as a result of “passionary” impetus, a Mongol world emerged bringing with it “a new original culture and language”. In 1240 AD, *Sokrovennoye skazaniye mongolov* (Mongol Mystery Legend), a masterpiece of written language, was created and in this work the *Oirats* were referred to several times as an independent ethnic group. It was not the only written document dating to the 13th century texts in Mongol script of this period were also inscribed on stones. Monasteries were the centers of book printing, while manuscripts could be written outside the monasteries. In 1269 AD, Phags-pa lama, the Buddhist monk, following the order of the emperor Khubilai invented the Mongol square script. In 1311 AD, Choidzhi-odser lama invented the Mongol script as we know it today. The migration resulted in a new name for the Oirats – "khal'mg" or "khalimag" (from the Mongol "separated") that was subsequently transformed into "Kalmyk".

Buddhism appeared in India in 5th century BC. It is widespread in South-east Asia, China, Mongolia, Korea, and Japan. When Khan (king) Puntsuk was swearing allegiance to Moscow kingdom in 1661AD, he kissed Buddha's image and the book of Buddhist prayers. Thus the Kalmyks were the first in Russia to adopt Buddhism – the most ancient world religion.

Nowadays, Kalmykia actively develops the traditional relationship with Mongolia in different spheres. In December 2006, the then President of Mongolia, N. Enkhbayar visited Kalmykia for the first time. "The Days of Mongolia" is being traditionally celebrated in our republic. The scientific contacts are developing very actively. Certain progress has already been achieved in the direction of the Mongolian Studies recently: several academic conferences were organized in Kalmykia, such as the International conference *Mongolian Studies in the New Millennium* in 2003. This conference attempted to integrate the scientific potential of the Mongolistics and to unite the efforts of Russian and foreign scholars to deal with the problems of modern Mongolian Studies. Recently the Dissertation Committee on Mongolian languages has been established at the Kalmyk State University. The Department of the Kalmyk language of the Kalmyk State University was transformed into Department of the Kalmyk language and Mongolistics. The Department of Mongolology and Tibetology of the Kalmyk Institute for Humanities was transformed into the Centre of Mongolology and Tibetology.

In summer 2007, a big group of scientists, teachers, journalists, artists of Kalmykia carried out study visit to Mongolia. A joint Russian-Mongolian expeditionary project *Folklore and Language of the Western Mongols* (the *Oirats*) in context of Central-Asiatic oral and written tradition was successfully carried out in the year 2007.

There are four national organizations:

1. Kalmyk Mongolian Society of Friendship;
2. Mongolian Cultural Information Centre;

3. "Fund of Mongolians";
4. Mongolian Scientific Centre.

Kalmykia can be called an ethnographic museum, the main core of which is people that preserved its original culture. Buddhism coexists with Pagan elements. Ancient shamanist ceremonies and even pre-shamanist cult of *Tsagan Aav* (The White Elder) – the keeper of life and all living beings – are preserved in national holidays. *Tsagan Sar* (The White Month) is considered to be the major and the most festive holiday. Famous Italian traveler of 13th century, Marco Polo has mentioned this festivity. The Kalmyks celebrate New Year (it is called *Zul*) according to the lunar calendar as the rest of the holidays. The holiday of the beginning of summer *Urs Sar* is connected with the process of driving cattle to summer pastures. It is full of symbolic features that imply ordinary hopes of a human-being for the better.

The Stupa of Enlightenment was erected in the year 1998. It was designed by a well-known Buddhist architect Voytek Kossovsky and named after Buddha's enlightened mind. Stupas-*suburgans* are usually built for energetical balance of the location, peace and prosperity. Each of the details has a symbolic meaning: the square foundation denotes the Earth, the round one – *Bumba* –water element, the golden rings denote fire, the umbrella-crown – air, a drop of water on the Sun and the Moon denotes ether – the source of life. The procedure of erecting a stupa is complicated and includes lots of Buddhist ceremonies. That is why monks from Nepal and India and a master of Tibetan painting came to Kalmykia. Stupa's wholesome effect "comes into action" as soon as it is sanctified which occurred on July 28, 1999. The ceremony of opening and sanctifying was mastered by the head of Nepal Buddhists Lopen Tsechu Rinpoche. About 2,500 local dwellers and 500 guests from Russia and Ukraine were present. The Buddhist name of the Stupa is *Monlam Tamched Drupa* – "Fulfilling all prayers".

Sacred Buddhist relics, texts of prayers are kept inside the *suburgan*. The walls are covered with pictures of Buddhas and various gods. In the center there is set a barrel with 50 million prayers. Beside the stupa there was built Makhakala's house. He is considered to be the main defender of Buddhist school *Karma Kagyu*. Makhakala's statue is cast in metal, painted and filled with prayers and is more than one meter high.

Kalmyk people take great interest in Buddhism as a philosophy. A branch of International Buddhist Karmala Institute (New Delhi, India) was opened in 1995, to further contribute to Buddhist tradition and practice in Kalmykia. It educates Buddhologists, translators-interpreters. Young people who are keen on studying the philosophy of Buddhism in India or Buryatia get every possible state support. Under the government's aegis supreme Buddhist monks can visit Kalmykia.

Many things have been lost and some of them are irrevocable but today opportunities are opening and may be one can recover some of the lost treasures. All circles of the Kalmyk society are well aware of their responsibility for the future of their people and much effort is underway to encourage all forms of ethnic revival.

Changes can be seen in all spheres of life in the Republic, as well as in its capital as its new architecture, sculptural pieces and constructions are aimed at creating an atmosphere of peace and friendliness. Recently Elista has also become the center of international communication.

The roads to temples built in the last decade are always crowded, favourite warriors of the epic *Djangar* are on guard in the streets of the town watching the people doing their peaceful work and the soft tinkling of the bells on the "Gold Gate" is filling us with hopes for a harmonious and creative life in the new millennium. Together with the Administration of Head of the Republic of Kalmykia, Government of the Republic, Parliament realizes the plan of cooperation and friendship. Kalmykia and Mongolia maintain contacts to develop their culture and traditions.

CHAPTER 28

PROBLEMS OF *ORALMANS* FROM MONGOLIA: THE MIGRATION POLICY IN KAZAKHSTAN

L.K. Shotbakova

Kazakhstan is one of the few states which follows a policy of preserving the ethnic identity and national character of the Kazakhs living abroad. The active immigration policy of Kazakhstan, the peak of which was in the 90s of the twentieth century was explained by a number of factors. The crisis of demographic situation inside the country, on the other hand those in conditions of globalization and integration of the Kazakh diaspora were considered as important components of foreign policy of the country. Besides, the Kazakhs living abroad, who virtually constituted one third of the population of Kazakhstan can be a powerful social resource of Kazakhstan. These factors became the basis for the consolidation and independence of the Kazakhs living all over the world, which was one of the important strategic goals of the Republic of Kazakhstan.

In the beginning of twenty first century about 4 million Kazakhs lived outside Kazakhstan. And there are more than 1.2 million people of the Kazakh nationality living all over the world. The most numerous diaspora were in Uzbekistan - up to one and half million people, in Russia – 740,000, in Turkmenistan – 70,000. In the far abroad countries the biggest number of ethnic Kazakhs lived in the Peoples Republic of China - about 1.5 million, in Mongolia – 100,000, in Afghanistan – 30,000 and in Turkey – 25,000.

By the end of 1990s, work on the formation of legal basis of the repatriation program of Kazakhs as stipulated in *The Concepts of repatriation of ethnic Kazakhs to the historical native land* and approved by governmental order of the Republic of Kazakhstan on September 16, 1998 was completed. On the whole, following the independence of Kazakhstan, several important legislative documents regulating the status of *Oralmans* were adopted. These are the State program of support of the compatriots living abroad, approved by the Decree 3308 of the President of the Republic of Kazakhstan, December 31, 1996, the Decree *About the State program of support of the compatriots living abroad for 2005-2007*, Law of the Republic of Kazakhstan *About the migration of population*, *The Branch program of migratory policy of the Republic of Kazakhstan for 2001-2010*, the Decree of the President of the Republic of Kazakhstan about a quota of *Oralmans* immigration for 2005-2007 dated December 27, 2004, the Instruction on the order of defining the status of the repatriate (*Oralman*), re-emigrant, the immigrant, and also the forced immigrant.

According to the Law of Migration, *Oralmans* are considered to be foreigners or persons without citizenship of Kazakh nationality who lived at the time of independence of the Republic of Kazakhstan, that is on December 16, 1991, beyond its borders and who arrived in Kazakhstan with the purpose of permanent residence. The Ministry of Labour and Social Protection of the population of the Republic of Kazakhstan, is the authorized body to the migration processes in Kazakhstan vide the governmental order №1132 of the Republic of Kazakhstan dated October 29, 2004. The quota of immigration of *Oralmans* is annually approved by the President of the Republic of Kazakhstan. Actually all the ethnic Kazakhs living abroad, have the right to return to their historical native land. This is especially relevant for the Kazakhs living in the People's Republic of China, Uzbekistan, Turkmenistan and Mongolia.

The Repatriation was at its peak during the mid-1990s when 164,000 repatriates returned to Kazakhstan. Actually the term *Oralman*, that is the ethnic Kazakhs coming to the Republic of Kazakhstan from other countries, appeared at that time. As a whole during the period from 1993 till October 1, 2005, 117,698 families of *Oralmans* or 464,426 persons arrived in Kazakhstan; 61.5 per cent from Uzbekistan, 15.4 per cent from Mongolia, and 17.6 per cent from other places. The positive balance of migration turned to be from the far abroad countries as China (the increase of population is in 31.8 times) and Mongolia - in 11.1 times. The number of Kazakh immigrants who arrived from Mongolia tinto Kazakhstan is on the second place after China: 36 per cent of immigrants arrived from China during 1999-2005 and 23.3 per cent from Mongolia.[1]

The share of persons of able-bodied age makes 53.4 per cent out of the whole number that arrived. The number of *Oralmans* with higher education accounts for 10.1 per cent out of the total and the number of students in higher educational institutions is 1.7 per cent out of the whole number of *Oralmans*.

In the year 2006, 1 billion 200 million *tenge* were allocated for *Oralmans* from the republican budget.[2] According to the decree of the President dated December 27, 2004, the quota of 15,000 families of *Oralmans* immigration was fixed for the period 2005-07. In 2000, this figure was 500 families, in 2001 – 2655 families, in 2003 – 5000 families and in 2004 – 10,000 families. That is, in each successive year the number of families having the opportunity to return home on a legitimate basis has grown in a positive proportion.

According to the law of the Republic of Kazakhstan *About the migration of population*, *Oralmans* have been included in the quota of immigrants receiving lumpsum and housing grants from the State. Besides, they receive transport charges on the basis of actual expenses. Each member of family receives 100,000 *tenge* in the form of the lumpsum financial assistance.

Oralmans are settled practically in all regions of Kazakhstan, but mostly in South Kazakhstan, Mangistau and Almaty regions. *Oralmans* also live in Karaganda region. So as per the data of the head of the migration and demography department of Karaganda region, G. Medeubayeva, 3,736 families or 17,561 *Oralmans* lived on the territory of Karaganda region by January 1, 2003, out of which 2,879 families (14,065 persons) were from Mongolia.[3]

The issue of repatriation of the Kazakhs from Mongolia,

being a part of the migration policy of the post-independent Kazakhstan has been one of the most complicated problems in the internal political life of the country. The history of formation of the Kazakh diaspora on the territory of modern Mongolia originates from mid- nineteenth century, when a part of the Kazakh clan Abak Kerey moved to the territory of Mongolia. The reasons attributed to their migration are both external and internal political circumstances. Mongolia at that time was a part of Tsinskaya empire and the authorities did not interfere with the resettlement of some Kazakh clans in the territory of Mongolia. Besides, Tai pei revolt, sharp reduction in the pasturable grounds and deterioration of social status of the Kazakh population as a result of colonial policy of Russia, contributed to their migration. The data of resettlement of the Kazakhs in the territory of Mongolia can be found in works of Russian travellers. According to G.E. Grumm-Grzhimaylo, "In the last century (eighteenth century) a part of the Kazakhs of a clan Kerey having lived on Chertyy Irtysh as a result of cross-clanish struggle for the ground has been compelled to leave for the territory of modern western Mongolia". Besides, those Kazakhs left for the territory of modern Mongolia after the defeat of Dzhungaria Khanate in the 60s of eighteenth century, when the Kazakhs began to occupy the grounds which were vacated.[4] In 1876, Mongolia was visited by G.N.Potanin during his expedition to Altay. He left a note about the Kazakhs living in western Mongolia in his records.[5] These records confirm the account of G.E. Grumm-Grzhimaylo about the resettlement of Kazakhs of a clan Kerey in the mentioned territory in the 18th-19th centuries. The same period, that is 1860s is mentioned in the works of Mongolian researchers, particularly, Tseven Zhamsranov.[6] It is clear that in the last few centuries mostly the Kazakhs of clan Abak Kcrey moved to the territory of modern Mongolia, part of them subsequently remained in China, and some of them moved from China to a number of European and Asian states.

Ethnic Kazakhs of Mongolia started returning to Kazakhstan in February 1991 when 97 Kazakhs moved to Kazakhstan from Mongolia.[7] They were placed in Saryozek in Taldy-Korgan region. After the beginning of immigration of the Kazakhs from Mongolia, the Kazakhstan Institute of Strategic Studies made sociological research in 1992 among the Kazakhs of one of the *aymaks* of the Mongolian National Republic, namely the Bayan-Ulgiyskiy where Kazakhs lived compactly. The results of investigation showed that the majority of the Kazakh population 80.5 per cent would like to return home to Kazakhstan and as a place of their future residence they chose East Kazakhstan, Karaganda, Almaty, Kokchetav and Kustanay regions. Among the reasons cited for their movement to Kazakhstan were their desires to give good education to children (24.6 per cent) and also to live in the native land of their ancestors (20.3 per cent).

During the period 1991-1994, 60,772 Mongolian Kazakhs moved from Mongolia to Kazakhstan.[8] A large settlement of Kazakh diaspora from Mongolia is located in the Kustanay region. One of the places of compact settlement of *Oralmans* from Mongolia, is the village Uspenovka of the Fedorovskiy district 60 kms. from Kustanai. They have faced the problem of employment because in Mongolia practically all of them were cattlemen and none had any specialisation. It was easier for those who had arrived earlier in the beginning of the 1990s, as they were provided with houses and other facilities. One of the *Oralmans* explained the perception of life in the new place: "There in Mongolia we lived in one village we knew each other well. I can not say that all thirty families live here well. But in fact anywhere either in Mongolia or here nobody will not simply give you anything if you do not work. We have arrived here to find the native land." All the *Oralmans* in Uspenovka have own allotments of land. All of them are very active and hardworking.

The Mongolian Kazakhs perfectly speak Kazakh language and that's why they do not face any problem of educating their children in the Kazakh schools. Many of them know Russian language, particularly those *Oralmans* who arrived in Kazakhstan at a mature age, having received their education in the former USSR or the countries of SEV. In total, during the period from 1991 to 1997, 64,000 Kazakhs were repatriated to Kazakhstan from Mongolia. They were settled in Kustanay, Pavlodar, Karaganda and some other regions of Kazakhstan.[9]

Practically all the immigrant Kazakhs initially wished to live compactly in one area, it was the general characteristic for all the *Oralmans*, irrespective of the country of resettlement. But, in practice *Oralmans* are settled in different regions of the Republic of Kazakhstan.

Nowadays many problems regarding the accommodation of *Oralmans* have been successfully solved with the help of the centers of adaptation in all the regions of Kazakhstan. However, there are some problems of *Oralmans* which need urgent attention:

- The main problems faced by *Oralmans* during the initial days of their arrival in Kazakhstan, are those of adaptation and receiving all necessary documents. Another problem is to find temporary dwelling and to solve their accommodation problem permanently;
- *Oralmans* who arrived from the far abroad countries face the problem of language barrier. For example, *Oralmans* from China do not know the system of Cyrillic writing and do not know Russian language, which complicates the process of their adaptation among the local population;
- The unemployment percentage among *Oralmans* is 40 per cent, even after the centers of population employment try to solve their problem. Since they do not have liquid depositable assets, they cannot receive bank loans;
- Numerous families of *Oralmans* which come to Kazakhstan out of the approved quota do not receive material support from the state. As a rule, the *Oralman* families settle in a countryside and sometimes are not received well by local population. Though there is no threat, the risk of social tension between *Oralmans* and local population, does exist;
- There is no balanced settlement of *Oralmans* in the regions and areas of the Republic of Kazakhstan.

REFERENCES

1. B.I. Rakisheva, "Migratory Processes in Kazakhstan: the Factor of the State policy", at http://www.cessi.su/index.php?id=168
2. Zh. Abdiyev at http://reflaw.narod.ru/HTMLs/lows/kazakh/print/migr_pr.htm
3. Medeubayeva at http://www.otandastar.freenet.kz/vregionah,html
4. G.E. Grumm-Grzhimaylo, *Western Mongolia and Urianhayskiy Region*, 1930, p. 413.
5. G.N. Potanin, *Essays on Northwest Mongolia* (Travelling across Mongolia), 1948, pp.38-39.
6. Tseven Zhamsranov, *Darhad, Hovsgol nuuryn Urianhay hasag, hamnigan naryn garal undes baydlyn oguulel*, Ulaanbaatar, 1927. p. 132
7. G.M. Mendikulova, *Historical Destinies of the Kazakh Diaspora: The Origin and Development*, Almaty, 1997, p.232.
8. *Ibid*, p.234.
9. *Ibid*.

INDEX